# TAKEOVER

# TAKEOVER

## The Return of the Imperial Presidency and the Subversion of American Democracy

### CHARLIE SAVAGE

LITTLE, BROWN AND COMPANY
New York  Boston  London

Little, Brown and Company
Hachette Book Group USA
237 Park Avenue, New York, NY 10017
Visit our Web site at www.HachetteBookGroupUSA.com

First Edition: September 2007

Library of Congress Cataloging-in-Publication Data

Savage, Charlie.
    Takeover : the return of the imperial presidency and the subversion of American democracy / Charlie Savage. — 1st ed.
        p.   cm.
    Includes bibliographical references and index.
    ISBN-10: 0-316-11804-4
    ISBN-13: 978-0-316-11804-0
    1. United States — Politics and government — 2001–   2. Bush, George W. (George Walker), 1946– — Political and social views.   3. Cheney, Richard B. — Political and social views.   4. Executive power — United States.   5. Official secrets — United States.   6. Supreme Court — United States.   7. Constitution — United States. 8. Presidents—United States—Biography.   9. Cheney, Richard B. 10. Vice-Presidents — United States — Biography.   I. Title.
    E902.S38  2007
    973.931 — dc22                                                                                 2007013077

10   9   8   7   6   5   4   3   2   1

Q-FF

Printed in the United States of America

*To Luiza*

# Contents

# TAKEOVER

# 1

## Inside the Bunker

### 1.

As the United States of America reeled, Vice President Dick Cheney took control.

At a quarter past ten o'clock on the morning of September 11, 2001, a choking cloud of debris and death, once the south tower of the World Trade Center, engulfed lower Manhattan. Flames and black smoke poured from the upper stories of the north tower. In northern Virginia, just across the Potomac River from downtown Washington, the Pentagon's western wall crumbled into its own blaze. Three miles away, the aboveground portions of the White House complex stood empty, evacuated just minutes earlier by the Secret Service as hijacked American Airlines flight 77, bound for the military headquarters, had barreled toward the nation's capital with its target yet unknown.

Three stories into the bedrock beneath the White House's East Wing, behind body armor–clad guards holding shotguns and MP5 machine guns, loomed a sealed vault door—the entrance to the Presidential Emergency Operations Center.[1] Originally built as an air-raid shelter for President Franklin D. Roosevelt during World War II, the cramped bunker had never before been used during a crisis. It had a few days' food and supplies, bunk beds, and a conference room with televisions, secure phones, and video links to key federal agencies and military installations. Inside, Cheney sat at a conference room table with a handful of other top officials. As they looked from one television screen to another, a military aide approached the vice president. The bunker had received reports of a second plane headed toward the capital. United Airlines flight 93, a Boeing 757, had veered off course over Ohio, banked sharply back over Pennsylvania, and was now believed to be just eighty miles away. The military had put fighter jets on patrol a few minutes earlier. The officer wanted to know whether the interceptors should shoot down the airliner, sacrificing the forty-four people aboard to prevent a potentially larger disaster from taking place.

Cheney's chief of staff, I. Lewis "Scooter" Libby, was sitting next to the vice president at the table, taking notes. Libby later described Cheney's decisive answer to the aide: "In about the time it takes a batter to decide to swing," Libby said, the vice president authorized the military to destroy United 93. Five days later, Cheney would describe the order as the toughest decision made that day, but one that was necessary. "Now, people say, you know, that's a horrendous decision to make. Well, it is. You've got an airplane full of American citizens . . . and are you going to, in fact, shoot it down, obviously, and kill all those Americans on board? And you have to ask yourself, 'If we had had combat air patrol up over New York and we'd had the opportunity to take out the two aircraft that hit the World Trade Center, would we have been justified in doing that?' I think absolutely we would have."[2]

Shortly after Cheney gave the order, the military aide returned and said the aircraft, now believed to be sixty miles out, had just been confirmed as a hijacking. The aide wanted to make sure that the military had the authority to attack the plane. As Joshua Bolten, later the White House chief of staff but then just one of several deputies, later recalled, "The vice president said yes again. And the aide then asked a third time. He said, 'Just confirming, sir, authority to engage?' And the vice president—his voice got a little annoyed then—said, 'I said yes.'"[3] The aide left and the conference room went quiet as the enormity of the exchange fell upon all who had heard it. Then, from down the table, Bolten broke the silence. Boldly, he suggested that Cheney call President George W. Bush to "confirm" the shoot-down order Cheney had just given.[4]

At that moment, the commander in chief was aboard Air Force One as it rapidly ascended into the atmosphere above Sarasota, Florida. Bush had been reading to children that morning at a photo-op at Booker Elementary School. When the second plane hit the World Trade Center, it became clear that the country was under attack. After a brief delay, Bush and his entourage had headed for the airport.

The president and Cheney had spoken at 9:55 a.m., just before Bush's plane took off. Cheney, standing at a secure phone just outside the vault doors of the White House bunker, had urged Bush not to return to Washington until the situation was stabilized. "Basically I called to let him know that we were a target and I strongly urged him not to return to Washington right away, that he delay his return until we could find out what the hell was going on," Cheney later recalled.[5]

Bush had taken Cheney's advice. The president had hung up and strapped himself in aboard Air Force One, which had gotten safely off the ground with its ultimate destination—Barksdale Air Force Base in Louisiana, as it would turn out—not yet chosen. Back in the tunnel, Cheney had hung up and entered the bunker, where he then learned that the military had just scrambled fighter jets around Washington.

Now Cheney took Bolten's advice. He called Bush back at 10:18 a.m. Aboard Air Force One, Bush's press secretary, Ari Fleischer, was with his boss and, like Libby, taking notes. Two minutes later, according to Fleischer's notes, Bush hung up the phone and said he had just authorized the military to shoot down any remaining planes.[6]

## 2.

Amid the initial turmoil, Cheney believed that the shoot-down order had been carried out. In a teleconference with Secretary of Defense Donald Rumsfeld at 10:39 a.m. Cheney said he believed that two planes had just been shot down. But, as it turned out, the question of whether to shoot down hijacked airliners was moot. Investigators would later determine that United 93, the last of the four hijacked planes, had already nose-dived into a Pennsylvania field at 10:03 a.m. amid a passenger uprising against the hijackers.[7] Confused officials had been looking at a computer-projected track of where United 93 would have been had the flight still been airborne, not at an actual radar image. Moreover, military commanders had never passed the shoot-down authorization on to the fighter pilots because, as they told the 9/11 Commission, "they were unsure how the pilots would, or should, proceed with this guidance" coming from the vice president. (As the 9/11 Commission report noted, "In most cases, the chain of command in authorizing the use of force runs from the President to the Secretary of Defense, and from the Secretary to the combatant commander."[8] The shoot-down order, then, ended up a minor and inconsequential footnote on a morning full of hugely complex and important events. Yet the sequence leading to the shoot-down order would later become the subject of a pointed dispute between the White House and the 9/11 Commission. This conflict would sharply illustrate Cheney's willingness to exercise extraordinary executive power, Bush's penchant for deferring to Cheney, and their administration's efforts to control the flow of information about their actions to Congress and the public.

More than two years after the attacks, on April 29, 2004, Cheney and Bush met with the 9/11 Commission in the Oval Office on the condition that they would not be placed under oath, that no recording or transcript would be made, and that Cheney would sit beside Bush the entire time so that they could answer questions together. During the meeting, Cheney insisted that the president had given him permission to authorize shooting down hijacked passenger jets some ten minutes or so before Cheney first gave the order at 10:15 a.m. Cheney claimed that he had called Bush back immediately after entering the bunker conference room, when he was first told there were fighters in the sky, and during this earlier call, Bush had given him authorization to issue a shoot-down order if it became necessary. The president backed Cheney's account.[9]

In an extraordinary and largely overlooked passage of its findings, the bipartisan commission sharply scrutinized the president and vice president's account. It reported that it found "no documentary evidence for this call"—and the commission had had plenty of evidence to look through. "Others nearby who were taking notes, such as the Vice President's chief of staff, Scooter Libby, who sat next to him, and Mrs. Cheney, did not note a call between the president and Vice President immediately after the Vice President entered the conference room," the commission report said.[10] Nor had Fleischer, who was keeping detailed notes of events aboard Air Force One, recorded any earlier call. Bolten told the commission that he had spoken up to tell Cheney to call Bush to confirm the shoot-down order because "he had not heard any prior conversation on the subject with the president." Tucked away in the footnotes of the commission report was further evidence casting doubt on whether there had been an earlier call. In order to reconstruct the events that occurred in the bunker that morning, the commission reported, it also obtained the White House secure switchboard log, Secret Service and White House Situation Room logs, the White House "President's Daily Diary" record, and four separate White House Military Office logs that tracked significant events and communications in the bunker.[11] None of these sources recorded the alleged earlier call that Cheney, much later, insisted he had placed. If Cheney and Bush were telling the truth, then their most trusted aides, Cheney's wife, and eight White House and military log keepers all somehow missed the single-most potentially momentous call of that morning.[12]

### 3.

The dispute over the existence of the phone call was no small detail. It embodied the central role that Cheney played in the second Bush presidency. The most powerful vice president in American history, Cheney literally called the shots for the administration on 9/11. He did not hesitate to take command, and Bush acquiesced to his vice president's actions. As the war on terrorism unfolded, Cheney would continue to play a central role in guiding Bush's policies. Cheney, after all, was one of the nation's most experienced vice presidents when he and Bush were sworn in on January 20, 2001. He had been a midlevel Nixon-administration official, a White House chief of staff in the Ford administration, an influential congressman for ten years, and a secretary of defense under the first President Bush. By contrast, the second President Bush was a term-and-a-half state governor thrust to national prominence by elements of his father's old political network. Bush's father had been a member of Congress, an ambassador to the United Nations and to China, a chairman of the Republican National Committee, a director of the Central Intelligence Agency for ten months, and a vice president for eight years. His son shared the first President Bush's name but had been none of those things. George W. Bush was one of the least experienced presidents ever to take the oath.

The upper ranks of the new administration quickly filled with two types of people. There were Bush People—mostly personal friends of the new president who shared his inexperience in Washington. These included Alberto Gonzales and Harriet Miers, Bush's first and second White House counsels, each of whom was a corporate lawyer in Texas before becoming attached to the governor's political network. And then there were Cheney People—allies from Cheney's earlier stints in the federal government who were deeply versed in Washington-level issues, a familiarity that would allow their views to dominate internal meetings. These included Rumsfeld and other cabinet secretaries, key deputies throughout the administration, and David Addington, Cheney's longtime aide who would become a chief architect of the administration's legal strategy in the war on terrorism.[13]

Given the stark contrast in experience between Cheney and Bush, it was immediately clear to observers of all political stripes that Cheney would possess far more power than had any prior vice president. William Kristol, the neoconservative editor of *The Weekly Standard* and former chief of staff to Vice President Dan Quayle, said in early 2001 that Cheney would play the role of "Bush's number one adviser" and "super chief of staff," giving him "unprecedented" influence. "The question to ask about Cheney," Kristol said, was, "will he be happy to be a very trusted executor of Bush's policies— a confidant and counselor who suggests personnel and perhaps works on legislative strategy, but who really doesn't try to change Bush's mind about anything? Or will he actually, substantively try to shape administration policy in a few areas, in a way that it wouldn't otherwise be going?"[14]

By the Bush-Cheney administration's second term, Kristol's question had been decisively answered. Cheney had used his influence to shape policy in hugely substantive ways. To be sure, some of the administration's signature domestic issues—such as establishing national school-testing standards, pushing to reform the immigration system by turning illegal aliens into guest workers, banning gay marriage, and creating faith-based initiatives throughout the federal bureaucracy—were a natural fit for Bush, the born-again Christian who had run a state that shared a border with Mexico, and who had tried to reform the Texas public education system. But in other key areas, the administration's policies emerged from Cheney's own experiences and interests. Indeed, while most of the media's attention was devoted to Cheney's influence in pushing the administration to invade Iraq, the vice president was also immersed in another, far less visible effort. This second project was rooted in an agenda he had been developing for thirty years, stretching back far longer than his interest in toppling the regime of Saddam Hussein, and if successful would mark American politics for generations to come.

Cheney was determined to expand the power of the presidency. He wanted to reduce the authority of Congress and the courts and to expand the ability of the commander in chief and his top advisers to govern with maximum flexibility and minimum oversight. He hoped to enlarge the zone of secrecy around the executive branch, to reduce the power of Congress to restrict presidential action, to undermine limits imposed by international treaties, to nominate judges who favored a stronger presidency, and to impose greater White House control over the permanent workings of government. And Cheney's vision of expanded executive power was not limited to his and Bush's own tenure in office. Rather, Cheney wanted to permanently alter the constitutional balance of American government, establishing powers that future presidents would be able to wield as well.

Cheney made no secret of his agenda of expanding—or "restoring"—presidential power. He repeatedly declared that one of his goals in office was to roll back what he termed "unwise" limits on the presidency that were imposed after the Vietnam War and the Watergate scandal. "I clearly do believe, and have spoken directly about the importance of a strong presidency," Cheney remarked at an awards ceremony for the Gerald R. Ford Foundation in June 1996. "I think there have been times in the past, oftentimes in response to events such as Watergate or the war in Vietnam, where Congress has begun to encroach upon the powers and responsibilities of the President; that it was important to go back and try to restore that balance."[15]

Cheney was not the first person to try to consolidate governmental authority inside the White House. Others had helped lay the groundwork for expanding executive power during the preceding thirty years, especially during the Reagan and Bush-Quayle administrations. Many of these "presidentialists" joined the Bush-Cheney administration. But as vice president, Cheney became the most important of the believers.

To understand what happened to presidential power during the Bush-Cheney administration, it is necessary to start by examining Cheney's own beginnings in public life, from his political apprenticeship in the Nixon administration, to his first taste of real power in the Ford administration amid the fallout from Vietnam and Watergate, to a decade he spent defending the Reagan administration from inside a hostile Congress, and to his tenure as a wartime secretary of defense under President George H. W. Bush. The 9/11 attacks would reenforce Cheney's view on the need for centralizing strong powers in the presidency. The war on terrorism's climate of perpetual emergency provided a vehicle for turning his vision of an unfettered commander in chief into a reality. But Cheney's agenda was forged years before Al Qaeda attacked the United States. His agenda's origins date to 1969, when a former congressman named Donald Rumsfeld hired Cheney, then a twenty-eight-year-old graduate student in political science, to be his aide inside the Nixon administration.

# 2

## The Fall of the Imperial Presidency and the Rise of Dick Cheney: 1789–1976

### 1.

Richard Bruce Cheney was born on January 30, 1941, in Lincoln, Nebraska. When he was thirteen years old, his father, a soil conservation agent with the U.S. Department of Agriculture, was transferred to Wyoming. The Cheney family moved to the last house on the east side of Casper, next to a vast empty prairie. Cheney grew up with an *American Graffiti* lifestyle, though he never showed as much interest as some of his friends in cruising between the town's two A&Ws on Friday nights.[1] He was a tough but popular teenager at Natrona County High School, where he was the class president and a football player. "Dick and I both made the varsity [football team] our sophomore years," boyhood friend Joseph Meyer recalled. "And the way we did it [was] one-on-one drills. We hit each other so hard that you could hear the sound. We did that about four times, and the sophomore coach called over the head coach and said, 'These guys are out of their mind!'"[2]

Cheney also learned to fight with his fists, recalled Tom Fake, who grew up with Cheney in Casper and became an all-state quarterback on the football team. (Cheney became a linebacker.) During Cheney's senior year, he and Fake crossed the railroad tracks to the poorer side of town and found an old boxer who taught them to spar. "We spent four months during our senior year fighting in each other's garage. He probably whipped me more than I whipped him," Fake said.[3]

Friends, teammates, and boxing partners, Cheney and Fake were also rivals. During their junior year, Fake dated Lynne Vincent, a popular girl who was the state baton-twirling champion. Vincent's father was a government engineer, and her mother was a sheriff's deputy.[4] A Casper native, Lynne would never grow taller than five foot two, but she had large ambitions. By senior year, she was Cheney's girlfriend—and his future wife. "I knew her when we were in the eighth grade, but she wouldn't have anything to do with me until I was a junior in high school," Cheney later recalled. "Actually, we double-dated with others first. And Lynne was dating my good friend Tom Fake, and shortly after that I asked her out. And when I first asked her out, she said, are you kidding? Which I took to mean she really wasn't very interested." It became an inside joke for the couple; Cheney's wife has always insisted that what she meant was she was surprised that he was interested in her.[5]

Cheney and Vincent would have a lifelong political partnership, and the relationship began paying dividends for Cheney immediately after he began dating her. The teenage Vincent had a part-time job as a secretary in the office of Alpha Exploration, a Casper-based oil company, and she introduced her new boyfriend to the owner, Tom Stroock. A graduate of the Yale College class of 1948, Stroock took a shine to Cheney and Fake and recruited them to attend his alma mater on full-ride scholarships. "In those days, you could do things you can't do now," Stroock later recalled, "so I called Yale and told 'em to take this guy" along with Fake.[6]

Cheney and Fake, popular jocks from Wyoming, found a different world when they arrived in New Haven, Connecticut, in 1959. Like many scholarship students from the heartland who made it to the Ivy League, they found that they were unprepared for the Eastern social and academic world. The Casper boys, who had effortlessly dominated the teenage social scene and never had to study hard back home, were overwhelmed.[7] They partied but failed to engage with the academic side of Yale. Cheney was forced to leave Yale after three semesters for academic reasons. He briefly returned to Wyoming, then went back to Yale for a second try at completing his sophomore year—but he again flunked out, and lost his scholarship.

Cheney withdrew from Yale for good in 1962. Three years later, a young George W. Bush would arrive on the Yale campus as a freshman. A New Haven native and the grandson of a U.S. senator from Connecticut, Bush shared Cheney's mediocre study habits and his youthful enthusiasm for partying. But Bush was much more comfortable in the Ivy League environment. He would be elected president of a fraternity and was inducted into the elite Skull and Bones secret society, coasting to graduation, where the Wyoming scholarship student had faltered.

Cheney returned to Wyoming and got a union job laying electrical lines in the blue-collar town of Rock Springs. He was arrested twice in the next year for drunk driving, and he would later speak of realizing that he was "headed down a bad road." In 1963, "when I should have been graduating from Yale, one of the world's finer universities, with a first-rate education, all paid for by the university, I found myself in Rock Springs working, building power lines, having been in a couple of scrapes with the law."[8] While Cheney drifted, his girlfriend, Lynne Vincent, was earning a BA with highest honors from Colorado College and an MA from the University of Colorado. Then Lynne put her foot down. The Dick Cheney she had fallen in love with was the king of his high school with a wide-open future, not a dropout and manual laborer who was running afoul of the law. To keep her, Lynne made clear, Cheney needed to get his life back on track.

Cheney refocused and went back to school — first completing a semester at a community college in Casper and then switching to the University of Wyoming in Laramie, where he earned a BA and an MA in political science. In 1964, Lynne agreed to marry him, and to convert from her Presbyterianism to his Methodism.[9] "Turned out I was a pretty good student when I worked at it," Cheney said. "And a year later Lynne and I got married. I must say I've got to give her a good deal of the credit for being a positive influence in my life. Stuck by me all those years. We'd gone to high school together and dated throughout this whole period of time. And she made it clear she wasn't interested in marrying a lineman for the county. That was really when I went back to school in Laramie. I buckled down and applied myself. Decided it was time to make something of myself."[10]

Marriage and a return to college studies had other advantages as well. The Vietnam War was heating up, and the government was drafting increasingly large numbers of unmarried young men who weren't in college to go fight in the jungles of Southeast Asia. Cheney earned four draft deferments. Then, in October 1965, the rules protecting married men changed — only parents would be eligible to avoid being drafted. Within weeks, Lynne was pregnant with the first of their two daughters, and Cheney applied for a new deferment. In all, the future secretary of defense and wartime vice president would receive five deferments during the Vietnam War, protecting him from service during his draft-eligible years.[11]

In 1966, the Cheneys moved to Madison and began work on PhDs—he in political science, she in English—at the University of Wisconsin. As more and more young American men were dying in Vietnam, an antiwar movement gained force on many college campuses. Protests fueled a growing antigovernment sentiment and counterculture lifestyle that would become the hallmark of the sixties. Cheney did not relate to the political winds blowing around him. While his classmates were marching on Washington, Cheney was crunching congressional voting pattern data, looking for trends that could be used to predict the outcomes of political fights. In an *American Political Science Review* paper, for example, Cheney showed that lawmakers tended to vote in line with their party leaders on tax issues, but they voted in line with their district's demographic makeup on welfare issues.[12]

Watching the increasingly unruly antiwar protests on campus convinced Cheney that liberalism was getting out of control and soured him on his chosen career as a college professor. In 1968, Cheney put off writing his dissertation and went to Washington, DC, to work as an intern in the office of Rep. William Steiger, a moderate Republican from Wisconsin. Cheney never returned to his studies. (Lynne Cheney completed her PhD in 1970, writing a dissertation on nineteenth-century British literature.) In 1969, Steiger provided Cheney with an entrée to Donald Rumsfeld, a rising star in the new Nixon administration. Rumsfeld, thirty-six, was a former Princeton wrestler and navy pilot. A moderately conservative Republican, Rumsfeld had been elected to Congress from a wealthy district in the suburbs north of Chicago in 1962. Rumsfeld had been an early supporter of Richard Nixon's 1968 presidential campaign, and in April 1969 Nixon had asked Rumsfeld to resign from Congress and join him in the executive branch.

Nixon gave Rumsfeld two roles: He was both a special assistant to the president—entitling him to a second-floor office in the West Wing of the White House—and the director of the Office of Economic Opportunity, an antipoverty agency headquartered a few blocks away. Later that year, Rumsfeld hired Cheney to be his executive assistant at the Office of Economic Opportunity. Cheney, then a twenty-eight-year-old former political-science student, was about to begin a very different kind of political education—experiencing the rush of exercising presidential power from inside the Nixon administration, at the very peak of what the historian Arthur Schlesinger called the era of the "imperial presidency."[13]

## 2.

The "imperial" power invested in the presidency during the first decades of the Cold War was an anomaly in American history, Schlesinger argued. It traced its existence back to the Truman administration and gained force with successive presidencies leading up to Nixon. Truman and his successors, especially Lyndon Johnson, had begun invoking national security to seize more and more power from Congress and the courts. The Constitution empowers Congress to regulate the presidency, but these presidents and their men began arguing that the modern world was too dangerous and complex for a president's hands to be tied. They advanced a philosophy that the president wields vast "inherent" and independent powers not spelled out in the Constitution that allow the president to defy the will of Congress. This centralization of power in the hands of the president intensified and peaked under Nixon, during the period of Cheney's apprenticeship in government. But the imperial presidency seemed to collapse amid the ruins of the Vietnam War and the Watergate scandal, a process that left a deep impression on Cheney.

During this brief period, presidents wielded far more power than America's Founders had intended when they created the office two centuries before. The first generation of Americans, having rebelled against a king whom they viewed as a tyrant who dominated the British parliament and abused his power over the colonies, well understood the threat that strong executive power poses to democracy. Indeed, their first attempt at forming a government after the American Revolution had no executive at all. Instead, under the Articles of Confederation, the Founders chose a weak national government consisting only of a Congress. But this system soon proved a failure because it allowed state governments to run rampant, preventing a cohesive national economy and identity from taking shape. Pressured by the need for collective action against such problems as attacks on American shipping by the Barbary pirates, the Founders convened in Philadelphia in 1787 to write a new constitution.[14]

The second time around, the Founders gave more power to the national government than it had wielded under the Articles of Confederation. But the changes created concerns that the new federal government would abuse its powers to destroy individual rights and freedoms. To prevent that from happening, the Founders limited the government's role to a specific set of functions. They divided control of the government into three separate powers—the presidency, the Congress, and the courts—giving each institution the ability to check the others if they got out of control. In debating the new executive branch, the Founders argued over whether the day-to-day manager of the government should be just one president or an executive committee, according to notes of the Constitutional Convention debates kept by James Madison. His convention notes and the *Federalist Papers*—essays written by three Founders to explain the Constitution and to urge states to ratify it—also show that the Founders decided it made sense to have just a single president so that the executive branch could act decisively, especially in times of war. But they were also bent on ensuring that this new president would not get out of control and become a king.

To that end, the Constitution gave Congress the power to pass laws setting all the "rules and regulations" it deemed "necessary and proper" for the execution of presidential powers. The executive branch, in turn, was charged with obeying these rules. If the president did not like the laws, he could veto them, but Congress could override a veto with a supermajority vote. And the Founders specifically took away from the executive the power to take the country to war—a chief provenance of the British king—leaving presidents the power to repel sudden attacks only without first getting the assent of Congress. The Founders vested in Congress the power to declare war, to authorize military conflicts that fell short of war, to create armies and devise rules for running them, to "make rules concerning captures on land or water," and to regulate how the president could call up the armed forces in emergencies such as an insurrection or invasion. Finally, the Founders were mindful that until the English Revolution of 1688, less than a century earlier, one of the chief ways in which the British king had acted as a tyrant was through his "prerogative power"—the asserted power to dispense with a law if the king, and he alone, decided that setting a statute aside would be good for the public. The Founders made sure that the American president would not have this prerogative power, writing in the Constitution that the president must "take care that the laws be faithfully executed."

The Founders' idea for preserving democracy, then, was simple. Congress would enact the general rules, and the president of the United States was bound to obey them. This system of checks and balances was designed to prevent the consolidation of too much power into any one person's, or one branch's, hands. Knowing that it was inevitable that from time to time foolish, corrupt, or shortsighted individuals would win positions of responsibility in the government, the Founders came up with a system that would limit anyone's ability to become a tyrant or to otherwise wreck the country.[15] And over the next century and a half, the system worked as the Founders had designed it to work.[16]

There were adjustments, of course, as Congresses and presidents filled in some of the blanks in the Constitution. For example, nothing in the Constitution gives the president the right to withhold any information about the government from congressional oversight committees. But over time, Congress allowed presidents to withhold information if disclosing it would be against the public interest. In practice, this meant carving out a series of limited exceptions to a general rule of disclosure, such as protecting details of an ongoing investigation or the identity of confidential informants.

Similarly, while the Constitution left decisions about going to war to Congress, presidents gradually claimed a right to deploy small numbers of troops on their own authority for quick strikes against foreign foes. Presidents took small-scale military action to pacify Indian tribes, capture pirates, or rescue Americans in third world trouble spots. In such cases, Congress acquiesced to the fact that some combat had occurred without its authorization because the deployments and hostilities were localized, brief, and over by the time Congress could act. And throughout the nineteenth century and the first half of the twentieth, presidents continued to seek Congress's authorization for major wars.[17]

The one major early jolt to this system came during the Civil War, the greatest threat to national survival that the United States has ever experienced. Southern rebels launched the war against the federal government while Congress was out of session, firing upon Fort Sumter on April 12, 1861. President Abraham Lincoln did not wait for Congress to return before taking steps to stop the country from breaking apart. Without a declaration of war, Lincoln enlarged the Union's army and navy, blockaded Southern ports, spent money not appropriated by Congress, and arrested Northerners suspected of being Southern agents without giving them legal rights—all steps that exceeded his authority under federal law and the Constitution. Lincoln did not claim that most of what he had done was lawful based on his own independent and inherent powers as president. Rather, Lincoln acknowledged that several of his dramatic steps were outside the constitutional framework of government.

As soon as Congress reconvened, Lincoln explicitly asked for its authorization of his emergency actions, arguing that the actions had been necessary in order to keep the nation from falling apart. "These measures, whether strictly legal or not, were ventured upon under what appeared to be a popular demand and a public necessity, trusting then, as now, that Congress would readily ratify them," he wrote to Congress on July 4, 1861.[18] Forgiving the trespass in light of the extraordinary circumstances, Congress passed a statute retroactively making legal the actions Lincoln had taken.

In 1866, the Supreme Court made clear that Lincoln's actions were to be viewed as a singular exception in American history, not as a new general rule about presidential power. A year after the Civil War ended, the Court struck down a military tribunal Lincoln had used to prosecute Northern civilians, ruling that the Constitution limits presidential power even in times of national emergency. "The Constitution of the United States is a law for rulers and people, equally in war and in peace, and covers with the shield of its protection all classes of men, at all times, and under all circumstances," the Court ruled. "No doctrine, involving more pernicious consequences, was ever invented by the wit of man than that any of its provisions can be suspended during any of the great exigencies of government. Such a doctrine leads directly to anarchy or despotism . . ."[19]

As the country stabilized, another seventy years passed with the system functioning basically as the Founders envisioned. Presidents generally hewed to the role the Constitution laid out for them, although some were more assertive than others. Perhaps the most assertive was Theodore Roosevelt, who was president from 1901 to 1909. Roosevelt declared that the president had a broad "residuum of powers" to do anything he was not specifically forbidden to do. Without seeking prior congressional approval, Roosevelt launched the project to build a canal in Panama, sent the U.S. fleet around the world, and dispatched U.S. troops to intervene in the Dominican Republic and Cuba. Roosevelt's views, a version of what would become known as the theory of inherent power, contained the seeds of the imperial presidency that would arise during the first decades of the Cold War. But his handpicked successor, future Supreme Court chief justice William Howard Taft, revived the traditional view that the presidency has only those powers specifically granted to it by the Constitution or federal laws. Taft thus restored the constitutional balance, preserving the Founders' vision for two more generations.[20]

Presidential power began to grow again under the stewardship of Theodore Roosevelt's distant relative, President Franklin D. Roosevelt, who was elected in 1932 during the Great Depression. The first push came when Congress agreed to pass Roosevelt's New Deal legislation. These laws greatly expanded the federal government bureaucracy and gave sweeping new powers over domestic issues to agencies controlled directly or indirectly by the president. The Supreme Court initially struck down these laws as unconstitutional. But in 1937, Roosevelt attacked the judicial branch, threatening to "pack" the Supreme Court by expanding its size and then appointing extra members who would vote the way he wanted. Congress rejected his plan but the Court bowed to the political pressure and began upholding the New Deal legislation, enabling the rise of the modern administrative state inside the executive branch.

Then, in the early days of World War II, before the United States had entered the war against Nazi Germany, Roosevelt sent supplies to Great Britain in violation of the Neutrality Act, under which Congress had sought to keep America out of World War II by prohibiting assistance to either side. Roosevelt did not simply claim that he had an "inherent" right to violate the Neutrality Act under his powers as commander in chief; instead, he used a stretched interpretation of federal statutes to justify his transgression, consulting with Congress at every step. Most important, Roosevelt did not claim that he could take the country to war against Germany and Japan on his own. When the time came, he asked Congress to authorize the war.

Congress typically reclaimed the authority that had been ceded to presidents during wartime. But World War II gave way to the early Cold War against the Soviet Union and the new threat of sudden nuclear annihilation. Rather than demobilizing, the U.S. armed forces stayed at large numbers. And President Harry S Truman used this climate of standing armies and perpetual emergency to expand his powers as commander in chief.

The Founders had intended only to ensure civilian control of the military by naming the president as the commander in chief of the armed forces—a title that Alexander Hamilton, who was among the strongest supporters of a powerful presidency, described in the *Federalist Papers* as amounting to "nothing more" than being the "first general" in the military hierarchy.[21] And the Founders explicitly sought to keep the commander in chief from having the power to decide when the country would go to war, leaving such a decision to Congress alone. As James Madison, the namesake for the city in which young Dick Cheney studied government, wrote in 1793: "Those who are to *conduct a war* cannot in the nature of things, be proper or safe judges, whether a *war ought* to be *commenced, continued,* or *concluded.* They are barred from the latter functions by a great principle in free government, analogous to that which separates the sword from the purse, or the power of executing from the power of enacting laws."[22]

But Truman, for the first time in American history, asserted that the title commander in chief brought with it the unwritten power to take the country into a major overseas war on his word alone. In 1950, Truman sent U.S. troops to fight North Korea without asking Congress for authorization, asserting that he had inherent powers to do so as the commander in chief. Truman did ask the foreign governments sitting on the United Nations Security Council to pass a resolution authorizing military action to turn back the North Korean invasion. But the permission of foreign states was irrelevant to the domestic legal issue of who got to decide whether the United States would go to war.[23] No president had ever before launched anything on the scale of the Korean War without prior permission from Congress, as the Constitution requires. Some thirty-seven thousand Americans would die in Truman's "police action," an unpopular and costly war that resulted in a stalemate. But members of Congress, eager to appear tough against Communism and to support a war effort, did nothing to block Truman.

Two years later, Truman went further. Again citing his inherent powers as commander in chief, Truman took over the nation's steel industry in order to avert a strike that he said could endanger the war effort. A steel-mill owner sued the government to regain control of his factory, putting Truman's legal theory before the Supreme Court. The Court struck down Truman's order as an unconstitutional usurpation of Congress's power to write the laws, noting that "the Founders of this Nation entrusted the lawmaking power to the Congress alone in both good and bad times."[24] But the steel seizure case turned out to be only a pause in the movement toward an increasingly authoritarian presidency.

Truman's successors picked up his claim to vast inherent powers, each citing special circumstances to use those powers. For example, seeking to protect government personnel files from Senator Joe McCarthy's anti-Communist witch hunts in 1954, President Dwight Eisenhower invented the phrase "executive privilege." Previous presidents had occasionally withheld information from Congress for a narrow and defined set of categories, but Eisenhower essentially proclaimed that the executive branch could withhold *any* internal documents—thereby creating a potentially boundless new category of government information a president could deny to Congress.[25]

Eisenhower also authorized the CIA to operate in foreign countries without congressional approval, expanding a new national security apparatus that gave the president the ability to undertake secret paramilitary actions at his own discretion. Such covert CIA interventions authorized by Eisenhower and his immediate successors facilitated coups in an attempt to assassinate foreign leaders and topple governments—often democratically elected but suspected of harboring Communist sympathies—in countries such as Iran, Guatemala, the Dominican Republic, Cuba, Brazil, Guyana, and Chile.[26] These operations, undertaken at a president's say-so alone and far exceeding the legal charter Congress gave the CIA when it created the agency after World War II, resulted in a mix of short-term successes and failures. But even where the aggressive operations achieved their goals, they often did long-term damage to the nation's reputation, creating new and lasting enemies for the American people in countries such as Iran.

Similarly, amid the urgency of the 1962 Cuban missile crisis, President John F. Kennedy launched a military blockade of Cuba and threatened imminent war with the Soviet Union without consulting congressional leaders. Further expanding presidential war-making powers in the absence of congressional approval, Kennedy's successor, Lyndon B. Johnson, greatly escalated U.S. troop levels in Vietnam and "Americanized" the combat against the Communist North without congressional authorization. In the Tonkin Gulf resolution of 1964, Congress approved defensive action only for the purpose of stopping attacks on U.S. troops stationed in Vietnam. Later, some in Congress proposed repealing the Tonkin Gulf resolution, but Johnson argued that such a move would be irrelevant. He said he had the inherent power, as commander in chief, to keep the country at war in Vietnam in order to defend America against a threat to its national security.

When Nixon became president in 1969, he inherited a presidency whose powers to act beyond the will of Congress were greatly inflated when compared with those the office held throughout most of American history, powers that had little basis in the Founders' constitutional system. This imbalance—the "imperial presidency"—was the result of the actions of a few recent presidents and of the inaction of Congress amid the confusion and fears of the early Cold War years. Nixon, with a young Cheney watching and learning inside his administration, then pushed the power of the presidency to its breaking point.

In 1977, three years after Nixon resigned to avoid being impeached for abuses of power, the former president remained defiant about his view of White House authority. In a famous interview with the British journalist David Frost, Nixon declared that presidents have the inherent power to authorize government officials to break laws if the president decides that doing so would be in the national interest. Citing Lincoln's example during the first few months of the Civil War as precedent, Nixon said that presidents have the power to take any action in order to protect national security, regardless of what the laws say. "When the President does it, that means it's not illegal," Nixon declared.[27]

This view represented the culmination of Nixon's grasp for nearly unlimited presidential power, a strategy that unfolded on many fronts. First, Nixon tried to impose greater political control over the permanent government bureaucracy. Under Johnson, Congress had passed a series of anti-poverty and civil rights laws, setting up agencies in the executive branch to enforce the statutes. Nixon disagreed with these laws, but Congress was unwilling to repeal them. So Nixon tried to block career civil servants from carrying out the tasks Congress assigned to them; young Cheney would be drawn into this effort. Nixon also sought to eliminate some of the agencies whose work he opposed by significantly escalating the practice of "impoundment"—refusing to spend money Congress had appropriated for programs that the president opposed. He greatly expanded the White House staff, centralizing political control of the government under officials who were not confirmed by Congress and not subject to testifying before them.[28]

Nixon also invoked executive privilege far more aggressively than his predecessors had done. Similarly, he tried to control what newspapers could print, seeking to prevent the publication of the leaked Pentagon Papers—a classified history of the Vietnam War showing that the government had knowingly lied to the public during the conflict's early years—but the Supreme Court refused to go along, upholding the right of the news media to report any information that came into their possession.

Nixon also took expansive action on the basis of inherent presidential powers, asserting that he had exclusive authority—meaning no act of Congress could affect it—across the entire realm of foreign policy and national security. Expanding the Vietnam War to encompass all of Indochina, he secretly ordered the military to begin bombing the neutral countries of Laos and Cambodia. Nixon also refused to acknowledge a role for Congress in deciding when to withdraw from the war, saying such issues were for him alone to decide. Congress repealed the Tonkin Gulf resolution in 1971, for example, but Nixon kept the war in Vietnam going until 1973.

Expanding on the practices of his immediate predecessors, Nixon authorized warrantless domestic wiretapping, burglaries, mail openings, and other illegal "black bag job" intelligence collection on U.S. soil in order to eavesdrop on his political enemies, including war protesters and civil rights leaders. Several of these illegal operations were carried out by a shadowy organization originally set up inside the White House; they were dubbed the "plumbers" because their first mission was to plug leaks about national security matters. Several members of the plumbers later tried to sabotage the 1972 Democratic presidential campaign, in part by burglarizing the Democrats' headquarters at the Watergate building in Washington. But they were arrested and charged in relation to the break-in, setting in motion a massive but ultimately unsuccessful cover-up operation inside the White House.

The Watergate scandal, which shocked the country as it unfolded through the media and congressional investigations, combined with disgust over the ill-advised war in Vietnam, temporarily collapsed an imperial presidency that had been building for two decades. But just as Nixon's story was ending, Cheney's was beginning.

3.

In 1969, when Cheney went to work for the Nixon administration as Rumsfeld's assistant at the Office of Economic Opportunity, he had been thrust into the middle of Nixon's effort to expand presidential control over federal agencies. Cheney's new workplace, the Office of Economic

Opportunity, had been established by Congress as part of Johnson's War on Poverty. As a measure of its importance under the previous administration, Johnson had asked Sargent Shriver, the Kennedy in-law and former head of the Peace Corps, to be the office's first director. But the agency was deeply unpopular among conservatives. Nixon had made the Office of Economic Opportunity's alleged faults a campaign issue during the 1968 election. In 1969, Rumsfeld's job, with Cheney beside him, was to help Nixon bring the agency to heel.

Nixon continually pressed Rumsfeld to impose greater political control over the agency and to curb its antipoverty programs he didn't like, such as the Office of Legal Services, which Congress created to provide free lawyers for the poor.[29] "Rumsfeld took the OEO job because Nixon saw him as a skillful dismantler," said Paul O'Neill, who oversaw the agency for the White House Office of Budget under both the Johnson and Nixon administrations, and later served as treasury secretary under the Bush-Cheney administration.[30]

Congress had given the agency a broad mandate "to further the cause of justice among persons living in poverty."[31] Some of the more aggressive Legal Services lawyers began developing high-profile class-action lawsuits on behalf of the poor. Although the class-action lawsuits were a small percentage of the total number of suits brought by the Legal Services program, they were having a major political impact. In 1967, for example, California governor Ronald Reagan tried to cut $210 million from the state's medical care budget, but Legal Services funded a lawsuit that reversed the cuts.[32] These lawsuits—against local, state, and federal agencies, police departments, major landlords, industrial farmers, and corporations—irritated Republicans and their donors. They saw the class-action lawsuits as trouble, and the poverty lawyers as taxpayer-funded radicals. Nixon expected Rumsfeld to take care of the problem.

Legal Services was then headed by a former federal prosecutor and civil rights trial attorney named Terry Lenzner. Just twenty-nine years old, Lenzner had been the captain of the Harvard football team, gone on to Harvard Law School, and then joined the Justice Department. After catching Rumsfeld's eye, Lenzner had preceded Cheney as Rumsfeld's assistant for his first several months at the agency. In July 1969, Rumsfeld put Lenzner in charge of the Legal Services program, which by that point had more than 2,000 lawyers and 850 offices around the country. Lenzner was Rumsfeld's first major appointment, and it came with a strong personal endorsement: "I have worked closely and personally with [Lenzner] on a daily basis since assuming this position, and I have confidence in his judgment, his ability, and his commitment," Rumsfeld said.[33]

As Legal Services' courtroom successes continued, top White House aides—including White House chief of staff H. R. "Bob" Haldeman and Nixon's top domestic adviser, John Ehrlichman—began pressuring Lenzner to fire the lawyers who were filing aggressive litigation. But Lenzner, who described himself as idealistic about the mission of the office, said he didn't want to fire anybody for political reasons. Moreover, he said, he could not fire the lawyers because of the way Congress had set up the agency. "I was being told, 'You have to put a stop to this, you have to control these lawyers,'" Lenzner recalled. "But I said that if I do what you want me to do, it will violate the law."[34]

The orders to fire lawyers, Lenzner emphasized, came from other Nixon White House officials, not Rumsfeld or Cheney personally.[35] Still, as Lenzner failed to rein in the Office of Legal Services, Rumsfeld turned his back on his former protégé. Increasingly, the only time they spoke was when Rumsfeld wanted to relay complaints from Republican congressmen and other local officials who were unhappy about certain lawsuits.

When Rumsfeld announced plans to reorganize Legal Services under a system of regional administrations, Lenzner directed his aides to analyze the fine print of the plan. They concluded that the apparently innocuous change was actually "an ingenious Nixon administration way to politicize the program and take the fangs out of Legal Services," Lenzner said, because the change would give regional power brokers the ability to quash lawsuits filed against powerful interests in their home state. Lenzner said that one of his assistants, without asking his permission, sent a copy of their memo to the office of Senator Walter Mondale, the liberal Minnesota Democrat who later served as Jimmy Carter's vice president. Mondale raised a stink about Rumsfeld's reorganization, scuttling the plan. Rumsfeld was, to say the least, not happy. "Don blew up," Lenzner recalled. "I was not a 'team player.'"[36]

During this period, Nixon repeatedly reminded Rumsfeld about a need to purge disloyal officials in order to gain greater political control over the permanent government, a message that surely was passed on to Cheney. As Rumsfeld was brought more into the inner councils, he began spending a greater percentage of his time at the White House. The change left Cheney with greater responsibilities for running the Office of Economic

Opportunity in Rumsfeld's absence, and for enforcing Nixon's agenda. Cheney quickly developed a reputation as both efficient and rather cunningly persuasive, despite his low-key manner. One former coworker, Ted Taylor, later recalled Cheney as "a very strong manager. And you didn't realize till afterward that he'd already gotten you to do something. You almost had to think, God, did I say yes to that?"[37]

Cheney appeared deeply skeptical about Legal Services. On numerous occasions, Lenzner said, "I would get calls from Cheney. Don was not around as much and Cheney was issuing orders, calling to say, 'You got to do this' and 'You can't do that.' The message was that 'I'm watching you and I'm not too happy with what's going on because of all the calls from the White House.' It was clear nobody was happy."[38]

In November 1970, shortly after the midterm elections, Lenzner was summoned to the director's office. Rumsfeld, with Cheney at his side, fired Lenzner on the grounds that he was "unable or unwilling to comply" with orders, according to Lenzner. Lenzner called a press conference and accused the Nixon administration of secretly hamstringing Legal Services on behalf of "powerful interests."[39]

With Lenzner out of the way, the agency's independence was sharply reduced. The firing drew front-page coverage in the next day's newspapers. It was an early milestone in the Nixon administration's efforts to undermine Legal Services in defiance of the federal law that created it. And for Cheney, whose own, lesser role went almost unnoticed in the press at the time, the experience represented his first hands-on lesson in how the presidency should operate: wresting control of an agency away from Congress in order to bend it to the White House's agenda.[40]

Rumsfeld's and Cheney's own days in the Office of Economic Opportunity were numbered. In December 1971, Nixon put Rumsfeld in charge of the Cost of Living Council, an agency that set price controls in an effort to control inflation, and Rumsfeld again brought Cheney along as his deputy. But their relationship was briefly severed in February 1973, when Nixon made Rumsfeld his ambassador to NATO, seeking to give his trusted young aide foreign policy experience that would help his later career. After Rumsfeld departed for NATO headquarters in Brussels, Cheney briefly left the government to work as a partner in an investing firm.

Both men watched from a distance as Congress battled Nixon and sought to counter his claims of presidential power. Congress passed laws in 1973 ordering Nixon to stop bombing Laos and Cambodia and demanding that presidents consult Congress for any future wars. Then, as Watergate revelations grew, Nixon resigned in August 1974 to avoid being impeached.

4.

On August 9, 1974, Nixon left the White House grounds in defiant disgrace aboard a marine helicopter shortly before Gerald Ford was sworn in as the new president. At that moment, Cheney was off to Dulles International Airport, forty-five minutes south of Washington, where he would meet Rumsfeld's flight from Brussels. Rumsfeld, then still the NATO ambassador, had been vacationing on the French Riviera with his wife when he got a call from Phil Buchen, soon to be Ford's new White House counsel.[41] Buchen told Rumsfeld that Ford wanted him to come back and head up the transition team that needed to quickly create a new administration from the ruins of the Nixon presidency. Rumsfeld's temporary assignment soon became permanent, as Ford made him White House chief of staff. Rumsfeld again tapped Cheney to be his deputy. The following year, when Ford made Rumsfeld the secretary of defense, Cheney replaced his mentor as White House chief of staff—an extraordinarily powerful position for a thirty-four-year-old.

In one sense, his timing was terrible. Cheney had gotten his chance to help wield the powers of the presidency from high in the executive branch hierarchy just as those powers had come under fierce assault. Congress had begun aggressively reining in the presidency during the last years of the Nixon administration. Among its most important moves was enacting the War Powers Resolution of 1973; overriding Nixon's veto, Congress required presidents to consult with Congress whenever deploying troops into likely combat, and required any deployments not explicitly authorized by Congress to end after sixty days. Years later, Cheney would describe the era as the "low point" of presidential power, and he singled out the War Powers Resolution as unconstitutional because it "made a change in the institutional arrangements that I don't think is healthy. I don't think you should restrict the president's authority to deploy military forces because of the Vietnam experience."[42]

Ford, a former House minority leader who had had nothing to do with Watergate, enjoyed a few weeks of harmony with Congress, but his surprise decision to grant Nixon a full and unconditional pardon a month after taking office ignited a new round of congressional action.[43] The first fight the new administration faced involved a bill to strengthen the Freedom of Information Act. The bill allowed judges to review documents the executive branch wanted to keep secret. Congress's goal was to prevent officials from stamping a document "classified" for political purposes. Ford was reluctant to veto the bill. In his first remarks after taking office, Ford had promised a new era of openness in government. Moreover, a midterm election was coming up, and vetoing such popular legislation would look terrible. "A veto presents problems," Ford scrawled on a memo to an aide three days after becoming president. "How serious are the objections?"[44]

But the CIA, the Pentagon, the State Department, and other agencies that dealt in classified information were adamantly against the bill. Leading the charge was the young head of the Justice Department's Office of Legal Counsel, which advises the president on constitutional matters. His name was Antonin Scalia. Scalia asserted that the bill unconstitutionally infringed on the president's "exclusive" power to withhold information to protect national defense and foreign policy.[45] Joined in argument by all but one of Ford's top advisers (Buchen, the White House counsel and a friend of Ford's from their college days[46]), Scalia and company convinced Ford to veto the bill because it could lead to leaks and "would violate constitutional principles."[47] The Ford administration then launched an all-out lobbying campaign to urge Congress to sustain the veto and instead pass alternative legislation that Ford's legal team would help craft. Congress, however, promptly overrode his veto.[48]

Ford officials soon had cause to worry that Congress would go even further in restricting the president's powers. In the November 1974 midterm elections, Democrats won huge victories at the polls as voters punished Republicans for the Watergate scandal and Ford's pardon of Nixon. The election meant that the opposition party would enjoy a greater than two-to-one majority in both houses of Congress—enough to easily override presidential vetoes.

One month after the midterms, the *New York Times* published a report by the investigative journalist Seymour Hersh alleging that the CIA had for two decades undertaken a massive and illegal program of domestic spying, including tapping phones, opening mail, breaking into homes and offices, and keeping files on ten thousand antiwar protesters and other dissidents. Hersh's article touched off an uproar in the new Congress, prompting vows to investigate and reform the intelligence community. Transcripts of National Security Council meetings from this period portray a White

House feeling under siege. Ford remarked that they were all "struggling . . . with the consequences of the Hersh article" and that he was "concerned that the CIA would be destroyed."[49] In a memo to the president, Cheney urged Ford to quickly create a White House commission to investigate the CIA as "the best prospect for heading off congressional efforts to further encroach on the executive branch."[50]

Ford, who would later remember getting to know Cheney and "develop[ing] a great admiration for his ability to analyze problems, his good judgment,"[51] took the young deputy's advice and created the commission, putting his vice president, Nelson Rockefeller, in charge of it. But the new Congress moved in anyway, launching eight separate hearings and demanding full access to secret documents. Soon, the probes were consolidated into one for each chamber. A special House committee, headed by Democratic representative Otis Pike of New York, focused on whether the intelligence community needed to be redesigned. The White House's fights with Pike were heated but paled by comparison with the battles with a separate Senate committee that was focusing on investigating past cases of severe abuses by the intelligence agencies.

This Senate committee, which generated the sharpest attacks on the presidency during the Ford years, was chaired by Idaho Democrat Frank Church. Church had been an intelligence officer for the army in Southeast Asia during World War II. He had joined the military shortly after graduating from high school in 1942. After his discharge in 1946, Church earned an undergraduate degree from Stanford and went on to law school. But his studies were interrupted again when he was diagnosed with cancer in his abdomen, underwent surgery, and was given just months to live. However, a second doctor subjected Church to an early form of radiation therapy, using X-rays to kill the remaining cancer cells. The treatment worked. Church later said that the early reminder of his mortality spurred him to be more aggressive in life. "I had previously tended to be more cautious—but having so close a brush with death at 23, I felt afterwards that life itself is such a chancy proposition that the only way to live is by taking great chances," he recalled.[52]

The young lawyer channeled that energy into politics. The youngest son of a staunch Republican who loved to argue politics over dinner, Church had often taken a contrarian stance simply in order to "furnish an argument." The dinnertime debates led Church to hone his political skills—he won a national American Legion oratory contest as a sixteen-year-old—and also converted him into a Democrat. He won a U.S. Senate seat in 1956 at age thirty-two, making him the fifth-youngest U.S. senator in history. He would serve for four terms, becoming one of the early opponents of the Vietnam War and a true believer in the dangers an imperial presidency poses to American democracy.

Church achieved his greatest fame heading one of the 1975 probes into severe abuses by the vast covert spy force that had grown up, almost without discussion, after World War II. In its final report, the Church Committee described the growth of illegal domestic intelligence activities as a product of excessive secrecy and unrestrained executive power. The report said that in order to preserve the Constitution, it was imperative to impose safeguards on what a president could do with spy agencies.

"For decades Congress and the courts as well as the press and the public have accepted the notion that the control of intelligence activities was the exclusive prerogative of the Chief Executive and his surrogates," the Church Committee report said. "The exercise of this power was not questioned or even inquired into by outsiders. Indeed, at times the power was seen as flowing not from the law, but as inherent, in the Presidency. Whatever the theory, the fact was that intelligence activities were essentially exempted from the normal system of checks and balances. Such Executive power, not founded in law or checked by Congress or the courts, contained the seeds of abuse and its growth was to be expected."[53]

Church's findings would ultimately prompt Ford to write a sweeping executive order imposing new limits on the intelligence community. The 1976 order for the first time established explicit rules for intelligence operations, banning most physical surveillance of U.S. citizens and legal residents as well as the collection of information about them. It also prohibited the infiltration of most domestic groups and made clear that the CIA was not to conduct operations on U.S. soil, nor to assassinate foreign leaders. Ford's order blunted efforts in Congress to lock down such rules in statute so that they could not be waived by future presidents at their own discretion, but the findings also prompted Congress to create intelligence oversight committees in each chamber and to require the president, by law, to tell the committees about all intelligence activities.[54]

As the Church Committee began pressing for access to secret documents in early 1975, Ford tapped Jack Marsh, one of his top advisers, to coordinate responses to the requests. A former congressman and Defense Department official, Marsh later said that being in the Ford White House during those years felt like being under relentless assault. "There was an avalanche of demands and requests," Marsh said. "If you want to get really whipsawed sometime, be in the White House when you got that kind of an issue, and the Congress is against you two to one."[55]

Meanwhile, the press was uncovering major new revelations. In 1973, at the height of the Watergate investigations, the director of the CIA had ordered the agency to compile a classified report on any past or present activities that might have been illegal. This report, which Ford-administration officials alternately called the "horror stories" and the "family jewels," leaked to CBS in February 1975. It included numerous allegations of attempted assassinations of foreign leaders over the previous twenty years.

Cheney instructed the White House press secretary to "stonewall" press inquires about the assassination report.[56] Rumsfeld urged a "damage-limiting operation for the president" as they sought to thwart congressional demands for secret documents while trying not to look like they were engaged in a Watergate-style cover-up.[57]

Years later, Scalia would recall attending daily morning meetings during this period in the White House Situation Room with Marsh, CIA director William Colby, and other top officials. At those meetings, "we decided which of the nation's most highly guarded secrets that day would be turned over to Congress, with scant assurance in those days that they would not appear in the *Washington Post* the next morning. One of the consequences of these congressional investigations was an agreement by the CIA that all covert actions would be cleared through the Justice Department, so, believe it or not, for a brief period of time, all covert actions had to be approved by me. Needless to say, I did not feel that this was an area in which I possessed a whole lot of expertise. Nor did I feel that the Department of Justice had a security apparatus to protect against penetration by foreign operatives. We had enough security procedures to frustrate *la cosa nostra*, but not the KGB."[58]

As late as mid-March 1975, Cheney wrote a note to himself saying that they had a "problem": "At the present time, we have no clear guidelines, no coherent policy developed for responding to Congressional requests generated by their investigation of the intelligence community."[59]

## 5.

A month later, the commander in chief endured a new humiliation. In the spring of 1975, North Vietnam invaded the South, violating the cease-fire that the Nixon administration had negotiated in 1973. By April, it was clear that the Communists would soon take Saigon. Ford and his advisers, especially Secretary of State Henry Kissinger, wanted to conduct a massive airlift that would rescue 175,000 Vietnamese whose lives were in danger because they had worked with the Americans. Because of the laws Congress had passed at the end of the Vietnam War, Ford was forced to ask Congress for permission to conduct the airlift. But Congress opposed a new round of military action in Vietnam. In an April 14, 1975, meeting in the Oval Office, the Senate Foreign Relations Committee told Ford that it was a terrible idea because the number of American troops that would be necessary to secure the area while the airlift unfolded could reignite the war.

Congress gave Ford permission to use the military only to evacuate any Americans who were still in Saigon. His hands tied, the president could only watch helplessly as the television news depicted chaotic crowds of desperate South Vietnamese trying to get aboard the last helicopter flights out of the American embassy on April 30, 1975. It was a heart-wrenching scene. But limiting the evacuation also probably prevented a new round of war in Vietnam.

Two weeks later, the Ford administration began to push back against Congress. On May 12, 1975, a U.S. cargo container ship called the SS *Mayagüez* was seized by the Cambodian navy in the Gulf of Siam. Kissinger urged military action to get the ship and its crew back, arguing that it was necessary to make a strong show of force to alert Communist regimes in the region that the United States would respond to attacks on its interests despite the fiasco of the Vietnam War. Ford took his advice, ordering the U.S. Marines to sink Cambodian warships and to storm an island where the crew was believed to be held—and he did so without consulting Congress ahead of time. Just two weeks after the Saigon airlift, Ford had revived the notion that he could order the military into combat without consulting Congress.

After Ford gave the orders to proceed with the assault, he called congressional leaders from both parties to come to the Cabinet Room in the White House and briefed them about what he had already done.[60] The congressional leaders agreed that the attack was the right decision as a matter of policy, but they sharply disagreed with how Ford had gone about it. A 1971 law prohibited the use of ground combat troops in Cambodia, and the 1973 War Powers Resolution required advance consultation with Congress "in every possible instance." Speaker of the House Carl Albert informed Ford, "There are charges on the Floor that you have violated the law." And Senate Majority Whip Robert Byrd, Democrat of West Virginia, asked, "Why were the [congressional] leaders not consulted before the decision to strike the mainland? I'm for getting the ship back, but I think you should have given them a chance to urge caution."

"That's a good question and I'll answer," Ford replied. "It is my constitutional responsibility to command the forces and to protect Americans. . . . We have a separation of powers. The president is the commander in chief so long as he is within the law. I exercised my power under the law and I complied with the law. I would never forgive myself if the Marines had been attacked. . . ."[61]

The *Mayagüez* and its crew were recovered, and Ford's decision was celebrated as a "daring show of nerve and steel," a "classic show of gunboat diplomacy," and a "four star political and diplomatic victory," as *Newsweek* told its readers, adding for good measure, "It was swift and tough — and it worked."[62]

But later, this heroic portrait was revealed to be false. The U.S. death toll from the assault was far higher than initially reported. Instead of one dead and thirteen missing, more than forty marines had died — fifteen in the initial assault on the island, twenty-three in a related helicopter crash, and three who had been accidentally left behind and were captured and executed by the Cambodians. The intelligence surrounding the operation had been terrible. The United States expected to find just two dozen Cambodian soldiers on the island; instead, there were ten times that many. Worse, the captured crew wasn't on the island — and never had been; they had been taken to the mainland at the beginning of the crisis. Worst of all, it turned out that the Cambodians had publicly announced that they were releasing the crew and the vessel before the attack began, but the message hadn't reached Ford before he rushed to attack. The crew was floating out to sea on a fishing boat when the marines launched their assault on the island, dying for nothing.[63]

But these facts did not come out for several weeks — and some facts took years. In the meantime, the operation was presented to the public as a stunning, morale-boosting victory just two weeks after the humiliating Saigon evacuation. An unnamed Ford administration official admitted to a *Newsweek* reporter that the White House release of information about the operation had been "the sheerest sort of jingoism," but his argument was that the operation had worked — "and nobody challenges success."[64] Indeed, it proved difficult for members of Congress to quarrel with an apparently successful operation, and their grumbles about the principles involved quickly died down.

The *Mayagüez* incident revealed just how difficult it would be for Congress to rein in a president once troops were committed. And Ford would not be the last president to chip away at the War Powers Resolution.

Another area in which lawmakers were newly vigilant had to do with treaties. The Constitution divided power over contracts with foreign nations, allowing presidents to negotiate such agreements but requiring presidents to submit them to the Senate for ratification. Over time, however, presidents began sidestepping this procedure by making more aggressive use of "executive agreements" with foreign governments—turning what were supposed to be limited understandings into major treaties under another name, which they never sent to Congress.

Nixon, who had taken this practice to unprecedented levels, even sometimes kept the agreements a secret from Congress. In April 1975, when the North Vietnamese forces neared Saigon, the South Vietnamese government produced confidential letters Nixon had sent them in late 1972 and early 1973 during peace negotiations with the North. The letters appeared to commit the United States to coming to the South's defense with "severe retaliatory action" if the North violated the peace agreement. "You have my assurance of continued assistance in the post-settlement period and that we will respond with full force should the settlement be violated by North Vietnam," Nixon had written, urging South Vietnam to sign the accord.[65]

The revelation of Nixon's promises caught both Congress and the Ford administration by surprise. In the White House, Cheney helped craft the White House reaction. There was no support in the United States for reopening the Vietnam War, and Congress had since passed laws against further military involvement in Indochina. For its part, the Ford White House had no desire to follow through on Nixon's promises, and Cheney's handwritten notes show that he struggled to understand whether Nixon's letter constituted a commitment on behalf of the United States. He also debated whether Nixon's other secret letters to South Vietnam should be released to the public—a point soon made moot when the South Vietnamese leaders made them all public before fleeing.[66]

Lawmakers quickly introduced legislation in both houses that would require the president to submit any executive agreements to Congress for approval, as he was supposed to do in the case of a treaty. On May 15, 1975, the Ford administration dispatched Scalia to the Senate to testify against the bills. He called the plan an unconstitutional attempt to usurp presidential power to carry out the nation's foreign affairs.[67] Although legislation to force presidents to submit their executive agreements to a vote in Congress would eventually falter, senators would succeed in getting Ford to show them classified letters he had exchanged with Saudi Arabia, even though the president felt "it would not be wise to establish the precedent of providing correspondence between the heads of state."[68] As the fight played out, Ford called several congressional leaders into the White House and urged them to slow down the legislation. Ford's deputy national security adviser, Brent Scowcroft, urged the lawmakers not to undercut the president's ability to speak for the United States with other foreign leaders. But Senator John Sparkman of Alabama told Scowcroft that the American president didn't have the power make a commitment on behalf of the country on his own. "Other presidents do speak with that kind of authority, and this is precisely the danger we want to avoid," Sparkman said, alluding to dictatorships.[69]

## 6.

Ten days after Scalia's testimony, Cheney spotted a way to push back against the Church Committee's investigations into what presidents had done with the intelligence community. On May 25, 1975, five months after Hersh's article about illegal domestic spying by the CIA touched off the congressional probes, Hersh published a new investigative piece about a different top-secret intelligence operation. For the past fifteen years, American submarines had been infiltrating Soviet Union waters and eavesdropping on their undersea communications lines, Hersh reported.

Rumsfeld and Cheney were furious. There was nothing legally questionable about the submarine operation, and it was an important ongoing source of intelligence about the Soviet military. Rumsfeld, who was leaving for a trip to Europe, instructed Cheney to lead a meeting to decide what to do about the disclosure. Cheney's handwritten notes show that he explored the ideas of launching an FBI investigation of Hersh and searching his home, and of asking a grand jury to indict both the reporter and the New York Times Company for having disclosed classified information. While it was not illegal for the media to publish secrets, Cheney proposed using a World War I–era law aimed at foreign spies to go after Hersh. Cheney argued that charging the reporter with a crime would discourage the media from aggressive investigation and also "create an environment" that could take the steam out of Congress's probes. He wrote, "Can we take advantage of it to bolster our position on the Church Committee investigation? To point out the need for limits on the scope of the investigations?"[70]

In a top secret cable sent back from Brussels, Rumsfeld indicated that he liked Cheney's ideas but sounded a note of caution. While "there is a desire to have the FBI investigation begin soon," Rumsfeld wrote, if it "would adversely affect the operation . . . do not initiate the investigation."[71] Cheney quickly ran into roadblocks. The navy had in fact seen no Soviet response to the article. If the Soviets had overlooked Hersh's story, the submarine eavesdropping operation could continue, and the navy did not want to jeopardize that stroke of luck by publicizing official displeasure with the article.

In addition, Cheney reported that Ford's new attorney general, Edward Levi, thought the case for indicting the reporter using the espionage law was weak. Levi was a formidable force. He had been a special assistant to Attorney General (and future Supreme Court justice) Robert Jackson during World War II, and he had spent twelve years as dean of the University of Chicago Law School and seven more as the university's president before becoming Ford's attorney general in 1975.

Now, pressed by Cheney to approve an FBI investigation of Hersh, Levi refused. He pointed out that the anti-espionage law was aimed at spies who gave classified information to foreign governments, not at journalists who provided information to the American public. And, Levi noted, despite Cheney's displeasure at the article, it actually contained very little new information. Tactically, any prosecution would have to focus on just a few tidbits that hadn't been published elsewhere, and without real prospects for a successful prosecution, he could not properly authorize an FBI probe.[72]

Based on Levi's continued opposition to an FBI investigation of Hersh and the military's recommendation that the operation continue, Cheney cabled back to Rumsfeld that they would have to back off from their plans to punish the reporter.[73] In the end, the Ford administration took no action—but thirty years later, when Cheney was vice president and the White House was facing a new round of leaks about intelligence operations to the media, the idea of using the espionage law to go after journalists would return.

As 1975 rolled on, Cheney and other top Ford officials stepped up their efforts to protect presidential powers from the fallout of the intelligence scandals. In July, a lawsuit seeking the public release of papers related to the CIA's report on illegal activities raised the prospect of a precedent that would render the president's own files subject to the Freedom of Informa-tion Act. Cheney strongly recommended to Ford that the White House re-lease the CIA report in full on its own in order to make the lawsuit moot.[74]

Four months later, in November 1975, the Church Committee bore down on reports that there had been CIA involvement in a 1973 coup in Chile, during which its democratically elected but Marxist-leaning presi-dent, Salvador Allende, was murdered. Congress subpoenaed all docu-ments related to Nixon's meetings about Chile, but Ford invoked executive privilege to avoid turning them over.[75] Ford allowed Kissinger to testify before Congress but told him, "I think you should be very firm. The coun-try is not behind the committee."[76]

Shortly afterward, Ford decided to shake up his cabinet. He made George H. W. Bush, the chairman of the Republican National Committee, the di-rector of the CIA, sent Rumsfeld to the Pentagon as his new secretary of de-fense, and elevated Cheney to White House chief of staff. In his memoirs, Ford recalled feeling no hesitation at asking Cheney to take over from Rumsfeld, despite the new chief of staff's youth: "If their personalities differed—Cheney was very low-key, Rumsfeld rather intense—their ap-proaches to the job were remarkably alike. Both were pragmatic 'problem solvers'; both worked eighteen-hour days and were absolutely loyal to me. I knew that I could ask Cheney to step into Rumsfeld's shoes and that the White House would function just as efficiently."[77]

Soon after the cabinet shake-up, Congress began drafting legislation to require the government to obtain a warrant when monitoring the phone calls of suspected spies or terrorists. One of the impeachment charges ap-proved in 1974 by the House Judiciary Committee against Nixon had been "illegal wiretaps"—Nixon, it found, had "caused wiretaps to be placed on the telephones of 17 persons without having a court order au-thorizing the tap, as required by federal law."[78] And the Church Commit-tee in 1975 had uncovered the use by several recent presidents of the National Security Agency to conduct widespread warrantless wiretapping on Americans, including civil rights and antiwar leaders. Lawmakers wanted to make sure that future presidents did not abuse their power to wiretap communications that touched U.S. soil, so they made clear that warrants were required in all circumstances—even when a president as-serted that domestic spying was necessary to protect national security.

Inside the Ford administration, a major fight broke out over how to re-spond to the warrant bill. Several of Cheney's allies were part of a faction that opposed having Ford endorse any such bill. This faction included Rumsfeld, Bush, Scowcroft, and Kissinger.[79] They argued that White House support for any warrant law "unnecessarily derogates" the president's "inherent Constitutional authority to conduct warrantless electronic surveillance for foreign intelligence purposes."

But two of the leaders of the Ford administration legal team, Levi and Buchen, sharply disagreed. Levi told Ford that "the step by the President in asking for special legislation and a warrant procedure will be reassuring and an appropriate step in presidential leadership."[80] And Buchen rejected the idea that a president had inherent powers; he once chastised a subordinate for using the word "inherent," saying, "If the President does not have the authority either under the Constitution or under statutes, he has no authority."[81] The fight dragged out for several months, but Levi and Buchen ultimately prevailed. Ford endorsed the warrant bill, granting Levi permission to negotiate with Congress over its details.[82]

These internal disputes made an impression on Cheney. In his new role as White House chief of staff, he soon moved to impose greater centralized control over the administration in its final year in office, inviting fewer people to key meetings in order to tighten control over information and stop leaks, and cutting down on access to the Oval Office by officials who disagreed with administration policies.[83] Ford's press secretary, Ron Nessen, later wrote in his memoir that under Cheney "sensitivity over news leaks rose almost to the paranoid level," and "by [1976], there was no question that Dick Cheney was firmly atop the White House chain of command. Cheney had taken on more and more power until he was running the White House staff and overseeing the campaign in an authoritative manner—his easygoing style had disappeared."[84]

Cheney would later acknowledge that he had cut down on access to the president by officials with competing viewpoints, narrowing the range of policy advice Ford received during his final year in office. "It's really a matter of trade-offs," Cheney told an interviewer in 1979. "There is no question that to the extent that you involve a number of people in the consultative process before you make a decision, you raise the level of noise in the system. You enhance the possibility of premature disclosures and leaks. You also take more time, cut down in efficiency."[85]

Twenty-four years later, Cheney would bring this management philosophy with him back to the White House as the top adviser to another president of the United States.

# 3

# "A Cabal of Zealots": 1977–2000

## 1.

Georgia governor Jimmy Carter defeated Gerald Ford in the November 1976 presidential election as voters expressed their lingering desire to clean house after Watergate and their anger at Ford's decision to pardon Richard Nixon. Dick Cheney, who turned thirty-six ten days after Carter's Inauguration Day, was out of a job. He returned to Wyoming, intending to start some kind of business career in Casper. But when the state's sole congressman retired that fall, Cheney decided to make a run for the at-large seat. "I set out to be a political science teacher," Cheney told a *Washington Post* reporter who flew out to write a story about the novelty of a former White House chief of staff running for Congress. "My years in Washington sort of got in the way of that, but it all ties in. What I want to do is political stuff. . . . So I said, what the hell. I'm going to take a shot sometime—why not now?"[1]

It was hard work slogging across the sparsely populated state in search of voters. Six months into the primary campaign, in June 1978, Cheney felt a stabbing pain in his chest. After he was rushed to the hospital, doctors diagnosed him with a heart attack and ordered him to rest for six weeks. Instead, Cheney toughed it out. He sent a letter to every registered GOP voter in the state, explaining that he still wanted to run. As his name recognition soared from news accounts of the heart attack, support for Cheney surged. He won the Republican primary and then coasted to victory in the general election.

Cheney returned to Washington in January 1979 and was sworn in as the distinguished representative from Wyoming. At first his efforts were mostly parochial. He took up a seat on the House Interior Committee and began pushing for looser regulation on mining and other economic issues important to westerners. Cheney sponsored just thirty-three bills during his decade in Congress, two-thirds of which involved land use, water rights, drilling for oil, and dams. Only two of Cheney's thirty-three bills became law. One created a federal floodplain below a dam on the Colorado River, and the other directed the government to pay $307,092.50 to a former American spy who had been imprisoned in Cuba from 1965 to 1979.[2]

As Cheney settled into Congress, a writer named Michael Medved — who would go on to be a nationally syndicated talk-radio host — was completing a 1979 book about presidential chiefs of staff from the Lincoln to the Carter administration. His chapter on the Ford administration was devoted to a profile of Cheney. Medved wrote that it was unlikely that much would come of the new lawmaker, who despite his experience was now just another member, with no seniority, in a chamber dominated by Democrats. "Whatever glories Cheney achieves in Congress, it is unlikely that he will ever again hold the power he enjoyed at Gerald Ford's right hand," he predicted. "That can be sobering knowledge for a man not yet 40, and Cheney must console himself with the certainty that he was one of the most effective, though least publicized, Presidential assistants of our time. He also has his store of memories to fall back on."[3]

But Cheney's memories — both of what it felt like to exercise the power of the presidency, and of the frustrating restrictions that Congress imposed on the presidency after Watergate — drove him to maximize his influence, defying the apparent weakness of his position. He joined the House Ethics Committee, a body that meets in private to oversee confidential investigations against other lawmakers, giving him leverage over his colleagues. He also joined the House Intelligence Committee, which conducts classified hearings of national security matters. And he became a member of the House Republican Policy Committee, shaping his party's positions and rising to minority whip — the No. 3 GOP leadership position in the House.

Cheney was quiet about executive-power issues during his freshman term in Congress. But after Ronald Reagan retook the White House for the

Republican Party in 1981, Cheney would become one of the White House's most outspoken defenders amid a hostile House of Representatives.

## 2.

Before Reagan, Democrats controlled both the White House and the Congress. But even with a president of their own party, Democrats pressed forward with their post-Watergate reforms. In 1977, Congress imposed new controls on a president's ability to declare a state of emergency in order to trigger statutes giving him extra powers to block financial transactions and freeze assets. In 1978, Congress passed the Ethics in Government Act, which enabled independent-counsel investigations of any White House wrongdoing. That same year, Congress also passed the Foreign Intelligence Surveillance Act, which established a secret national security court made up of life-tenured federal judges who had to approve requests to wiretap. The law made clear that its warrant procedures were the "exclusive means" by which the executive branch could monitor calls where at least one end touched U.S. soil; violating the law was a felony punishable by a $10,000 fine and a five-year prison sentence. And in 1980, Congress passed a law requiring presidents to keep newly created intelligence oversight committees in each chamber fully informed about all secret spy activities and programs.

Carter signed the bills imposing new controls on the presidency into law, generally adopting a modest stance toward his constitutional role. Once the secret Foreign Intelligence Surveillance Court came into existence, for example, the Carter administration began asking it to approve warrants not only for wiretapping, but also to cover "black-bag jobs" — secret break-ins of homes and offices of suspected spies or terrorists on U.S. soil. On its face, the original 1978 FISA law covered only electronic surveillance, not physical searches. But the Carter administration voluntarily submitted to the new court's oversight anyway, applying for secret warrants when the FBI wanted to undertake a black-bag job against suspected KGB spies. (Later, the Reagan administration would roll back Carter's concession by challenging the national security court's authority to issue warrants for clandestine physical searches. A judge on the court agreed with Reagan's legal team that the statute did not give the court oversight of black-bag jobs. Reagan and his successors then resumed warrantless break-ins for national security purposes—subject only to the approval of the attorney general—until 1994, when Congress modified the intelligence law to explicitly regulate black-bag jobs as well.)[4]

But even Carter was aggressive at times about protecting or even expanding his institutional muscle to act without the approval of Congress. The power of the presidency is a neutral, nonpartisan issue; liberal presidents are as tempted as conservatives to do whatever they can to impose their agendas, and in several disputes that arose during Carter's presidency, he created precedents that his successors would pick up on and greatly expand in frequency and breadth.

One of the most important Carter moves began in June 1978, when he publicly attacked Congress's increasing habit of passing laws that gave one of its committees or chambers the power to veto executive branch actions.[5] These laws tended to grant the executive branch more power to do something, such as to make a rule or regulation over some matter, but checked that new power by allowing the legislature to reverse any particular use of the authority. For example, Congress passed a law giving the Immigration and Naturalization Service the power to suspend the deportation of illegal immigrants if it found that the deportation would cause "hardship," but Congress also reserved the right to overrule any such decision by a vote of either chamber. When the House voted to overrule the INS and force the deportation of a certain foreign exchange student whose visa had expired, the immigrant sued on the grounds that the legislative veto was unconstitutional. The Carter administration joined the student in the case, saying Congress could tell the executive branch what to do only if both chambers voted on something and then gave the president a chance to veto it. The litigation was still grinding on when Carter left office, but in 1983 the Supreme Court struck down all legislative vetoes as unconstitutional—a landmark victory for presidential power that eliminated many hundreds of similar checks across the federal statutes.[6]

Carter also battled Congress over control of treaties. In December 1978, he announced that the United States would pull out of a 1954 mutual-defense treaty with Taiwan in order to improve relations with the Communist government of mainland China. Senator Barry Goldwater of Arizona, the 1964 GOP presidential nominee and a conservative icon, led a group of senators in suing Carter, saying he had to consult them before abrogating a treaty. "Just as the president alone cannot repeal a law," Goldwater said, "he cannot repeal a treaty, which itself is a law."[7] But the Supreme Court decided that the judicial branch should stay out of the fight, saying that Congress and the White House would have to work it out politically. Controlled by Democrats who approved of Carter's policy, Congress let the fight lapse and left the constitutional question unresolved.

On November 4, 1979, a group of radical Iranian students overran the American embassy in Tehran, taking fifty-two U.S. citizens hostage for 444 days. During negotiations with Iran over getting the hostages back, Carter agreed to shut down lawsuits in U.S. courts by American businesses whose property in Iran had been nationalized and who wanted to seize Iranian property inside the United States as compensation. In turn, the business owners sued the U.S. government, arguing that their lawsuits were authorized by a federal statute, so the president could not summarily end them. The Supreme Court sided with Carter.

In April 1980, without consulting Congress, Carter commanded the military to launch what turned out to be a disastrous aborted attempt to rescue the American hostages. Amid the fallout from the debacle, in which eight American servicemen died, some in Congress criticized Carter for ordering the high-risk mission without consulting with them ahead of time under the War Powers Resolution. But Carter argued that consultation had not been required because the rescue mission had depended on total secrecy and was not combat. His answer did not satisfy the critics, but Congress made no move to sanction him.

On November 4, 1980, Reagan and his running mate, George H. W. Bush, won a landslide victory over Carter and Vice President Walter Mondale. Reagan's tidal wave swept the Senate into Republican control for the first time since 1954. Among the liberals who lost that year was Senator Frank Church, whom the Ford administration had battled over control of intelligence secrets. Democrats held on to control of the House but lost thirty-five seats.

The era of the "Reagan Revolution" would usher in a new period of conservative political action — and with it, the most aggressive push for a muscular presidency since Watergate. It would also mark a return to prominence for Cheney. Just four years earlier, Cheney had helped run Ford's 1976 presidential campaign as it defeated Reagan in the Republican primary, thereby delaying Reagan's ascent by four years. Now, however, Cheney forged strong ties with the Reagan team with help from Reagan's first White House chief of staff—another 1976 Ford campaign veteran and a lifelong friend of Cheney's, James Baker.

Two weeks after the election, Baker met with Cheney to seek advice about being a White House chief of staff. Baker took four pages of handwritten notes based on what Cheney told him that day, November 18, 1980. The notes mostly consist of recommendations about such matters as personnel and the president's schedule. But Cheney also offered one piece of substantive policy advice: "Pres. seriously weakened in recent yrs. Restore power & auth to Exec Branch—Need strong ldr'ship. Get rid of War Powers Act—restore independent rights." Cheney must have been emphatic in conveying this idea. Baker marked the comment with two double lines and six asterisks, and went back to the margin to add: "Central theme we ought to push."[8]

3.

The Reagan presidency marked a widespread revival of conservative social and economic policies, coupled with an optimistic outlook and a revival of national confidence after the dark days of the 1970s. Rejecting the legacy of Lyndon B. Johnson's Great Society programs as excessive, Reagan declared that America had put too much faith in big government programs as the solution to social and economic problems. Calling for lower taxes, fewer regulations, and weaker labor unions, he argued that everyone benefited from an economy that unleashed entrepreneurialism. The Reagan administration also pushed a social-conservative agenda, calling for a more "restrained" judiciary and seeking Supreme Court rulings that would roll back abortion rights and quota-style affirmative-action policies. And Reagan was staunchly anti-Communist, calling for increased military spending and a more confrontational stance with the Soviet Union and its proxy states around the globe.

These policies coincided with many positive developments for American society. The economy took off in a record-breaking expansion that led to strong job growth and low unemployment. And just a few years after Reagan's term ended, the Berlin Wall fell and the Cold War came to a decisive end, with democratic capitalism the clear winner. (There were downsides as well; for example, Reagan's surge in defense spending had helped bankrupt the Soviet Union, but it also led to enormous American budget deficits.)

None of these signature policies for Reagan depended upon any particular conception of the authority of the presidency. But along the way, a desire to increase the executive power became attached to the Reagan team's agenda in the face of a liberal Congress. And as the White House team began looking for ways to achieve its conservative goals without congressional approval, a new partisan split emerged over the proper powers of the presidency. While Democrats in Congress continued to view the presidency through the lens of Watergate, supporters of Reagan sought to rehabilitate the early Cold War faith in a strong centralized authority inside the White House, and a subordinate role for Congress.

"Watergate was seen [by others] as a confirmation that those who govern must not be trusted with the means or discretion of governing effectively," wrote Charles Fried, a conservative Harvard Law School scholar who served as solicitor general during Reagan's second term, in his memoir. ". . . The presidency was seen as a particularly dangerous elite that had to be hemmed in by Congress, by a permanent bureaucracy, and by legal procedures and rules of all sorts."[9] But Reaganites increasingly rejected this view. Instead, they believed that Watergate was at worst an individual failing on the part of Nixon—an aberration from which the wrong lessons had been drawn. Alongside the other aspects of the Reagan ideology, a new tenet soon emerged. This was, as Fried put it, that "the President must be allowed a strong hand in governing the nation and providing leadership."

In previous generations, presidents embracing imperial tendencies had often been Democrats—notably Franklin Roosevelt, Harry Truman, and Johnson—and their power grabs were opposed by Republicans who embodied a traditional conservative distrust of concentrated government power. But the new generation of conservative activists, who had no first-hand memory of those fights, began to associate unchecked presidential authority with their desire for lower taxes, a more aggressive stance against Communism, and domestic policies that advanced traditional social values. To them, Congress was the bastion of liberal Democrats and liberal values, and the executive branch was for conservatives.[10]

The Federalist Society, a club founded the year Reagan took office, was an important driver of this new ideology. A trio of conservative law students at Yale and the University of Chicago established the club for an initially modest purpose: According to Steven Calabresi, one of its founders, the friends thought their law school faculties were too liberal, and they wanted to bring conservative speakers on campus to debate their professors in order to gain exposure to another point of view.[11] But as its first members graduated from law school and moved on, the Federalist Society quickly grew into an enormously influential conservative network. Soon, it was no longer limited to campuses, as chapters and conferences sprang up for working lawyers. Although its membership was not monolithic, conservative legal activists tended to hone their ideas and make valuable connections at Federalist Society meetings and events, spreading the new way of thinking about executive power. And many of its first generation ended up working for the Justice Department in the Reagan and Bush-Quayle administrations. Especially under Edwin Meese III, Reagan's second-term attorney general, the Justice Department became a giant think tank where these passionate young conservative legal activists developed new legal theories to advance the Reagan agenda.

"We wanted the Justice Department to be a dynamic place where we had people thinking beyond their day-to-day activities—thinking about the state of the law, and how the law and the legal profession could be improved, how the government could do a better job," Meese later recalled. "We wanted to be a place of intellectual ferment."[12]

Some of the older attorneys on the Reagan legal team thought the new generation sometimes went too far. In his memoir, Fried referred disparagingly to Meese's "cadre of committed young assistants" who "thought of themselves as revolutionaries." He blamed these "young advisers—many drawn from the ranks of the then fledgling Federalist Societies" for writing a series of provocative speeches for Meese to read in which he laid out "extreme positions, such as questioning the constitutionality of independent agencies or suggesting that the president need not obey Supreme Court decisions with which he disagrees."[13]

Fried was not the only one to notice this. In an April 30, 1986, internal report generated by the Meese Justice Department on presidential power, one anonymous contributor warned that the short-term political contingencies in Washington were clouding their thinking about the long-term importance of the legislative branch and maintaining checks on executive power. "Conservatives traditionally have valued separation of powers because it operates to limit government," the writer said. "However, some conservatives now are also finding separation of powers frustrating because it is sometimes an obstacle to the conservative political agenda, thereby serving to preserve the liberal status quo. They are thus inclined to make an exception to their usual respect for separation of powers and advocate a very strong President—primarily for the practical reason that an activist conservative currently sits in the White House, and they fear he may be the last."

Mindful that liberal Democrats had been president before and would be again, the more senior members of the Reagan and Bush-Quayle legal teams kept a lid on some of the more extreme ideas their younger colleagues were coming up with. But two decades later, when the Bush-Cheney administration put together its legal team, the old generation was retired. Coming into their own, the Reagan Revolution generation of the conservative legal movement would revive two ideas about presidential power developed during the Reagan years—one arising from a fight over control of "independent" officials inside the executive branch, the other from a fight over funding anti-Marxist militants in Nicaragua—and push them to extremes.

## 4.

Reagan's effort to deregulate the national economy initially met with little resistance from Congress. With the Senate in GOP hands and the House Democrats cowed by Reagan's overwhelming electoral success in 1980, Congress generally went along in the first two years of his presidency as he pushed to eliminate rules in banking, media ownership, shipping, and a host of other areas. But Democrats picked up 27 seats in the House in the 1982 midterm election and started using their stronger majority to frustrate Reagan's attempts to further deregulate the government.

The Reagan team increasingly turned to other tactics for achieving their goals. Reagan issued two executive orders requiring regulatory agencies to submit their proposed rules to the White House for cost-benefit analysis by political appointees, enabling the administration to quash or delay new regulations opposed by business interests. Reagan signed his first such executive order in 1981, days after taking office, then revisited the subject with a much more forceful version in 1985. The Reagan administration also put political appointees hostile to regulation in charge of several key regulatory agencies, where they had the unspoken mandate of stopping that agency from doing much. The tactic sparked a confrontation with Congress that led to the most dramatic fight over a president's domestic powers during the Reagan era.

Reagan's appointee to lead the Environmental Protection Agency, Anne Gorsuch Burford, opposed aggressive regulations to stop air and water pollution. Accusing her of dismantling the agency instead of directing it to faithfully enforce environmental laws, Congress began holding hearings into alleged political interference at the EPA. After the hearings, a dispute arose over whether Reagan administration officials had obstructed the investigation by illegally withholding documents and lying under oath. In December 1985, the House Judiciary Committee demanded an independent-counsel investigation into the actions of several current and former Reagan officials during the EPA investigation.

The independent-counsel law was one of Congress's most important post-Watergate reforms. In 1974, Nixon had tried to derail the Watergate investigation by firing the prosecutor investigating the White House. To prevent such abuses of power in the future, Congress enacted the Ethics in Government Act of 1978. The law set up a special independent counsel who could look into high-level wrongdoing in the White House but who reported to a court and could not be fired by the president for political reasons.

Under the terms of the statute, Attorney General Meese had little choice but to comply with the committee's demand by April 10, 1986.[14] When the deadline arrived, Meese asked a court to appoint an independent counsel to investigate whether the former head of the Justice Department's Office of Legal Counsel, Theodore Olson, had committed perjury in his sworn testimony to Congress during the EPA hearings. By 1986, Olson was out of government and working in private practice, but as a former high-ranking administration official, he still fell under the 1978 independent-counsel law.

Two weeks later, Meese was handed a confidential eighty-page memo with a deceptively bland title: "Separation of Powers: Legislative-Executive Relations."[15] Meese had commissioned the April 30, 1986, report from the Justice Department's Domestic Policy Committee, one of his think tank groups of conservative activists. Among the Reagan legal team's most detailed manifestos for stronger presidential power, the report noted approvingly in a cover letter that "the strong leadership of President Reagan seems clearly to have ended the congressional resurgence of the 1970s," and it laid out ways to start recovering lost ground.[16] It called for refusing to enforce statutes that "unconstitutionally encroach upon the executive branch," vetoing more legislation, making greater use of "signing statements" to leave behind a record of the president's interpretation of new laws, and attacking the constitutionality of the War Powers Resolution and other limits on a president's national security authority. The report also laid out a revolutionary new vision of the president's powers under the Constitution that would play a key role in the Olson case.

The Meese team argued that for two hundred years, courts and scholars had misunderstood what the Founders meant when they created the "separation of powers" system. The team rejected the mainstream view that the Constitution creates three separate institutions and then gives them overlapping authority over the government as a means of preventing the tyranny of concentrated power. Instead, they said, the Founders cleanly divided the powers of government, assigning to each institution exclusive control of its own universe. "The only 'sharing of power' is the sharing of the sum of all national government power," the April 30 report said. "But that is not jointly shared, it is explicitly divided among the three branches."

The report's writers argued that the White House ought to be able to exercise total control over anything in the executive branch, which could be conceived of as a unitary being with the president as its brain. Thus, it was unconstitutional for Congress to pass laws giving executive branch officials independence from presidential control. Such a "checks and balances" law, they argued, was actually an invalid attempt by Congress to encroach on the rightful power of the president. Thus, if the White House didn't like the interest rates set by the board of the Federal Reserve, or if it didn't like how an "independent counsel" was prosecuting a case, the president should be able to remove such officials at will—even though statutes say that such officials cannot be fired by the president.

This vision was soon dubbed the "Unitary Executive Theory." Its name was adapted from one of the *Federalist Papers*. In *Federalist 70,* Alexander Hamilton explained that the Founders had decided to put one president instead of a presiding council atop the executive branch because they thought that good government requires the "energy" that comes from having one person make decisions. "That unity is conducive to energy will not be disputed," Hamilton wrote. "Decision, activity, secrecy, and dispatch will generally characterize the proceedings of one man in a much more eminent degree than the proceedings of any greater number; and in proportion as the number is increased, these qualities will be diminished."[17]

There were obstacles. The Constitution empowers Congress, not the president, to pass laws it deems "necessary and proper" for the overall structure of how the executive branch goes about its business. And the Supreme Court unanimously decided in 1935 that Congress has the power to set up independent agencies inside the executive branch to handle specialized tasks without political interference.[18] But the Meese team wondered if it could get the modern Court to overturn that precedent and embrace the Unitary Executive Theory.[19] In early 1987, Olson refused to comply with a subpoena in the EPA case, challenging the constitutionality of the independent counsel under the Unitary Executive Theory. The Reagan administration jumped in on Olson's side, setting up a momentous test of its idea.

At first it looked as if the Reaganites would achieve an historic victory. In January 1988, a federal appeals court sided with Olson and the Reagan team. Judge Ruth Bader Ginsburg, a Carter appointee, argued that the independent-counsel law was perfectly constitutional because it fit within the Founders' "system of mutual checks and balances" by preventing presidents from abusing their power. But Ginsburg was outvoted 2–1 by Judges Laurence Silberman and Stephen Williams, both recent Reagan appointees. Silberman, the author of the majority opinion, was a former Nixon and Ford official who had long been allied with advocates of strong executive powers—and he was a friend of Cheney's.[20] In 1975, Cheney had pushed Ford to make Silberman, then the deputy attorney general, the top domestic policy official in the White House, and Henry Kissinger had told Ford that "Silberman would be a good director of CIA."[21] Instead Ford had decided to make Silberman ambassador to Yugoslavia. Now wearing black robes, Silberman declared that the independent-counsel law was an unconstitutional infringement on the president's rightful powers because the statute was "inconsistent with the doctrine of a unitary executive."

But in June 1988, the Supreme Court upheld the independent-counsel law by a 7–1 vote. Stunning the Reagan legal team, the author of the majority opinion was Chief Justice William Rehnquist, the former head of the Office of Legal Counsel in the Nixon administration and usually a reliable vote for executive power. In upholding the power of Congress to pass laws setting up officials inside the executive branch who were independent from the president, Rehnquist's opinion did not even bother to mention the Unitary Executive Theory. Only Justice Antonin Scalia—put on the bench by Reagan in 1986—supported the Meese Justice Department's view.[22]

For Olson personally, the defeat became irrelevant. The independent counsel, freed to proceed, decided not to file any charges against him. Cleared of taint, Olson later argued the *Bush v. Gore* case before the Supreme Court in 2000 on behalf of the Bush-Cheney campaign, and then became the new administration's first solicitor general.

For enthusiasts of the Unitary Executive Theory, however, the defeat was devastating. Fried said the decisive ruling meant the Reagan legal team's "separation-of-powers initiative was dead."[23] Yet although he expressed disappointment, in his memoirs Fried also said that the Unitary Executive Theory was in some ways hard for a traditional conservative to defend. Despite its "perfect logic" and "beautiful symmetry," he wrote, the Unitary Executive Theory "is not literally compelled by the words of the Constitution. Nor did the framers' intent compel this view."[24]

## 5.

Throughout its fights to expand presidential power at the expense of the legislative branch, the White House would find no greater ally in Congress than Representative Cheney. Taking sides with his party over his institution, Cheney used his position as a member of the Intelligence Committee to support Reagan's national security agenda at every turn. An ardent anti-Communist, Cheney was a strong supporter of U.S. assistance to the Contras, the anti-Marxist rebels waging a civil war in Nicaragua against the Soviet-supported Sandinista government. Cheney often went to the White House and met with members of the National Security Council staff to work out strategies for overcoming Democratic opposition to funding the Contras.[25] When Democrat Jim Wright later became Speaker of the House in 1987 and began meeting with Nicaraguan leaders in an effort to soften American policy in Central America, Cheney was among those who bitterly attacked Wright for challenging the president's role in running foreign affairs.

Former representative Mickey Edwards, an Oklahoma Republican who served in Congress from 1977 to 1994, worked closely with Cheney throughout this period. Like Cheney, Edwards was both a passionate supporter of the Contras and a member of the House GOP leadership team. Two decades later, Edwards became a sharp critic of the Bush-Cheney administration's attempt to expand presidential power, calling it an affront to traditional conservative principles. But, looking back at the early 1980s, Edwards said that Cheney showed few hints of radicalism. "We all knew he had once been White House chief of staff, but no one thought of it as whether he was a champion of executive power," Edwards recalled. "It didn't come up. We were busily engaged in the conflict with the Democrats in the Congress, and I never had a reason to ask him. . . . If Cheney supported doing things to give the president more power, no one would have noticed because that is where almost all the Republicans were. And that was out of frustration, because what mattered was the policy outcome."[26]

Cheney staunchly backed Reagan's decisions to deploy the American military aggressively. In 1982, Reagan sent U.S. Marines to Beirut as part of a multinational peacekeeping force. When a suicide bomber killed 241 servicemen on October 23, 1983, several members of Congress attacked Reagan for ordering the deployment. But Cheney played defense for the White House, telling reporters that Congress bore equal responsibility, since they had voted for an agreement—after the forces were already in Beirut—to let the marines stay in Lebanon for eighteen months: "I don't think it's right for us to say we got bagged," he said. "We had our eyes open."[27]

Two days after the Beirut bombing, Reagan sent U.S. troops to invade the tiny island nation of Grenada in order to stop a Marxist-backed coup. The intervention was controversial in part because Reagan did not ask Congress for prior approval; instead, Reagan justified the massive invasion by saying that he sent the troops to protect a small group of American medical students.[28] Some lawmakers said the invasion was illegal, but Cheney was a loud supporter. He traveled to the island, praising the intervention as a "selfless and courageous act by a great nation" and assuring reporters that the Grenadians felt the United States had "rescued and liberated them."[29]

Cheney forged other ties with the White House. According to James Mann's *Rise of the Vulcans,* once a year in the 1980s, the Reagan administration flew Cheney to a secret bunker to practice rebuilding the government if the Soviets destroyed Washington. Cheney's role, Mann reported, was to use his White House chief of staff experience to run the government in the name of any surviving cabinet member who made it to the bunker. The Reagan plan ignored the Presidential Succession Act, a 1947 law that put two top congressional leaders higher in the line of succession than cabinet secretaries. The program also made no plan for reconstituting Congress, because "it would be easier to operate without them," a participant told Mann.[30]

Cheney made no secret of his continuing loyalty to the executive branch during this era. In January 1985, on the eve of Reagan's second inauguration, Cheney told a reporter that his experience as Ford's chief of staff outweighed his more recent time as a member of Congress. "I retain strong feelings of the importance of the executive branch, views that were shaped by my time at the White House," Cheney said. "But I believe I'm in a minority up here. The President has to have broad leeway to operate. The Congress too often interferes in areas in which he has primacy."[31] The following year, on March 24, 1986, the Reagan team rewarded their close ally by naming Lynne Cheney to head the National Endowment for the Humanities, giving her the power to distribute $125 million a year in grants to fund intellectual projects.

A few weeks later, Dick Cheney stepped up his rhetoric in defense of Reagan's wartime powers. On April 5, 1986, terrorists bombed a West Berlin discotheque frequented by American soldiers. The Reagan administration blamed the bombing on Libyan dictator Mu'ammar Gadhafi, who had called for acts of violence against Americans following clashes between the U.S. Navy and Libyan patrol boats in disputed waters off the Gulf of Sidra. As the U.S. military prepared to attack Libya, some lawmakers, including Senate Armed Services Committee chairman Sam Nunn, Democrat of Georgia, complained that Reagan was about to commit an act of war without consulting Congress, as he was required to do by the War Powers Resolution. Some also argued that the government should make public its case against Gadhafi before essentially launching a war.

But on April 11, 1986, four days before Reagan would bomb Libya, Cheney went on *The MacNeil/Lehrer NewsHour* and argued that "if the president of the United States reviews it and feels it's adequate," then the public should trust what he says about classified intelligence. "I am satisfied that I know all I need to know at this point, and I would disagree with what we often hear from the Hill, the cry for consultation in advance, let us in on the decision, we want to share responsibility," Cheney said. "It seems to me that this is a clear-cut case where the president as commander in chief . . . is justified in taking whatever action he deems appropriate and discussing the details with us after the fact."[32]

## 6.

Any lingering discontent in Congress over how Reagan handled the April 1986 Libyan bombing was quickly eclipsed by the emerging Iran-Contra affair.

The origins of the scandal traced back to 1982, when Congress decided to roll back U.S. involvement in the "secret war" in Nicaragua between the CIA-supported Contras and the Soviet-supported Sandinista government. Congress passed a statute called the Boland Amendment, which set a limit on humanitarian aid to the Contras and prohibited the use of funds "for the purpose of overthrowing the Government of Nicaragua."

But the Reagan administration found a way around this ban by saying that its actions were intended to force the Sandinistas to reach a peace agreement with the Contras, not to bring down the government. In 1984, the CIA placed mines in three Nicaraguan harbors, damaging several ships, including a Soviet oil tanker.[33] Furious both at the outlaw operation—deemed a violation of international law by the International Court of Justice—and at the fact that the Reagan administration had not briefed the intelligence oversight committees about the sabotage plan ahead of time, Congress passed a new and much more draconian Boland Amendment. This second law was a flat ban on expending funds to support the Contras in any way.

"There are no exceptions to the prohibition," Rep. Edward P. Boland, a Massachusetts Democrat who chaired the House Intelligence Committee, explained when introducing the second version of the law in October 1984.

Supporters of the Contras in Congress immediately recognized its sweep. Cheney denounced it as a "killer amendment" that would force the Contras "to lay down their arms."[34] But Congress passed the bill, and Reagan signed it into law. Cheney would spend the next several years trying to get his colleagues to repeal the ban.

Meanwhile, inside the White House, several members of Reagan's National Security Council staff—including National Security Adviser John Poindexter and his deputy, Lieutenant Colonel Oliver North—conspired to circumvent the ban with a complex scheme. Investigators later found that NSC staff had arranged to secretly sell U.S. arms to Iran, at inflated prices, in exchange for the release of some American hostages held by Iranian-backed terrorists in Lebanon—violating the president's stated policy of not negotiating with terrorists and illegally withholding information about the covert deal from congressional oversight committees. Then they steered the proceeds from the sale to the Contras. They separately solicited third-party countries, such as Saudi Arabia, to fund the Contras in return for implied favors. Just after the midterm election in November 1986, the scheme began to come to light in foreign media reports. Days earlier, the Democrats had won back control of the Senate, and 1987 would be dominated by a joint House-Senate committee investigation into the affair.

Cheney landed a seat on the Iran-Contra committee, where he was the ranking House Republican. Instead of delving deep, when it was his turn to ask questions of witnesses during the hearings, Cheney merely encouraged them to explain why preventing a Marxist government from taking hold in Nicaragua was the right policy for the United States. In between hearings, while working with the Republican staff on the committee, Cheney made an important new connection. One of his fellow House Republicans on the committee had contributed a young staff attorney named David Addington to the effort. Addington would soon become Cheney's own aide, and they would become a powerful duo for the next two decades.

Like Cheney, Addington was an ardent hawk who had never served in the military, although his father was a retired general and a veteran of World War II and the Korean War. Addington had been a smart, sarcastic teenager in New Mexico, graduating from high school in 1974 during the end of the Vietnam War and the peak of the Watergate scandal. Eschewing the anti-authoritarian counterculture, Addington was a sharp-tongued conservative; his former high school history teacher told *The New Yorker* that Addington felt strongly that America "should have stayed and won the Vietnam War, despite the fact that we were losing."[35]

Addington attended the U.S. Naval Academy in Annapolis, Maryland, for a year, but dropped out and went home to New Mexico, working at a Long John Silver's fast-food restaurant. Like Cheney, he got his life back on track, graduated summa cum laude from Georgetown, and went on to earn a law degree from Duke in 1981. He went straight from law school to the general counsel's office of the CIA, where former colleagues said he strongly opposed the new restrictions that Congress had imposed in the wake of the Church Committee investigations. He later took a job as a GOP staffer on the House Intelligence Committee before transferring to the Iran-Contra investigation.

Just thirty years old in 1987, Addington shared Cheney's deeply held belief that Congress ought to leave intelligence and national security matters to Reagan. Addington was also developing a philosophy about why the president, as a matter of constitutional law, might have inherent and exclusive powers that would allow him to take action in foreign affairs and national defense without congressional approval.

As Cheney got to know Addington and the Iran-Contra investigation progressed, his defense of the Reagan administration became sharper. Instead of merely attacking the Boland Amendment as bad policy, Cheney now began to question whether it was constitutional — meaning that Reagan and his top aides on the National Security Council might have been free to ignore it all along. This new constitutional theory bolstered an otherwise strained argument for why the operation might not have been illegal; maybe, some White House defenders had been arguing, Congress had meant for the Boland Amendment to cover only intelligence operations run by the CIA, which left those run out of the White House unfettered. On July 20, 1987, Cheney flipped on his hearing room microphone and, in his characteristically measured tone, declared his support for this entire line of argument: "I personally do not believe the Boland Amendment applied to the President, nor to his immediate staff or to the NSC staff."[36]

Most of Cheney's colleagues did not share his vision of a presidency empowered by the Constitution to ignore laws that control its foreign policy options. Four months later, the Iran-Contra committee issued a scathing and bipartisan report accusing a "cabal of zealots" inside the White House of having broken "the letter and spirit of the Boland Amendment" with "pervasive dishonesty and inordinate secrecy." More than just breaking a law, Congress said, the administration officials had "undermined a cardinal principle of the Constitution" and the Founders' "most significant check on Executive power: the president can spend funds on a program only if he can convince Congress to appropriate the money."

"The common ingredients of the Iran and Contra policies were secrecy, deception, and disdain for the law," the report declared. "A small group of senior officials believed that they alone knew what was right. . . . In the Iran-Contra Affair, officials viewed the law not as setting boundaries for their actions, but raising impediments to their goals. When the goals and the law collided, the law gave way."[37]

This majority report was signed by eighteen lawmakers on the twenty-six-member committee, including three Republicans. Cheney was not among them. Refusing to sign the report, he instead commissioned Addington and other GOP staffers to write an alternative assessment. It declared that the real lawbreakers were Cheney's fellow lawmakers, because the Constitution "does not permit Congress to pass a law usurping Presidential power." Signed by Cheney and seven other Republicans, the minority report declared that the Boland Amendment infringed on the presidency's rightful powers: "Judgments about the Iran-Contra affair ultimately must rest upon one's views about the proper roles of Congress and the president in foreign policy. The fundamental law of the land is the

Constitution. Unconstitutional statutes violate the rule of law every bit as much as do willful violations of constitutional statutes. . . . Congressional actions to limit the President in [foreign policy and national security] should be reviewed with a considerable degree of skepticism. If they interfere with core presidential foreign policy functions, they should be struck down. Moreover, the lesson of our constitutional history is that doubtful cases should be decided in favor of the President."[38]

Cheney's alternate report did not make a big splash. Senator Warren Rudman of New Hampshire, the senior Republican senator on the joint Iran-Contra committee and one of the signatories to the majority report, called the rival effort "pathetic." Cheney and the other White House allies who signed his report had, Rudman said, "separated the wheat from the chaff and sowed the chaff."[39]

After the Iran-Contra hearings ended, Cheney moved quickly to ensure that fallout from the scandal did not lead to new restrictions on presidential power. When other lawmakers pushed a bill forcing presidents to notify Congress of all covert operations within forty-eight hours, the Senate passed it, but Cheney led a fight to block it in the House.

"On the scale of risks, there is more reason to be concerned about depriving the president of his ability to act than about Congress's alleged inability to respond," he wrote in a May 1988 *Wall Street Journal* column.

But something was different this time. In addition to making his usual pragmatic arguments in favor of giving the president flexibility to decide when to disclose sensitive operations to Congress, in his May 1988 column Cheney also mounted a sophisticated legal argument. He wrote that as a matter of constitutional law, Congress could decide only whether or not to fund the CIA. Once Congress provided the agency with a budget, he said, only the commander in chief could decide how to run it. If presidents had to tell Congress about all covert operations within forty-eight hours, creating the risk that a lawmaker might leak the operation's existence, then presidents might not be able to run some operations that lasted longer. Thus, the forty-eight-hour rule was unconstitutional, he said.

"At the heart of the dispute over this bill is a deeper one over the scope of the president's inherent constitutional power," Cheney wrote. "I believe the president has the authority, without statute, to [order covert operations]. . . . Congress may not use the money power to invade an inherently presidential power."[40]

The public record contains almost nothing like this coming from Cheney prior to his service on the Iran-Contra committee. In retrospect, it seems likely that the embryo of the Bush-Cheney administration's legal strategy began incubating at the moment Cheney's career-long drive for a policy of expansive presidential power encountered Addington's theories. The logic of the minority views Iran-Contra report pointed toward the prospect of a total victory for "presidentialists" without the need for any more frustrating debates with Congress. Indeed, if Addington was right, then the unfettered presidential powers Cheney dreamed of already existed, regardless of what Congress said. The powers were just slumbering in wait for the day that a bold president would pick them up and wield them.

The minority views Iran-Contra report would be virtually ignored for almost two decades. Then, in December 2005, the *New York Times* revealed that the Bush-Cheney administration had authorized the National Security Agency to monitor Americans' international phone calls and e-mails without warrants, violating the Foreign Intelligence Surveillance Act of 1978. As Congress erupted, Cheney told reporters that he believed the president had all the authority he needed to bypass the law based on his inherent powers as commander in chief. And he directed the reporters, if they wanted a road map to the central operating principles of the Bush-Cheney presidency, to go back and read his Iran-Contra report.[41]

## 7.

In the November 1988 presidential election, Vice President George H. W. Bush defeated Massachusetts governor Michael Dukakis for the right to succeed Reagan. Bush and his vice president, the former Indiana senator Dan Quayle, arrived in the Oval Office hobbled by a Democratic-controlled Congress whose members were still upset about the Iran-Contra scandal, and who harbored lingering suspicions that Bush himself may have known more about the illegal operation than he let on. Bush also lacked Reagan's charismatic ability to advance his policy agenda in the face of a hostile Congress by communicating directly with the American people. Instead, the former vice president had to find other ways to advance his policies unilaterally.[42]

On July 27, 1989, the newly appointed general counsels of every executive branch agency received a memo from William P. Barr, the new head of the Office of Legal Counsel.* Entitled "Common Legislative Encroachments on Executive Branch Authority," the memo laid out the top ten ways in which Congress tried to meddle with powers that should be the president's alone. Among them were "4. Micromanagement of the Executive Branch," "5. Attempts to Gain Access to Sensitive Executive Branch Information," and "9. Attempts to Restrict the President's Foreign Affairs Powers."

Perhaps the most startling part of the memo was its unqualified support for the Unitary Executive Theory, despite its 7–1 defeat at the hands of the Supreme Court just a year earlier. Barr also reiterated the belief that the Constitution required the executive branch to speak "with one voice" — the president's — and told the general counsels to watch out for any legislation that would protect executive branch officials from being fired at will by the president. He also said the administration should try to narrow the impact of the ruling by arguing that the Court's reasoning applied only to independent counsels. "Only by consistently and forcefully resisting such congressional incursions can executive branch prerogatives be preserved," Barr wrote.[43]

"Never before had the Office of Legal Counsel . . . publicly articulated a policy of resisting Congress," Georgia State law professor Neil Kinkopf,

---

*The leadership of the Office of Legal Counsel during the Bush-Quayle administration demonstrates the long-range connections of the activist conservative lawyers who have played key roles in the push to expand presidential power. Barr's views on executive power were shaped by his experiences working as an analyst for the CIA during the Nixon and Ford administrations — including during the Church Committee's investigation into intelligence abuses — while taking law school classes at night. Bush later promoted Barr to attorney general. Barr's first replacement at the Office of Legal Counsel was J. Michael Luttig. Bush then nominated Luttig to be a federal appeals court judge, and Luttig would play a key role in litigation over the Bush-Cheney administration's claims that it could hold U.S. citizens without trial as "enemy combatants." After Luttig became a judge, he was replaced at the Office of Legal Counsel by Timothy Flanigan, who went on to become deputy White House counsel for the Bush-Cheney administration. Flanigan told the *New York Times* that the idea of using military commissions to try Al Qaeda detainees was first suggested by Barr in a phone call a few days after 9/11; Barr had explored using military tribunals to try terrorists a decade earlier after the Libyan-backed bombing of Pan Am flight 103 over Lockerbie, Scotland. On November 18, 2001, the *Washington Post* published an op-ed by Barr contending that Bush's plan to try terrorists for 9/11-related crimes was "well grounded in constitutional law, historical precedent and common sense"; the piece did not disclose Barr's role in creating the policy.

who worked in the Office of Legal Counsel during the Clinton years, later wrote. "The Barr memo did so with belligerence, staking out an expansive view of presidential power while asserting positions that contradicted recent Supreme Court precedent. Rather than fade away as ill-conceived and legally dubious, however, the memo's ideas persisted and evolved within the Republican Party and conservative legal circles like the Federalist Society."[44]

Bush adopted a relatively measured approach to a president's power to act independently of the will of Congress. But one of his most fiery moments in defense of presidential power came in a speech on May 10, 1991, at the dedication ceremony for a new social sciences complex at Princeton University. "The most common challenge to presidential powers comes from a predictable source . . . the United States Congress," Bush declared, accusing lawmakers of trying to "micromanage" executive branch decisions, especially in foreign policy.[45] In the fifteen-minute speech, Bush denounced Congress for trying to accumulate power at the president's expense by making excessive demands for information and by "writing too specific directions for carrying out a particular law." He said that six of the twenty vetoes he had cast to that date were to defend the presidency against such meddling. And he criticized lawmakers for passing complex bills full of earmark provisions for unjustifiable expenditures like "a federal grant to study cow belches," demanding that Congress give him a line-item veto.

But at Princeton, as he consistently did elsewhere, Bush tempered his remarks. "The great joy and challenge of the Office I occupy," he said, "is that the President serves, not just as the unitary executive, but hopefully as a unifying executive."

That moderation meant that the first President Bush eschewed some of the more extreme suggestions he received from his advisers. Among those pushing him was Cheney, whom Bush had tapped to be his secretary of defense in 1989.

8.

In March of 1989, Representative Cheney was preparing to deliver a talk at a conference sponsored by the American Enterprise Institute, a conservative think tank, about what he called "congressional aggrandizement" and "congressional overreaching in foreign policy." In a forty-two-page essay submitted ahead of time to AEI, Cheney argued that "the legislative branch is ill-equipped to handle the foreign policy tasks it has taken upon itself over the past 15 years."[46] Cheney urged his readers to look up the minority views report of the Iran-Contra committee. But he said he wanted to get beyond the legal arguments over the possible meanings of the "parchment document" and explain why, for pragmatic and "real world" reasons, he endorsed an interpretation that gave stronger powers to the president and a lesser role for Congress.

As a leak-prone 535-member body, he said, Congress is simply not capable of acting with the speed, secrecy, and decisiveness of a single president. Moreover, since the majority of its members have to stand for reelection in the next two years, they are looking for "quick results—something to show the voters before the next election." As such, he said, Congress cannot be trusted to make important decisions affecting national security and foreign policy. "When Congress steps beyond its capacities, it takes traits that can be helpful to collective deliberation and turns them into a harmful blend of vacillation, credit-claiming, blame avoidance and indecision," Cheney wrote.

Any rule in which the body of elected representatives must reach a consensus about whether it is a good idea to launch a covert or military attack, Cheney said, would diminish the likelihood of the proposed attack's going forward. Thus, "the real world effect often turns out, as Caspar Weinberger has said, not to be a *transfer* of power from the President to Congress, but a *denial* of power to the government as a whole." (Weinberger had been secretary of defense under Reagan and was indicted for perjury as part of the Iran-Contra scandal.)

Based on this principle, Cheney went on to argue that the president must have total and exclusive control of the nation's diplomacy, decisions over launching covert operations and determining when it is safe to tell Congress about them, and decisions about launching military attacks against a foreign enemy. Once Congress learns about an action, Cheney said, they can still check the president: If lawmakers disagree with what the president has done, they can vote to cut off funds for any ongoing operation when they pass the next year's budget. But if Congress "does not have the will to support or oppose the president definitively," he added, then "the nation should not be paralyzed by Congress' indecision." Therefore, Cheney called for the repeal of the War Powers Resolution—the 1973 law that required the president to both consult with Congress before going to war and pull out of any combat after sixty days if Congress had not explicitly authorized the operation to continue. The law was both "unworkable and of dubious constitutionality," Cheney said, adding, "I cannot accept such a limited view of the president's inherent constitutional powers."

Cheney never delivered his talk. As he was writing the paper, the Senate was in tumult over Bush's first choice to be the new secretary of defense, former Texas senator John Tower. After Tower was accused of having questionable ties to defense contractors, his nomination failed. A week before the American Enterprise Institute conference, Cheney got a phone call from the White House. They needed a replacement defense secretary nominee who could get easily confirmed, and they wanted the House minority whip to take the job. Cheney bowed out of the conference, shelving his sharp-tongued comments, and easily won confirmation by the Senate. When he left Congress for the Pentagon, he took Addington with him as his top aide.

As defense secretary, Cheney would soon get a chance to oversee military action. In December 1989, Bush ordered U.S. troops to intervene in Panama, where they arrested strongman leader Manuel Noriega. Bush cited several justifications for the invasion, including the protection of American citizens in the Canal Zone, the restoration of democracy in Panama, and Noriega's links to drug trafficking. Bush did not go to Congress for authorization, but U.S. troops involved in the combat began pulling out again by January 1990, well before the War Powers Resolution's sixty-day clock was up.

After Saddam Hussein invaded Kuwait in August 1990, Bush sent five hundred thousand U.S. troops to Saudi Arabia—more than ten times as many as had been involved in Panama. The United Nations Security Council voted to approve the use of force to liberate Kuwait if diplomacy failed. But Congress had not voted to authorize the United States to participate in any war, as both the Constitution and the War Powers Resolution required. Nevertheless, Cheney urged Bush to launch the Gulf War without asking Congress for authorization. He told Bush that it was unnecessary and too risky to seek a vote in Congress, where both chambers were dominated by Democrats.

"I was not enthusiastic about going to Congress for an additional grant of authority," Cheney recalled for a 1996 documentary on the Gulf War. "I was concerned that they might well vote 'no' and that would make life more difficult for us."[47]

By urging Bush to ignore the War Powers Resolution on the eve of the first major overseas ground war since Congress enacted the law, Cheney was attempting to set a powerful precedent. Had Bush taken his advice and survived the political fallout, the Gulf War would have restored Truman's 1950 claim that as president he had "inherent" power to send American troops to the Korean War on his own.

But the president rejected his defense secretary's advice. Although Bush continued to insist that he had the authority to launch the war on his own, in January 1991 the president asked Congress for a vote in "support" of the use of force against Iraq. Bush won the authorization vote—barely. The margin in the Senate was 52–47. Had Congress voted no, Cheney later said, he would have urged Bush to ignore them and launch the Gulf War anyway. "From a constitutional standpoint, we had all the authority we needed," he argued.[48]

As the Gulf War proceeded, Cheney fought with Congress on other fronts. The defense secretary thwarted Congress by refusing to issue contracts for the V-22 Osprey, a plane that was plagued with technical problems. Cheney opposed the V-22 program, but Congress decided to appropriate funds for it anyway. By refusing to issue contracts, Cheney revived the Nixon-era tactic of "impounding" funds, declining to spend money Congress had appropriated for programs that he didn't like. In fact, Congress had passed a law in 1974 to ban impoundment, but Cheney—who believed the anti-impoundment law unconstitutionally infringed on executive power—was ignoring it.

Further in defiance of Congress, Cheney also pushed to impose greater political control over uniformed military. During the run-up to the Gulf War, the civilian general counsel of the army, William James Haynes II, clashed with the army's top uniformed lawyer, a two-star general, over whose office should control legal issues that might arise from the war, such as the handling of any contaminated bodies of soldiers who might be killed by Iraqi biological weapons. Jim Haynes, a protégé of Addington, pressed for greater executive power over the army. In 1991, Cheney formally asked Congress to change the law to place all military attorneys under the control of civilian political appointees. Congress rejected Cheney's proposal. But in March 1992, Cheney's deputy issued an administrative order making the changes anyway.

Cheney's fights with Congress over the V-22 Osprey contracts and the independence of the uniformed lawyers came to a head in the summer of

1992, when Addington appeared before the Senate Armed Services Committee for a confirmation hearing. Addington had been Cheney's personal aide for the first three years of his tenure at the Pentagon, controlling what papers reached the secretary's desk and fighting internal battles with military brass. Colonel Lawrence Wilkerson, who served as chief of staff to General Colin Powell, the chairman of the Joint Chiefs of Staff during Cheney's tenure as defense secretary, said Addington had developed a reputation around the Defense Department as an intense bureaucratic infighter devoted to concentrating ever more authority in Cheney's office. "Addington was a nut," Wilkerson recalled. "That was how everybody summed it up. A brilliant nut, perhaps, but a nut nonetheless."[49] Now Cheney wanted Addington to become the Defense Department's general counsel, a position that required Senate confirmation.

On July 1, 1992, Addington, for the first and only time in his career in government service, had to answer in public to an authority other than Cheney. He endured a rocky confirmation hearing as one senator after the next used his appearance to express their displeasure with Cheney's policies. Throughout, he calmly defended himself by denying that he and Cheney had any intent to defy Congress.

"How many ways are there around evading the will of Congress? How many different legal theories do you have?" Senator Carl Levin, Democrat of Michigan, thundered at Cheney's aide.[50]

"I do not have any, Senator," replied Addington.

Eventually, Addington was confirmed, but only after promising that the Pentagon would restore the military lawyers' independence and issue V-22 contracts as quickly as possible. His tenure as the top lawyer at the Defense Department was brief. That November, Bush lost the 1992 presidential election to Arkansas governor Bill Clinton and his running mate, Tennessee senator Al Gore. Once again, Cheney was out of a job.

# 9.

The tenure of President Clinton, like that of Carter before him, showed that presidential power is not a partisan issue. As the Clinton-Gore administration sought to advance its generally liberal policy agenda — especially after conservative Republicans retook Congress in 1995 — the White House used the tools of unilateral presidential power it inherited from Republican administrations. As one scholar has written, Clinton's legal team was "relatively cautious in its assertion of executive power, with a little more respect for congressional prerogatives, but it still mostly embraced the Reagan and Bush administrations' views" of its rightful powers.[51]

Early in his presidency, Clinton refused to release documents showing who had attended meetings of First Lady Hillary Clinton's task force on reforming the nation's health-care system. The move presaged a later fight by Vice President Cheney to keep his similar energy task force records secret. But unlike Cheney, Clinton eventually reversed course and agreed to release the names.[52] Clinton also reversed a Reagan-Bush clampdown on the Freedom of Information Act, ordering government agencies to comply with requests by the public for documents if possible. And he ordered a massive review of classified documents, resulting in the release to historians of numerous government files.

While Clinton never invoked the Unitary Executive Theory as justification for seizing greater control over the permanent government, he did advance some of its principles in modest ways. He issued an executive order strengthening the Reagan-Bush practice of forcing executive agencies to submit proposed rules to the White House for review before they could take effect. (Because his administration was less ideologically hostile to the idea of regulation, these procedures did not generate much impact until after Clinton left office.) Especially after 1994, Clinton also made aggressive use of executive orders to advance his agenda without going to Congress on such issues as protecting the environment and implementing international human rights treaties. The executive orders prompted some conservatives to accuse Clinton of acting like a dictator. Phyllis Schlafly, the leader of the conservative Eagle Forum, denounced Clinton's "power grab" and complained that his executive orders "function in a Never Never Land of almost unlimited power."[53] And in 1996, when Congress banned placing U.S. troops under United Nations command, Clinton declared that he could bypass the law under his power, as commander in chief, to decide how best to structure the military's hierarchy of command.[54]

Clinton's attempts to invoke muscular presidential powers did not always succeed. After Democrats lost control of Congress, he issued an executive order banning the government from issuing federal contracts to any company that hired permanent replacements for striking workers. The move, which embodied how the Unitary Executive Theory might play out in the hands of a liberal president, outraged conservatives, and the Chamber of Commerce filed a lawsuit to stop the secretary of labor from carrying out the order. The Clinton legal team argued that federal courts had no power to review such presidential actions, but they lost the case in 1996.[55]

Clinton suffered similar setbacks in federal courts as a result of his affair with a White House intern, Monica Lewinsky. Seeking to keep his conversations with White House attorneys secret, Clinton lost a pair of decisions that reduced the level of attorney-client privilege enjoyed by presidents. But though the Lewinsky affair led to Clinton's impeachment, it also had the long-term effect of strengthening the presidency as an institution. Independent counsel Kenneth Starr's relentless and expensive investigation of Clinton convinced Democrats to join Republicans in wanting to get rid of the Ethics in Government Act. Congress allowed the law to expire in 1999, freeing all future presidents from the threat of a prosecutor they could not fire.

Perhaps the most dramatic fight over presidential power during the Clinton years concerned his overseas interventions. When Clinton arrived in office in 1993, he inherited from Bush a peacekeeping operation in Somalia. After a Republican congressman sought to force Clinton to pull the troops out under the War Powers Resolution, Clinton's legal team declared that the law did not apply to Somalia because U.S. forces were not in sustained combat—a claim that prompted the conservative *National Review* to crow that Clinton had "set a precedent that the next Republican President will cheerfully embrace."[56] However, after the October 1993 "Black Hawk Down" incident, in which nineteen U.S. servicemen were killed in Mogadishu, Congress and Clinton agreed to withdraw the forces by April 1994.

As Clinton's presidency progressed, he deployed peacekeeping troops to such trouble spots as Haiti and Bosnia and launched missile strikes on Iraq, Afghanistan, and Sudan—all without seeking prior congressional authorization. Like his predecessors, Clinton refused to acknowledge that the War Powers Resolution restricted his actions as commander in chief. But, also like his predecessors, Clinton mostly complied with other aspects of the law. He made reports to Congress when he sent troops into a hostile zone, and none of the fighting lasted longer than the statute's sixty-day cutoff for deployments that did not receive congressional authorization. There was one notable exception: On March 24, 1999, Clinton ordered the U.S. Air Force to take part in a NATO bombing campaign in

Kosovo. The air war kept going for seventy-nine days. This was the first time since the War Powers Resolution became law that any president had deployed U.S. forces into overseas combat for more than sixty days without explicit congressional authorization, as the post-Vietnam law required. The Clinton legal team argued that the president had all the authority he needed because Congress had approved an emergency supplement spending bill to fund the Kosovo war on May 22, 1999—just a few days before the sixty-day clock ran out. They argued that by funding the war, Congress had implicitly authorized it.[57] This theory was controversial, in part because the War Powers Resolution explicitly said that appropriations cannot count as authorization—just because Congress refuses to cut off supplies for U.S. troops who are already engaged in combat doesn't mean they approve the war.

Clinton's Kosovo campaign sparked a dramatic role reversal among Washington politicians. Democrats who had previously insisted that the War Powers Resolution be obeyed by Republican presidents now offered little or no criticism of Clinton. Indeed, some of the most ardent doves during the Reagan and Bush-Quayle years, such as House minority whip David Bonior, Democrat of Michigan, declared their strong support for Clinton's actions and urged him to do "whatever it takes" to win the war in Yugoslavia, including using ground troops "if necessary."[58] Bonior offered little convincing explanation for why he had suddenly abandoned the principles he had embraced during the previous decade, when he opposed Reagan's military interventions in Central America and voted against authorizing Bush's Gulf War. Republican politicians were no less hypocritical and partisan than Democrats. House majority whip Tom DeLay of Texas, who in 1991 said that the first President Bush had the power to fight the Gulf War without Congress's interfering like "535 commander in chiefs," became one of 127 House Republicans who unsuccessfully voted in May 1999 to invoke the War Powers Resolution—demanding that Clinton remove all U.S. forces from the Balkans within thirty days. In a floor statement, DeLay explained that he had trusted Bush to make the right decisions, but Clinton had provided "no explanation defining what vital national interests are at stake. . . . Many who argue we cannot pull out say we should stay to save face, if for no other reason. I would like to ask these people, was it worth it to stay in Vietnam just to save face?"[59]

In the last year of his presidency, Clinton further eroded restrictions on the commander in chief. In 1972, the United States and the Soviet Union had agreed to the Anti-Ballistic Missile Treaty. One of its provisions forbade building a missile-defense system. But after the Cold War ended and rogue states such as North Korea began pursuing their own nuclear programs, some called for the United States to revisit the idea of a missile shield. In 2000, Clinton's legal team asserted that he could simply "interpret" the treaty as allowing him to do what it clearly prohibited: start building a radar facility that could be used for a missile defense system.[60] Invoking the revisionist interpretation of the treaty, Clinton began building such a facility in Alaska—keeping the option of a missile-defense system available for his successor while avoiding pulling out of the ABM treaty.

Clinton's stance toward the Kosovo air war and the ABM treaty prompted a harsh critique from conservatives, including a Berkeley law professor named John Yoo. At a conference on executive power in 2000, Yoo declared that "the Clinton administration has undermined the balance of powers that exist in foreign affairs, and [they] have undermined principles of democratic accountability that executive branches have agreed upon well to the Nixon Administration." And in the Clinton administration's strained legal interpretation of the ABM treaty, he added, "the legal arguments are so outrageous, they're so incredible, that they actually show, I think, a disrespect for the idea of law, by showing how utterly manipulatable it is."[61]

Yoo would be heard from again in years to come.

## 10.

After leaving government in 1993, Cheney joined the American Enterprise Institute, the conservative think tank where he had planned to present his paper on congressional overreach in March 1989, and he seriously explored running for president himself. He talked about the idea on CNN's *Larry King Live* in December 1993 and asked Addington to help run an exploratory committee for him.[62] In 1994, Cheney embarked on a long speechmaking tour and campaigned for 160 Republicans in forty-seven states, an exhausting effort designed to raise his profile in preparation for the 1996 primary.

But Cheney's Washington experience did not translate into a connection with voters outside the Beltway, and he lacked the charisma necessary to win support in early polls. He also had a bad heart, and he faced the potential ugliness of a smear campaign among social conservatives about the fact that one of his daughters, Mary Cheney, was a lesbian. On January 3, 1995, Cheney faxed a terse statement to news organizations announcing that he would not run for president. Reporting the "surprise" decision by the "moderate conservative," the Associated Press quoted an unnamed confidant as saying that Cheney had told friends that he wanted to avoid putting himself and his family through the ordeal of a campaign, and that he was "not enthusiastic about campaigning on the social-dominated domestic agenda that he saw shaping up, preferring greater emphasis on security and broad economic issues."[63]

The former defense secretary soon found lucrative employment as CEO of Halliburton, a Dallas-based oil services and military contracting company. It appeared that his political career was over.

Three years passed. Then, in December 1998, Cheney was invited to Austin to visit the governor of Texas, George W. Bush. Fresh off a resounding reelection victory the previous month, the governor was eyeing his own run at the presidency. A host of his father's old political allies were linking up with the younger Bush in the belief that he had the charisma and name recognition to restore them to power. They were helping Bush organize a national campaign and tutoring him in foreign policy and national security, where the governor's experience was weak. Cheney became one of those tutors, and he began making regular visits to the governor's mansion.[64]

Later, as Bush was locking up the Republican presidential nomination, he tapped Cheney to lead the search for a vice presidential running mate. Campaigning in Ohio, Bush told the reporters that he was honored that Cheney would take the time to help him, saying, "He has enormous experience and great judgment." Bush also said he wanted Cheney to determine the best way to decide whom Bush should pick. "I found somebody who can handle the search, to put the committee together, to put the plan together," Bush said.

In a statement issued by the campaign, Cheney said: "Fortunately, there are many good candidates to choose from in our party. We will look at them all. And we will make sure we have the best ticket possible this fall."[65]

On July 25, 2000, Bush announced the results of Cheney's search. Presidential campaigns often select a running mate who is likely to help the ticket win a large battleground state in the general election. But his campaign's search, Bush said, had instead emphasized finding someone who was a "distinguished and experienced statesman" and who was "capable of serving as president." As Cheney had laid out the strengths and weaknesses of many different candidates for the governor to consider, Bush said the answer slowly became clear to him.

"As we worked to evaluate the strength of others, I saw firsthand Dick Cheney's outstanding judgment," Bush said. "As we considered many different credentials, I benefited from his keen insight. I was impressed by the thoughtful and thorough way he approached his mission. And gradually I realized that the person who was best qualified to be my vice presidential nominee was working by my side."

When Bush finished speaking, Cheney—who would bring to the ticket Wyoming's three electoral votes, certain to vote Republican anyway—stepped to the microphone. He said he honestly had not expected to become the nominee when he agreed to head up Bush's search team, but Bush's vision for the country had persuaded him to return to public service. Cheney talked about helping Bush undertake entitlement reform, improve public schools, cut taxes, and rebuild the country's military. He talked about wanting to help "restore a spirit of civility and respect and cooperation" in the nation's capital.

"Big changes are coming to Washington, and I want to be a part of them," Cheney said.[66]

In laying out his program if they were to be elected, the future vice president did not utter a word to voters about expanding—or "restoring"—the powers of the presidency. The agenda that Cheney had been cultivating for nearly thirty years, and that would be a guiding principle from the first day he and Bush took office, had no place on the campaign trail.

# 4

## The Agenda

### 1.

The first White House Counsel's Office staff meeting of the Bush-Cheney presidency fell on a Sunday, to the best of one participant's recollection — the day after Inauguration Day. Just twenty-four hours earlier, George W. Bush had stood in the cold rain beside Dick Cheney, placed his hand on a Bible, and solemnly sworn that he would, "to the best of my ability, preserve, protect and defend the Constitution of the United States." When Bush uttered those words, at noon on January 20, 2001, the era of Bill Clinton had ended.[1]

The members of the new White House legal team believed that the scandal-plagued Democrat had been unworthy of the office — that Clinton's personal peccadilloes and liberal policies showed that he could not be trusted with the awesome powers and responsibilities of the presidency. Much of the conservative legal community in Washington had played roles in one of the many investigations of Clinton administration scandals, the most dramatic of which had resulted in Clinton's impeachment and then acquittal by the Senate. Many had also volunteered in the epic legal battles surrounding the Florida recount, culminating in the Supreme Court's 5–4 decision in *Bush v. Gore*.[2] Now it was a new day. A Republican president, having pledged to "restore honor and dignity to the White House," was installed in the Oval Office, bringing the conservative legal activist movement back into the executive branch.

As the new White House legal team filed into the second-floor corner office of their boss, Alberto Gonzales, they saw that the White House counsel had already moved into the stately, wood-paneled room—filling its bookcases and display shelves with family photographs and memorabilia from his time in Texas government. The grandson of Mexican immigrants, Gonzales had been born into poverty in San Antonio and worked his way to Harvard Law School. But Gonzales had shown no early interest in legal politics or affinity for constitutional law. Instead of landing a high-profile clerkship after law school, Gonzales had returned to Houston to work for a corporate law firm, where he had specialized in handling the paperwork details of large real-estate transactions. In 1991, Gonzales had helped host a reception at his undergraduate alma mater, Rice University, for President George H. W. Bush. The Bush family machine had recognized the political value of a conservative-minded Hispanic with an inspiring life story and a penchant for loyalty. After George W. Bush was elected governor of Texas in 1994, he had named Gonzales as his general counsel.

One of Gonzales's most important tasks had been to prepare briefings for Bush about death row prisoners on the mornings of their scheduled executions so that the governor could decide whether to grant clemency or to allow the sentence to be carried out. During Bush's six-year watch, 152 inmates were executed—a number unmatched by any other modern American governor. Gonzales had written clemency memos for the first 57 of them. Almost all of the petitions were marked "Confidential" and none of them was intended to see the light of day, but *The Atlantic Monthly* later obtained them through an open-government law. After comparing each briefing memo with the actual facts of each case, the magazine concluded that Gonzales had "repeatedly failed to apprise the governor of crucial issues in the cases at hand: ineffective counsel, conflict of interest, mitigating evidence, even actual evidence of innocence." Instead of telling Bush the best argument for why it might be appropriate to commute a given death sentence to life without parole—such as the fact that one thirty-three-year-old convict was severely retarded and had been abused as a child, two issues that his defense lawyer had incompetently failed to bring up at sentencing—Gonzales largely confined his briefings to reciting details of the convict's crimes.[3] But Bush, a strong supporter of the death penalty who had made clear that he was not interested in stopping executions, was pleased with his counsel's approach. Bush appointed

Gonzales to be the Texas secretary of state in 1997, then, two years later, to be a judge on the Texas Supreme Court. When Bush made the leap from the statehouse to the White House in 2001, he asked Gonzales to resign his judgeship and join him in Washington.

The transition team had helped Gonzales quickly put together a new White House counsel's office, including by recruiting eight associate White House counsels. One of them was a thirty-five-year-old lawyer named Bradford Berenson.

Berenson had assumed that the transition team would offer him a position in the new administration. After all, he was an active member of the Federalist Society and had consulted with the independent-counsel investigation of Clinton's secretary of housing and urban development, Henry Cisneros, who was accused of lying to the FBI during a background check about having once paid hush money to a mistress. Berenson had also been an early and robust supporter of Bush. In 1997, he had made his first campaign donation to the then-governor, and in 1999, he had joined Lawyers for Bush, a brain trust of conservative attorneys who later coordinated the Bush-Cheney campaign's legal battle in Florida.

But Berenson had been thinking about a job in the Justice Department, which has hundreds of positions for attorneys. When Gonzales unexpectedly offered him one of eight spots as an associate White House counsel, Berenson was uncertain whether he wanted it. He called his old mentor, appeals court judge Laurence Silberman—the former Nixon and Ford official whom Reagan had put on the bench in 1985 and who wrote the 1988 opinion, later overturned by the Supreme Court, asserting that the Unitary Executive Theory was true. Silberman had grown into a key junction in the conservative legal network—a "feeder" judge known for sending his clerks, including Berenson, on to Supreme Court clerkships, and for staying in touch with them afterward. More members of the Bush-Cheney legal team had once clerked for Silberman, a close friend of Cheney's, than for any other appeals court judge. Silberman told Berenson that he was crazy to hesitate. The White House counsel's office was a small and elite group—offering an extraordinary opportunity to inhabit the beating heart of governmental power. "I'd jump at it," the judge said.[4]

Berenson had called Gonzales back and taken the job. Now, a whirlwind of background checks and office moves later, it was time for the first staff meeting. The team settled into the sofas and chairs in Gonzales's office and after a genial introduction got down to business. Of course, Gonzales said, much of the work of the White House counsel's office would be handling the everyday legal tasks for the West Wing, from reviewing speeches and letters to answering questions about ethical issues. These tasks were the same in every administration, regardless of who held power. But Gonzales said that he had spoken with the president about an affirmative mandate for the office. Bush had told Gonzales that the White House legal team was to make two missions their top priority.

The newly hired associates leaned forward to receive their charges.

First, Gonzales relayed, they were to move quickly on finding nominees to fill the numerous vacancies on the federal courts. In the last few years of the Clinton administration, Republicans in the Senate had slowed the confirmation process down by refusing to schedule hearings for many of Clinton's nominees, keeping them from coming to a vote. The delay tactics had created an unusually large number of slots to fill. The 2000 election had left the Senate with a 50–50 split, meaning that Cheney, in his role as president of the Senate, was empowered to cast tie-breaking votes. With Republicans now in control of both the White House and the Senate—but just barely—for the first time since 1986, it was time to move fast. They were to find as many conservative "judicial restraint"–minded lawyers as there were judgeships to be filled, and to get them confirmed, Gonzales said.

The assembled lawyers nodded. Helping to screen potential judicial nominees, in partnership with the Justice Department, was one of the most important jobs the White House counsel's office had. They all understood how precariously their party was now clinging to power in the Senate. Such control was likely to be lost after 2002, since the party in the White House usually did poorly in midterm elections, and it might even end sooner, if one of the older Republican senators died or became incapacitated.* This first mission, then, was predictable.

Gonzales moved on to the second, equally important mandate for the legal team: They were to be vigilant about seizing any opportunity to expand presidential power. Bush had told him, Gonzales said, that the institutional powers of the presidency had been weakened by his predecessors

---

*Indeed, though they did not know it at the time, just a few months later the moderate Republican senator Jim Jeffords of Vermont would abruptly leave the GOP, shifting control of the chamber back to the Democrats.

For example, Clinton, in attempting to defend himself against numerous scandal investigations, had lost several key decisions in the federal appeals courts. The decisions had narrowed the scope of presidential privilege, holding that Secret Service bodyguards and White House attorneys could be forced to testify about their communications with a president. In addition, the GOP-led Congress had inundated the Clinton White House with a flood of subpoenas demanding all kinds of documents and information, turning a previously rare tool of congressional oversight power into a routine intrusion on the executive branch. It was time to turn back this tide, Gonzales said. The president wanted Gonzales and his associates to do everything in their capacity to defend, and if possible expand, the prerogatives and privileges of the White House.

Scholars of presidential power tend to reject the depiction of a White House left unusually weak at the end of the Clinton administration. Most of the important controls imposed on the presidency following Watergate and Vietnam had already eroded by the time Bush and Cheney took office. Despite Ford's fears about the expanded Freedom of Information Act, courts had proven highly reluctant to overturn an executive branch official's decision that a document should be classified. The Supreme Court had struck down legislative vetoes in 1983. The independent-counsel statute expired in 1999. In Kosovo, Clinton's defiance of the War Powers Resolution's sixty-day limit for overseas battles not authorized by Congress had nearly returned the commander in chief's power to send troops into action to what it had been under Nixon. As Andrew Rudalevige, a professor of political science at Dickinson College, has argued, "Already . . . the ground lost by the presidency after Watergate seemed largely to have been retaken: as the twenty-first century dawned, the institutional landscape no longer reflected the vision of those who had sought to rein in presidential unilateralism."[5]

But Gonzales did not mention this broader context when laying out Bush's second mandate — to fortify and increase the powers of the presidency — to his new staff. Viewed from the narrow context of Clinton's court battles over executive privilege, the premise of the mandate seemed to make sense. Although Republicans such as Berenson had spent the 1990s pushing investigations that narrowed Clinton's presidential immunities, Clinton was gone now and the institution itself, with a proper president in the Oval Office, needed repair.

Berenson was struck by the specific words the new White House counsel used when conveying the central agenda from the president to his legal
team, and he remembered them years afterwards. Gonzales had said they
were all instructed by Bush "to make sure that he left the presidency in
better shape than he found it."

The object wasn't just to strengthen President Bush's powers personally, but rather to strengthen the office, institutionally, for all future presidents of both parties.

"Well before 9/11, it was a central part of the administration's overall
institutional agenda to strengthen the presidency as a whole," Berenson
later said. "In January 2001, the Clinton scandals and the resulting impeachment were very much in the forefront of everybody's mind. Nobody
at that point was thinking about terrorism or the national security side
of the house."

## 2.

As Berenson and his new colleagues filed out of Gonzales's office, they
had no reason to think that the instructions they had just received were
anything other than what they appeared to be. The potential role of Vice
President Cheney and his counsel, David Addington, in helping to formu-
late these instructions did not initially cross Berenson's mind. "As far as
we were concerned, these were the president's own wishes, and that's all
you need to know as a member of the White House staff," Berenson
said.[6]

It wasn't until January 2002 that Cheney openly took ownership of the
agenda of using his and Bush's time in office to expand the powers of the
presidency. His public unveiling of this long-held agenda came in an interview with Cokie Roberts on ABC's *This Week*. During the interview,
Cheney talked about his quest to reverse the restraints placed on the powers of the presidency after Watergate, all of which he characterized as "unwise compromises" that served to "weaken the presidency and the vice
presidency." He explained that in the thirty-four years since he had first
come to Washington, he had "repeatedly seen an erosion of the powers
and the ability of the president of the United States to do his job."

Cheney disclosed that he had made a similar case to Bush, who had
found his vice president's perspective persuasive. And in laying out his

argument to ABC's audience, Cheney uttered precisely the same metaphor that Bush had used one year before when conveying the instructions to Gonzales: "One of the things that I feel an obligation on—and I know the president does too, because we talked about it—is to pass on our offices in better shape than we found them to our successors."[7]

## 3.

The unfolding crisis that began with the terrorist attacks of September 11, 2001, provided an enormous opportunity to expand presidential power. As national security concerns rushed to the fore, the Bush-Cheney legal team aggressively seized the opening. A former senior member of the administration legal team who did not want to be identified by name recalled a pervasive post-9/11 sense of masculine bravado and one-upmanship when it came to executive power. A "closed group of like-minded people" were almost in competition with one another, he said, to see who could offer the farthest-reaching claims of what a president could do. In contrast, those government lawyers who were perceived as less passionate about presidential power were derided as "soft" and were often simply cut out of the process. "The lawyers for the administration felt a tremendous amount of time pressure, and there was a lot of secrecy," the former official said. "These things were being done in small groups. There was a great deal of suspicion of the people who normally act as a check inside the executive branch, such as the State Department, which had the reputation of being less aggressive on executive power. This process of faster, smaller groups fed on itself and built a dynamic of trying to show who was tougher on executive power."[8]

On paper, the leaders of the administration's legal team on 9/11 were Gonzales and Attorney General John Ashcroft. But in practice, neither of these men was the leading architect of its legal strategy in the war on terrorism. Although he was a vocal public supporter of the administration's policies in the war on terrorism, Ashcroft was not a member of the inner circle and sometimes disagreed with the White House's legal moves, former officials say. Moreover, like Gonzales, Ashcroft had little prior experience in the legal issues surrounding executive power and national security; the attorney general had spent most of his career in Missouri state politics before serving a single term in the U.S. Senate, where he had primarily focused on conservative Christian issues, such as opposing "activist" judges. The heavy legal lifting in support of the administration's war-on-terrorism policies was instead performed by a brain trust of influential lawyers who were less well known to the public or Congress. Although these figures were lower in the official hierarchy than Gonzales and Ashcroft, they had been thinking through ways to expand White House power for much of their professional lives. This expertise allowed them to dominate the meetings at which legal policy was debated and decisions were reached.

At the Justice Department, the real power resided in the Office of Legal Counsel. Few outside Washington or the nation's law schools have ever heard of the Office of Legal Counsel, or OLC, but it is one of the most important agencies in government. The Office of Legal Counsel advises the president and other executive branch officials, often in secret, about the lawfulness of proposed executive actions. By statute, an advisory opinion by the office becomes the binding interpretation of the law that the rest of the executive branch, including the CIA and the Pentagon, must follow. That means that the small group of politically appointed lawyers who run the Office of Legal Counsel get to act like an internal Supreme Court for the executive branch — they have the power to simply say what the law is, especially in national security matters that are unlikely to see the inside of a courtroom. This role gives the Office of Legal Counsel attorneys an extraordinary responsibility: If the executive wants to do something illegal, the duty of the office's attorneys is to say that it cannot be done. But this role also gives the Office of Legal Counsel attorneys the power to preemptively absolve officials of wrongdoing: If the OLC says a thing can be done lawfully, then a government official who takes an action relying on their pronouncement is safe from prosecution.

Because the Office of Legal Counsel is so powerful, its leader — the assistant attorney general for the OLC — is required to undergo the vetting of Senate confirmation. (This director supervises the work of four or five deputies, who are appointed by the president without congressional involvement, along with some fifteen to twenty career government lawyers.) But on 9/11, the OLC had no real boss — the result of an early feud between Ashcroft and the White House over who would control the legal team.

Initially, Ashcroft wanted Paul Clement, a former clerk to Judge

Silberman and Supreme Court justice Antonin Scalia who ended up going to the solicitor general's office. The White House instead wanted Douglas Cox, a Washington lawyer who played a prominent role in the *Bush v. Gore* case and who had been the No. 2 official in the Office of Legal Counsel under the Bush-Quayle administration.[9] The dispute—part of a larger tug-of-war between Ashcroft and a White House team bent on keeping unusually tight control over the appointment of subcabinet officials—delayed the naming of an OLC head for the first two months of the administration. In late March, the two factions settled on a compromise choice: Columbia University law professor John Manning, a clerk to Judge Robert Bork and Scalia who had worked in the Reagan and Bush-Quayle administrations. But Manning later withdrew his name before confirmation, reopening the dispute for another three months. Finally, in July, the White House and Ashcroft agreed on a University of Nevada, Las Vegas law professor named Jay S. Bybee.[10] The Senate did not confirm Bybee as head of the Office of Legal Counsel until more than a month after 9/11. Moreover, Bybee stayed out in Nevada until late November because he had a prior commitment to finish teaching a compressed term of classes at the UNLV law school. Bybee finally moved his family to Washington and assumed leadership of the Office of Legal Counsel after Thanksgiving 2001.[11]

As a result of these delays, the Office of Legal Counsel was without Senate-confirmed supervision for almost three months after 9/11. By the time Bybee arrived, the administration legal team had already established a very aggressive legal framework for dealing with the war on terrorism, and the government had already taken several bold actions based on its view of what was lawful. Even if Bybee had been inclined to disagree with the course the office had taken, by December 2001 it would have been very difficult for him to change its course. In addition, Bybee was not in a good position to balk at the legal theories the administration had adopted. He was a solid conservative—a graduate of Brigham Young, Bybee had come of age in the Meese Justice Department and had served as an associate White House counsel in the Bush-Quayle administration. But he had no particular expertise in national security issues.[12] When he finally started work, Bybee let deputies continue to spearhead the review of matters related to the war on terrorism. On December 6, 2001, in the midst of momentous decisions about the laws on war and terrorism, Bybee had his coming-out event as the new titular head of the Office of Legal Counsel:

He testified at a House subcommittee hearing about a government broadcasting license deal.[13]

4.

These factors meant that the real power to shape the Office of Legal
Counsel's wartime advisory opinions was wielded by an aide to Bybee
who specialized in national security and international law: Deputy Assistant Attorney General John Yoo. This deputy wrote the first confidential
memos about the extent of the president's war powers in the weeks after
9/11, establishing a framework from which everything else would follow.
And Yoo continued to draft most of the important memos after the putative boss finally arrived—although they sometimes went out with Bybee's
signature attached. Adding to Yoo's power was the fact that his writings
dealt with classified matters, so they were not reviewed by his colleagues,
most of whom had no idea what Yoo was working on. And while Yoo's
lower rank on paper meant that he was not subject to the scrutiny of a
Senate confirmation hearing, like all deputies in the office, he wielded
"signing power"—the ability to make his opinion the binding interpretation of the law for the entire executive branch simply by signing his name
to a memo.

Yoo was born in South Korea in 1967, emigrating from there to the
United States with his family when he was just a few months old. His parents had both lived through the Korean War and held strongly anti-
Communist views. As a teenager growing up in Philadelphia in the early
1980s, Yoo absorbed his parents' outlook about North Korea and Communism around the dinner table. Yoo said that he began to identify with the
Republican Party and to be "attracted to Reagan's message" as an adolescent because of Reagan's aggressive stance against what the president called
the "Evil Empire."[14] A high achiever, Yoo went on to graduate from Harvard College in 1989 and then from Yale Law School in 1992, where he
joined the Federalist Society.

As an undergraduate, Yoo gravitated toward the study of American
diplomatic history, in part because of his strong interest in the Korean
peninsula. As a law student, this interest pushed him into the study of
muscular assertions of presidential power. The Korean War has a bad reputation in American history—it was an unpopular and bloody war that

resulted in a stalemate, and President Truman launched it without asking Congress for authorization. But constitutionally illegitimate or not, the Korean War had saved the people of South Korea, including Yoo's family, from life under a Communist dictatorship. Yoo told a Seoul newspaper that his familial connection to the Korean War had influenced his decision to devote his academic career to mounting a defense for the kind of sweeping presidential powers Truman had claimed for his office. "Maybe some of it is from being Korean," Yoo said. "The Korean War is an example where the president, at that time Harry Truman, decided to use force without the permission of Congress."[15] He later elaborated: "I'm conscious of the fact that if it weren't for presidents like Truman, or maybe even like Johnson, there would be a lot more people who would be living under Communist dictatorships today than there are. You have a track record where presidential powers led to benefits for other people abroad." He conceded, however, that "you also have examples where the use of presidential power was harmful to the country, too."[16]

After graduating from Yale, Yoo landed clerkships with two of the most aggressive "presidentialists" on the bench — appeals court judge Silberman and Supreme Court justice Clarence Thomas. Yoo spent most of the Clinton years as a professor at Boalt Hall, the law school of the University of California at Berkeley, although he took one year off to be counsel to then–Senate Judiciary Committee chairman Orrin Hatch of Utah. A regular speaker at Federalist Society events, Yoo also began to specialize in writing law journal articles and op-eds that took a provocatively strong stance on presidential power. He first made a name for himself in 1996 by writing a lengthy essay in the *California Law Review* arguing that the Founders intended to empower presidents to launch wars without congressional permission.[17]

Yoo argued that generations of legal scholars and historians had misread the history of the Constitution. Far more than everyone realized, Yoo wrote, the Founders embraced rather than rejected the British model of executive power, under which the king got to decide when the country went to war. When the Constitution gave Congress the power to "declare war," he said, the Founders were merely referring to the ceremonial role of deciding whether to proclaim the existence of a conflict as a diplomatic nicety. But the Founders had left the power to *commence* war with the executive, he said. Most other scholars, however, believed that Yoo was wrong. Notes of the Constitutional Convention, they argued, clearly show that other than in the narrow case of repelling sudden attacks, the Founders wanted Congress, not the commander in chief, to decide whether the country should go to war.[18] James Madison, the "Father of the Constitution" and fourth president, wrote in 1795, "Of all the enemies to public liberty war is, perhaps, the most to be dreaded"—since it invariably leads to higher taxes, public debt, propaganda, and expanded governmental control. Yet history had shown that monarchs tended to like a state of war, because it increased their own power, while its costs were borne by ordinary citizens. Thus, Madison wrote, giving America's executive the power to decide on his own to wage war "would have struck, not only at the fabric of our Constitution, but at the foundation of all well organized and well checked governments. The separation of the power of declaring war from that of conducting it, is wisely contrived to exclude the danger of its being declared for the sake of its being conducted."[19]

Before 9/11, Yoo's sometimes idiosyncratic writings, which rejected Madison's view, made him a welcome presence in law journals and at legal symposiums; because Yoo's perspective ran contrary to what most other constitutional scholars believed, his arguments sparked vigorous and entertaining conversations. And his heavily footnoted articles, which stood out because they said something new and surprising, were published by law journals, which are edited by law students rather than professors. Yoo thus succeeded in doing what all ambitious young academics try to do: He carved out a unique niche for himself, raising his profile enough that Berkeley granted him tenure in the 1997–1998 academic year.

After 9/11, however, Yoo's legal philosophy had far more serious consequences, prompting a closer examination of the quality of his scholarship. Although his tenure remained intact, Yoo became something of an outcast among mainstream legal scholars. Some of his colleagues denounced Yoo in highly personal terms. Their numbers did not include Cass Sunstein, a prominent law professor at the University of Chicago who repeatedly went out of his way to defend Yoo as a "very interesting and provocative scholar" who "doesn't deserve the demonization to which he has been subject."[20] Yet in reviewing a 2005 book by Yoo, essentially a compendium of the pre-9/11 academic writings that had landed Yoo his Justice Department job, even Sunstein concluded that Yoo was a "good lawyer" only in the pejorative sense—an advocate willing to write a one-sided opinion that tries to "justify a particular set of predetermined conclusions."

"Yoo's reading would require us to ignore far too many statements by prominent figures in the founding generation," Sunstein said. "There are not many issues on which James Madison, Thomas Jefferson, John Marshall, Alexander Hamilton, George Washington, James Wilson, John Adams, and Pierce Butler can be said to agree. Were all of them wrong?"[21]

Yoo's opinions may have left most of his colleagues in the academic world shaking their heads, but those same views made him an attractive recruit to the ranks of the Bush-Cheney legal team. In April 2001, when John Manning accepted the administration's invitation to be head of the Office of Legal Counsel, he contacted Yoo and asked him to join him at OLC. Yoo accepted. Later, when Manning withdrew his name before being confirmed, the administration asked Yoo to stay on.[22] In July 2001, Yoo took a leave of absence from Berkeley and joined the Justice Department. Assuming the title of deputy assistant attorney general, Yoo was charged with overseeing any legal opinions about presidential power that might arise in the area of national security and international law.

Then came 9/11. At thirty-four years old, Yoo found himself the primary official entrusted with telling the president whether or not his proposed policies for fighting Al Qaeda were legal. And with Jay Bybee not yet confirmed and still in Nevada, Yoo had a free hand to lay down the first legal opinions that charted the course for all that followed. On September 25, 2001, he delivered a confidential memorandum asserting that no statute passed by Congress could limit the war powers of the commander in chief; as authority for this claim, Yoo cited his own academic writings six times in thirty-two footnotes. In the weeks that followed, Yoo developed close working relationships with White House officials such as Addington, relationships that were well established by the time the new OLC boss arrived. From the first memos written after 9/11 until the summer of 2003, when he left the Justice Department and returned to his tenured position at Berkeley, Yoo did what his previous scholarship strongly suggested he would do if asked where the limits of presidential power might lie. He said that Cheney was right: For the commander in chief, everything was permitted.

5.

There were other important figures on the Bush-Cheney legal team in the early days after 9/11. One was Timothy Flanigan, the deputy White House counsel and Gonzales's No. 2. Having headed the Justice Department's

Office of Legal Counsel himself during the last two years of the Bush-Quayle administration, Flanigan had deep experience as an advocate for strong presidential powers. Another key personality was William James Haynes II, the Pentagon's general counsel. Jim Haynes's career also dated back to the Bush-Quayle administration, when he had been the army general counsel and a protégé of David Addington's in Cheney's Pentagon.

But by far the most important member of the legal team when it came to orchestrating its presidential-power agenda was Addington himself. As counsel to the vice president, Addington, like Cheney, officially had no power—a point his colleagues say he liked to raise before launching into an aggressive and well-prepared argument that almost unfailingly carried the day. After the war on terrorism commenced, his informal clout grew. The former CIA and Pentagon lawyer had once helped Cheney defend the Reagan administration during the Iran-Contra scandal; now he took a central role in shaping policies that both relied upon and expanded the president's power to act in defiance of Congress and treaties. And while most of the other key players on the legal team that was in place on 9/11 eventually moved on, Addington stayed—and became even more powerful. In 2005, after Cheney's first chief of staff, I. Lewis "Scooter" Libby, was indicted for perjury and resigned, Cheney handed Addington Libby's powers and responsibilities as well.

Addington's power in internal disputes stemmed from his intellect, his personality, his bureaucratic skills, and—above all—the fact that he spoke for Cheney. The White House routed every memo related to national security through Cheney's office, where Addington could review it, and he attended all the important legal and national-security meetings, where his aggressive view of executive power dominated the debate. A relentlessly hard worker who put in long hours, Addington routinely helped draft memos—both monitoring and advising those who did the drafting of advisory opinions at the Justice Department's Office of Legal Counsel. According to the *Washington Post*, on at least one occasion when a matter arose concerning presidential power and detainees, Addington ghost-wrote a key memo that went to Bush's desk in Gonzales's name.[23]

The younger conservative lawyers on the administration legal team admired Addington for his intelligence, his power, and his purity; showing no interest in the trappings of power even as he worked to accumulate it, Addington eschewed his access to an official government car service and instead rode to work on the Washington subway. For many of the attorneys who had come of age after the Reagan Revolution and had no personal memories of Watergate, Addington, and his concerns about presidential prerogatives, became a larger-than-life guidepost. "Addington is a colorful figure," said one former White House attorney who asked not to be named. "David carries the Constitution around in his jacket pocket. And he's a very good lawyer, and frankly a role model and mentor for many of the lawyers in the counsel's office."[24]

But former secretary of state Colin Powell's chief of staff, Lawrence Wilkerson, said that Addington came across quite differently to those who questioned his view of presidential power. Wilkerson described Addington as a force who both used Cheney's influence and influenced Cheney in turn. Addington, he said, was the leader of the small group of ideological lawyers "who had these incredible theories and would stand behind their principals [elected officials such as Cheney and Bush], whispering in their ears about these theories, telling them they have these powers, that the Constitution backs these powers, that these powers are 'inherent' and blessed by God and if they are not exercised, the nation will fall. He'd never crack a smile. His intensity and emotions and passion for these theories are extraordinary."[25]

Even Addington's allies acknowledged his fierce manner. Several years after leaving the White House, Flanigan said of his former colleague: "David could go from zero to 150 very quickly. I'm not sure how much is temper and how much is for effect. At a meeting with government bureaucrats he might start out very calm. Then he would start with the sarcasm. He could say, 'We could do that, but that would give away *all* of the president's power.' All of a sudden here comes David Addington out of his chair. I'd think to myself we're not just dancing a minuet, there's a little slam dancing going on here."[26]

# 5

# "Behind Closed Doors": Secrecy I

## 1.

At just before noon on Monday, January 29, 2001, at the start of the second week of the new administration, a handful of reporters on White House pool duty were hustled into the Cabinet Room. President Bush and Vice President Cheney were sitting at a dark wood conference table, surrounded by other key members of the government. Bush told the reporters they were witnessing an important event: the inaugural meeting of a task force that would draw up a new national energy policy, the first major public policy initiative of his presidency. Out of the administration's concern for "the people who work for a living . . . who struggle every day to get ahead," Bush said, the task force was going to come up with a plan for the country to meet the rising demand for energy and to avoid the shortfalls that were causing electricity blackouts in California. Bush announced he had decided that the task force should be led by Cheney.

"Can't think of a better man to run it than the vice president," the president said.

Bush thanked the reporters for coming. One of them asked whether he would answer a few questions. Bush declined. "Next time," the president offered. "Give you a chance to think of some good ones. I've got some suggestions. I've got some suggestions. First answer — you can think of the question — first answer is 'Ravens.' "[1] A day earlier in Tampa, the Baltimore Ravens, led by MVP linebacker Ray Lewis and a stifling defense, had crushed the New York Giants 34–7 in Super Bowl XXXV. The reporters laughed as they were led from the Cabinet Room. The door closed behind them. Bush left by another exit, and Cheney's energy task force, concealed from the public eye, went to work.

The way Cheney conducted the task force would result in litigation that reached the U.S. Supreme Court. That dispute—over whether the White House could keep the task force's records secret from Congress and the public—became the first battleground on which the Bush-Cheney administration would fight to expand the power of the presidency.

Over the three months of its existence, the energy task force met with large numbers of oil, gas, coal, nuclear, and electric company lobbyists. Among the officials who offered advice about what should be in the energy plan was a not-yet-indicted leader of the Enron Corporation, a company that would later be revealed to have played a role in the 2000–2001 California blackouts by calculatedly manipulating the electricity market. These industrialists urged the White House to put together a package of billions of dollars in new tax breaks, reduced fees for drilling on public lands, relaxed environmental regulations, and other incentives for their companies. Many of these influential outside advisers had been major financial backers of the Bush-Cheney campaign.

A typical bit of the advice the task force received behind closed doors came on March 1, 2001, in the form of a confidential memo to Cheney from Haley Barbour. A jowly, white-haired former chairman of the Republican National Committee, Barbour enjoyed a level of access in the Bush-Cheney White House that prompted *Fortune* magazine to name his firm as the single-most influential lobbyist group in Washington in 2001.[2] Barbour would later become governor of Mississippi, where his defining moment would be heading up the state response to the 2005 Hurricane Katrina disaster. But in 2001 Barbour was working for fossil fuel companies, and in the March 1 memo, he urged Cheney to block any attempt to limit carbon dioxide emissions at power plants in the name of stopping global warming.[3]

Barbour's policy advice was candid because it was never intended to reach public ears. And his memo was typical of the recommendations the energy task force was secretly receiving—and secretly soliciting. There was no pretense of openness or democratic process. Indeed, a top political appointee on the task force put it this way in an e-mail sent to a natural gas executive on March 18, 2001: "If you were King, or Il Duce, what would you include in a national [energy] policy, especially with respect to national gas issues?"[4]

Although no one from the public was allowed into the meetings, word of the outsized influence enjoyed by industry lobbyists began to seep out in leaks to the media. A month after the "Il Duce" e-mail, two Democratic members of the House of Representatives, Henry Waxman and John Dingell, decided that Congress ought to look into how the energy task force was going about its business. Since 1975 Waxman had represented a district that includes Hollywood, and Dingell was the longest-serving member of the House, having represented the western suburbs of Detroit since 1955. Both were known for their vigorous approach to oversight investigations, and the energy task force was well within their jurisdiction: Waxman was the ranking member of the House Committee on Government Reform, and Dingell was the ranking member of the House Committee on Energy and Commerce.

On April 19, 2001, Waxman and Dingell wrote to the task force's executive director, Andrew Lundquist, demanding access to the task force's records. Lundquist, a political appointee in the Energy Department, was a native of Fairbanks, Alaska, and had been an aide to Republican Alaska senators Frank Murkowski and Ted Stevens—both of whom were strong supporters of the oil and gas industries and backed opening the Alaska National Wildlife Refuge to drilling.[5] In their letter to Lundquist, Waxman and Dingell asked with whom the task force had met and what had been said at those meetings.[6] They based their request on the 1972 Federal Advisory Committee Act, an open-government law. It said that when nongovernment officials help craft public policy, the government must pick a balanced representation of viewpoints and have open meetings so that interested members of the public and the press can attend.

Two weeks later, on May 4, 2001, the counsel to the vice president, David Addington, sent back a reply. The information the lawmakers had sought would not be provided to Congress, Addington wrote, because the open government law did not apply to the task force. Addington directed the lawmakers to a six-page attachment, signed by Lundquist. Lundquist acknowledged that members of the task force and its staff had "met with many individuals who are not federal employees to gather information relevant to the group's work." But these meetings with industry officials, Lundquist said, did not count, because the energy lobbyists weren't *official members* of the task force.

Firing a warning shot across the bow of Congress, Addington went further. He invoked "due regard for the constitutional separation of powers" and reserved the right to assert executive privilege over the information. Congress, Addington implied, was not entitled even to the brief answers from Lundquist, which the White House had provided only out of good manners—"as a matter of comity between the executive and legislative branches."[7]

Four days later, Congress escalated the stakes. The General Accounting Office—the nonpartisan investigative arm of Congress—faxed Addington another letter, declaring that it intended to review the composition and workings of the task force. Dingell and Waxman had asked David Walker, the comptroller general, for help in their investigation. (After Democrats regained control of the Senate later that year, several Senate committee chairmen with jurisdiction over energy matters also asked the GAO to investigate on behalf of their committees.) Walker had been appointed to a fifteen-year term as the head of the GAO by President Clinton in 1998. But Walker was not a partisan Democrat. He had been a political appointee in both the Reagan and Bush-Quayle administrations, and he had been a delegate for George H. W. Bush to the 1980 Republican National Convention.[8]

The GAO's legal authority to probe the task force came from a statute empowering it to examine what the government does with the money Congress appropriates. For eighty years—ever since the office was established by an act of Congress that was signed into law by President Warren Harding in 1921—the GAO's legal right to probe the executive branch had been taken for granted. Its reports had long played a critical role in helping Congress conduct oversight of government operations.

But the GAO was about to run into a level of resistance that was unprecedented in its history. On May 16, 2001, the day Cheney's secret task force completed its work, Addington sent the GAO a letter. The agency, Addington declared, had no authority under the Constitution to inquire into how the task force had come up with the energy plan, because such matters were the executive branch's business alone. As a part of the legislative branch, Addington wrote, the GAO could not "inquire into the exercise of authorities committed to the executive by the Constitution." The president could keep any such government deliberations secret from Congress, he said, in order to "ensure the candor" of the advice he received.[9]

The next day, Walker's office sent a reply to Addington, rejecting the White House's interpretation of the GAO's legal authority.[10] In response,

Addington followed injury with insult. Conceding that the congressional watchdog might be entitled to know about the direct costs incurred by the task force, but nothing else, the Office of the Vice President sent over seventy-seven pages of expense reports, highlighted by a receipt for a pizza that Lundquist had put on his credit card.[11]

The opening battle in the Bush-Cheney administration's war to expand presidential power had begun.

## 2.

The power to control information is both a shield and a sword. It was no accident that the Nixon administration, which went further than any predecessor in centralizing power and eroding democratic checks and balances, made expanding secrecy a major part of its strategy. When government officials can select which fragments of information reach the public, they can shape public opinion in a way that will improve their chances of being returned to office. Conversely, a freer flow of information about what the government is doing serves as one of the most sweeping checks on abuses by those in power. As Supreme Court justice Louis Brandeis famously wrote of transparency in 1933, "Sunlight is said to be the best of disinfectants; electric light the most efficient policeman."[12]

As the imperial presidency stumbled amid Vietnam and Watergate, Congress began passing a series of laws designed to prevent future abuses of executive power. One of its key strategies was making the government as open as possible. The new legislation empowered the public to scrutinize the executive branch's internal workings and required the government to share information about its intelligence activities with courts and Congress. Such laws represented the ethos of the era, summed up in 1976 by the Church Committee's warnings against excessive secrecy: "Abuse thrives on secrecy. . . . Knowledge is the key to control. Secrecy should no longer be allowed to shield the existence of constitutional, legal and moral problems from the scrutiny of all three branches of government or from the American people themselves." The Church report acknowledged that there were areas, of course, in which government secrecy served the public interest and not just the private interests of those in power. Details about ongoing criminal investigations, the identities of spies, troop movements during wartime, and technological know-how for building a nuclear bomb are all properly kept secret from the public. But beyond such limited exceptions, a free flow of information about the government's activities is a fundamental principle of democracy, serving as a key check on the power of the president.

Cheney, however, saw things differently. He believed that transparency limited the quality of the advice that the president received before making a decision. The executive branch needed to be able to keep its internal dealings hidden from Congress and the public so that the president's advisers felt free to be candid. To advance this principle, Cheney fostered a culture of secrecy in the administration, denounced leaks, and used the energy task force case and then 9/11 to expand the shield of confidentiality around the White House. He also set an example by his own conduct. Any investigator seeking to uncover what Cheney was up to would find few writings by the vice president. Four years into the Bush-Cheney presidency, Cheney would remark that because of Watergate, he refused to keep a diary or engage in correspondence and barely wrote anything down — he didn't even use e-mail.[13]

Beginning with the fight over the energy task force records, the Bush-Cheney administration systematically set out to expand government secrecy wherever it found an opportunity for doing so. Although 9/11 would be invoked as justification for the administration's efforts to seize greater control over information, the curtain of secrecy had begun to descend across the federal government long before the terrorist attacks.

"If you can control the flow of information, you often can control the process itself," said Peter Weitzel of the Coalition of Journalists for Open Government. "I think they believe that's the most effective way to govern, and so that's what they sought out to do."[14]

3.

As Addington and the GAO exchanged increasingly irate letters over the spring and summer of 2001, the White House counsel's office began to debate the road down which Cheney's office was leading the administration. Then–associate White House counsel Brad Berenson, who worked on the case, later recalled looking through the records sought by the GAO. There was nothing of interest in them, he said, that had not already come out in the media — yes, fossil fuel and nuclear energy executives were meeting with the task force and providing wish lists. But thanks to media reports, everyone knew that already.* Yet the White House was willing to take the short-term hit over withholding the documents. The long-term payoff was an opportunity to establish a high principle of presidential power: Communications involving the office of the presidency should be secret, whatever a law passed by Congress and signed by some previous president might say.

At every step, Addington was there to help the legal team grasp the importance of advising Bush to pay the political price of shielding these generally uninteresting papers. Helping to enforce Cheney's views in all matters, Addington became a regular at the morning staff meetings of the White House Counsel's Office even though he didn't work for Gonzales.[15]

As Cheney and the GAO dug in their heels, the growing fight began to attract greater media attention. In May, *Newsweek* ran an article entitled "Big Energy at the Table" that caught the eye of Chris Farrell, the director of investigations and research at a conservative government watchdog group called Judicial Watch. The group, which was partially funded by the conservative billionaire Richard Mellon Scaife, had made a name for itself during the 1990s by launching lawsuit after lawsuit against the Clinton administration. Farrell, a former army counterintelligence agent who had hunted spies in Europe during the Cold War, had joined Judicial Watch in 1999. His first assignment had been to fly down to Little Rock, Arkansas, to interview former Clinton administration officials about whether the White House had abused its access to FBI files to dig up dirt on Republicans. When Farrell read the *Newsweek* article, the whole secret process struck him as no different from what Hillary Rodham Clinton had tried to do when her health-care policy task force had met behind closed doors eight years earlier. Conservatives had been outraged at the Clinton administration's secrecy during the health-care fight, yet here the same thing was happening.

"The government can't operate in secret," Farrell later explained. "They are answerable to the people. There are appropriate times for secrecy on military and intelligence matters, but the notion that national policy on a

---

*There was at least one exception to this description of the papers as uninteresting. One document, later obtained by Judicial Watch, showed that Cheney's energy task force was studying Iraqi oil fields, and the companies that had drilling rights on them, as early as March 2001, two years before the invasion of Iraq.

matter like energy or health care can be developed in secret is offensive and counter to the Constitution."[16]

Sitting around a circular glass table in the seventh-floor conference room at Judicial Watch's headquarters, some six blocks south of the Smithsonian National Air and Space Museum on the National Mall, Farrell and the other top leaders debated about whether they ought to move in. Judicial Watch's chairman, Larry Klayman, and its president, Thomas Fitton, had become widely viewed as GOP hatchet men because of their aggressive pursuit of the Clinton administration. But they all agreed that the secrecy surrounding Cheney's energy task force was repugnant to core conservative principles, as they saw them.

Farrell drafted a letter to Cheney that went out on June 25, demanding access to the energy task force's records. Their letter noted that the rules were very clear on such matters: If the executive branch chooses to solicit outside advice when writing policy, the Federal Advisory Committee Act requires the government to make such discussions open to public scrutiny. "Judicial Watch respectfully requests that, in light of the questionable legal and ethical practices, negative publicity, and public outrage surrounding Hillary Rodham Clinton's 1994 national health-care policy development group, you direct the [energy task force] to abide by the FACA," they wrote, adding that such openness "will instill public trust and confidence in the operations of the [task force] and insure that the national policy is formulated, discussed, and acted upon in a manner consistent with the best traditions of our Constitutional Republic."[17]

The letter was written on Judicial Watch's letterhead, emblazoned with the pointed motto it had used as a weapon against the Clinton administration for the previous five years: "Because no one is above the law!"

On July 5, Addington offered a terse three-sentence reply. Repeating the argument he had made to the members of Congress, but with even less explanation, Addington wrote that no open-government laws applied to Cheney's task force, so there would be no "disclosure of the materials you requested."[18]

Eleven days later, Judicial Watch filed a lawsuit in federal district court against the White House. They asked a federal judge to force Cheney to turn over the records.

Initially, the lawsuit got little attention in the media or in the White House. Cheney's fight with Congress was the main event. On July 31, 2001, Walker partially backed down. Instead of demanding access to the full minutes of Cheney's meetings with energy lobbyists and copies of any materials the lobbyists submitted for the task force to use, Walker told Addington that the GAO would scale back its request and accept just the names of the lobbyists, the dates of the meetings, their general subject matter, and their cost.[19]

But Walker's offer to compromise just spurred Cheney to press harder for a total victory. On August 2, 2001, Cheney signed a letter to congressional leadership demanding that they order the GAO's Walker to stand down. Although the GAO was no longer asking for access to notes from the vice president's meetings, Cheney asserted that complying with the GAO's request would still violate "the confidentiality of communications among a President, a Vice President, the President's other senior advisers and others." And again raising the stakes, Cheney's letter informed the lawmakers of what he described as "actions undertaken by an agent of the Congress, the Comptroller General, which exceeded his lawful authority and which if given effect, would unconstitutionally interfere with the functioning of the executive branch."[20]

Washington, built on a swamp, essentially shuts down throughout the eighth month of the year, as everyone who has the means flees for a less muggy locale. Congress was in recess for the entire month, so responding to Cheney's pugilistic attack on its comptroller general would have to wait until lawmakers returned in September. The congressional leadership had not yet taken action on the GAO issue when nineteen Al Qaeda terrorists simultaneously hijacked four airliners and used them to kill nearly three thousand people inside the United States.

4.

The Bush-Cheney administration seized the atmosphere of emergency and uncertainty that followed 9/11 to dramatically expand the zone of secrecy surrounding the executive branch. It broke the ice by seizing greater secrecy powers in matters directly related to terrorism investigations. Later, however, the clampdown moved into areas that, like the energy task force papers, had nothing to do with national security.

The first blow fell ten days after 9/11. In the wake of the attacks, the FBI had begun arresting hundreds of foreign Arab and Muslim men around the country. None of the more than twelve hundred cab drivers, students, restaurant workers, and shop clerks who were detained had any connection to the attacks, but in the atmosphere of fear and urgency following the hijackings, few questioned the sweeps. Plus, there was a lawful reason to go after the detainees: Many of them were in the country on immigration visas whose time limits had expired.

As the government began holding deportation hearings to expel the detainees from the country, the Justice Department took an unusual step. On September 21, 2001, Michael Creppy, the chief U.S. immigration judge — an executive branch official in the Justice Department despite the title "judge" — issued a blanket directive closing all the deportation hearings to the public, press, and family members. Creppy also prohibited immigration court administrators from listing the detainees' names or cases on public dockets. In demanding this unprecedented control of information, the Bush-Cheney administration did not argue that there was reason to believe that any particular detainee was a terrorist. Instead, it said, national security demanded blanket secrecy because terrorist cells, reading about the deportation proceedings in the media, might piece together bits of information, harmless by themselves, that could provide useful insights into the government's investigation. Thus, the public would just have to trust that the government had arrested and deported the right people, even though their names were kept a secret and the decision to expel them from the country was made behind closed doors.

By invoking the chance that the enemy might detect a pattern in otherwise harmless information, the government would be justified in withholding *everything*. The implication of its theory was that the public had no right to know anything, no matter how innocuous, because any tidbit of trivial information could potentially be stitched together with other minor bits of information to conceivably provide some useful insight for terrorists. Recognizing the danger that the administration's move posed to fundamental principles of open government, the *Detroit Free Press* and several New Jersey media organizations sued the Justice Department. Citing the First Amendment, they demanded access to the deportation proceedings.

District court judges in both cases would rule against the administration, citing a long string of cases protecting access by the media to government proceedings. Cited in one of the rulings was the conservative justice George Sutherland, who had written for a unanimous Supreme Court in a 1936 case, "An informed public is the most potent of all restraints upon misgovernment."[21]

The Bush-Cheney administration would appeal both losses.

On August 26, 2002, the U.S. Court of Appeals for the Sixth Circuit, in Cincinnati, would hand down its decision in one of the cases, *Detroit Free Press v. Ashcroft*. By a 3–0 vote, the appeals court panel said the administration's secret-deportation-hearing policy went too far in trampling the public's right to know what the government was doing. While the government should be able to selectively close individual deportees' hearings if there is a particular reason to do so, the court ruled, it could not simply shut down public access to all of them. "In an area such as immigration, where the government has nearly unlimited authority . . . the press and the public serve as perhaps the only check on abusive government practices," wrote appeals court judge Damon Keith for the panel.

Keith was eighty years old and had encountered presidents bent on seizing greater powers for themselves before. As a district court judge in 1971, Keith presided over a criminal trial based in part on warrantless wiretapping ordered by Nixon's attorney general, John Mitchell. The Nixon administration argued that the president's men had "inherent" power to wiretap without a warrant people they suspected of being domestic terrorists, but Keith rejected the claim, noting, "Such power held by one individual was never contemplated by the framers of our Constitution and cannot be tolerated today."[22] Nixon appealed Keith's decision to the Supreme Court, but the Court unanimously upheld it. Six years after Keith's famous decision, President Carter elevated him to an appeals court seat.[23]

Now Keith once again found himself declaring that the Constitution does not allow presidents to assume kingly powers. "The executive branch seeks to uproot people's lives, outside the public eye and behind a closed door," Keith wrote. "Democracies die behind closed doors. The First Amendment, through a free press, protects the people's right to know that their government acts fairly, lawfully and accurately in deportation proceedings. When the government begins closing doors, it selectively controls information rightly belonging to the people. Selective information is misinformation. The Framers of the First Amendment did not trust any government to separate the true from the false for us. They protected the people against secret government."[24]

But on October 2, 2002, the other appeals court would issue its own ruling, directly contradicting the Sixth Circuit. In the New Jersey case, the U.S. Court of Appeals for the Third Circuit, sitting in Philadelphia, voted 2–1 to uphold the administration's power to conduct all the deportation hearings in secret. Writing for the majority, Chief Judge Edward Becker—who was named to the district court by Nixon and elevated to the appeals court by Reagan—concluded that if a president or his top advisers declared that blanket closures of deportation hearings were necessary for national security reasons, then courts ought to defer to their judgment. "We are quite hesitant to conduct a judicial inquiry into the credibility of these security concerns, as national security is an area where courts have traditionally extended great deference to executive expertise," Becker wrote.[25]

Usually when two appeals courts issue conflicting opinions about the same legal question, the Supreme Court steps in to resolve the question. But the administration did not appeal its loss in the Michigan case, since the deportation proceedings for the post-9/11 sweeps were by then already over. And the Supreme Court decided not to hear an appeal in the New Jersey case, offering no explanation. As a result, even though four of the six appeals court judges who reviewed the Creppy directive rejected it as unconstitutional, the administration managed to create a precedent for a presidential power to impose blanket secrecy over immigration hearings that stands in forty-six states—everywhere except the Sixth Circuit's Kentucky, Michigan, Ohio, and Tennessee.

The Creppy directive was just the first move in a wave of new government secrecy measures that followed the 9/11 attacks. On October 12, 2001, Attorney General John Ashcroft issued an order dealing a severe blow to the Freedom of Information Act. Under the Clinton administration, Attorney General Janet Reno had ordered FOIA officers to operate with a "presumption of disclosure" unless it was "reasonably foreseeable that disclosure would be harmful."[26] Ashcroft turned Reno's "foreseeable harm" policy on its head. Reviving a Reagan-era policy aimed at undermining the Freedom of Information Act, Ashcroft instructed the government to reject FOIA requests if it was at all possible to do so, under any legal reason for withholding documents—even if the information sought was harmless. And he promised to back up any decision to reject a FOIA request in court. The Ashcroft policy quickly discouraged the release of information to the public because few people were willing to go to the trouble and expense of an inevitable lawsuit.

Then, on November 1, 2001, Bush signed an executive order imposing sharp new restrictions on public access to historical presidential records.

In 1978, as part of its post-Watergate reforms, Congress had passed the Presidential Records Act, declaring White House files to be public property and requiring the government to systematically make most such files, including "confidential communications . . . between the president and his advisers," available to the public twelve years after any administration leaves office. The first administration to which this law applied was the Reagan-Bush presidency, whose records by law were supposed to become widely available on January 21, 2001. But Alberto Gonzales had earlier sent a series of letters to the National Archives ordering them to delay the release of President Reagan and Vice President George H. W. Bush's papers while the White House considered "the many constitutional and legal questions raised by potential release of sensitive and confidential Presidential records."[27] The delay was still in place as Bush declared that all records would remain sealed if either the current president or the past president (or his relatives) wanted them withheld from the public as "privileged." Moreover, instead of giving the current and former presidents a one-time opportunity to go back and withhold a few key documents, the order declared that all requests for documents would have to be routinely screened as they came in, meaning that responses could be delayed indefinitely.

And, Bush declared, the same screening rights and restrictions would apply to the papers of current and former vice presidents—the first beneficiaries of which were Bush's father, who had been Reagan's vice president, and Cheney, the current officeholder.

<h2 style="text-align:center">5.</h2>

On December 13, 2001, the House Government Reform Committee, chaired by Rep. Dan Burton, a conservative Republican from Indiana, issued a subpoena to the Department of Justice seeking records on former attorney general Janet Reno's decision not to appoint an independent counsel to investigate allegations of illegal campaign fund-raising by the Clinton-Gore campaign in 1996. Bush, for the first time in his eleven-month-old presidency, invoked executive privilege to shield the related papers from Congress, saying that turning over the records would inhibit candid discussions inside the executive branch.[28]

The White House announced that Bush was invoking executive privilege over the papers on the eve of a House Government Reform Committee hearing on the Clinton fund-raising scandal. Infuriated, Burton confronted a lower-level Justice Department official sent to testify about the administration's position. During the ritual pre-hearing handshake with the witnesses, Burton jabbed his finger at his fellow Republican and told him Bush was making a big mistake. "We've got a dictatorial president and a Justice Department that does not want Congress involved," Burton said. "Your guy's acting like he's king."[29] The committee's Republican chairman was only slightly more diplomatic in his official comments from the dais, where he denounced the White House for setting a "terrible, terrible precedent" in the name of executive power. "This is not a monarchy," Burton said. "The legislative branch has oversight responsibilities to make sure there is no corruption in the executive branch."[30]

Burton wasn't alone among Republicans in expressing alarm about the growing pattern of secrecy. Although Bush's move was targeted at a House investigation, several lawmakers in the Senate — then embroiled in a dispute with the White House over access to records about changes to air pollution regulations — also took notice. Among them, Senator Chuck Grassley, Republican of Iowa, questioned the White House argument that it would be contrary to the public interest to allow Congress to access the Clinton fund-raising documents. "Anything that limits legitimate congressional oversight is very worrisome," Grassley said. "This move needs to be carefully scrutinized, particularly in an atmosphere where Congress is giving the Justice Department additional powers and authority."[31]

But politics defeated such principles. Most Republicans were unwilling to challenge Bush, and many Democrats opposed Burton's probes of the Clinton campaign fund-raising, so few members of either party were interested in fighting the White House about it. And because Bush's first invocation of the power was done in part to protect Clinton and the Democrats, not himself, the gesture seemed principled rather than self-serving. It was tactically brilliant.

Bush also used the Clinton scandals to expand the zone of executive privilege in the courts. Judicial Watch, still fighting with the administration over the energy task force papers, also went to court seeking records about controversial pardons that Clinton had issued during his last days in office. Previously, the rule had been that communications that reached the president were privileged and exempt from disclosure, but documents seen only by lower-level officials could be made public. Judicial Watch sought access to several thousand pages of documents about the pardons prepared by subordinate officials, which Clinton never personally saw. The Bush-Cheney administration refused to hand them over, arguing that the "presidential communications privilege," a part of executive privilege, ought to be expanded to all such documents. And in a key March 28, 2003, ruling, U.S. District judge Gladys Kessler—a Clinton appointee— upheld the administration's broad claims, ensuring that Clinton's pardon papers would stay secret and handing the Bush-Cheney legal team another victory in its bid to expand the White House's power to keep its inner workings secret.

Judicial Watch's president, Tom Fitton, accused Kessler of endorsing Bush's theory of executive privilege in order to cover up a scandal by the president who had put her on the bench. But the White House hailed the expansion of the presidency's right to keep documents secret from the public. And White House spokesman Scott McClellan noted approvingly that the courts had now recognized that the privilege "applies to former, current, and future presidents."[32]

## 6.

Sidelined temporarily by the 9/11 attacks, the energy task force fight began moving forward again a few months later. The Enron Corporation, whose executives had met six times with Cheney or his aides about energy matters, had subsequently fallen apart in one of the largest corporate fraud scandals in history. As Congress began deliberating over whether to enact the president's energy bill, several committee chairmen in the Senate—then controlled by Democrats—joined in asking the General Accounting Office to press forward with its investigation into the influence of energy industry lobbyists in crafting the administration's policy. By January 2002, David Walker was openly talking about filing a lawsuit against the executive branch to get the White House to turn over the information—something that had been threatened but that had never turned out to be necessary in the history of the agency.

Inside the White House, the deliberations over how to respond to the GAO's demands reached a turning point. With each letter between Addington and Walker, the positions had hardened and the stakes had been raised. It was clear that if the vice president did not back down, an unprecedented GAO suit might go forward, which—if nothing else—would certainly prove to be an embarrassment for the White House. The legal team went to Bush to see whether he wanted to back down and turn over some of the records. But the president, whose post-9/11 standing in the public opinion polls was at historic highs, didn't hesitate. He told Gonzales to keep backing Cheney.

In January 2002, Cheney talked about the reasons for his uncompromising stance about the energy task force papers on ABC's *This Week*. As noted earlier, the interview represented the first time that the vice president laid out publicly his agenda of rolling back three decades of restrictions on presidential power. The interviewer, Cokie Roberts, pointed out that Republicans in Congress were saying that it was politically unwise for Bush to withhold the records because "it just looks like they're hiding something. People are beginning to ask that age-old Washington question with a new twist, which is, what did the vice president know and when did he know it?"[33]

Cheney wasn't put off by the Watergate reference. The vice president readily acknowledged that his view of the ideal level of presidential power was the level the office enjoyed when Cheney had first arrived in Washington, at the height of Nixon's pre-Watergate imperial presidency. Cheney also denounced the "unwise" erosion of executive authority he had witnessed after Nixon's fall, saying that he would not compromise away the powers of his institution the way other administrations had. Moreover, Cheney said, his counsel—Addington—had assured him that the constitutional case for withholding the energy task force papers was sound.

The vice president further promoted his position three weeks later on NBC's *The Tonight Show*. Cheney told host Jay Leno, "What's at stake here is whether a member of Congress can demand that I give him notes of all my meetings and a list of everybody I met with. We don't think that he has that authority." By then, as noted earlier, the GAO didn't want the notes and minutes of the meetings, just a list of the lobbyists' names. But as Cheney described his tough stand against congressional encroachment on executive power, the studio audience applauded enthusiastically.[34]

Walker deeply resented Cheney's mischaracterization of the case to the public, later referring to Cheney's false description of the GAO's request as "disinformation." But Walker also had larger concerns about the long-term ability of the GAO to do its job. If he quietly acquiesced to Cheney's stonewalling over the energy task force records, Walker feared, every other executive branch agency would start taking the same approach. "It was pretty clear to me that we would have faced a proliferation of records-access problems throughout the federal government had we not shown our resolve in connection to this matter," Walker later said. "There was an attempt to redraw the lines in separation-of-powers doctrine between what Congress has a right to obtain and what the executive had a right to [keep secret]."[35]

On February 22, 2002, Walker filed the lawsuit. *Walker v. Cheney* sought a court order forcing the vice president to disclose to the congressional watchdog agency the identities of the oil company executives who participated in the task force. In its court filings, the GAO argued that a loss would "either be extremely damaging to the General Accounting Office or fatal to its ability to perform functions that it has [carried out] in the past for Congress and the public." If Cheney's position were accepted, the GAO warned, it would be "literally devastating to the General Accounting Office's ability to obtain any information from the executive branch under any circumstances."[36]

7.

As the Bush-Cheney administration's fight to keep its energy papers from the congressional watchdog agency shifted into court, its broader secrecy campaign marched on. On March 19, 2002, White House chief of staff Andrew Card instructed government agencies to be vigilant about safeguarding records containing any "information that could be misused to harm the security of our Nation and the safety of our people." Because Card's order did not define those terms, agencies were free—indeed, encouraged—to interpret them very broadly.[37]

One consequence of Card's instructions was the acceleration of a tactic by the executive branch of blocking access to information under an array of loosely defined security designations.[38] The information that the administration was removing from public access was not considered risky enough to national security to be officially classified as "Confidential," "Secret," or "Top Secret" under rules in place for decades. Now large amounts of less-risky information were being stamped "For Official Use Only," "Sensitive but Unclassified," "Not for Public Dissemination," or one of what the Congressional Research Service estimated to be fifty to sixty other designations that were developed by executive agencies in an attempt to keep unclassified information from the public.

Although some of these terms predated the Bush-Cheney administration, their use grew sharply after 9/11. Precise numbers of documents being shielded are unknown because the administration kept no records. And there were only vague standards governing the types of documents that could be made secret. Under the official classification system, each level of secrecy comes with clearly defined criteria. There are strict limitations on who is authorized to decide whether a piece of information should be classified. (In 2005, precisely 3,959 officials had this power.) There are time limits after which most classified secrets can become public. There is a process for appealing a classification. And the government tracks how many classified secrets it creates each year.

By contrast, the new terms such as "Sensitive but Unclassified" have vague criteria that vary from agency to agency. In some departments, any employee, even a clerk, can stamp a document as off-limits. All 180,000 employees of the Homeland Security Department, for example, are empowered to decide a document is "For Official Use Only." There is no system for tracking who stamped it, for what reason, and how long it should stay secret. There is no process for appealing a secrecy decision.

The explosive growth in the executive branch's use of "Sensitive but Unclassified" markings under the Bush-Cheney administration was part of a larger pattern in shutting down the flow of unclassified information to the public. Websites went dark, periodic reports that compiled politically inconvenient information were shut down, and Freedom of Information Act requests began running into new walls.

Across the federal government, information that had previously been available to the public vanished. For years, a citizen who wanted to know the name and phone number of a Pentagon official could buy a copy of the Defense Department directory at a government printing office. After 9/11, the directory was stamped "For Official Use Only."

After a 1984 chemical plant accident had killed thousands of people in Bhopal, India, Congress in 1986 passed the Emergency Planning and Community Right-to-Know Act, giving Americans the right to know if they lived downwind from dangerous chemicals. Until 2001, the Environmental Protection Agency had posted on its website each plant's plans for dealing with a disaster, leading to public pressure on the chemical industry to maintain safer conditions. After 9/11 the database was removed from the website for security reasons.

For decades, the Defense Department's map office had made its topographic charts available to the public. Biologists use them to map species distribution, and airlines use them to create flight charts. But after 9/11, the administration moved to stop selling larger maps to the public to keep the maps away from "those intending harm" to the United States.

In July 2004, *Forbes* magazine reported that even old press releases—documents the government had specifically created for public dissemination—were being declared secret. The Justice Department cited "unwarranted invasion of personal privacy" in rejecting an FOIA request for press releases it had already issued concerning terrorism-related indictments.[39]

On August 4, 2004, the Nuclear Regulatory Commission announced that it would no longer let the public know whether nuclear plants had passed or failed security tests. The NRC said its change was to keep the information out of the hands of terrorists; watchdog groups accused the commission of taking away a key tool that allowed communities to pressure corporate executives to improve their safety measures.[40] And early the next year, the Nuclear Regulatory Commission put in place plans to block Americans from viewing what had previously been public, unclassified nuclear information. The new rules ensured that only officials employed by the nuclear industry could discuss regulatory changes with the government. Sue Gagner, a spokeswoman for the Nuclear Regulatory Commission, said the agency was "very mindful of the public's need to know," but its "concern is not to release information that could be helpful to a terrorist." (Among the documents withheld was a National Academy of Sciences report challenging the idea that the industry-preferred way of storing spent nuclear fuel rods was safe from terrorism.) The change prompted Rep. Edward J. Markey, Democrat of Massachusetts and a homeland security hawk, to accuse the commission of using security threats as a "pretext to prevent the public from accessing documents that do not pose a security risk." The agency, he claimed, was suppressing information "based on the fact that it disagrees with the conclusions, not on any legitimate security" fears.[41]

In April 2005, an employee of the group Human Rights Watch found an unclassified draft of a new policy on a Defense Department website. The document proposed holding suspected Iraqi insurgents without trial in the same way that accused Taliban members have been imprisoned at Guantánamo Bay. After the group issued a press release denouncing the idea, the Pentagon took down its entire electronic library of unclassified documents, including many hundreds of unrelated papers. The military later put part of the website back up, but dozens of documents that had previously been available to the public were still gone.[42]

Such moves were increasingly criticized across the political spectrum. Senator John Cornyn, a Texas Republican, introduced a bill to strengthen the Freedom of Information Act, but his colleagues in the GOP-led Congress never took it up. Moreover, a report coauthored by the Heritage Foundation, a conservative think tank, attacked "overzealous" decisions to dismantle entire websites over security fears. It also said that the Bush-Cheney administration had not conducted a systematic review of formerly public information that had been made secret, by weighing the likelihood that it could help terrorists against the "countervailing public safety and other benefits of providing" the information.[43]

The Bush-Cheney administration argued that it was just being cautious about keeping sensitive information from terrorist hands. But skeptics said that the administration was also suppressing politically awkward information that had no connection to national security.

Starting in October 2002 and extending into 2003, for instance, a political appointee on the White House Council on Environmental Quality, Philip A. Cooney, used his position to alter drafts of reports by the Environmental Protection Agency about scientific findings related to global warming. Handwritten notes by Cooney, a former oil industry lobbyist with no scientific training, showed that he adjusted the language of draft reports and sometimes crossed out whole paragraphs in order to cast doubt on what climate scientists said were solid links between the burning of fossil fuels and global warming.[44]

On Christmas Eve of 2002, the administration announced that the Bureau of Labor Statistics would stop publishing its monthly Mass Layoffs Statistics Report, which detailed factory closings around the country.[45] The administration said the report was too costly; labor unions said the government was seeking to suppress negative economic news.

Three months later, in March 2003, the administration announced that it would no longer publish an annual report that laid out how much money each state received from each federal program. At the time, governors of both parties were loudly complaining that budget cuts in Washington were creating huge shortfalls in state capitals. Without the annual four-hundred-page report, however, it became much harder to track how the budget cuts were affecting each state. An administration official said that such information would still be available "in a different mode" from each of the many federal agencies that handle grants, but Democrats accused Bush of simply trying to conceal the cuts.[46]

In October 2003, the Department of Justice posted on its website a copy of a report it had commissioned about its own record on racial diversity in the workplace. But half the report's 186 pages had been censored, including its summary and conclusions. In Tucson, Arizona, a First Amendment activist named Russ Kick downloaded a copy of the report and realized that he could digitally remove the redaction lines to see what had been kept from the public. Kick, the author of books such as *50 Things You're Not Supposed to Know,* unmasked the black lines and revealed that the administration was hiding the fact that minority lawyers at the department perceived their work climate to be rife with "stereotyping, harassment and racial tension." After Kick posted the uncensored diversity report on his website, TheMemoryHole.org, civil rights lawyers and Democrats in Congress accused the administration of ignoring its own report because it didn't like the findings, and unjustifiably hiding those findings from the public. But a Justice Department spokesman said that the portions of the report that had been blacked out—including its conclusions—were "deliberative and predecisional" under the administration's interpretation of the Freedom of Information Act, so it was legal to exclude them from the public version.[47]

That same month, October 2003, Kick read a small news story about how the administration had quietly banned news coverage of America's war dead arriving at military bases. Incensed, he immediately filed a Freedom of Information Act request for any photos of caskets at the base. The military rejected his request, and, without hoping for much, Kick appealed. Four months later, he received a package in the mail. To his amazement, some military official had reversed the decision. The package contained a CD with 361 photographs of flag-draped coffins, mostly the caskets of soldiers killed in Iraq, arriving at the Dover Air Force Base. There was no personally identifiable information visible in the images—just row upon row of anonymous coffins strapped down in the hold of transport planes. Kick immediately posted the photographs on his website, writing, "Score one for freedom of information and the public's right to know."[48] The images soon appeared on the front pages of newspapers and on television news. The Bush-Cheney administration quickly ordered the Pentagon to conceal such photographs in the future, citing privacy concerns, even though no names were attached to the pictures. (This would prove to be a common tactic. After *60 Minutes II* broadcast pictures of the Abu Ghraib torture scandal in 2004, the Pentagon would ban troops from taking cell-phone cameras into detention facilities. After the *Washington Post* reported about substandard conditions for injured Iraq war veterans at Walter Reed Army Medical Center in 2007, the Pentagon would order all patients not to speak with reporters.) The move to block the release of pictures from Dover drew a rebuke from Rep. Jim McDermott, a Washington Democrat who served in the navy during the Vietnam War. "This is not about privacy," McDermott told reporters. "This is about trying to keep the country from facing the reality of war."[49]

In August 2004, Education Department researchers released a surprising study of test scores showing that students at charter schools were performing worse than comparable students at regular public schools.[50] The findings were a disappointment for those in the Bush-Cheney administration who favored charter school funding. Less than two weeks later, the Education Department decided to sharply cut back on the information it collected about charter schools.[51]

In January 2006, Dr. James Hansen, the director of NASA's Goddard Institute for Space Studies and a top climate scientist, revealed that the Bush-Cheney administration had ordered the agency's public affairs staff to review his lectures, papers, website postings, and interview requests after he gave a lecture calling for the reduction of emissions of greenhouse gases linked to global warming. "They feel their job is to be this censor of information going out to the public," Hansen said, vowing to ignore the restrictions. A space agency spokesman denied any attempt to muzzle Hansen, saying the restrictions applied to all NASA officials and that it was inappropriate for government scientists to make policy statements.[52]

In February 2006, the Family Research Council, a conservative Christian group, sent a letter to the Department of Health and Human Services complaining about a government website that for six years had provided the public with information about gay-oriented health issues. Two weeks later, the entire website disappeared.[53]

In December 2006, the administration imposed unprecedented controls on scientists at the U.S. Geological Survey, an agency that studies environmental issues such as global warming and endangered species. Under the new rules, scientists were required to submit research papers and prepared speeches to higher-ups for screening prior to dissemination. The rules also required the scientists to alert the public affairs office of "findings or data that may be especially newsworthy, have an impact on government policy, or contradict previous public understanding to ensure that proper officials are notified and that communication strategies are developed." Scientists at the agency complained about the prospect of political appointees looking over their shoulders. "The explanation was that this was intended to ensure the highest possible quality research," said Jim Estes, a marine biologist who had worked for the agency for more than thirty years. "But to me it feels like they're doing this to keep us under their thumbs."[54]

And in March 2007, the U.S. Fish and Wildlife Service issued new rules for scientists about to attend an international meeting on the Arctic. The guidelines said the scientists were not allowed to talk about climate change, polar bears, and sea ice — even if asked. The Bush-Cheney administration said it wanted to have one person in the delegation be the official spokesman for such issues simply out of diplomatic protocol. But Deborah Williams, a former Interior Department official in the Clinton administration who obtained the memos, criticized the Bush-Cheney administration's efforts to impose political control over what government scientists could talk about to their peers. "This sure sounds like a Soviet-style directive to me," Williams said.[55]

## 8.

Back in June 2002, three months after Card instructed the executive branch to tighten its control over information in light of the war on terrorism, a Justice Department legal ethics adviser named Jesselyn Radack faxed a set of internal government e-mails about a key terrorism legal case to a *Newsweek* reporter. The e-mails, which Radack herself had written, concerned the case of John Walker Lindh.[56]

A California-born twenty-year-old who had converted to Islam, Lindh had traveled to Pakistan and Afghanistan to study religion. Attracted to the Taliban's attempt to build a so-called perfect Islamic society, he had joined them in their civil war against the Northern Alliance — all before 9/11. After the attacks, when U.S. bombers helped the Northern Alliance sweep over the Taliban, Lindh was among the prisoners taken to Mazar-e

Sharif, and he was among the handful of surviving prisoners. His discovery had prompted a sensation—Lindh became notorious as the "American Taliban." It had also prompted the first major terrorism prosecution after 9/11. With a dramatic flourish, Attorney General Ashcroft personally unveiled a ten-count indictment against Lindh, including charges of conspiracy to kill Americans and to provide material support to international terrorists.

Almost the entire basis for the indictment was his own statement to interrogators after he was taken prisoner, and without a defense attorney present. Ashcroft declared that Lindh had no attorney at the time, so his statement should be admissible. But Radack, who had been consulted early on about the case, had e-mails that proved otherwise. Investigators had known that Lindh's father had already retained a defense attorney for his son before they interrogated him. Radack had warned the FBI not to question Lindh without his attorney present—but the FBI interrogated him anyway. Moreover, when a judge had ordered the department to turn over all its internal correspondence about Lindh, department supervisors had tried to conceal the order from Radack, and her e-mails had disappeared from the Lindh files. At the same time, Radack's supervisors suddenly forced her out of her job with an unscheduled performance evaluation giving her terrible ratings, less than a year after they had given her a merit bonus and a promotion.

Radack still had a copy of her e-mails. As the Lindh case unfolded and the administration continued to swear that it knew nothing of the fact that Lindh already had a defense attorney at the time of his interrogation, she decided to send them to a reporter. "I wasn't in my mind saying, 'Gee I want to be a whistle-blower,'" Radack later recalled. "I was just trying to correct the wrong, just trying to set something straight."[57]

The resulting article added to questions about whether Lindh's interrogation had been mishandled. Already a photograph had leaked showing the conditions of Lindh's initial interrogation: he was naked, blindfolded, strapped to a board with duct tape, and not given immediate medical treatment for a bullet wound in his leg. Three weeks after *Newsweek* published its article about Radack's e-mails, the Department of Justice announced a surprise plea bargain deal to end Lindh's case on the eve of an evidence-suppression hearing that would have probed the facts surrounding his interrogation. The government dropped most of the more spectacular charges against Lindh, and in return, Lindh pled guilty to simply aiding the Taliban regime and carrying a weapon while doing so. He was sentenced to twenty years without parole.

As Lindh's case was abruptly ending, however, Radack's ordeal was just getting going. Radack had done nothing illegal. The Lindh e-mails were not classified, and there is no law against leaking unclassified materials. But the Bush-Cheney administration came down hard on Radack for revealing information to the public that it had wanted to keep secret. While working for a private law firm, Radack was informed by her supervisors that the government told them she was a "criminal" who could not be trusted. The firm forced her out as well. The Justice Department also launched a yearlong criminal investigation of Radack, though she had broken no law; investigators never identified a potential charge against her, and no charges were ever filed.

"My attorneys asked what I was being investigated for and never got an answer," she said. "There is no law against leaking. This was nonclassified stuff. I think they were just trying to get me to slip into making a false statement. Beyond that, it never seemed like they were really going to bring charges. This was just to harass me."

The harassment did not end there. The Bush-Cheney administration also referred her for "discipline" to the bar associations in the states where she was licensed to practice law, submitting a secret report she was not allowed to see and making it almost impossible for her to fight the allegations or find a new job. And the government further harassed Radack by putting her on the "selectee" version of the "no-fly list," forcing her every time she went through airport security to endure the kind of invasive extra screening that is supposed to be for potential security risks.[58] After missing one too many flights while being forced, once again, to remove her underwire bra at security, Radack gave up.

"I quit trying to fly," she said. "I just got sick of being told, for the nineteenth time, that I'd been 'randomly selected' to go through secondary screening measures. I just drove to Disney World from Washington, DC, with three young children rather than flying because I can't have them go through security while I'm stuck going through a full body search."

Whatever one thinks of Lindh's actions and his ultimate fate, the Justice Department had no legal standing in attempting to conceal Radack's e-mails from the judge. Moreover, Congress has passed numerous laws, including the Whistleblower Protection Act of 1989, making the rules clear: Whistle-blowers are supposed to be protected from retaliation when they bring government misconduct to light. But the existing laws contain no mechanism by which a victim can enforce the limits, such as a right to sue the government for breaking the law. Instead, the protections rely only on the willingness of high-ranking executive branch officials to obey a statute.

The whistle-blower laws did nothing to help Radack when the Bush-Cheney administration decided to make an example of her, sending a clear warning to other officials who might be inclined to bring secret executive branch wrongdoing to light.[59] And Radack would not be the last.

## 9.

In November 2002, President Bush signed two bills passed by Congress that would have a dramatic—and opposite—impact on his administration's ability to control government secrets.

The first bill, which Bush signed on November 25, 2002, was the Homeland Security Act. Most media coverage of the bill focused simply on its plan to create a new federal cabinet department, pulling together agencies such as immigration services, customs, border patrol, airport security, and the Coast Guard into a single organization. Other coverage focused on a political dispute between Republicans and Democrats over whether employees of the department should be exempted from normal worker protection rules; in a win for the White House, the final law granted unusual powers to the president's political appointees to hire, fire, promote, and move career officials around at will. Much less covered was the bill's grant of vast new secrecy powers to the executive branch. Lawmakers included sweeping new powers to withhold information from the public about "critical infrastructure" such as emergency plans for major industrial sites, criminalizing the release of such information to the public by a government official. Ostensibly aimed at preventing terrorists from obtaining a "road map" for planning attacks, the new law virtually eliminated the public's right to know about risky practices at industrial sites in their communities.[60]

Two days later, Bush signed a bill creating the 9/11 Commission to look into how the disastrous Al Qaeda terrorist attacks had succeeded and what should be done to prevent such a thing from happening again. For months, the White House had resisted the creation of such an independent panel. When it became increasingly clear that Congress, prompted by victims' families, would go forward with the creation of the commission, the White House lobbied to prevent the panel from looking into secret intelligence. But the pressure from victims groups for a full investigation became too much to resist, and the 9/11 Commission was given a legal mandate to look into everything.

That mandate would hit home in early April 2004, when Bush's national security adviser, Condoleezza Rice, appeared before the 9/11 Commission to testify about steps the administration had taken, and failed to take, to stop Al Qaeda before the attacks. The White House had resisted allowing Rice to provide such information to the commission — and the public — for months but relented under the increasingly heavy pressure from the commission and family members of the victims. During her testimony, Rice let slip the title of a heavily classified Presidential Daily Briefing that Bush had received thirty-six days before the attacks. Written by the CIA, the memo was entitled "Bin Laden Determined to Strike Inside US."

Rice would insist that the briefing was purely "historical" and that it contained no specific threats that should have served as cause for additional action by the administration. But several family members of victims as well as panelists on the commission said the document should be declassified so that the public itself could determine the report's significance. Again buckling under the pressure, the administration declassified the two-page memo on April 10, 2004. As the administration hastened to point out, the pre-9/11 briefing did not mention using hijacked planes as missiles, and it did not give specific times or places for any attack. But the document summarized a series of indicators that bin Laden, Al Qaeda's leader, was trying to hit the United States. It also said that Al Qaeda members "have resided or traveled in the US for years, and the group apparently maintains a support structure that could aid attacks." Bush had also been told that the FBI had detected "patterns of suspicious activity in this country consistent with preparations for hijackings or other types of attacks."[61]

It would not be the last time that the 9/11 Commission would bring to light information the administration did not want the public to know—including the lack of documentary evidence supporting the claim that Bush had given Cheney prior authorization to order the shoot-down of hijacked planes on the morning of the attacks. The existence and perseverance of the bipartisan panel represented the single greatest failure for the White House's secrecy agenda. But such setbacks were rare amid a sea of victories.

## 10.

On December 9, 2002, about two weeks after Bush signed the Homeland Security and 9/11 Commission bills, a federal district judge shut down the General Accounting Office's lawsuit in the energy papers case, handing Cheney a clear victory in his attempt to keep the information from the congressional watchdog agency.

The case had been randomly assigned by the court computer to district judge John Bates. A Republican, Bates had forged his political connections as deputy independent counsel in Kenneth Starr's Whitewater investigation of President Clinton. Bush appointed Bates to a federal judgeship in 2001, and now Bates sided with Cheney and dismissed the case. Walker might be the comptroller general and the head of the GAO, Bates ruled, but he was just one man and so had no standing to sue the executive branch on behalf of Congress.

After the ruling, members of Congress initially focused on the short-term political issue of the energy task force. "It is regrettable, but not surprising, that a newly appointed federal judge chose to look the other way," said Representative Dingell, one of the original two lawmakers who had sought access to the task force records. "Vice President Cheney's cover-up will apparently continue for the foreseeable future unless the Republican Congress demands appropriate disclosure. I'm not holding my breath."[62]

But Bates's ruling had far more momentous implications. By taking away the GAO's ability to threaten to file a lawsuit, his decision severely damaged the congressional watchdog's capability to persuade executive branch agencies to comply with its requests for information. While a district court ruling is not a binding precedent, unlike a decision by an appeals court or the Supreme Court, it was still the first and only ruling on the books about a lawsuit between the GAO and the executive branch. Bates had established a principle that, if left undisturbed, could change the attitudes of executive branch officials when the GAO asked for documents they did not want to disclose.

Alarmed, open-government advocates urged Walker to appeal the ruling. But in January 2003, Republicans took over the Senate, and the new leadership joined with House Republicans in opposing further litigation against Cheney. Walker reluctantly dropped the case.[63] "Despite GAO's conviction that the district court's decision was incorrect, further pursuit of the [energy task force] information would require investment of significant time and resources over several years," he said when announcing his decision.

A congressional newspaper later reported that Walker had decided not to appeal because the Republican chairman of the Senate Appropriations Committee, Ted Stevens of Alaska, threatened to slash the GAO's budget unless Walker dropped the case.[64] But Walker denied that report. He acknowledged that some U.S. senator, whom he would not name, had threatened his agency's funding over the case at one point but said the threat had been made a year earlier, as he was first mulling over whether to file a lawsuit. Instead, Walker said, he decided not to press on with an appeal for damage-control reasons. He didn't want to fight a protracted battle that might damage the GAO's reputation as nonpartisan, and he didn't want to risk an even more damaging ruling against the GAO by an appeals court. If the GAO was going to fight that legal battle, Walker explained, it was strategically unwise to use a case that involved records inside the White House itself instead of a less prominent part of the executive branch.[65]

As the GAO's ability to pry information out of the executive branch on behalf of Congress was taking a hit, tension between lawmakers and the administration increased. Throughout 2002 and early 2003, members of Congress began to complain that the Bush-Cheney administration was not being forthcoming with the information that oversight committees needed in order to do their jobs.

One of the first flash points concerned the administration's refusal to answer questions about how often the FBI was using the new law enforcement powers provided by the USA Patriot Act. The Ashcroft Justice Department had presented a draft of the bill to Congress shortly after the 9/11 attacks, saying the FBI needed extra powers to seize business records, wiretap, and secretly search homes in order to protect the country from Al Qaeda. Lawmakers eagerly passed the law in October 2001 as a symbol of their support for fighting terrorism. The Senate approved the Patriot Act by a vote of 98 to 1, and the House approved it 357 to 66.

In the following months, however, civil libertarians started to raise questions about whether Congress had been too hasty in expanding the executive branch's police powers and loosening its oversight restrictions.* As privacy advocates began pressing Congress to take a harder look at the law's impact on basic freedoms, the Patriot Act's symbolic meaning shifted. Instead of being a sign of Congress's bipartisan stance against terrorism, the law came to represent fears that the government security clampdown after 9/11 was going too far in curtailing individual rights. Against this backdrop, both the House and Senate Judiciary committees sent letter after letter to the administration, seeking to know how often the administration had used its Patriot Act powers. But even though the committees had staffers with security clearances who regularly dealt with classified information, the Bush-Cheney administration refused to answer their questions.[66]

The executive branch's stonewalling eventually became too much for House Judiciary Committee chairman James Sensenbrenner of Wisconsin, usually a loyal Republican ally of the president. In August 2002, Sensenbrenner declared he was about to "start blowing a fuse." He said that if Ashcroft did not provide answers to fifty questions about the Patriot Act, such as how many times the Justice Department had obtained wiretaps under the act, he would subpoena the attorney general and block the law from being renewed when it expired in 2005.[67]

But the moment did not long endure. On October 17, 2002, the Justice Department provided some information about its use of the Patriot Act to

---

*Subsequent events would demonstrate that these concerns were not without merit. For example, one of the things the Patriot Act did was ease the standards by which FBI agents could seize telephone, Internet, banking, and credit-card records without having to get a warrant from a judge. The changes caused the FBI to dramatically increase its use of the warrantless seizure power, from eighty-five hundred times in 2000 to forty-five thousand times a year after the Patriot Act. And freed of judicial oversight, FBI agents would sometimes abuse their expanded powers. In March 2007, an audit by the Justice Department's inspector general would find that the FBI had made numerous "improper and illegal" uses of its new tools. The "serious misuses" had included collecting information not permitted by the law, collecting information about people who were not proper subjects of an FBI investigation, a failure to report such errors, and undercounting its real use of the powers by as much as 20 percent in reports to Congress. "A Review of the Federal Bureau of Investigation's Use of National Security Letters," Department of Justice, Office of the Inspector General, March 2007, http://www.usdoj.gov/oig/special/s0703b/final.pdf.

the House Judiciary Committee. Although the administration did not fully answer the fifty questions, saying some of the information was classified, its gesture was enough that Sensenbrenner removed himself from the ranks of those who were criticizing the White House for being too secretive. "I am satisfied that the Department of Justice has produced answers that are sufficient for the committee's oversight and legislative efforts at this time," he explained.[68]

Sensenbrenner's quick fold may have emboldened the administration to further frustrate Congress's ability to perform oversight. On July 17, 2003, Cheney received a very unusual handwritten letter. It came from Sen. Jay Rockefeller of West Virginia, the ranking member on the Senate Intelligence Committee. Earlier that day, the vice president had personally delivered a briefing about a top secret program to Rockefeller and three other leaders of the intelligence oversight committees. Under the program, which Bush had authorized after 9/11, the National Security Agency was monitoring Americans' international phone calls and e-mails without warrants. According to laws passed in 1974 and reinforced in 1980—the last of the post-Watergate reforms—the administration was required to brief the Intelligence committees in both chambers about all such secret intelligence programs. There was one exception: For ultrasensitive covert missions abroad, where leaks could be especially devastating, the White House was allowed to brief merely the chairman and ranking member of the committees. Cheney invoked that exception for the wiretapping program, even though it did not meet the legal definition of a covert program. Cheney also refused to allow the lawmakers to discuss the program with any of their expert staff, despite the fact that their staff had top secret security clearance.

In his letter, Rockefeller complained that the few details the vice president had provided were inadequate. From what he could understand of the program, the senator said, it reminded him of the Total Information Awareness program—a vast data-mining scheme to track Americans' credit-card transactions, website visits, travel records, bank transactions, and other database files at the Pentagon. Led by Iran-Contra figure John Poindexter, the Total Information Awareness program had raised alarms among privacy advocates, such as conservative former Nixon speechwriter William Safire.[69] At the time of Rockefeller's letter, Congress had recently ordered the program suspended, and it would soon cut off funding for the program entirely. The data-mining aspects of the National Security

Agency surveillance program suggested that the military might still be using the same techniques Congress had just been saying it did not want the government to use.

"Clearly the activities we discussed raise profound oversight issues," Rockefeller wrote. "As you know, I am neither a technician nor an attorney. Given the security restrictions associated with this information, and my inability to consult staff or counsel on my own, I feel unable to fully evaluate, much less endorse these activities. . . . Without more information and the ability to draw on any independent legal or technical expertise, I simply cannot satisfy lingering concerns raised by the briefing we received." He also made clear in his letter that he was helpless to do anything about his concerns, since it was a criminal offense to break the secrecy rules the White House had invoked, but he wanted to record his objection. However, after the program was revealed, Rockefeller would release a copy of his handwritten letter that he had been keeping in a secure safe in his office.[70]

The administration also kept from Congress critical information that had nothing to do with national security. In November 2003, Congress narrowly approved a prescription drug benefit program favored by the White House as a key means to convincing senior citizens to vote the Bush-Cheney ticket in the coming year's presidential election. The program was highly controversial among fiscal conservatives, who opposed the idea of creating an expensive new entitlement program. To convince skeptical lawmakers that the program was affordable, administration officials testified that its cost would not exceed $400 billion over the coming decade. Later, it emerged that the chief actuary for Medicare, a career bureaucrat named Richard Foster, had developed information showing that the cost of the program was likely to be some $550 billion. But one of Bush's political appointees to the Medicare program, Thomas Scully, threatened to fire Foster if he told Congress about his findings before it voted.[71] The revelation outraged lawmakers. Several Republicans said they would not have voted for the program had they known its true cost.[72]

The Bush-Cheney administration took steps to stop Congress from discussing information that was already public, too. In March 2004, the General Accounting Office handed Congress a report about problems with the development of the missile-defense system. The GAO document reproduced an unclassified list of fifty recommendations for improving the system that came from a public report the Pentagon generated four

years earlier. The Defense Department declared that the list of fifty recommendations was now retroactively classified, so members of Congress
could not discuss them in public. The two members who had asked the
GAO to write the missile-defense report, Democratic representatives John
Tierney and Henry Waxman, sent an angry letter to Defense Secretary
Donald Rumsfeld, calling the decision to classify the information "highly
dubious" and "an attempt to stymie public debate through the use of the
classification system."[73] The administration ignored the protest.

The lawmakers' agitation was hardly unique. Rank-and-file committee
members from both parties increasingly complained that the Bush-Cheney
administration gave them too little information to perform effective oversight on a wide variety of intelligence issues. "Is the administration giving
us everything we want or need? Of course not," said Rep. William "Mac"
Thornberry, Republican of Texas and chairman of the oversight subcommittee of the House Intelligence Committee.[74] On several occasions, the
administration told them about a program only when the White House
learned that the information had been leaked and was about to be published anyway.

Other secrecy rules helped thwart effective congressional oversight of
the administration's intelligence programs. All lawmakers were entitled
to read the secret intelligence authorization bills, including the details of
covert programs. But under the rules congressional leaders had negotiated with the White House, members were not allowed to mention the
contents of those bills if they read them—even if that information was
later leaked by someone else to the media—on penalty of criminal prosecution and expulsion from Congress. By the middle of the Bush-Cheney
administration, most lawmakers had simply abandoned their opportunity to read the intelligence bills or receive the intelligence briefings because they did not want to be gagged from talking about important issues
in the war on terrorism. In April 2006, for example, the House voted 327
to 96 to pass a bill authorizing the administration's plans for fighting the
war on terrorism, but only a dozen House members had read the bill. "It's
a trap," said Rep. Russ Carnahan, Democrat of Missouri, referring to the
rule that members must refrain from discussing items in the bill. "Either
way, you're flying blind." And Rep. Walter Jones, a North Carolina Republican, acknowledged, "We ought to be doing a better job of oversight,
[but] if you're not going to be able to question it or challenge it, that makes
it difficult."[75]

Party politics further kept Congress from using its constitutional power over spending to pry secrets loose from the administration. Democrats tried to enact a budget bill slicing funds from the Pentagon and CIA unless the administration answered lawmakers' questions about detainee treatment, the Pentagon's relationship with the controversial Iraqi exile leader Ahmed Chalabi, and, later, the warrantless surveillance program. Each time, Republicans voted down the amendments, branding them as "completely irresponsible in a time of war."[76]

# 6

# The Unleashing: Laws and Treaties I

## 1.

Rain and gloom blanketed Washington on Friday, September 14, 2001, a date proclaimed by President Bush to be a National Day of Prayer and Remembrance for the victims of 9/11. The Pentagon still burned despite days of intense firefighting; when the rubble shifted, new air pockets opened and fed fresh flare-ups. In New York, emergency workers continued to hunt through the debris at the site of the former World Trade Center, now renamed Ground Zero. In Washington, military vehicles were a common sight on the streets, and anti-aircraft missile batteries circled the White House. Adding to the sense of dread, the capital city's central airport, Reagan National, was shut down indefinitely to keep planes at a distance. Vice President Cheney had been moved to a "secure, undisclosed location"—later reported to be a Cold War–era command bunker under Raven Rock Mountain in Pennsylvania, about seven miles north of Camp David—where he was busy working on the nation's response to the attacks.[1] Bush, by contrast, was making a series of public appearances.

At 1 p.m., Bush stepped to the pulpit at Washington National Cathedral, a Gothic church rising above a leafy northwest Washington neighborhood. Before him, much of the nation's political leadership had assembled, including most of Congress as well as former presidents Gerald Ford, Jimmy Carter, George H. W. Bush, and Bill Clinton. Bush's voice echoed off the sanctuary walls as he read an eight-minute speech about the nation's sorrow and resolve. America had a responsibility to "answer these attacks and rid the world of evil," Bush said, and he lauded the new spirit of national unity that had "joined together political parties in both houses of Congress."[2]

Just a week earlier, Congress had been sharply divided by partisan feuding over such issues as the secret energy task force. After the terrorist attacks, the conflict seemed trivial and was temporarily put aside. On the morning of September 14, before boarding buses that would take them to National Cathedral, America's lawmakers had convened beneath the marble dome of the U.S. Capitol. Carrying out the solemn responsibilities assigned to it by the Founders and reinforced by the War Powers Resolution of 1973, Congress decided that the United States of America would go to war. By votes of 98–0 in the Senate, and 420–1 in the House, Congress authorized the president to "use all necessary and appropriate force against those nations, organizations, or persons he determines planned, authorized, committed, or aided the terrorist attacks that occurred on September 11, 2001, or harbored such organizations or persons."[3]

Shortly after Congress authorized war, the White House press office put out a terse prepared statement in Bush's name. It read: "I am gratified that the Congress has united so powerfully by taking this action. It sends a clear message—our people are together, and we will prevail."[4] The wording of this statement was, upon close inspection, curiously vague—why had the White House said "taking this action" rather than given a more specific description of what Congress had done, such as "authorized war"? But few were paying close attention to semantics amid the day's other dramatic events. That same day, Congress also approved a $40 billion aid-and-recovery package. Bush called up thirty-five thousand military reservists. And in a dramatic moment of unscripted theater later that afternoon, Bush stood near the debris pile in lower Manhattan, put his arm around a firefighter, and, in response to calls that he could not be heard by the crowd, vowed through a bullhorn that "the people who knocked these buildings down will hear from all of us soon."[5]

The scene showed up on all the nightly newscasts and was splashed on the front pages of newspapers nationwide the next day, becoming an iconic high point of Bush's presidency. But for the administration's legal team, the vote by Congress to authorize Bush to use military force against the perpetrators of 9/11 was the most important event that took place on September 14, 2001. And it was something of an affront. The president's men believed that the commander in chief *already* had the power on his own to decide whether to take the country to war over the attacks, so "authorization" from the legislative branch was at best redundant. They also believed that the War Powers Resolution of 1973, which required presidents to consult with Congress when deploying troops into hostilities, was unconstitutional. And the legal team resented especially key limitations that Congress had placed on the otherwise expansive grant of wartime authority to the president.

The days after 9/11 had been intense ones for the Bush-Cheney legal team. Those who worked at the White House were initially barred from the evacuated compound, and some of them had convened at the nearby lobbying offices of the DaimlerChrysler Corporation, just off Lafayette Park, to hammer out a legal strategy.[6] On the evening of September 12, as Congress worked on the resolution's wording, representatives from the White House, led by Deputy White House Counsel Timothy Flanigan, had urged the lawmakers to adopt far broader language. Congress, the administration suggested, should endorse the president's power to use the military to "deter and pre-empt any future acts of terrorism or aggression against the United States." Such language would represent an open-ended blank check to go to war against anybody or any nation the president might later deem to pose a threat of any kind, whether or not the target was connected to 9/11. But Congress rejected the White House's request, specifically limiting the war authorization to Al Qaeda.[7]

Then, on the morning of September 14, just minutes before the final vote in the Senate, the administration's legal team tried a different way of expanding the war powers Congress was about to endorse. A White House lobbyist asked then–Senate majority leader Tom Daschle, Democrat of South Dakota, to amend the resolution by adding the words "in the United States and" after "appropriate force." Under this new plan, Bush would be authorized to "use all necessary and appropriate force *in the United States and* against those nations, organizations, or persons" linked to 9/11. In other words, Bush wanted Congress's support for exercising full battle field powers—from holding enemies prisoner without giving them legal rights, to shooting suspected enemies on sight—on U.S. soil. Congress again balked.[8]

Congress went ahead with its vote to authorize limited war powers. But even as Bush rose to speak at National Cathedral, his legal team was secretly going to work to seize the unlimited powers Congress had declined to grant. Meeting behind closed doors, the Bush-Cheney lawyers drew up a secret Office of Legal Counsel memo describing the war powers the presidency considered itself free to wield. Addressed to Flanigan and signed by Deputy Assistant Attorney General John Yoo, the advisory opinion was completed on September 25, 2001, but kept secret for more than three years. Yoo's memo laid out powers that went far beyond the authority that Congress had just granted.[9] The secret memo asserted as fact that "the President's powers include inherent executive powers that are unenumerated in the Constitution," among them a right to use military force as he saw fit, regardless of the views of Congress. The Founders intended to vest "all federal executive power in the President to ensure a unity in purpose and energy in action," especially in matters of foreign affairs and national security. Thus, Congress had no power to limit how the president defended the nation. If Bush wanted to use military force on U.S. soil, or if he wanted to attack countries that he determined posed a threat even though they had no connection to 9/11, he could do so.[10]

In short, as far as the executive branch was concerned, the modest boundaries on Bush's wartime authority that Congress had tried to impose in its September 14 resolution were meaningless. Congress may have thought it was granting the president limited wartime powers after 9/11, but the Bush-Cheney administration decided in secret that it wielded unlimited wartime powers. "We think it beyond question," Yoo concluded, that Congress cannot "place any limits on the President's determinations as to any terrorist threat, the amount of military force to be used in response, or the method, timing, and nature of the response. These decisions, under our Constitution, are for the President alone to make."[11]

It would not be long before the Bush-Cheney administration discovered opportunities to turn its aggressive theory into real-world action. Each time a problem arose—and many problems would arise in the weeks and months after 9/11—the inner circle of key decision makers at the White House looked at their options and then picked the solution that relied upon the greatest possible assertion of presidential power. These policies, usually enacted in secret, transformed their theory into precedent.

## 2.

Like most lawyerly writings, the Bush-Cheney administration's confidential legal opinions are long and full of scholarly-seeming jargon and citations, and present a dense thicket for the nonspecialist to navigate. But boiled down into everyday language, their thrust is simple to understand. With a revolutionary one-two punch, they eliminate nearly all the checks and balances that have been traditionally understood to limit the power of the president.

First, the Bush-Cheney team embraced a theory that the president, as head of the executive branch and the commander in chief of the armed forces, has vast "inherent" powers that are not spelled out in the Constitution or federal law. Especially in matters of national security, these unlisted powers provide for an enormous potential scope of action. The government can do virtually anything the president believes is necessary to defend the country.

But even for believers in inherent executive authority, there remained an obstacle to maximum presidential power. An inherent executive power is not the same thing as an exclusive executive power. It's one thing to say that if necessity arises, the president can direct the government to do something that he was not specifically authorized to do by the Constitution or a federal statute—monitoring phone calls that touch U.S. soil in search of spies and terrorists, for example. But it's a very different thing to say that Congress cannot pass a law regulating how the president goes about doing that thing—as Congress did when it passed a law in 1978 requiring the government to start obtaining warrants for such eavesdropping, for instance.

The gap between inherent and exclusive power posed an impediment to the White House during the era of the so-called imperial presidency, between World War II and Watergate. As noted earlier, the most famous example came in 1952, when President Truman, citing his inherent power, authorized the government to seize the nation's steel mills. A labor dispute between steelworker unions and mill owners had raised the prospect of a strike, one that could cut off critical supplies for the Korean War effort. But Congress had previously passed a law that provided certain ways for the government to try to avert a strike, and the statute did not include the option of simply taking over the plants. Since Congress had already spoken, the Supreme Court struck down Truman's order, saying he had exceeded the limits of his authority as president. Even the commander in chief had to obey the law, the court said. "No penance would ever expiate the sin against free government of holding that a President can escape control of executive powers by law through assuming his military role," wrote Justice Robert Jackson.[12]

But three decades later, the Reagan legal team planted the seed for an idea that might erase the distinction between inherent and exclusive powers, thereby scrapping Congress's ability to regulate *any* executive power, inherent or otherwise. This seed was the Unitary Executive Theory. Back in the 1980s, advocates of the theory had been thinking about domestic issues—control of the independent agencies—not national security matters, but after 9/11, the Bush-Cheney legal team revived the Unitary Executive Theory and dramatically expanded its sweep. They again invoked Hamilton's words in *Federalist 70:* The Founders had put a single president in charge of the executive branch in order to give it a "unity" so it could act with "decision, activity, secrecy, and dispatch." Such characteristics, Hamilton also noted, were especially important in a time of war, when "energy in the executive is . . . essential to the protection of the community against foreign attacks." Thus, the Bush-Cheney team argued, statutes and treaties that restrict what the military and other security forces can do are unconstitutional; because of the new and improved Unitary Executive Theory, only the commander in chief could decide how the executive branch should go about defending America.[13]

During the years when Reagan's legal team invented the Unitary Executive Theory, television commercials for Reese's Peanut Butter Cups celebrated the combination of chocolate with peanut butter—the result, the commercials suggested, was more delicious than the sum of its parts. The Bush-Cheney legal team had discovered another kind of potent combination. The old "inherent power" theory greatly expanded what the executive branch could do, but it was silent about whether Congress could impose restrictions on how the president carried out those responsibilities. The new and improved Unitary Executive Theory said that Congress could not regulate *any* executive power, but the theory said nothing about the potential scope of such power. When fused, the two theories transformed any conceivably inherent executive power into an exclusive one. The president could do virtually anything, without any check by Congress.

Yet most outside legal scholars from across the political spectrum rejected the theories of unfettered presidential power that were developed and advanced by the Bush-Cheney legal team. These skeptics noted, for example, that the Constitution empowers Congress, not the president, to make laws that are "necessary and proper" to organize the executive branch and to regulate the general conduct of executive branch officials. Adherents of the Unitary Executive Theory, who believe the president should wield exclusive authority over how the executive branch goes about its business, tend to ignore this specific grant of lawmaking authority to Congress.

Moreover, the skeptics noted, the Supreme Court has repeatedly upheld the power of Congress to pass laws limiting the president's absolute control over lower-ranking officials. Such precedents, including a 1935 case upholding Congress's power to create independent agencies inside the executive branch, and the 1988 independent-counsel case, are simply incompatible with the Unitary Executive Theory. The Bush-Cheney administration legal team regularly ignored the existence of such precedents in its secret advisory opinions.

Then there is Alexander Hamilton's discussion of the executive branch's "unity" in *Federalist 70*, the most important document for adherents of the Unitary Executive Theory. Hamilton's essay in *Federalist 70*, it is true, described many virtues of putting one president in charge of the government instead of multiple decision makers, especially in a time of war. The presidentialists left their readers with the impression that Hamilton was contrasting the president with Congress—describing why the Founders did not want a body of several hundred lawmakers to intrude on the commander in chief's decisions and so restricted them from passing statutes that limited his options.

But skeptics say this reading of *Federalist 70* is extremely misleading. Hamilton was not talking about Congress. He was talking about why the Founders had decided to have one president instead of a small committee atop the executive branch, which had been a rival proposal at the Constitutional Convention. The virtues Hamilton was extolling were those of a system of day-to-day decision making in which there is no need for the executive branch to reach an internal consensus between rival factions before deciding what to do next, and these virtues have nothing to do with whether Congress can pass laws regulating how the executive branch carries out its responsibilities. Indeed, in a passage of the very same essay that the presidential power advocates have consistently failed to mention, Hamilton went out of his way to praise Congress as the place best suited for the devising of general rules within which the government acts: The Founders, he wrote, considered the legislative branch "best adapted to deliberation and wisdom, and best calculated to conciliate the confidence of the people and to secure their privileges and interests."

Even more important, Hamilton wrote another *Federalist* paper that much more squarely addresses the president's wartime powers: *Federalist 69*. In this essay, Hamilton explained that even though the American president would oversee the nation's military, just as the British king did, the American commander in chief's powers would be subject to much stronger checks and balances than were the monarch's, including submission to regulation by laws passed by Congress. Hamilton described the "commander in chief" title as meaning "nothing more" than that the president would be the "first general" in the military hierarchy, ensuring civilian control of the military. The commander in chief's powers were "much inferior" to a king's because all the power to declare war and to create and regulate armies is given instead to Congress, he explained.

Some state governors, Hamilton also noted, had even greater security powers as head of their state militias than the president would wield. "It may well be a question whether [the constitutions] of New Hampshire and Massachusetts, in particular, do not . . . confer larger powers upon their respective governors than could be claimed by a president of the United States." A look at the Massachusetts Constitution of 1780 shows clearly what this means. The commonwealth's constitution made its governor the commander in chief of its own armed forces and spoke expansively of his duty and power to use those forces to defend the commonwealth from invasion or rebellion. Yet in the same section, the Massachusetts Constitution made clear that all of these powers were subject to a key limit: They were to be "exercised agreeably to the rules and regulations of the constitution and the laws of the land, and not otherwise."[14] The Massachusetts governor had no monarchical "prerogative power" to set aside laws in the name of a security necessity. And the U.S. president's authority as commander in chief, Hamilton said, was even weaker than the Massachusetts governor's.

Over and over again, the presidentialists' most important legal writings failed to make any mention of *Federalist 69*, even as they selectively quoted tidbits of *Federalist 70*—and quoted them out of context—as proof for their notion that the Founders intended the commander in chief to have sweeping power to act beyond the limits of statutes passed by Congress. The 1987 Iran-Contra minority views report talked about *Federalist 70* but not *Federalist 69*. So did Cheney's 1989 manifesto on congressional overreach in foreign policy. So did many of the Bush-Cheney Office of Legal Counsel memorandums. And so did a forty-two-page "white paper" the Justice Department issued in January 2005 in support of the claimed legality of the National Security Agency's warrantless wiretapping program after it became public.[15]

Some defenders of the Bush-Cheney administration argued that its critics were exaggerating the importance of *Federalist 69*. Douglas Kmiec, a Pepperdine University law professor who had worked for the Reagan Justice Department, said that *Federalist 69* must be read alongside other *Federalist Papers* that cut the other way, such as *Federalist 70*. Yoo, after leaving government, said that *Federalist 69* is just one among many records of the Founders' thinking, some of which are contradictory or misleading. (In his 2005 book, *The Powers of War and Peace*, Yoo did briefly address the existence of *Federalist 69*, dismissing it as rhetorical excess that exaggerated the difference between a king and an American president.[16]) *Federalist 69* "should not be read for more than what it is worth," Yoo argued. The Bush-Cheney administration, he added, is "following the general view of presidents of both parties for many years, since probably FDR," so its legal reasoning is not "unserious."[17]

But David Golove, a New York University law professor who specializes in executive power issues, cited the Massachusetts Constitution text as one example of why Yoo's arguments, both in his book and in his administration memos, were "radically misleading if not outright false."[18] And, he noted, the buildup of executive power beginning with Franklin D. Roosevelt is "completely irrelevant" from the originalist perspective that the Bush-Cheney administration espoused in other areas of the law. If the proper way to interpret the Constitution is by looking to what the Founders intended, he said, then it is *Federalist 69*, not the record of the imperial presidency era, that matters.

And Richard Epstein, a conservative law professor at the University of Chicago who embraces originalism, said *Federalist 69* shows that the administration's legal theory is "just wrong." He called the presidentialists' failure to acknowledge the essay "scandalous" because it is one of the most important records of the Founders' views on the balance of power between Congress and the commander in chief. "How can you not talk about *Federalist 69*?" he said. "All you have to do is go on Google and put in 'Federalist Papers' and 'commander in chief' and it pops up."

3.

The U.S. Air Force began dropping laser-targeted bombs on Taliban militia units on October 7, 2001. That same day, President Bush sent a letter to Congress informing them that he had ordered the U.S. armed forces into combat. Although few noted it at the time, Bush did not rely upon Congress's Authorization for Use of Military Force as the source of his legal power to take the country to war. Rather, Bush announced that he had the power to move the nation from peace to war on his own, and that is what he had done. "I have taken these actions pursuant to my constitutional authority to conduct U.S. foreign relations as Commander in Chief and Chief Executive," Bush's letter said, adding only that he appreciated "the continuing support of the Congress, including its enactment of [the war resolution], in these actions to protect the security of the United States of America and its citizens, civilian and military, here and abroad."[19]

Meanwhile, unknown to Congress or the public, the administration was taking steps to tear down the legal distinction between "here" and "abroad." As the government's overseas forces—the military and the CIA—went on the offensive in Afghanistan, domestic security forces were working feverishly to uncover any other Al Qaeda sleeper cells already inside the United States. Then, at a critical meeting, General Michael Hayden, then the head of the Department of Defense's National Security Agency, proposed using the military spy agency to detect future planned attacks on U.S. soil. President Bush later recalled: "After September the 11th, I spoke to a variety of folks on the front line of protecting us. And I said, is there anything more we could be doing, given the current laws? And General Mike Hayden of the NSA said there is."[20]

Created by President Truman in 1952 to spy on the Soviets, the National Security Agency is a high-tech military operation headquartered at Fort Meade, Maryland. It gathers "signals intelligence"—intercepted phone calls, faxes, and e-mails that can reveal what America's enemies are saying to one another. In its modern form, the agency uses powerful computers to hunt for the needle of a conversation of interest amid the haystack of millions of unrelated phone calls and e-mails traveling together through telecommunications switches and intercepted microwave transmissions. Using complex algorithms, computers mine these vast data streams for suspicious patterns that help the agency identify the associates of suspected terrorists. The computers can also sift through millions of communications for certain phone numbers and e-mail addresses, filtering out specific conversations and messages for humans to analyze. Before 9/11, the National Security Agency limited itself to spying on non-U.S. citizens living overseas, where neither domestic wiretapping laws nor the Constitution's protection against unreasonable government searches applies. But given the gravity of 9/11, Hayden suggested, it might be a good idea for the military to turn its powerful surveillance technology inward, to hunt for possible terrorism-related phone calls and e-mails that touch U.S. soil.[21]

There was, however, a major legal obstacle to the program Hayden proposed. A 1978 law called the Foreign Intelligence Surveillance Act, or FISA, requires the government to obtain warrants from a secret national security court whenever it wants to monitor a communication on U.S. soil. To get a judge's permission to eavesdrop on a phone call or e-mail, the government must show evidence that there is probable cause to believe the targeted caller is a terrorist or spy.[22] The statute says this warrant procedure is the "exclusive" legal means for the government to eavesdrop on communications that reach U.S. soil, and violating it is a felony offense.

The warrant law was one of the key reforms Congress enacted after Watergate to reassert democratic checks and balances on the presidency. The law targeted one of the central pillars of the "imperial" presidency: its previously unchecked control over the powerful new intelligence community created after World War II. In the first decades of the Cold War, the new spy bureaucracies, including the CIA and the National Security Agency, gave presidents the opportunity to order assassinations, spy on enemies, and undertake all kinds of warlike acts in secret with no real oversight. Handed such power, presidents came to abuse it. Presidents Johnson and Nixon, for example, had the government secretly eavesdrop, without warrants, on their domestic political opponents. Both presidents justified listening to antiwar leaders on the grounds that they posed a risk to national security because they might be agents of the Soviet Union. There was never evidence to support such a connection, but under the old system the president did not have to justify his decision to anyone.

After the Church Committee investigation of 1975 brought decades of intelligence abuses to light, Senator Frank Church reserved his greatest alarm for the "tremendous potential for abuse" if the National Security Agency "were to turn its awesome technology against domestic communications."[23] It would mean the end of privacy, Church said, and could be a devastating tool of political repression. The Church Committee's findings led directly to Congress's decision to enact the warrant law. By making sure that a federal judge signed off each time executive branch officials wanted to eavesdrop on a person on U.S. soil, the regulation would ensure that the government invaded a person's privacy only when there was a good reason for doing so. In 1976, President Ford endorsed the concept of a warrant requirement, overruling subordinates such as then–defense secretary Donald Rumsfeld and then–CIA director George H. W. Bush, who both believed that accepting the law would derogate the presidency's inherent power to wiretap without warrants for national security purposes. Two years later, President Carter signed the warrant law without complaint. Since then, the Carter, Reagan, Bush-Quayle, and Clinton administrations had obeyed it.

The Bush-Cheney administration recognized that the warrant law appeared to forbid what Hayden proposed. As they considered the NSA idea, officials debated whether they should ask Congress to amend the warrant law so that the statute would allow the program. At that moment, Congress was rushing to pass the USA Patriot Act, giving the government expanded police powers to secretly search homes and seize papers. The White House could have asked Congress to include in the Patriot Act a provision allowing the National Security Agency to spy on U.S. soil without warrants. In fact, one of the provisions in the Patriot Act, which became law on October 26, 2001, altered the warrant law—expanding from twenty-four hours to seventy-two hours the time the government can wait before seeking a warrant retroactively for spying it has already undertaken in an emergency. But the administration decided that Congress was unlikely to simply exempt the National Security Agency from the traditional warrant procedure. "We have had discussions with Congress in the past—certain members of Congress—as to whether or not FISA could be amended to allow us to adequately deal with this kind of threat, and we were advised that that would be difficult, if not impossible," Alberto Gonzales explained in January 2006, after the program was revealed.[24]

But there was another way. In response to a joint request from Gonzales and Jim Haynes, the Pentagon's general counsel, John Yoo completed another secret advisory opinion, on October 17, 2001.[25] Its title was "Authority for Use of Military Force to Combat Terrorist Activities Within the United States." The text of this advisory opinion has remained secret, but it was referenced and described in other memos that have become public. The memo looked at statutes passed by Congress that restrict the use of the military on U.S. soil, and it concluded that such statutes do not apply when the commander in chief wants to use military force to prevent and deter terrorism within the United States.[26] Its reasoning was that 9/11 showed that U.S. soil was a battlefield, and Congress had no power to restrict the president's tactics in confronting the enemy on a battlefield. Thus, if the president decided that it was necessary to use the military's spy agency to collect "battlefield intelligence" on U.S. soil, no law enacted by Congress could regulate how he went about doing that, such as by forcing him to get warrants.[27]

"Our legal system had been built on the idea that the home front could operate under normal rules of the criminal justice system, and that wars are things that happened abroad," Yoo would later explain. "Nine-eleven showed that that clean line doesn't exist as strongly as it used to. The NSA wiretapping is a good example of that. The commander in chief's authority to prevent attacks on the United States has to follow the terrorists. If the terrorists come into the United States and are sending communications into and out of the country, then the president's authority should be able to follow them."[28]

Or, as Yoo put it in another interview, the president would be justified in monitoring U.S. communications—even when there was insufficient evidence to get a court warrant. "I think there's a law greater than FISA, which is the Constitution, and part of the Constitution is the president's commander-in-chief power. Congress can't take away the president's powers in running war."[29]

Simply declaring, in secret, that the executive branch no longer needed to obey the warrant law had other attractions as well. By launching the classified program without consulting Congress, the administration could ensure its secrecy and avoid a tug-of-war over its details. "Within the executive branch there is a general suspicion that Congress can't keep secrets—especially if you're asking for legislation," a former senior administration attorney said. "Plus, you will never get everything that you want. So, why wait weeks and get eighty-five percent of what you want, if you can get a hundred percent of what you want, and get it immediately, by doing it on your own?"[30]

The only question was how far to go. According to the *New York Times*, Cheney and Addington pushed to allow the National Security Agency to monitor *all* calls and e-mails, including those that both began and ended on U.S. soil. One senior intelligence official said Cheney and Addington argued that purely domestic eavesdropping without warrants "could be done and should be done."[31] But the NSA's lawyers balked. The intelligence community had spent more than twenty years living down the stigma of lawlessness that followed the Church Committee investigations. Its attorneys were wary of the fallout that would come if it should ever be exposed that they had violated the law, even with the president's permission.

Hayden finally negotiated a compromise: The agency would monitor calls and e-mails going in and out of the United States without seeking warrants, but for monitoring purely domestic communications, the government would continue to get warrants. Such a split made little sense as a matter of law; if the warrant law was constitutional, then it was just as illegal for the government to monitor either kind of communication without seeking permission from a judge. And if the president had the wartime power to set aside the warrant law, then it was just as lawful for the government to monitor purely domestic calls, too. But the compromise stuck, and the Bush-Cheney legal team assured the president that he had ample legal cover to proceed with defying the statute. Bush later said: "I was concerned about the legality of the program, and so I asked lawyers — which you got plenty of them in Washington — to determine whether or not I could do this legally. And they came back and said yes."[32]

## 4.

The rule of law is the enemy of the powerful. The essence of law is that everyone obeys the same rules regardless of weakness or strength, so the law chafes most keenly against those who, in a world without rules, have the power to simply impose their will. When America's Founders granted enormous power to the presidency, they also made clear that they wanted Congress to be the place where the country's rules were determined. This does not mean that the presidency is defenseless against statutes and treaties, of course. A president must sign a bill for its provisions to become law.[33] And a president must negotiate and sign a treaty before the Senate gets to decide whether to ratify it. But once in place, they become binding rules on the presidency that outlast the current officeholder. Under the rule of law, the president is bound to obey existing statutes and treaties unless and until he can persuade Congress to rescind them.

After 9/11, the Bush-Cheney administration embarked on a series of policies that systematically loosened the legal force of statutes and treaties that bound a president's hands. By and large, these policies represented reactions to real-world problems that arose as the war on terrorism unfolded. Every time a problem presented itself, the administration had many different options for solving it. Guided by Cheney and Addington, and covered by Yoo's advisory opinions, the administration systematically selected the option that relied upon the most aggressive theory about a president's power to defy laws and treaties.

By basing its real-world actions on its controversial theory of presidential power, the Bush-Cheney administration created one historical precedent after another. On the few occasions when a dispute over the administration's legal theory came before a court, the Bush-Cheney legal team warned the judges against disturbing key elements in the nation's defenses against terrorism, not so subtly implying that any judge who rejected their actions would have blood on his hands. Sometimes judges nonetheless refused to dismiss the case, and then ruled against the White House on the merits. But such setbacks were rare, and the fallout from them was quickly contained. And in the majority of cases, the White House succeeded in keeping its programs away from a forum where their legal basis could be tested.

This systematic effort to expand presidential power began with Bush's order authorizing the warrantless surveillance program after 9/11. After the program's existence was revealed in December 2005, administration officials repeatedly insisted that they had looked only for terrorists and did not abuse their power to listen in on private conversations for personal or political gain. No evidence to suggest the contrary emerged, but the point was not whether the program made sense as a matter of policy or whether the program had been abused. The point was that a president had secretly claimed the power to ignore a law, and then he had acted on that power. In so doing, the Bush-Cheney administration unleashed imperial presidential power. Even if they had not personally abused their power, there was no guarantee that future presidents would show the same restraint. Moreover, there was no difference in principle between the warrant law and any other law that regulates how the president can carry out his national security responsibilities. By demonstrating that a president can set aside a statute or a treaty at will, the administration had set a precedent that future presidents, liberal and conservative alike, would be able to cite when they, too, wanted to violate a legal restriction on their power.

"This is a defining moment in the constitutional history of the United States," Bruce Fein, a conservative lawyer who served as a deputy attorney general in the Reagan administration, told Congress in February 2006. "The theory invoked by the president to justify eavesdropping by the NSA in contradiction to FISA would equally justify mail openings, burglaries, torture or internment camps, all in the name of gathering foreign intelligence. Unless rebuked it will lie around like a loaded weapon, ready to be used by any incumbent who claims an urgent need."[34]

5.

In late October of 2001, Tim Flanigan, the deputy White House counsel, summoned Brad Berenson to his office on the second floor of the West Wing. The young associate White House counsel hurried across the street from his desk in the Old Executive Office Building, a dark Gothic structure next door to the White House that sits inside the compound's security fence. Flanigan was waiting in his small office, just two steps to the left of White House counsel Alberto Gonzales's grander room. The deputy handed Berenson a draft presidential order. Under the order, Bush would invoke his wartime powers to establish a system of military commissions. The tribunals would be used to put Osama bin Laden and other high-ranking Al Qaeda figures on trial if and when U.S. forces captured them in Afghanistan.

Military commissions offered several advantages. First, they were a way to mete out swift justice without the spectacle, delay, and security risks of an ordinary criminal trial before civilian courts. They also potentially offered greater flexibility for the admission of evidence gathered on a battlefield, which might not live up to civilian criminal justice standards. And commissions enhanced presidential power by concentrating the process in the executive branch alone. Under normal trials, Congress defines a crime and sets the sentence for it; the executive branch investigates and prosecutes people who are accused of committing the crime; and the judicial branch runs the trial, decides whether to admit evidence, determines whether the defendant is guilty or innocent, and hears any appeal. With a military commission, all those powers were collapsed into the hands of the armed forces and, ultimately, their commander in chief. Although fairly common in nineteenth-century conflicts, military commissions were a relic: They had not been used by the United States since World War II.

Flanigan's move to set up military commissions was a departure from the customary way the government would handle such an important issue as deciding how to prosecute terrorists. Usually, experts from every part of the government affected by a proposed policy work together in an interagency process to develop it—a system designed to help officials vet major new policies and avoid making mistakes. Indeed, the issue of prosecuting captured terrorists had initially been handled in exactly that way. Just over a week after the 9/11 attacks, a group of lawyers from across the administration had met in Gonzales's office to figure out what they would do if they captured bin Laden. Those at the meeting had included Gonzales, Flanigan, Addington, Haynes, National Security Council lawyer John Bellinger, and Pierre-Richard Prosper, a former career prosecutor who was the State Department's new ambassador-at-large for war crimes issues. The officials had decided that Prosper would lead an interagency task force that would study ways to bring terrorists to trial.

Prosper's group had met for the next month in a windowless conference room on the seventh floor of the State Department. It had brought together experts from around the government, including military lawyers and Justice Department prosecutors. The group had analyzed a range of options, weighing the pros and cons of each. The Justice Department advocated regular trials in civilian federal courts, as the United States had done after the 1993 World Trade Center bombing. But holding terrorist trials in a regular courthouse on U.S. soil presented security risks. The uniformed lawyers had advocated using courts-martial, which could take place anywhere in the world. But courts-martial had well-established rules of evidence and procedure. Setting up a new system of military commissions, the third option on the table, would provide greater flexibility. There were problems, though: Some lawyers believed that the president might need to go to Congress for specific authorization.

Then, before Prosper's group could complete its work, Flanigan had abruptly short-circuited the interagency process. Without telling Prosper, Flanigan had secretly decreed that the answer was military commissions, and that the president had the inherent wartime authority to create them on his own. Flanigan wrote up the draft order himself. In completing it, he worked with just two other government lawyers. One was Berenson, his junior subordinate, chosen because he had been the White House's representative at Prosper's group and so was already steeped in the issue. The other contributor was Addington.

Berenson later said he knew that Flanigan and Gonzales had been "unhappy with the slow pace of the interagency group," but he was surprised when Flanigan called him over and handed him a copy of the draft order as a fait accompli.

"It's easy to forget now the intense atmosphere of urgency that existed at that time," Berenson said. "People were anticipating that there could be additional attacks any day. Nobody knew that a period of years would go by in which there would be no further attacks. So even slight delays were a cause for a lot of distress."[35]

Throughout late October and early November of 2001, Addington and Berenson met frequently in Flanigan's office, sitting on its small sofa surrounded by built-in bookshelves. Plowing through the research Prosper's group had gathered, the trio debated the text of an order setting up the commissions for Bush to sign. Their work was bolstered on November 6, 2001, when Patrick Philbin, a Justice Department attorney who had also taken part in Prosper's aborted interagency group, delivered a secret thirty-five-page memo to Gonzales that backed up the claim that Bush had the authority to unilaterally set up military commissions.

Philbin was another deputy assistant attorney general at the Office of Legal Counsel, and the other political appointee besides John Yoo to be given major responsibilities over classified post-9/11 national security matters. Philbin and Yoo were old colleagues. Both had gone to Yale as undergraduates and to Harvard Law School. Both had clerked the same year for appeals court judge Laurence Silberman, and in different years for Supreme Court justice Clarence Thomas. But Philbin himself was not a specialist in the laws of war. He had spent the 1990s working for a corporate law firm helping telecommunication companies sue the Federal Communications Commission. When Philbin started work at the Office of Legal Counsel on September 4, 2001, the expectation was that he would handle only questions involving administrative law. But after 9/11, so much was happening on the national security front that it was too much for Yoo to handle alone, and Philbin had been drafted to help carry the load. Philbin's memo, titled "Legality of the Use of Military Commissions to Try Terrorists," was his first major contribution to the effort.[36] It argued that 9/11 had been an act of war instead of a crime, triggering full war powers for the president, including an inherent authority to create military commissions.

As its primary precedent for saying that Bush had this power, the Philbin memo cited a 1942 case in which President Roosevelt had created military commissions to try eight Nazi saboteurs captured inside the United

States during the first year of America's involvement in World War II. The Nazis challenged Roosevelt's power to prosecute them in a military commission instead of a regular court, but the Supreme Court unanimously backed Roosevelt, and the saboteurs were quickly executed. The Nazi saboteur case was controversial: The Supreme Court made its decision in a snap, without going through its usual slow and careful procedures; in fact, the defendants had already been executed by the time the court wrote the opinion explaining its ruling. Several justices who participated in the hasty 1942 decision later said they regretted it, and the executive branch, too, was leery about what it had done; when several more Nazi saboteurs were captured later in the war, it did not prosecute them in the same way.[37] Moreover, since World War II, the last time America had convened a military commission, the laws of war had undergone major changes. Congress had enacted a set of laws called the Uniform Code of Military Justice, which said that any future military commissions must, to the extent practical, use the same procedures and defendant rights as American troops receive in courts-martial. And the Senate had ratified the 1949 Geneva Conventions, which afford all wartime prisoners a basic right to a fair trial.

But the Philbin memo brushed aside the ways in which the laws of war had changed since 1942. If the commander in chief had inherent and exclusive powers to set up military commissions as he saw fit, then no act of Congress or treaty could limit his options. Citing the memo as the definitive word on the president's authority, Flanigan, Addington, and Berenson drafted a military order authorizing the Pentagon to create military commission trials for terrorists.

On Thursday, November 8, 2001, Pentagon general counsel Jim Haynes called Major General Tom Romig, the judge advocate general of the U.S. Army, and informed him that the administration was close to finishing an order setting up military commissions.[38] Haynes said the army could send one representative to his office to help review the draft order, but he would not allow the officer to take a copy of the order away or even write down notes about it. Romig sent Colonel Lawrence Morris, an army attorney with significant experience in military justice and the laws of war. The next day, the two met in Romig's basement to go over what Morris had seen. Both were alarmed. The order was modeled on a World War II military commission. The Bush-Cheney team seemed bent on ignoring all the changes to military law over the past sixty years and instead reinstituting a rough-justice trial system that, Romig said, "was going to be perceived as unfair because it was unnecessarily archaic." Romig, Morris, and a third JAG officer, Brigadier General Scott Black, worked through Veteran's Day weekend on suggestions for modernizing the system. Morris took them to Haynes, but none of their proposed changes showed up in the final order.

Meanwhile, on Saturday, November 10, 2001, Vice President Cheney chaired a meeting in the Roosevelt Room at the White House to complete the order. He invited Haynes, Attorney General John Ashcroft, and several top White House lawyers—but no one from Condoleezza Rice's National Security Council or from Colin Powell's State Department. Cheney had decided not to tell the two cabinet members about the proposal until after Bush had signed the order. At that meeting, according to the *Washington Post,* Ashcroft angrily dissented from the plan to give the military sole power over prosecuting captured terrorists. Invoking his role as the nation's top law enforcement officer, Ashcroft said that the Justice Department must have a say in such decisions. But Cheney brushed off Ashcroft's objections. The vice president personally brought a copy of the order to his regular one-on-one lunch with Bush on November 13, 2001, and within an hour the president had signed the document, even though most of his staff had not reviewed it.[39] Powell, Rice, and Prosper were blindsided, first finding out about the new policy from the media that evening.[40]

Bush's order established the idea of commissions, but it provided few specifics about the procedures the trials would follow. The president officially delegated that task to Secretary of Defense Donald Rumsfeld, although once again government lawyers outside the public eye would actually write the order. Over the next few months, the JAGs worked closely with several political appointees—including Haynes, Yoo, and Philbin—in drawing up the commission rules. The meetings were sometimes tense. The JAG corps lawyers saw themselves as the real experts on the laws of war, and they believed that the rules as drafted would violate the Geneva Conventions and lacked sufficient due process. But the political appointees saw the JAGs as too closed minded and stuck in their way of doing things to grasp that the Geneva Conventions might not apply to the war on terrorism.

Initially, Romig said, some of the political appointees were interested in a very draconian system, which, among other things, could convict defendants under a low standard of proof; would deny them the right to have outside civilian defense attorneys; and could impose the death penalty without unanimity by the panel of officers judging the case. The JAGs objected strongly to these and other deviations from military law. One of the top JAGs threatened to resign if some of the harshest proposed rules became final, arguing that they would force military lawyers to violate their legal ethical standards and possibly put them at risk of later prosecution for war crimes.

In the end, the political appointees backed down from some of the most extreme proposals they had been floating. When Rumsfeld signed an order fleshing out what the commission trials would look like in March 2002, the system was closer to what the JAGs wanted: Defendants could be convicted only if guilt was proven beyond a reasonable doubt, outside defense counsel was allowed, and a unanimous vote was required for the death penalty. But the order, Romig said, was still not what the JAGs would have designed had they been allowed to create the commission system from scratch on their own. While less draconian than the political appointees' initial plans, the military commissions were still legally objectionable in several respects. The commission rules, for example, allowed secret evidence that would be kept hidden from a defendant and allowed the admission of evidence obtained through coercive interrogations. Moreover, the special trials still had no explicit congressional authorization. But it would take more than four years before such problems played out.

6.

Just before 10 a.m. on Thursday, December 13, 2001, Bush walked to a podium in the White House Rose Garden. Flanked by Rumsfeld and Powell, Bush read a momentous announcement: Invoking his executive powers, he had decided to renounce the Anti-Ballistic Missile Treaty.

"Today, I have given formal notice to Russia, in accordance with the treaty, that the United States of America is withdrawing from this almost thirty-year-old treaty," Bush said. "I have concluded the ABM treaty hinders our government's ability to develop ways to protect our people from future terrorist or rogue-state missile attacks."[41]

Signed by President Nixon and ratified by the Senate in 1972, the ABM treaty outlawed building missile-defense systems. The idea in 1972 was to avoid a costly new arms race between the United States and the Soviet Union, and to prevent either side from obtaining technology that might make its leaders think they could launch a nuclear strike on the other side without their own country being destroyed in retaliation.

Bush's national security team—especially Rumsfeld, who had been on a task force calling for a missile-defense program in the 1990s—had wanted to scrap the treaty well before 9/11. Notably, Bush's acceptance speech at the Republican National Convention in Philadelphia, in August 2000, had denounced restrictions on a president's ability to do whatever he thinks necessary to protect the country. Referring to the ABM treaty, then-governor Bush had declared, "Now is the time, not to defend out-dated treaties, but to defend the American people."[42]

Media coverage of the ABM controversy tended to focus on the policy merits of Bush's decision to pull out of the treaty. Some questioned the wisdom of pulling out of a treaty that had kept the peace for three decades in order to invest in a costly and unproven technology. Others expounded on the ways in which the treaty was outdated—the Soviet Union no longer existed, and the new threat came from rogue states such as North Korea that might not behave rationally. But whatever its policy merits, Bush's act had enormous consequences on another front. By unilaterally scrapping the ABM treaty, Bush seized for the presidency the power to pull the United States out of *any* treaty without obtaining the consent of Congress.

The Founders, perhaps not anticipating a need to pull out of a treaty, did not include a clear procedure for doing so in the Constitution. But they made clear that they did not want the presidency to have exclusive control over the country's decisions about treaties; the president can negotiate a treaty, but the Senate must vote to ratify it before it becomes binding on the United States. As Alexander Hamilton wrote in *Federalist 75*, treaties are simply too important to entrust to the decision of one man who will be in office for as little as four years: "The history of human conduct does not warrant that exalted opinion of human virtue which would make it wise in a nation to commit interests of so delicate and momentous a kind, as those which concern its intercourse with the rest of the world, to the sole disposal of a magistrate created and circumstanced as would be a President of the United States."[43]

The previous August, when Bush signaled his intent to pull out of the ABM treaty if Russia did not agree to modify it in a way that would allow the building of a missile shield, Yale Law School professor Bruce Ackerman had tried to sound the alarm about the serious implications of the proposal. "Presidents can't terminate statutes they don't like. They must persuade both houses of Congress to join in a repeal. Should the termination of treaties operate any differently?" Ackerman had written. "If President Bush is allowed to terminate the ABM treaty, what is to stop future presidents from unilaterally taking America out of NATO or the United Nations?"[44]

Advocates of strong presidential power, however, saw things differently. Prior to taking his leave of absence from Berkeley in July 2001 to join the Justice Department—just a month before Ackerman's article—Yoo had written extensively about his belief that a president should be able to pull out of a treaty on his own. Yoo, Addington, and other advocates of sweeping executive power asserted that the president is the sole and exclusive organ of the government in foreign affairs.* Because the Constitution is silent about how to pull out of a treaty, they said, the president has the inherent power to do so on his own.[45]

For most of the nation's history, presidents confronted with obsolete treaties did not break them on their own. Instead, they pulled out of treaties with the approval of Congress. But this system was tested in 1979, after, as noted earlier, President Jimmy Carter decided on his own to withdraw from a mutual-defense treaty with Taiwan in order to recognize the Communist government in mainland China. Outraged, conservative senators led by

---

*Supporters of the proposition that the president has unchecked powers of executive discretion in national security matters (such as the power to wiretap, indefinitely detain, torture, or wage war regardless of any acts of Congress) frequently cite a 1936 Supreme Court case, *United States v. Curtiss-Wright*, 299 U.S. 304. The opinion's author, Justice George Sutherland, made reference in an aside to the supposed "plenary and exclusive power of the President as the sole organ of the federal government in the field of international relations—a power which does not require as a basis for its exercise an act of Congress." *Curtiss-Wright* enthusiasts, however, often fail to acknowledge that Sutherland's remark was dicta—meaning that it was not necessary to the ruling and so has no legal effect. Moreover, many scholars agree that Sutherland was misquoting his own source, a remark made in 1800 by then-representative John Marshall in a House debate. In context, most scholars say, it is clear that Marshall was saying only that that president is the official charged with carrying out the nation's treaty obligations to other governments and the exclusive channel for diplomatic communications. Marshall was not saying that the other two branches of government share no power over foreign relations, an idea he never espoused when he became chief justice of the Supreme Court. See, e.g., Louis Fisher, "The 'Sole Organ' Doctrine," *Studies on Presidential Power in Foreign Relations*, The Law Library of Congress, August 28, 2006.

Barry Goldwater, Republican of Arizona, sued Carter. But the lawsuit ended inconclusively: The Supreme Court dismissed the case without resolving the constitutional issue, saying that such a question, involving both treaty breaking and the recognition of foreign governments, was "political," so Congress and the president had to work it out on their own.[46] Since Congress was controlled by Carter's fellow Democrats in 1979, the question of how to break a treaty faded without clear resolution.[47]

But in December 2001, just three months removed from 9/11, Bush stood at a 90 percent approval rating.[48] Instead of putting up a fight against a president with record-breaking popularity by taking a stance that could easily be misconstrued as softness on national defense, Congress simply went home for winter vacation. The president now indisputably had the power to dispense with even a major ratified treaty—which the Constitution calls the "supreme law of the land," equal to federal statutes—at his sole discretion. The Bush-Cheney team had poured reinforced concrete around a major expansion of presidential power that will resonate for generations to come.

7.

On January 11, 2002—four months to the day after the attacks of 9/11—the smoky silhouette of mountains came into view from the cockpit of a U.S. Air Force cargo plane. As the northbound C-141 Starlifter drew closer to the shoreline and began its descent toward the azure waters of the Caribbean Sea, the water grew brighter, a brilliant turquoise flecked by whitecaps.

The view would soon become less inviting.

The plane banked, passed over craggy rocks lapped by waves, and landed on a small airstrip surrounded by brown scorched grass, heavy scrub brush, and dusty hills. At the center of the small airport, a rusty hangar was decorated with a picture of a lighthouse and palm trees, and the logo "U.S. Naval Station Guantánamo Bay." Awaiting the plane's arrival were scores of marines wearing full battle gear—Kevlar vests, helmets, and face shields—and wielding heavy machine guns and rocket launchers. Quickly, the troops surged forward to surround the aircraft. Overhead, a navy Huey helicopter circled with a gunner hanging off its side. Offshore, an armed navy patrol boat moved back and forth within sight of the plane. Then, one by one, twenty manacled prisoners from Afghanistan were led from the cargo hold in orange jumpsuits and black-out goggles. A warren of kennel-like outdoor cages, dubbed Camp X-Ray, was waiting for them.[49]

The scene was unique in the history of the century-old base, but it would soon become routine. Guantánamo was once a coaling station for U.S. Navy ships in the Caribbean, but its original relevance dwindled as technology reduced the need for refueling. For years, the sleepy naval port had been used mainly by Coast Guard helicopters searching for drug smugglers and Florida-bound Cuban and Haitian refugees on rafts. In 1998, the Clinton administration had briefly considered bringing some refugees from Kosovo to Guantánamo, then rejected the plan. But the plane that arrived that day launched a prison operation that would make the name of the base notorious around the globe. Several months later, Camp X-Ray would be closed and replaced by Camp Delta, a more permanent set of metal-sided cell blocks with running water. As years passed, the open-air cell blocks would in turn be replaced by concrete-walled prison structures. With each step, workers from Kellogg, Brown & Root — a subsidiary of Halliburton, Cheney's old company, which was handed a no-bid contract worth tens of millions of dollars to build up Guantánamo — helped make the operation more permanent.

The policy, however, had had a hasty beginning. On Thanksgiving weekend in 2001, about three hundred Taliban and Al Qaeda fighters in the Afghan city of Konduz had surrendered to the forces of a Northern Alliance warlord supported by American bombers and a handful of U.S. Special Forces. The warlord took his sudden influx of prisoners to a nineteenth-century fortress near the city of Mazar-e Sharif. On November 25, 2001, some of the prisoners staged an uprising, killing a CIA agent who had been questioning them.[50] It took days to regain control of the fortress after firefights that left more than two hundred of the original prisoners dead. Unprepared to handle so many prisoners and determined to prevent a repeat of the fiasco, the commander of U.S. forces in Afghanistan, General Tommy Franks, asked Washington to move the survivors of Mazar-e Sharif and other detainees out of the combat zone so that their prison would not become a target of insurgent attacks.

In Washington, war crimes ambassador Prosper got a call at home. His interagency group, originally set up to research terrorist trials, had a new problem to solve: finding a place where the prisoners could be moved to. Prosper's task force met in a seventh-floor conference room at the State Department and spread a big map of the world out on the table. They knew they didn't want any prison based in the territorial United States; there would be too many security risks, and civilian courts might try to interfere. Some possible host countries lacked good infrastructure; others simply said no when asked. The group also considered putting a prison at the huge U.S. military base in Germany, a relic of the Cold War, but scrapped the idea before asking the German government for permission. "We looked at our military bases in Europe and ruled that out because (a), we'd have to get approval from a European government, and (b), we'd have to deal with the European Court of Human Rights and we didn't know how they'd react," Prosper recalled. "We didn't want to lose control over it and have it become a European process because it was on European soil. And so we kept looking around and around, and basically someone said, 'What about Guantánamo?'"[51]

Guantánamo presented its own problems. A decade earlier, during a rafter crisis, the U.S. government had put Haitian and Cuban refugees on the base, only to get involved in protracted litigation over the fate of some HIV-positive refugees the government did not want to bring into the United States. Prosper's group began researching such matters. But before they had finished working out the potential issues, the interagency process got short-circuited again. Rumsfeld decided that Guantánamo was the answer. And since the prisoners were in his control, as was Guantánamo, Rumsfeld decided that he had the authority to begin moving war prisoners to Cuba without further discussion.

During a Pentagon press conference on December 27, 2001, Rumsfeld announced the administration's intention to set up a makeshift prison camp at Guantánamo. The decision met with immediate skepticism. Noting that "we've gotten into trouble every time we've tried to use Guantánamo Bay in the past to hold people," a reporter asked why the administration had decided to fly prisoners halfway around the world from Afghanistan — why was Cuba the best place?

Rumsfeld corrected the reporter. "I would characterize Guantánamo Bay, Cuba, as the least worst place we could have selected. It has disadvantages, as you suggest. Its disadvantages, however, seem to be modest relative to the alternatives."[52]

But the defense secretary was not being entirely forthcoming. The day after Rumsfeld's press conference, Yoo and Philbin completed a secret Office of Legal Counsel opinion laying out a very clear advantage to putting a military prison at Guantánamo. The base was a unique place on the planet. It was outside the United States itself, so—the administration asserted—U.S. courts had no jurisdiction to oversee what happened there.[53] And yet the base was not on soil that was under the control of any other court system, either. Moreover, unlike other overseas military bases, which were located on the territory of friendly governments with whom the United States had lease and status of forces agreements, Guantánamo was on the soil of a Communist dictatorship whose predecessor had signed a perpetual lease with the United States. Thus, the base appeared to be under the absolute and unfettered control of the United States military and its commander in chief, beyond any independent review.

Guantánamo was chosen because it was the best place to set up a law-free zone.[54] And it would be no ordinary wartime prison.

## 8.

Two days before the first prisoners arrived at the base, on January 9, 2002, Yoo and another Justice Department lawyer completed a second secret memo. This time, Yoo concluded that the president, invoking his power as commander in chief, could declare that prisoners from the conflict in Afghanistan were not protected by the laws of war—especially by a set of treaties called the Geneva Conventions.

The 1949 Geneva Conventions, enacted after World War II and ratified by the Senate after the terrible mistreatment of American prisoners in the Korean War, famously established elaborate rights and procedures for captured enemy soldiers, who are officially called "Prisoners of War." But the treaties also give everybody else who is taken prisoner during wartime, whether they qualify for POW status or not, a basic right to humane treatment. Specifically, the treaties forbid inflicting on *any* wartime prisoner such abuses as "cruel treatment and torture," "outrages upon personal dignity, in particular, humiliating and degrading treatment," or criminal trials that lack "all the judicial guarantees which are recognized as indispensable by civilized peoples." The treaties say that a violation of these basic safeguards against the mistreatment of prisoners is a "grave breach" and a war crime in the eyes of international law. And the treaties give all wartime detainees a right to an individual hearing to determine what their status should be.

Inside the United States, a long line of presidents and lawmakers from both parties had embraced the Geneva Conventions. The treaties were signed by President Truman in 1949 and ratified by the Senate in 1955. Some forty-one years later, a Republican-controlled Congress added further domestic force to the treaties by passing the War Crimes Act. Signed into law by President Clinton, the statute embeds the restrictions of the Geneva Conventions in federal law by making it a felony for any U.S. official to commit a "grave breach" of the treaty. For nearly fifty years, one president after another obeyed the Geneva Conventions; even at the height of the "imperial presidency," Johnson and Nixon gave Geneva protections to captured insurgents in Vietnam, despite the fact that they wore no uniforms.

On January 9, 2002, the Bush-Cheney legal team wrested the presidency free from this long-standing restriction on its power. In a secret legal opinion, Yoo declared that Bush had the executive authority either to suspend the Geneva Conventions or to creatively interpret the treaties as allowing him to "determine" that their restrictions did not apply to the war against Al Qaeda and the Taliban. Yoo warned that such a stance would be controversial among scholars of international law both inside the United States and around the world. There was no precedent giving a country the authority to suspend its commitment to a humanitarian treaty such as the Geneva Conventions, or to interpret them into meaninglessness. But, Yoo said, by invoking "the President's Commander in Chief and Chief Executive powers to prosecute the war effectively," Bush could simply override the objections.[55] Wrote Yoo, "Importing customary international law notions concerning armed conflict would represent a direct infringement on the President's discretion as the Commander in Chief and Chief Executive to determine how best to conduct the Nation's military affairs."[56]

When Yoo completed his memo, Addington was waiting for it. On January 25, 2002, Bush received a separate memo urging him to base his Geneva Conventions policy on Yoo's conclusions. Former White House officials later told the *Washington Post* that the January 25 memo was entirely ghostwritten by Addington, although it was signed by Gonzales.[57] The memo told Bush that he had the "constitutional authority" to declare that the Geneva Conventions would not apply to detainees in the war on terrorism, and it urged him to set the treaty aside, because doing so "substantially reduces the threat of domestic criminal prosecution under the War Crimes Act." If some future administration decided to indict former Bush-Cheney administration officials or military and CIA interrogators for violating the Geneva Conventions, the memo told Bush, then his "determination would create a reasonable basis in law that [the act] does not apply, which would provide a solid defense to any future prosecutions."[58]

This radical approach was indeed controversial, even inside the administration. Among those who tried to fight it were Powell and his top legal adviser at the State Department, William H. Taft IV—the great-grandson of the former president and Supreme Court chief justice who, in 1909, rolled back Theodore Roosevelt's early attempt to establish "inherent" powers for the presidency. In a series of memos that later became public, Taft and Powell each insisted that Yoo was wrong. "The President should know that a decision that the Conventions do apply is consistent with the plain language of the Conventions and the unvaried practice of the United States in introducing its forces into conflict over fifty years," Taft told Gonzales. "It is consistent with the advice of [State Department] lawyers and, as far as is known, the position of every other party to the Conventions."[59]

But the Powell-Taft faction was no match for the Cheney-Addington faction. On February 7, 2002, Bush signed a decision memo addressed to Cheney and the other members of his war cabinet, settling the questions raised by "our recent extensive discussions" regarding prisoners. Citing his "authority as Commander-in-Chief and Chief Executive of the United States," Bush officially declared that all suspected Al Qaeda and Taliban detainees were unlawful combatants who did not qualify for Geneva Conventions protections.[60]

Bush's declaration that detainees captured in Afghanistan would not receive Geneva Conventions protection was immediately condemned around the world as an affront to the rule of law. But the White House dismissed such concerns. "These are the worst of a very bad lot," Cheney said of the Guantánamo prisoners on *Fox News Sunday* on January 27, 2002. "They are very dangerous. They are devoted to killing millions of Americans, innocent Americans, if they can, and they are perfectly prepared to die in the effort. And they need to be detained, treated very cautiously, so that our people are not at risk."[61] That same day, en route to a tour of Guantánamo, Rumsfeld assured reporters that the detainees being taken there were "among the most dangerous, best-trained, vicious killers on the face of the earth."[62]

Only later would it emerge that hundreds of the prisoners being hastily shipped to Guantánamo were not hardened terrorists at all. Aside from a handful of hard-core terrorists, most were mere peasants conscripted against their will into Taliban militias, while others had been turned over to U.S. forces on false pretenses in exchange for $5,000 bounties. In 2006, Seton Hall University School of Law released a study of the military's own records on 517 Guantánamo detainees. It found that 86 percent had been turned over to U.S. forces by either Pakistan or the Northern Alliance at a time when the United States was offering its cash bounties, rather than being captured by the United States directly in combat. The records also showed that military analysts eventually concluded that just 8 percent of those sent to Guantánamo had committed attacks on U.S. forces or its allies, while another 30 percent were actual "members" of a terrorist group or the Taliban, though they had not fought. Sixty percent had no definitive connection to Al Qaeda or the Taliban.[63]

In short, hundreds of the detainees who were flown to Guantánamo did not belong there. Such facts might have emerged had the detainees been given hearings before a "competent tribunal," a right guaranteed by the Geneva Conventions and obeyed by the United States in every war up to and including the Gulf War. But there were no such rules anymore.

## 9.

On March 13, 2002, the Office of Legal Counsel delivered another secret memo to Haynes, the Pentagon general counsel. Signed by Assistant Attorney General Jay Bybee but largely drafted by his deputy Yoo, the opinion was entitled "The President's Power as Commander-in-Chief to Transfer Captive Terrorists to the Control and Custody of Foreign Nations." The memo concluded that the president has the power to hand detainees over to foreign governments whose interrogators are known to have used torture, despite a treaty precisely forbidding such a move.

The treaty in question, the Convention Against Torture, was signed by President Reagan in 1988. When Reagan sent the treaty to the Senate for ratification, he strongly embraced its principles in an accompanying message. "The United States participated actively and effectively in the negotiation of the Convention," Reagan said. "It marks a significant step in the development during this century of international measures against torture and other inhuman treatment or punishment. Ratification of the Convention by the United States will clearly express United States opposition to torture, an abhorrent practice unfortunately still prevalent in the world today."[64]

The Senate waited until 1994 before it ratified the Convention Against Torture, but after the vote, the United States was bound to obey its restrictions. One key provision forbids the government from transferring a prisoner to a country "where substantial grounds exist for believing that he would be in danger of being subjected to torture." But, the March 13, 2002, memo asserted, the president was free to ignore such a restriction. Using now-familiar logic, Bybee and Yoo declared that because the Constitution named the president as commander in chief of the armed forces, he had the power to do anything with wartime prisoners, regardless of statutes or treaties.[65]

Covered by this secret legal opinion, the Bush-Cheney administration launched a policy of transferring terrorist suspects to the custody of security forces for such countries as Egypt and Syria—whom the State Department's own reports accused of regularly torturing prisoners—for further questioning. The United States had used a version of this process of "extraordinary rendition" in the 1990s, under the Clinton administration, but for a different purpose: to send fugitives back to their home countries to face open criminal trials. Now, suspects were simply disappearing into foreign gulags—and sometimes they were being delivered to the security forces of countries where they were not citizens. When this policy came to light, the administration insisted that its hands were clean because it had obtained diplomatic "assurances" from the countries that the prisoners would not be abused. Critics charged that, given the countries' track records, such assurances were a purely cynical exercise. In testimony before Congress in April 2007, Michael Scheuer, a CIA officer who helped run the rendition program until he retired in late 2004, candidly acknowledged that assurances from an Arab dictatorship that it would not torture a suspected Islamist weren't "worth a bucket of warm spit."[66]

Some of the detainees who were summarily transferred to such countries, often after being kidnapped on foreign streets, were probably terrorism supporters. But others turned out not to be. Although a strong supporter of the program, Scheuer told Congress that he knew of at least three mistakes that the CIA had made in its overseas rendition operations. One innocent victim of the transfer policy was a dual Canadian-Syrian citizen named Maher Arar. He was arrested on September 26, 2006, during an international flight stopover at New York City's JFK airport.[67] Canada had told the United States that Arar, a software engineer who emigrated from Syria to Canada in 1987 as a teenager to avoid mandatory military service, was associated with an Ottawa man suspected of having ties to Al Qaeda. Despite his Canadian passport, the United States shipped Arar to Syria, where he was imprisoned and interrogated for nearly a year. Arar claimed he was held in a small, dark underground cell where he could overhear other prisoners being tortured, and was himself regularly beaten and threatened with electrocution until he signed a false confession that he had trained at Al Qaeda camps in Afghanistan.

In October 2003, Syria released Arar back to Canada. A Canadian government inquiry later found that their suspicions of Arar had been unfounded; he had no associations with Al Qaeda and had never been to a terrorist training camp.[68] The Canadian government apologized to Arar and paid him $10 million, and the head of the Royal Canadian Mounted Police resigned over the affair. The Bush-Cheney administration, by contrast, refused to issue an apology or to take Arar off its terrorist watch list, meaning he could not fly through the United States—not that he wanted to.

Congress, in conjunction with a previous president, had ratified the Convention Against Torture to prevent innocent prisoners such as Arar—as well as genuinely bad people—from being sent off to certain torture, even though it knew that such a restriction would sometimes chafe. Whether or not this rule was wise, it was the rule. But the executive branch no longer recognized a need to obey such limits.

## 10.

On April 5, 2002, an American C-130 transport plane left Guantánamo and flew to Dulles International Airport, some forty-five minutes south of Washington. Aboard the plane was a twenty-one-year-old prisoner named Yaser Esam Hamdi. Shackled and clad in an orange jumpsuit, Hamdi was being transferred to a navy brig in Norfolk, Virginia. He would live there in isolation and under twenty-four-hour surveillance for the next two and a half years.

Hamdi had been captured in Afghanistan by the Northern Alliance in late November 2001. He was later turned over to the U.S. military, which believed that he was a Saudi citizen and a member of Al Qaeda. (His father claimed that Hamdi was a humanitarian relief worker, not a terrorist.) In early 2002, Hamdi was among the first prisoners to arrive at Guantánamo. But interrogators soon discovered that Hamdi was no ordinary detainee.

He had been born in Baton Rouge, Louisiana, in 1980. Although his parents had taken him back to their native Saudi Arabia when he was just a toddler, Hamdi's birth on U.S. soil made him legally an American citizen.

Hamdi's identity raised unanticipated problems. The administration had specifically chosen Guantánamo as the site of its interrogation prison out of a belief that the base was beyond the jurisdiction of American courts. But the presence of an American citizen among the detainee population might allow a judge to start looking over the president's shoulder at prison conditions. They got Hamdi out but decided to keep treating him as an "enemy combatant" rather than charging him with a crime.[69]

A month later, on May 8, 2002, a thirty-one-year-old man named Jose Padilla stepped off a plane from Switzerland at Chicago O'Hare International Airport. Born in Brooklyn, Padilla had grown up as a thug in Chicago and served time in connection with a street-gang killing as a teenager. In the mid-1990s, he had converted to Islam and moved to the Middle East. When he returned to the United States, federal agents were waiting for him at O'Hare. The FBI took Padilla to New York, where he was locked up for a month as a "material witness" to a terrorism investigation. Then, on June 10, two days before Padilla was to go before a federal judge for a hearing, Bush signed an order designating him as an "enemy combatant." Padilla was handed over to the military, which transported him to a brig in Charleston, South Carolina.

After moving Padilla to military custody, the administration disclosed his existence with fanfare. Ashcroft interrupted a trip to Moscow to announce that Padilla was an "Al Qaeda operative" who was "involved in planning future terrorist attacks on innocent American civilians in the United States." By arresting Padilla, Ashcroft said, the administration had "disrupted an unfolding terrorist plot to attack the United States by exploding a radioactive dirty bomb."[70]

Much of the initial coverage of the Padilla case focused on what Ashcroft said the prisoner had been planning to do. But, hidden beneath the flash of the sensational allegations, a startling legal precedent had just been established. Padilla was a U.S. citizen in the fullest sense — he had been raised in the United States, not just born here. Even more important, Padilla was not captured on a foreign battlefield by military forces, as Hamdi had been. Padilla was arrested on U.S. soil by a civilian law-enforcement agency. If the president had the power to hold Padilla as an enemy combatant, then every single American citizen was equally subject, as a matter of law, to being imprisoned on the president's orders, without charges or a trial or even access to a lawyer, and cut off from all interaction with the outside world—forever.

The Bush-Cheney administration's claim that a president could summarily imprison a U.S. citizen as an "enemy combatant" challenged one of the most important restrictions on executive power in Anglo-American history. Generations before the American Revolution, the Founders' forebears in England had grown fed up with the king's habit of declaring people "enemies of the state" and then throwing them in jail without charges or a trial. The king had been forced to give up his unrestricted authority to put people in "executive detention," and after the English reforms, only judges and juries decided whether someone should be imprisoned. Furthermore, judges had the power to order a prisoner's release if they decided there was no legal basis for holding him.

The Founders, who wanted the American president to be a far weaker executive than the British king, incorporated this vision into the Constitution. Only during a rebellion or an invasion, they wrote, could someone's right to challenge their detention in court be temporarily suspended. In 1792, the Founders went a step further when they amended the Constitution with the Bill of Rights. Among its key provisions was the absolute rule that the government could not imprison anyone "without due process of law." Congress later further strengthened this right by statute. During World War II, President Roosevelt had issued an executive order that caused thousands of innocent Japanese Americans living on the West Coast to be imprisoned in "relocation camps," an act that was later universally viewed as a terrible stain on the country's history. To prevent such a thing from happening again, Congress in 1971 passed, and President Nixon signed, the Non-Detention Act. It states that "no citizen shall be imprisoned or otherwise detained by the United States except pursuant to an Act of Congress."

Unwilling to let the administration's asserted legal theory harden into fact without challenge, several criminal defense lawyers filed lawsuits on behalf of Hamdi and Padilla. In both cases, federal district judges ruled that the government had to give them access to a lawyer as a preliminary step, suggesting that the next would be to force the government to charge them with crimes or release them. But the Bush-Cheney administration appealed, saying that any contact with the outside world would interfere with the detainees' interrogations. Moreover, they said, it was up to the president and his men alone to decide whether a prisoner was a terrorist, so courts had no right to demand access to the evidence, and prisoners had no need for an attorney. "The court may not second-guess the military's enemy combatant determination," the administration argued on June 19, 2002. ". . . Going beyond that determination would require the courts to enter an area in which they have no competence, much less institutional expertise, [and] intrude upon the Constitutional prerogative of the Commander in Chief (and military authorities acting under his control)."[71]

On July 12, 2002, the Fourth Circuit Court of Appeals in Richmond, Virginia, handed down its opinion. Hamdi would not be allowed to meet with his lawyer, and the lower courts were instructed to be far more deferential to the president's power as commander in chief in any future such cases. "The authority to capture those who take up arms against America belongs to the Commander in Chief under [the Constitution]," Judge Harvey Wilkinson IV, a 1984 Reagan appointee often touted as a potential Supreme Court nominee, wrote for the unanimous three-judge panel.[72]

But on December 18, 2003, the Second Circuit Court of Appeals in New York reached the opposite conclusion in the Padilla case. By a 2–1 vote, the appeals court panel ruled that the administration must charge Padilla with a crime or release him. Neither the Authorization for Use of Military Force nor the president's inherent power was enough to hold him without trial. "The President, acting alone, possesses no inherent constitutional authority to detain American citizens seized within the United States, away from a zone of combat, as enemy combatants," the court held. (Of the two judges in the majority, one was a 1998 Clinton appointee, and the other was one of Bush's first appointees in 2001. The dissent, who endorsed more sweeping executive powers, was a 2003 Bush appointee.)[73]

The conflicting rulings meant that the Supreme Court would have to step in, setting up an election-year showdown over presidential power.

## 11.

On August 1, 2002, less than three weeks after the Fourth Circuit's sweeping endorsement of the president's power to hold Hamdi without charge or access to a lawyer, another secret advisory opinion was delivered to Gonzales at the White House. The memo was signed by Bybee, the Office of Legal Counsel head whom Bush had recently nominated to be a life-tenured federal appeals court judge. But the memo had actually been drafted by Yoo, and the deputy himself signed a short cover letter to Gonzales that summarized the memo's conclusions. Its title was "Standards of Conduct for Interrogation." Its subject was torture.

Four months earlier, CIA agents working with Pakistani police had descended upon an apartment building suspected of being an Al Qaeda safe house. In the assault, they captured a trove of computer equipment and a man named Abu Zubaydah, whom they believed to be a high-ranking Al Qaeda operative. CIA interrogators wanted to extract everything Zubaydah might know about Al Qaeda's plans. But they grew frustrated by the early summer of 2002, believing that Zubaydah might know more than he was telling them. The CIA asked if it could start using bigger sticks, reportedly including "water-boarding," a technique that produces the sensation of drowning and that the U.S. military considers to be torture; mock executions, such as making the prisoner believe he is being buried alive; and threatening to let interrogators from countries known to use more direct forms of torture take custody of him. But the agency was also mindful of the backlash its less savory practices had engendered when they came to light during the Church Committee investigation. They wanted written authorization to show they had done nothing illegal.[74]

According to Newsweek, Gonzales convened high-level meetings to discuss whether there was a way for specific harsh interrogation techniques to be considered legal. Among the officials at the meetings were Yoo, Flanigan, Addington, and Haynes. Flanigan later described the meetings this way: "My overwhelming impression is that everyone was focused on trying to avoid torture, staying within the line, while doing everything possible to save American lives."[75]

Skeptics, however, suggest that not everyone in the administration was focused on avoiding torture, at least as the term is commonly understood. Five days after 9/11, Cheney had said the United States would soon have to work on the "dark side" of the intelligence world, adding, "It's going to be vital for us to use any means at our disposal, basically, to achieve our objective."[76] Many interpreted Cheney's vague remarks to have been a reference to brutal interrogation techniques. Cheney's personal support for such tactics would be confirmed in October 2006, when he told a radio interviewer that it was a "no-brainer for me" that water-boarding suspected terrorists was the right thing to do. Cheney added that he didn't count such coercive methods as torture, as he narrowly defined it. "We don't torture," Cheney said. "That's not what we're involved in. We live up to our obligations in international treaties that we're party to and so forth. But the fact is, you can have a fairly robust interrogation program without torture, and we need to be able to do that."[77]

Back in the summer of 2002, however, it seemed at first glance that the president was prohibited from authorizing any kind of "robust interrogation program" that involved tormenting prisoners in order to get them to talk. The Convention Against Torture, which, as noted earlier, had been ratified by the Senate in 1994, prohibits government officials from inflicting "torture and other cruel, inhuman or degrading treatment or punishment" on prisoners in order to obtain information. The treaty said that its ban was absolute and could not be waived: "No exceptional circumstances whatsoever, whether a state of war of a threat of war, internal political instability or any other public emergency, may be invoked as a justification of torture." And after the Senate had ratified the treaty, Congress bolstered the commitment by passing a domestic statute that also prohibited U.S. officials, anywhere in the world, from intentionally inflicting "severe physical or mental pain or suffering" upon another person in their control.[78] If a U.S. interrogator broke this law, he could be fined or imprisoned for up to twenty years. If the prisoner died as a result of the abuse, the interrogator could be sentenced to life in prison or death. And any American official who conspired to have a prisoner abused was subject to the same penalties as the actual interrogator.

But the Bush-Cheney legal team came up with a justification for CIA officials to circumvent the law. The Office of Legal Counsel issued one classified memo, whose text is still secret, signing off on a list of specific harsh techniques the CIA could use. And it backed that approval up with the August 1, 2002, advisory opinion drafted by Yoo and signed by Bybee, claiming that interrogators could, without triggering the antitorture law, inflict pain up to a level just shy of that "associated with serious physical injury so severe that death, organ failure, or permanent damage resulting in a loss of significant bodily function will likely result." The law, Yoo further asserted, banned only the sadistic infliction of pain as an end in itself, not the infliction of pain as a means of obtaining information that could protect the public. In case an interrogator was ever prosecuted for violating the antitorture law, Yoo laid out page after page of legal defenses he could mount to get the charges dismissed. And should someone balk at this strained interpretation of the law, Yoo offered his usual trump card: Applying the antitorture law to interrogations authorized by the president would be unconstitutional, since only the commander in chief could set standards for questioning enemy combatants.[79]

<h1 style="text-align:center">12.</h1>

In August 2002, during the annual monthlong congressional recess, speculation began to mount about whether Bush intended to launch a war against Iraq over Saddam Hussein's suspected weapons of mass destruction programs. The administration publicly downplayed such chatter, saying it had no plans or desire for war with Baghdad, and that it wanted to work with the United Nations before settling on a course of action. But inside the White House, Flanigan developed a legal position, relayed to Bush by Gonzales, that the president did not need congressional authorization to attack Iraq.[80] The major justification Flanigan cited was that Bush had inherent power as commander in chief to take the country to war as he saw fit; as backup, Flanigan added, Bush could still rely on the vote by Congress in 1991 giving its approval to Bush's father for the first Gulf War, and the United Nations Security Council resolutions on Iraq from that era.

Nevertheless, the next month, when Congress returned in September for a few last weeks of lawmaking before the midterm election, administration officials abruptly demanded that Congress immediately approve a hypothetical invasion of Iraq, just in case Bush later decided that diplomacy had failed and war was necessary. Such a preemptive vote, the White House said, would let Saddam Hussein know that the United States was serious as diplomatic negotiations over weapons inspections heated up. At the same time, administration officials escalated alarming rhetoric about the threat posed by Iraq, warning that the "smoking gun" for Iraq's alleged weapons programs and its alleged links to Al Qaeda could come in the form of a "mushroom cloud."[81] (On September 6, 2002, White House chief of staff Andrew Card discussed the abrupt shift in tone in an interview with the *New York Times*. He candidly explained, "From a marketing point of view, you don't introduce new products in August."[82])

The proposed hurry-up vote on the eve of the first election since 9/11 presented a win-win scenario for the White House: If Democrats voiced caution or skepticism about the proposed war resolution, then the GOP could portray them as weak on terrorism ahead of the election, and if

Democrats supported the bill, then the Bush-Cheney administration would fortify its powers by eliminating even the suggestion that it might later need to ask for permission to launch any war against Iraq.

Leading up to the vote, the administration flooded the airwaves with grave pronouncements, such as Cheney's claim on September 9, 2002: "We know based on primarily intelligence reporting . . . [that Saddam Hussein] is continuing to expand and improve his biological weapons capability both in terms of production and delivery systems; we know he is working once again on a nuclear program."[83] There were many unanswered questions about the strength of the evidence for such claims.[84] Nevertheless, the politics of presidential power helped sway the outcome. By mid-September 2002, GOP congressional candidates across the country were making Iraq a central issue—emphasizing their unwavering support for granting war authority to Bush, and focusing on any reservations about war with Baghdad on the part of their opponents as if that were the same thing as not wanting to go after Al Qaeda. In a race for an open House seat in New Mexico, for example, Republican Steve Pearce ran an ad against Democrat John Arthur Smith, who did not immediately voice support for the Iraq war resolution, saying, "While Smith 'reflects' on the situation, the possibility of a mushroom cloud hovering over a U.S. city still remains." In Minnesota, Republican Norm Coleman, challenging the incumbent senator Paul Wellstone, denounced the Democrat for refusing to "stand with the president."[85] Similar tactics showed up in campaigns around the country.

Hoping to get the Iraq vote out of the way so that they could change the subject to domestic issues such as the economy, most Democrats facing competitive reelection races joined nearly every Republican in approving the Iraq war resolution. Thus, even though the Founders wanted Congress to make the final decision about when the United States should go to war, lawmakers abdicated their responsibility and delegated their power to the president.*

The hurry-up Iraq vote, along with a simultaneous fight over whether

---

*In the months that followed, the GOP-led Congress would also largely abdicate its responsibility to hold oversight hearings on the executive branch's planning for the war and especially the occupation that would follow it. One notable and rare exception was the Senate Foreign Relations Committee under the chairmanship of Senator Richard Lugar of Indiana, but the administration largely ignored his efforts.

employees of the new Department of Homeland Security should have civil service–worker protections limiting the president's authority over personnel decisions, allowed Republicans to accuse Democrats of being soft on terrorism if they voiced skepticism about giving more power to the president. The impact of this strategy in the November 2002 midterm election was stunning. Republicans picked up eight seats in the House to expand their narrow majority, and they picked up two seats in the Senate to retake control of the upper chamber. Historically, the party in control of the White House has almost always lost seats in Congress during midterm elections. The 2002 election was the first midterm since 1934 in which the president's party managed to pick up seats in both chambers.

Yet, despite having pressured Congress for the Iraq vote, Bush would not rely upon their resolution six months later when he announced that diplomacy had failed and that war with Baghdad was necessary. In a letter to Congress on March 21, 2003, the first day of the Iraq war, Bush would briefly note the resolution's existence, but he would say that he had ordered U.S. troops into battle "pursuant to my authority as Commander in Chief."[86]

## 13.

Two years later, on the eve of the second Bush-Cheney inauguration, Cheney would be interviewed for a History Channel documentary about the presidency. Once again, the vice president brought up his frustrations during the years when he had worked for the Ford White House — a period he called the "low point" of presidential power. Once again, he argued that all the constraints Congress had imposed on the White House after the Vietnam War and the Watergate scandal had been mistakes. "I'm not sure that that justified reducing or restricting presidential power and authority or making changes in the fundamental institutional balance between the two," Cheney said.[87]

But something was different this time. Cheney no longer seemed as upset about the loss of presidential power. In fact, as he looked back over the changes the administration had made during its first term in office — some of which were known to the public, some of which were not — Cheney celebrated, in his low-key way, the return of what he believed to be the proper levels of executive power. "I think, in fact, there has been over time a restoration, if you will, of the power and authority of the president," Cheney said.

He reflected on the fact that when he and Bush had taken office in January 2001, they had done so with no mandate from the voters to support their agenda. They had lost the popular vote nationally to Vice President Al Gore, and it had taken one of the most controversial 5–4 Supreme Court decisions in history to ensure that they would win the election, anyway. Yet despite coming into power under such a cloud, Cheney said the two of them had been able to accomplish many things because they had made an "absolutely" conscious decision to implement their agenda "full speed ahead."

"A win is a win is a win," Cheney said. "It would not have been appropriate for him to be a timid president. In the aftermath of 9/11, that was especially true. Faced with a whole new threat, set of challenges, you needed a strong, decisive president, and that's exactly what we had. And that was possible because we didn't allow the closeness of the 2000 election, or the controversy that surrounded the outcome of the 2000 election, to, in any way, diminish our use of the power and authority of the office of the president."

# 7

# "A Hollow Shell": Secrecy II

## 1.

After Vice President Cheney turned aside the attempt by the General Accounting Office to look at his energy task force records, the White House's tightening grip on information soon faced a second—and more determined—challenge.

When Comptroller General David Walker announced in February 2003 that the GAO would not appeal the court ruling that threw out its lawsuit, he pointed to the ongoing public-interest lawsuits by Judicial Watch and a coalition of environmentalist groups as evidence that hope remained. That second front in the legal battle over the task force records had begun to heat up in July 2002, when the Bush-Cheney administration asked a federal district court judge to dismiss the Judicial Watch lawsuit. Two Cheney aides submitted affidavits saying that only government officials had been "members" of the task force. The White House said the Federal Advisory Committee Act's rules about open meetings did not matter, since the law applied only when a government task force had outside lobbyists as members, so the Judicial Watch case ought to be summarily thrown out.

Lawyers for the watchdog groups scoffed. They argued that there was no way to know whether the Cheney aides were telling the truth unless the judge looked at the records for himself. Moreover, they argued, it was entirely possible that energy lobbyists had played such a significant informal role in shaping the policy that they had been members in all but name. To bolster their case, they noted that in 1993, a federal appeals court had ruled that the same open-government law would apply to Hillary Clinton's health-care task force if outsiders had played such an important role that they were de facto members of it, regardless of whether Clinton called them "members."

The district court judge who was to decide the case, Emmet Sullivan, had impeccable bipartisan credentials. He had been appointed to a District of Columbia judgeship by President Reagan, elevated to a higher DC court by President George H. W. Bush, and then elevated again to the federal bench by President Clinton.[1] On August 2, 2002, Sullivan announced his decision. If Cheney wanted the case dismissed, the judge said, the White House first had to show him documents from the task force. This could be done privately in his chambers, and no one else need ever know the contents of the documents. But, citing the Clinton health-care task force precedent, Sullivan said that he needed to examine the records to see how much the energy company lobbyists and executives had participated in its work. "It is not appropriate to say, 'This request is unconstitutional,'" Sullivan told Cheney's lawyers. "I need to know what the basis is."[2]

Sullivan gave the White House one month to begin bringing records to his chamber. That night, as Judicial Watch's Chris Farrell drove home along the George Washington Memorial Parkway in his blue 1994 Geo Prizm, he was jubilant.

"It was very encouraging," Farrell later recalled thinking. "It looked like the judge had the intellectual honesty and courage to at least give it an evaluation and a fair look. If, in fact, everything the administration was saying was true, then the judge would look at it and draw that conclusion. At least then the public would have some sense of confidence and trust that the right thing was being done, because a fresh set of eyes had looked at it. Without that check, you don't know."[3]

But Cheney refused to comply with Sullivan's order. In the fall of 2002, the White House asked a federal appeals court to overrule Sullivan and throw out the case without first making Cheney show the documents to a member of the judicial branch. The appeals court again rejected Cheney, ruling that Sullivan was entitled to see the papers before deciding whether the open-government law applied to the energy task force.

Cheney decided to take his appeal to the Supreme Court. And in December 2003, the high court agreed to hear the case before its term was out, setting up a potentially dramatic showdown over the energy papers — and the larger issue of executive branch secrecy and presidential power — in the very midst of the 2004 presidential election campaign.

**2.**

Meanwhile, the Bush-Cheney administration's information-control project was also relentlessly moving forward on other fronts. On March 25, 2003, while Cheney's lawyers worked on their briefs for the federal appeals court and the country focused on the just-launched war in Iraq, President Bush quietly signed an executive order making sweeping changes to federal guidelines for classifying information.[4]

Bush's order made it much easier for government agencies to reclassify documents that had already been made public, removing them from the open stacks at the National Archives.[5] According to a later audit by the Archivist of the United States, Allen Weinstein, a reclassification program, which dated back to the 1990s but was significantly bolstered by Bush's executive order, enabled executive branch officials to remove more than twenty-five thousand records from public access — many illegitimately — because they supposedly contained classified information. Weinstein said the program had to be shut down. "More than one of every three documents removed from the open shelves and barred to researchers should not have been tampered with," Weinstein said. "That practice, which undermined the National Archives' basic mission to preserve the authenticity of files under our stewardship, must never be repeated."[6]

Bush's executive order also made it easier for the government to create new classified secrets. Each year, the National Archives Information Security Oversight Office tracks the number of documents that government officials stamp "Classified." It also tracks the number of pages of old material made public. This annual report allows a rare glimpse into the level of secrecy at any given time inside the executive branch. For example, in 2000, the final year of the Clinton administration, government officials had classified 220,926 secrets. The office's data shows that by 2004, the final year of Bush's first term, the number of newly declared classified secrets had jumped to 351,050. Because those secrets were recorded on more than one document, moreover, the 351,050 figure translated into 15.2 million new classified documents — the highest total ever recorded since the government had begun keeping track in 1980, at the height of the Cold War.[7]

As the record-breaking numbers for 2004 were piling up, the director of the National Archives Information Security Oversight Office, Bill Leonard, candidly acknowledged to Congress that it was "no secret that the government classifies too much information." And, Leonard warned, the growing culture of excessive secrecy was putting everyone at risk. Excessive secrecy, he said, discouraged the very information sharing between agencies that the 9/11 Commission said could help connect the dots and stop the next attack, and it could "serve as an impediment to sharing information with another agency, or with the public, who have a genuine need-to-know for the information."[8] And Thomas Blanton, director of the National Security Archive at George Washington University, said the rising wave of national security classifications, coupled with disclosures of formerly secret information that "doesn't pass the guffaw test," jeopardized the protection of legitimate secrets such as the names of covert operatives or the designs of weapons systems. "If people inside the system see dubious secrets being placed into the security system or see strategic declassifications being done for purely political reasons, they are less likely to be bound by their own oaths," he concluded.[9]

Bush's March 2003 executive order also gave the vice president, for the first time in U.S. history, the highest power to classify and declassify documents across the entire government. Most officials who have classification power can wield it only over information generated by their particular agency. The exception to this limitation is the president, since he is the head of the executive branch. The vice president, by contrast, officially isn't the head of anything—but now Cheney had been made the full equal to the president when it came to deciding whether to make something secret or to selectively release such information.[10]

But Cheney was not satisfied with the secrecy powers Bush had given him and moved to make himself the equal of the president in other ways as well. The president himself, along with a few top aides, is exempt from a longstanding requirement that executive agencies annually report to the Information Security Oversight Office the number of times each has used its power to make a document secret or to declassify a former secret. Bush's revised executive order said nothing about making the vice president's office exempt from this rule. But even though Cheney's office had complied with the oversight rule in 2001 and 2002, starting in 2003 Cheney began refusing to report how often his office had exercised its classification powers. Pressed for an explanation, Cheney's spokeswoman said Addington had opined that the vice president was "not under any duty" to comply with the disclosure rules. His legal theory was that because the Constitution gives the vice president the role of president of the Senate, enabling him to cast tie-breaking votes, the vice presidency partially exists outside the executive branch, and so it is not subject to its internal rules.[11]

Leonard would write several letters to Addington protesting the claim that the vice president's office was legally exempt from executive branch rules, but his letters went unanswered. In January 2007, Leonard asked the Justice Department to resolve the dispute with a formal legal opinion. As department lawyers studied the question, Cheney's staff urged a committee that was considering further revisions to the executive order on classified information to explicitly exempt the vice president's office from oversight — and to abolish Leonard's agency. In the end, Bush acquiesced to Cheney's defiance of the executive order. In June 2007, the White House stated that the reporting requirement does not apply to the vice president's office.[12]

Back in the summer of 2003, three months after Bush's first executive order on classified information, questions were mounting about why U.S. troops had found no weapons of mass destruction in Iraq. Amid the rising urgency, Cheney's office demonstrated the political power that accompanies the ability to selectively declassify government secrets at will. On July 6, 2003, a former ambassador named Joseph Wilson published an op-ed piece in the *New York Times* questioning the White House's public statements about the case for invading Iraq. Wilson revealed that the CIA had sent him to Niger in February 2002 to investigate a report that Iraq may have sought to buy uranium there in the late 1990s. Wilson had reported back his finding that no such transaction had taken place. Nonetheless, on January 29, 2003, Bush had cited the Africa uranium claim in his State of the Union speech as one of two key pieces of evidence that Iraq had reconstituted a nuclear weapons program.[13] The implication was that the administration may have knowingly misled the public in order to build support for the war.

Cheney used the power to control information to undercut Wilson's accusation. Two days after the op-ed piece was published, Cheney's chief of staff, I. Lewis "Scooter" Libby, met a New York Times reporter, Judith Miller, for breakfast at an elegant hotel near the White House. Libby showed Miller excerpts from a highly classified document representing the pre-war consensus of the intelligence community about Iraq. Among the key judgments of the National Intelligence Estimate was the conclusion that Iraq was "vigorously trying to procure" uranium, as a general matter. Libby also said Wilson's report had shown that in 1999, "an Iraqi delegation visited Niger and sought to expand commercial relations," which Libby said was "understood to be a reference to a desire to obtain uranium." Libby and Miller also apparently discussed the fact that Wilson's wife, Valerie Plame Wilson, was a CIA agent who had arranged to have her husband sent on the trip. The leak of her identity by several officials that month would prompt an investigation, leading to Libby's conviction on charges of perjury and obstruction of justice. Libby would be fined and sentenced to thirty months in prison in 2007, but Bush would commute his jail time.[14]

But Libby was not indicted for having leaked a classified intelligence document about Iraq. As Libby testified before a grand jury, Cheney had ordered him to get the selected excerpts of the National Intelligence Estimate out — and that made all the difference. He said Cheney told him it was "very important" for this information to come out, instructing his chief of staff to give it to Miller. Libby said he told Cheney that he could not have such a conversation with Miller because the excerpts were classified, but the vice president told him that he had spoken with Bush about the matter, and both agreed that the information should come out. Libby said he then spoke with Addington, who told him that such high-level permission to leak classified information "amounted to a declassification."[15]

The Office of the Vice President was not alone in exercising the power to declassify information for political purposes. In late April 2004, Attorney General John Ashcroft decided to declassify a 1995 Justice Department memo showing deliberations involving Jamie Gorelick, a former deputy attorney general under Clinton who had been named to the 9/11 Commission. The memo discussed long-standing limits on the ability of the CIA and the FBI to share terrorism information. Ashcroft, facing accusations that he had failed to take the Al Qaeda threat seriously prior to 9/11, brandished the Gorelick memo in his commission testimony in an effort to blame Clinton-era policies for the failure to prevent the attacks. The performance earned Ashcroft a rare public rebuke by Bush. White House spokesman Scott McClellan said at the time that the president was "disappointed" that the document was released, and made it clear that the decision was made by Ashcroft's Justice Department, not by the White House.[16] Some political analysts interpreted the unusual repudiation as a sign that the White House did not want to play politics with the 9/11 Commission, but there was an alternative explanation: Ashcroft had broken its ironclad rule that internal executive branch memos were never to be made public.

Selective retention and release could be a useful tool for the executive branch in court as well. In April 2004, a federal trial began in a Patriot Act–related case against a graduate student in computer science named Sami Omar al-Hussayen. The Justice Department accused Hussayen of conspiring to provide material support to terrorists because he had helped maintain websites that hosted videos and documents of Islamic groups who advocated holy war in Israel and Chechnya, among other places, and contained links to donation sites for Hamas. (A jury later acquitted Hussayen of all the terrorism charges.) While preparing for the trial, Hussayen's lawyers repeatedly asked for access to documents from the government's surveillance of their client, but the Justice Department fought that release on national security grounds. Three days before the trial, however, the government abruptly decided to declassify about thirty thousand intercepted Arabic-language phone calls and e-mail messages it was using as evidence in the case, raising questions about whether the delay was for security reasons or an attempt to prevent the defense from having sufficient time to review the documents.

## 3.

On April 17, 2004, a beautiful spring day in the midst of a ferocious presidential campaign, the Supreme Court convened to hear oral arguments in the Cheney energy task force case. The hearing drew a huge crowd. Adding to the controversy, one of the nine justices, Antonin Scalia, had recently gone on a duck-hunting trip with Cheney. Critics had called on Scalia not to take part in the case, but Scalia refused.

Chris Farrell watched the arguments unfold from a bench about two-thirds of the way back in the court, surrounded by more than a dozen colleagues. Nearly the entire Judicial Watch office had emptied out to see its director of litigation, Paul Orfanedes, appear before the court alongside Alan Morrison for the Sierra Club. The group had received enough reserved seating for most of the staff to attend, and the rest had gotten up early to line up outside the courthouse on the long marble steps for a spot with the general public.

From the start, the administration sought to drive home its point that the White House enjoys a "constitutional immunity" that protects the president from all legal demands for information unless the president himself is under criminal investigation. To the extent that the Federal Advisory Committee Act might force the president to make public or even show a judge any information about the advice he or other top White House officials received, the law itself was unconstitutional, it argued.

"This is a case about the separation of powers," began Ted Olson, the U.S. solicitor general. Olson, the former head of the Office of Legal Counsel for the Reagan administration had been the plaintiff in the landmark 1988 Supreme Court ruling rejecting the Unitary Executive Theory, asserted that presidents have an absolute right to seek confidential advice from outsiders. Neither Congress nor the courts, Olson argued, could force presidents to disclose information in court cases, as the district judge wanted to do in the energy task force dispute—not even very limited information necessary to establish whether there was a basis for letting the lawsuit proceed or dismissing it, a process called discovery.

"We are submitting that the discovery itself violates the Constitution," Olson said.

Justice Ruth Bader Ginsburg, the liberal jurist appointed by President Clinton in 1993, was startled by the sweep of the claim. If the presidency were simply immune from discovery, it would dramatically limit the ability of courts to review any civil lawsuit.

"All discovery?" she asked.

"Yes," Olson replied.[17]

Throughout the questioning, a majority of the justices appeared to be sympathetic to the administration's general constitutional concerns about a need to solicit candid advice. But they also seemed uncomfortable about siding with the White House on the technical legal issues at hand.[18]

On June 24, 2004, Farrell was down in South Florida, investigating a potential case involving the government's immigration policies, when he got a call on his cell phone. The court had issued its ruling. It appeared at first glance, he was told by his colleagues, to be a "punt"—they had neither ordered Cheney to turn over the papers nor dismissed the case. Instead, by a 7–2 vote, the Supreme Court simply ordered the appeals court to take a second look at its decision that Cheney had to show the district judge his energy task force records. Most of the national media similarly portrayed the ruling as a deflating nonevent, since it ensured that a final decision about the energy task force papers would not be made until after the fall's presidential election.

But it was not a mere punt. Lurking in the dry prose of the court's majority opinion were instructions to the appeals court for how they should go about taking that second look at the case. Next time, Justice Anthony Kennedy wrote, the appeals court—as well as all other district and appeals courts around the country that encountered a similar case—must use a legal standard that would be much more tilted toward the president's claim that documents should be kept secret, even from a judge. Courts must afford "presidential confidentiality the greatest protection consistent with the fair administration of justice," he wrote, lest the executive branch be distracted by too many lawsuits.[19]

At least one commentator—Shannen Coffin, a former Justice Department official who had worked on the Cheney case at earlier stages—immediately recognized that this decision was not a punt, but instead a "major victory" for presidential power. Writing on the conservative *National Review* website, he said that, thanks to "the vice president's resolute assertion that he and the president should have the right to receive in confidence the advice necessary to the performance of their duties," the White House had already won an expansion of its power to keep things secret—regardless of what happened when the appeals court reconsidered the energy case.[20]

"It is a decision that will be cited by many a president to come—Democrat and Republican," wrote Coffin approvingly.

In 2005, after Scooter Libby was indicted for perjury and resigned, Cheney made Addington his chief of staff, while letting him keep his old duties as counsel. But the workload became too much, so Cheney and Addington cast about for another lawyer who shared their eye for leveraging the law to expand presidential power.

They hired Coffin.

4.

One month after the Supreme Court heard oral arguments in the Cheney energy task force papers case, on May 13, 2004, Ashcroft took a dramatic step in an unrelated lawsuit involving an FBI whistle-blower he wanted to silence.

The case involved a translator named Sibel Edmonds, whom the FBI had hired on a contract basis shortly after the 9/11 attacks. In the spring of 2002, Edmonds had alleged that a colleague in her office had passed FBI information on to a Turkish spy group with ties to terrorism. According to a later inspector general report, Edmonds's allegations had merit, but, rather than getting to the bottom of her suspicions, her supervisor fired her for being disruptive. Shortly after Edmonds was let go, the Senate Judiciary Committee began to look into her allegations, and the FBI provided Congress with unclassified briefings and documents about Edmonds's work. Later, however, Edmonds filed a whistle-blower lawsuit against the Justice Department, alleging that she was improperly fired in retaliation for embarrassing her employer.

Urging a judge to dismiss the case, Ashcroft invoked the State Secrets Privilege, saying that the lawsuit could not go forward without discussion of Edmonds's work, and that such discussion could reveal information that might endanger national security. To bolster his argument, Ashcroft declared that he was retroactively classifying as top secret information related to the case that had previously been available to Congress. Then Ashcroft asked a judge to dismiss the lawsuit. After Ashcroft issued his order, two senators who had written letters to the Justice Department critical of its handling of Edmonds's allegations had no choice but to remove the letters from their website.

The gambit worked. A judge dismissed the case without giving Edmonds a day in court, accepting Ashcroft's invocation of the State Secrets Privilege. Edmonds was also barred from testifying about problems in the government's counterterrorism translation program in a class-action lawsuit by family members of victims of 9/11.

The Edmonds incident would not be the last in which the Bush-Cheney administration made aggressive use of the State Secrets Privilege to shut down awkward court cases. The administration repeatedly invoked the doctrine to declare that momentous questions about its use of executive power simply could not be adjudicated, in cases from lawsuits involving detainee abuse by the CIA to its warrantless domestic-surveillance programs.

This use of the State Secrets Privilege essentially established the president himself as the sole arbiter of which matters could receive judicial review. Yet nothing in the Constitution itself gives the executive branch the right to dispose of lawsuits by uttering the magic words "state secrets." Indeed, the first time the Supreme Court recognized such a privilege had been just fifty years earlier, at the beginning of the Cold War and amid the first real stirrings of the "imperial presidency." And a closer look at that precedent, *U.S. v. Reynolds,* shows that it was based on a lie that allowed the executive branch to cover up its own mistakes.

The *Reynolds* case arose after three civilian scientists working on guided-missile research were killed in the crash of a B-29 bomber in Georgia in 1948. Their widows sued the government, seeking compensation and access to the crash investigation report. A federal district judge said the government had to turn over the report, but the Truman administration refused. The administration said that discussion of the crash report would endanger national security by revealing important details about the classified research the scientists had been working on. The judge said he might be willing to dismiss the case, but he first wanted to see the crash report himself—secretly, in his chambers—in order to make sure the government was telling the truth.

Instead of complying, the Truman administration appealed the district judge's order, repeating its arguments that showing the report to anyone would endanger state secrets. Amid the fears of the early Cold War, this new claim of an expansive presidential power found a receptive audience. In 1953, without looking at the report, the Supreme Court upheld the claim on the grounds that there was a "reasonable danger that the accident investigation report would contain references to the secret electronic equipment." And, over the next five decades, presidents would invoke the *Reynolds* precedent to get rid of more than sixty uncomfortable lawsuits, with judges rejecting the State Secrets Privilege just five times.[21]

But something extraordinary happened in the year 2000. Judith Palya Loether, the daughter of one of the scientists who had been killed in the 1948 plane crash, was surfing the Internet for information about the accident. She had been seven years old when her father, Albert Palya, died, and she had always wondered about the mysterious circumstances around his death. A Google search led her to a website selling recently declassified military documents—including the long-withheld crash report. For a small credit-card fee, she got the report mailed to her home. When she opened it, she was astonished. There was nothing in the crash report about top-secret electronics. Instead, the accident report contained only incriminating evidence that the air force mechanics had neglected to install heat-deflector shields required by regulations to keep the engines from overheating. The engines had caught fire, causing the crash; several servicemen had bailed out and survived the crash, but one told an investigator that the civilians had not been briefed about how to escape the airplane—another violation of regulations.

"As I discovered more and more about it, I got more and more angry," Loether told a reporter. "It didn't have to do with state secrets; it had to do with embarrassment and negligence. You can't look at that accident report and not be overwhelmed by the amount of negligence involved."[22]

The central case on which the State Secrets Privilege rests, then, was a fraud. The Truman administration had lied to the courts and gotten away with it. In the process, it had won a precedent that significantly expanded presidential power to keep information from the courts and from the public, one that the Bush-Cheney administration would later wield with unusual vigor.

Loether tracked down Susan Brauner, the daughter of another of the dead civilian scientists, and shared her findings. Then one day Brauner heard on the radio about a court case being fought by the widow of one of the 9/11 victims. The widow had sued the airlines and was fighting to get documents about the airport security system in Boston, where two of the four hijacked flights had taken off. But the government refused to give the widow the documents or even to show the documents to the judge, citing the *Reynolds* case.[23] Incensed, the two daughters of the dead scientists decided to try to reopen their mothers' lawsuit. They asked to have the *Reynolds* decision overturned, hoping the government would correct the mistake now that it had come to light. "I even had fantasies that President Bush would call me and apologize," Loether said.[24]

That didn't happen. Recognizing the danger to a key tool of presidential power, the Bush-Cheney administration's legal team fought hard against Loether to protect the *Reynolds* precedent, arguing that too much time had passed to alter the old ruling. A federal district judge dismissed the case, and then a federal appeals court panel upheld the dismissal. One of the appeals court judges who refused to disturb the State Secrets Privilege precedent was Samuel Alito Jr., whom Bush would soon elevate to the Supreme Court.[25]

## 5.

On January 7, 2005, *USA Today* published the results of an investigation it had conducted using the Freedom of Information Act. Documents provided to the newspaper by the Education Department showed that a political commentator, Armstrong Williams, had been paid $240,000 of taxpayer funds to promote President Bush's controversial No Child Left Behind law on his nationally syndicated television and radio shows, and to urge colleagues to do the same. The contract required Williams to "regularly comment on NCLB during the course of his broadcasts" and to interview Education Secretary Rod Paige about the program. Williams, a former aide to Supreme Court justice Clarence Thomas and one of the most prominent black conservative columnists in the country, had not disclosed the payments as he regularly extolled the White House's signature domestic policy during the run-up to the 2004 election.[26]

The disclosure of the secret payments to Williams prompted outrage in the media community as a violation of journalistic ethics. It also focused sharper attention on some of the Bush-Cheney administration's most aggressive practices for controlling the flow of information to the public: fake news. The Williams deal was set up by a public relations firm that had contracts with other administration agencies to promote Bush administration policies. That same firm also produced "video news releases" that looked just like local TV news stories, complete with fake reporters interviewing administration officials and explaining administration programs in a very positive light. The government sent these videos to local television stations around the country. Local producers ended up broadcasting the professional-looking free content to fill airtime in their nightly newscasts—without alerting viewers that they were watching a government product.

Controversy over the video news releases first flared in the spring of 2004, when a prepackaged story praising the new Medicare drug benefit was widely disseminated. The story featured a hired narrator who ended the segment by saying, "In Washington, I'm Karen Ryan reporting."[27] Karen Ryan later showed up again, "reporting" in praise of the No Child Left Behind Act, just like Armstrong Williams.[28] Some video news releases explained fairly innocuous programs, such as government-sponsored anti-bullying and anti-obesity campaigns, but others were nakedly geared toward putting a positive spin on core White House policies featuring, for example, Iraqis who were happy that the U.S. military had deposed Saddam Hussein.

The video news releases prompted a new confrontation between the White House and the GAO—the nonpartisan congressional watchdog agency headed by Comptroller General David Walker, who had unsuccessfully sued Cheney over access to his secret energy task force records. In a series of reports to Congress, GAO auditors declared that the administration's prepackaged news segments were illegal under multiple laws that banned the use of taxpayer dollars for covert propaganda.[29]

But the Bush-Cheney legal team offered its own interpretation of the laws Congress had written, absolving the government of any wrongdoing. In March 2005, the acting head of the Justice Department's Office of Legal Counsel, a Bush-appointed lawyer named Steven Bradbury, would hold that while the video news releases might be "covert," since the government misled viewers about the source of the news segments, they weren't "propaganda," because they supposedly merely explained programs and facts rather than expressing a political viewpoint.[30] By statute, the Office of Legal Counsel's interpretations of the law are binding interpretations for the executive branch, so Bradbury's "advisory opinion" meant that there could be no prosecution of the officials who had signed off on the video news releases—and that the practice could continue.

But the GAO rejected the Bush-Cheney legal team's interpretation, continuing to insist that the video news releases were illegal—and unethical to boot. The dispute would come to an end in May 2005, when Congress passed a new law, clarifying that its ban on spending federal money for "covert propaganda" extended to producing and distributing *any* news story that does not openly acknowledge the government's role.[31] But other efforts by the administration to control news coverage of its activities were just around the corner.

## 6.

On May 5, 2005, the FBI arrested an Iran analyst for the Pentagon named Lawrence Franklin, opening a major new front in the Bush-Cheney administration's attempts to control the information received by the public.

A strong supporter of Israel, Franklin was accused of giving top-secret information about American policy toward Iran to two lobbyists with the

American Israel Public Affairs Committee, a group that lobbies the U.S. government to support Israel. The AIPAC lobbyists, Steve Rosen and Keith Weissman, were in turn accused of relaying the information to the government of Israel and to members of the media. Three months later, a federal grand jury indicted Franklin, Rosen, and Weissman under a law called the Espionage Act of 1917.

Congress had enacted the law shortly after the United States entered World War I, a time of a great crackdown on civil liberties in America. The following year, Congress strengthened the law with the Sedition Act of 1918. The two acts allowed the administration of President Woodrow Wilson to censor newspapers that were not supportive of the war effort, and to arrest people who spoke out against military recruiting. Congress repealed most of the laws in 1921, but it left on the books a section from the Espionage Act that prohibited the transmission of national defense information to people not authorized to receive it.

Using the Espionage Act against Franklin was not particularly remarkable. He was a government official who had access to secret information and had given it to people who were not authorized to receive it. (Franklin pled guilty and was sentenced to twelve years in prison in January 2006.) But using the law to indict Rosen and Weissman, the lobbyists, was unprecedented. By indicting the outside recipients of the information, the administration was declaring that private citizens were under the same obligation as government officials to keep quiet about any classified secrets that happened to come into their possession.

One of the first to recognize the sweeping implications of the administration's new legal strategy was the journalist Eli Lake. Writing in *The New Republic,* Lake observed that "if it's illegal for Rosen and Weissman to seek and receive 'classified information,' then many investigative journalists are also criminals. . . . While most administrations have tried to crack down on leaks, they have almost always shied away from going after those who receive them — until now. At a time when a growing amount of information is being classified, the prosecution of Rosen and Weissman threatens to have a chilling effect — not on the ability of foreign agents to influence U.S. policy, but on the ability of the American public to understand it."[32]

Under the Bush-Cheney administration, federal prosecutors had already become increasingly aggressive in jailing reporters on contempt charges if the journalists refused to turn over notes or disclose the identities of confidential sources to grand juries. Critics charged that the tactic was a means for intimidating both investigative reporters and would-be leakers, thereby eroding the ability of the free press to uncover wrong-doing in the executive branch. Some countries have laws such as Great Britain's Official Secrets Act that criminalize the dissemination of gov-ernment secrets by private citizens. But the United States, where freedom of speech is protected by the First Amendment, has never had such a law. The prospect of prosecuting investigating reporters for "espionage" took the United States into territory where it had never been.

The end of 2005 brought two major revelations about government se-crets that would further reveal the Bush-Cheney administration's get-tough attitude on investigative journalists. The *Washington Post* published an exposé of the CIA's system of secret prisons scattered around the world where detainees suspected of terrorist ties were held outside of the legal system, hidden from the Red Cross, and subjected to harsh interro-gations that sometimes left them dead. The following month, the *New York Times* revealed that Bush had signed off on allowing the National Security Agency to wiretap Americans' international phone calls and e-mails without a warrant. Both articles won Pulitzer Prizes and sparked controversies that led to sharp criticism of the administration's policies from some Republicans as well as Democrats in Congress, along with a series of oversight hearings and legislative proposals.

In response, the president and the vice president denounced the news-papers for endangering national security and quickly commenced an in-vestigation into who leaked the information to the reporters. Then, in May 2006, Alberto Gonzales went on ABC's *This Week* and unleashed a stunner: The administration was exploring the idea of prosecuting the journalists on charges of unauthorized disclosure of classified informa-tion under the 1917 Espionage Act. "I understand very much the role that the press plays in our society, the protection under the First Amendment we want to promote and respect . . . but it can't be the case that that right trumps over the right that Americans would like to see, the ability of the federal government to go after criminal activity," Gonzales said.[33]

The idea of using the Espionage Act to prosecute journalists was not new. It had been floated thirty-one years before, almost to the day, by a deputy chief of staff in the Ford White House named Dick Cheney. Then, Cheney had wanted to use the law to make an example of Seymour Hersh and the *New York Times* after it published Hersh's article about a classified Cold War–era spy program involving submarines. Back then, Ford's attorney general, Edward Levi, balked at the idea. Now Gonzales embraced it.

7.

Five days after the FBI arrested Lawrence Franklin, on May 10, 2005, the U.S. Court of Appeals for the District of Columbia handed down a decision that ended the second energy task force papers case. During oral arguments the previous January, several judges had indicated that they read the Supreme Court's ruling—insisting that they take a second look at the case using a much more pro–White House standard—as meaning that the higher justices did not want the judiciary to get further entangled in a showdown with the executive branch. The appeals court got the message loud and clear. It issued an 8–0 ruling that Cheney need not disclose the energy task force records to the federal district judge after all. And because, without access to such records, the court had no evidence that the lobbyists had cast a vote during the group's deliberations, they said the energy task force was not covered by the Federal Advisory Committee Act. With the bang of a gavel, they dismissed the case.

This decision relied entirely upon the assertion of two Cheney aides that the lobbyists had not cast any votes, a claim no judge ever verified by looking at the records. The court's ruling also dismissed arguments that "influential participation" by outsiders made them de facto members of the task force whether or not they cast votes, rejecting the standard the same court had used a decade earlier to force Hillary Rodham Clinton to disclose her health-care task force files.

The decision, said Judicial Watch's Chris Farrell, left the 1972 open-government law "a hollow shell." David Bookbinder, the Sierra Club's lead attorney on the case, told reporters that the outcome was a double blow: "As a policy matter, we see the Bush administration has succeeded in its efforts to keep secret how industry crafted the administration's energy policy. As a legal matter, it's a defeat for efforts to have open government and for the public to know how their elected officials are conducting business."[34]

# 8

## The Perseverance and the Purge:
## Laws and Treaties II

### 1.

In October 2002, while Congress was debating the Iraq war resolution, military interrogators at Guantánamo secretly began asking the same question as the CIA had asked two months earlier: How far were they authorized to go in questioning detainees they believed to be withholding information? The Guantánamo interrogators were particularly interested in Detainee 063, a Saudi named Mohammed al-Qahtani. Born in 1975, Qahtani had been captured along the Afghanistan-Pakistan border in December 2001. Although he had initially claimed to know nothing, officials figured out that Qahtani had been turned away by immigration officials at Orlando International Airport in August 2001. Moreover, at the very moment a suspicious official had refused to let Qahtani enter the country, 9/11 ringleader Mohamed Atta had placed a phone call from the airport lobby. Circumstantial evidence strongly suggested, then, that in front of them was the fabled twentieth hijacker—the missing man who should have been on the team that took over United 93, which had only four terrorists while the other hijacked flights all had five.

After several months of questioning, however, Qahtani had failed to provide any information about other planned terrorist attacks that might be in the works. Meanwhile, interrogators began asking themselves another question: If the twentieth hijacker had been hidden among the crowd of seemingly low-level prisoners that had been shipped from Afghanistan to Cuba, what other high-ranking Al Qaeda figure might be lurking in those cell blocks, pretending to be a nobody? Frustrated, the interrogators pushed harder. Then, on October 11, 2002, they asked for official permission to use more severe tactics, such as sleep deprivation, forcing the prisoners to stand until they were exhausted, shackling them into contorted stress positions, and water-boarding them.[1] With the request, the commander of the interrogators included a legal analysis prepared by the operation's uniformed lawyer, Lieutenant Colonel Diane Beaver, who concluded that since the president had decided that detainees "are not protected by the Geneva Conventions," all of the desired techniques were allowable because "no international body of law directly applies."[2]

Pentagon counsel Jim Haynes also told Secretary of Defense Donald Rumsfeld that the requested techniques were all legal, although Haynes recommended holding off on water-boarding and mock executions as "not warranted at this time." Rumsfeld signed off on the rest of the list December 2, 2002, adding a handwritten note questioning whether the techniques were still too lenient, in the form of a comment: "However, I stand for 8–10 hours a day. Why is standing limited to 4 hours?"[3]

Later that month, an expert in interrogations for the navy, Dr. Michael Gelles, was reading through top secret interrogation logs for an internal military study, when he stopped short. As the head forensic psychologist for the U.S. Naval Criminal Investigative Service for twelve years, a position in which he oversaw interrogations in Yemen following the 2000 USS *Cole* bombing by Al Qaeda agents, Gelles had seen a lot of ugly things. But he couldn't believe what he was reading now. The interrogation logs contained a meticulously bureaucratic, minute-by-minute account of physical torments and degradation being inflicted on prisoners by American servicemen and women. Gelles went to his superior, Naval Criminal Investigative Service director David Brant, and showed him the logs. Brant, too, was disgusted. Declaring that the NCIS would pull its interrogators out of Guantánamo if the abuses continued, Brant asked the navy's general counsel, Alberto Mora, for help.

Mora was a Bush-Cheney administration political appointee. A Cuban American who became a career foreign service officer out of college, Mora had been the top lawyer in the United States Information Agency for the Bush-Quayle administration. In 1993, both Mora and Vice President Cheney's counsel David Addington had ended up at the same Washington law firm, Holland & Knight. (Mora later said he knew Addington socially and by reputation. "He was known as an exceptionally skilled attorney and a true intellect, the kind of person who can quote passages from legal opinions by memory along with the citation number," Mora recalled.[4]) When the Bush-Cheney transition team assembled a new government in 2001, Mora was invited to fill the slot of navy general counsel. During his interviews for the position, his opinions about the president's power as commander in chief never came up.[5]

When the two career professionals from the navy came to Mora with alarm about what was happening at Guantánamo, Mora agreed with them. He thought interrogators could do anything to detainees up to cruel treatment, but that crossing that line was illegal—and what was happening at Guantánamo crossed the line. According to a statement he later provided to a general investigating detainee abuses, Mora immediately went to Haynes and warned him that the interrogation policy put in place by Rumsfeld was "unlawful and unworthy of the military services." Weeks passed and nothing changed, so Mora wrote down his concerns in a draft memo declaring that many of the techniques Rumsfeld had formally approved were illegal under both domestic and international law, despite the legal advice he had previously received. Mora noted, "They constituted, at a minimum, cruel and unusual treatment and, at worst, torture."[6]

Mora sent the draft memo to Haynes on January 15, 2003, saying he would sign it by the afternoon if he had not heard that the interrogation policy was rescinded. The implicit threat meant that there would be a paper trail showing that Rumsfeld's legal adviser had been warned that his boss had signed off on an illegal policy. Haynes called Mora in for an awkward meeting. The memo would not be necessary, Haynes told him. Rumsfeld would immediately withdraw permission for all the coercive techniques. He was also setting up a detainee policy working group at the Pentagon to come up with a comprehensive policy for prisoners at Guantánamo. Mora's colleague, air force general counsel Mary Walker, would chair the effort.[7]

Mora was relieved. But the promised careful review process was short-circuited from the beginning when Haynes contacted a friend and racquetball partner: deputy assistant attorney general John Yoo at the Justice Department's Office of Legal Counsel. He asked Yoo to write an advisory opinion that would settle how far military interrogators legally could go in inflicting suffering on detainees. Replicating his six-month-old secret memo for the CIA, Yoo quickly drew up a draft document that repeated the same arguments for military interrogators. He declared that it would be lawful to inflict cruel, inhuman, and degrading treatment on Guantánamo detainees, and that the anti-torture statute "does not apply to the conduct of U.S. personnel" at Guantánamo.

Mora was amazed when he read the first draft of the Yoo memo. Despite its "seeming sophistication," Mora later wrote, Yoo's memo was "profoundly in error," contradicted by both domestic law and treaties to which the United States was a party. Moreover, "the memo espoused an extreme and virtually unlimited theory of the extent of the President's commander-in-chief authority." On February 6, 2003, Yoo came to the Pentagon to talk with Mora and his deputy. The navy general counsel later recalled that Yoo "glibly" defended his memo without taking seriously Mora's concerns about the assertion that a president has the power to bypass anti-torture laws.

Yoo also said that his job was only to state what the law was. Mora's contrary view, Yoo asserted, was an expression not of the law, but of the policy Mora preferred. Yoo said that the president might wish to discuss and adopt a policy of not abusing detainees, but he was not legally required to do so.

"Where can I have that discussion?" Mora asked.

"I don't know," Yoo replied. "Maybe here in the Pentagon?"[8]

But a debate over the law substituted for a debate over the policy. Based on Yoo's legal opinion, the political appointees in the Pentagon working group wanted to tell Rumsfeld that it would be lawful for military interrogators to use abusive techniques such as mock executions and water-boarding.

Then they ran into another group of dissidents: Like Mora, the top uniformed lawyers—the judge advocates general, or JAGs—erupted. In a series of vehemently argued memos, they said that such techniques were illegal, no matter what Yoo claimed. Among the critics was Major General Jack Rives, a top JAG in the air force. In a memo dated February 6, 2003, Rives said that "several of the exceptional techniques, on their face, amount to violations of domestic criminal law," and that U.S. interrogators who used them would risk prosecution. In addition, he wrote, telling troops that it was acceptable to brutalize prisoners could lead to a general breakdown in their discipline: "We need to consider the overall impact of approving extreme interrogation techniques as giving official approval and legal sanction to the application of interrogation techniques that U.S. forces have consistently been trained are unlawful," Rives wrote.[9]

But Haynes ordered the detainee working group to consider Yoo's memo as the "controlling authority" on all legal issues, shutting down further debate.[10] Walker, the working group chair, embedded Yoo's views in the final detainee policy report for Rumsfeld, which she completed on April 4, 2003. The members of the working group who disagreed with Yoo's analysis were simply not told that the report had been finalized. Instead, they were led to believe that the report was so flawed that the project had been abandoned.[11]

After receiving the working group report, Rumsfeld signed off on a new interrogation policy for Guantánamo on April 16, 2003, restoring permission for coercive interrogations.[12] The new list of allowed techniques was slightly less expansive than what he had approved the previous December but still included isolation for up to a month at a time, sleep disruption, dietary manipulation, sensory assault with sound, and prolonged exposure to heat or cold—all tactics that could be piled atop one another for lengthy periods. It also included a set of vague categories such as "fear up harsh" and "pride and ego down," which were open to interpretation by interrogators on the ground.

And Rumsfeld also said any other technique not listed could still be used as long as he personally granted permission for it. In other words, there were no binding laws and treaties about torture anymore—the only limit was the judgment and goodwill of executive branch officials.

## 2.

While the military debated presidential power and the treatment of detainees during the winter of 2002–2003, the Bush-Cheney legal team was undergoing major changes. In a short span of several months, many of the strongest allies of David Addington, advocates who supported Vice President Cheney's view of presidential power, left the executive branch. The wave of departures began in December 2002, when deputy White House counsel Timothy Flanigan said good-bye to his colleagues. Flanigan had been a key "presidentialist" on the legal team and one of the closest allies to Addington for nearly two years. But Flanigan, a Mormon, had fourteen children, meaning fourteen college tuitions to pay. As the year drew to a close, Flanigan resigned his post to become general counsel of the industrial conglomerate Tyco International.[13]

Three months later, the Senate confirmed Jay Bybee, the head of the

Office of Legal Counsel, to be a federal appeals court judge. Bybee, the former UNLV law professor who had signed off on Yoo's still-secret advisory opinions, had expected a rough confirmation hearing.[14] But the Senate Judiciary Committee scheduled Bybee's confirmation hearing for February 5, 2003, at the same time that Secretary of State Colin Powell was giving the United Nations Security Council "facts and conclusions based on solid intelligence" about Iraq's alleged weapons of mass destruction and its ties to Al Qaeda.[15] Bybee's Democratic critics opted to watch Powell present what turned out to be a questionable case to justify the coming American invasion, and only friendly senators showed up at Bybee's hearing.[16] He coasted to confirmation.

The day after the Senate confirmed Bybee to a life-tenured judgeship, Yoo completed his interrogation memo for the Pentagon working group that was developing a detainee treatment policy for Guantánamo. This memo would be among his last major writings for the Office of Legal Counsel. According to *Newsweek,* Addington and White House counsel Alberto Gonzales wanted Yoo to replace Bybee as head of the office. But Attorney General John Ashcroft refused to go along with the choice, apparently because he "resented Yoo going behind his back to give the White House a private pipeline into the OLC."[17] Denied the promotion, Yoo resigned from the Office of Legal Counsel in the summer of 2003 and returned to his position as a tenured law professor at Berkeley.

When replacements arrived to fill these and other newly opened vacancies on the Bush-Cheney legal team, the White House discovered that it had inadvertently allowed several relatively moderate and mainstream legal thinkers into its inner circle. Like Mora, the navy general counsel, some of these newly arrived political appointees tried to hit the brakes on some of the more extreme manifestations of the systematic effort to undercut legal limits on presidential power, setting off a series of vicious internal bureaucratic battles.

Adding to the intensifying conflict, the Supreme Court and several lower courts would soon weigh in with rulings on presidential power that initially appeared to knock down some of the administration's more aggressive claims. Finally, media reports would begin to uncover some of the most important secret policies, from torture to warrantless wiretapping, subjecting them to public and congressional scrutiny.

Together, these setbacks posed a major potential obstacle to Cheney's push to lock down the expansion of presidential power as a permanent change to American government. But Cheney and his remaining allies would fight relentlessly to preserve their vision.

## 3.

By the summer of 2003, Bybee was gone and Yoo had been blackballed by Ashcroft, so the Bush-Cheney administration needed someone else to fill the crucial position at the head of the Office of Legal Counsel. They settled on Jack Goldsmith, a former University of Chicago law professor who had joined the Pentagon's general counsel office in 2002. On paper Goldsmith must have looked like an acceptable substitute for Yoo. Back in 1999, Goldsmith and Yoo had coauthored a *Wall Street Journal* opinion article saying that ratified human rights treaties were not binding on the United States unless Congress separately passed a statute echoing their provisions.[18] In May 2001, Goldsmith and Yoo coauthored an article arguing that Bush had the power to pull out of the Anti-Ballistic Missile Treaty without consulting Congress.[19] And in November 2001, Goldsmith was one of the only brand-name law professors in the country to support Bush's military commissions order, with its limited rights for defendants. "The idea is, you need swift justice," Goldsmith had explained.[20]

Bush nominated Goldsmith to take over the Office of Legal Counsel in May 2003, and the Senate confirmed him to the position on October 2. But almost immediately he began making waves. During the previous summer, an insurgency had unexpectedly grown up in newly occupied Iraq. Inside the administration legal team, a split had emerged about the rights of suspected insurgents who were detained in Iraq. One faction, led by Addington, wanted to declare that the Geneva Conventions did not protect fighters in Iraq who did not wear uniforms, just as they had previously said the treaty did not apply to such enemy combatants in Afghanistan. The other faction, led by Office of Legal Counsel deputy Patrick Philbin, disagreed.[21] Philbin had backed Addington's view on detainees from the Afghanistan war back in 2001, but he said Iraq was different: As an official occupying power in Iraq, unlike in Afghanistan, the United States had no choice but to give all detainees basic Geneva Conventions rights to humane treatment.[22]

The dispute had simmered while the legal team waited for Goldsmith to be confirmed and make the call. In his first major act as head of the Office of Legal Counsel, Goldsmith took the bold step of opposing Addington. The Geneva Conventions, Goldsmith opined, protected all wartime prisoners in

Iraq—including suspected terrorists—and the commander in chief could not override that restriction.[23] Two months later, in December 2003, Goldsmith went further. He sent a memo to Haynes, the Pentagon general counsel, withdrawing the Office of Legal Counsel's support for Yoo's March 2003 interrogation memo. Goldsmith said the memo was "under review" and "should not be relied upon for any purpose" as the military considered the limits of how it could treat detainees at Guantánamo and elsewhere.[24]

The steps enraged Addington, prompting several confrontations between the two men, former administration attorneys say. For Addington, the interrogation memo incident was the final straw with Goldsmith. "Now that you've withdrawn legal opinions that the president of the United States has been relying on, I need you to go through all of [the Office of Legal Counsel's opinions relating to the war on terror] and let me know which ones you still stand by," he sarcastically told Goldsmith, an eyewitness told *Newsweek*.[25] Indeed, Goldsmith was just getting started. His predecessors had also signed off on the legality of Bush's order authorizing the National Security Agency to monitor Americans' international phone calls and e-mails without a court warrant, which was seemingly prohibited by the Foreign Intelligence Surveillance Act. According to the way the Bush-Cheney administration had set up the secret program, Bush had to reauthorize it every forty-five or ninety days. As part of that process, the attorney general had to recertify that the program was legal. Ashcroft had routinely done so, based on the advice of the Office of Legal Counsel during the Yoo era. But Goldsmith, with Philbin's help, was now taking a fresh look at all of his predecessors' findings about the commander in chief's supposed power to bypass laws, and he apparently concluded that the program violated the rule of law.

There was another newcomer at the Justice Department: Deputy Attorney General James Comey. Comey had recently been confirmed to replace Ashcroft's politically hard-line former deputy, Larry Thompson,[26] and was known as a straight-shooting former career prosecutor, not a partisan. One of Thompson's last acts had been to promote Philbin from the OLC to the top legal adviser to the deputy attorney general, so Comey inherited Philbin. According to later congressional testimony by Comey, Goldsmith and Philbin came to raise concerns about the program's legality.[27] Comey agreed with Goldsmith, and Comey asked Ashcroft to come talk about the issues as well. After an hour-long deliberation in early March 2004, Comey said, Ashcroft decided that he would not recertify that the program was lawful when it next came up for renewal, on March 11.

But hours later, Ashcroft was abruptly rushed to George Washington Hospital with abdominal pain. He was diagnosed with gallstone pancreatitis and had to undergo surgery to remove his gall bladder.[28] After his abdominal surgery, Ashcroft's wife gave orders that he was to receive no telephone calls or visitors so that he could recover. During his convalescence, Ashcroft transferred his legal powers to Comey, who became the acting attorney general. The next week, on Tuesday, March 9, 2004, Comey, Goldsmith, and Philbin went to the White House to talk about the program with Cheney, Addington, Gonzales, White House chief of staff Andrew Card, and undisclosed members of the intelligence community. Goldsmith and Philbin had been communicating for weeks with the White House about the legal problems with the program. Cheney and Addington were furious. They insisted that Goldsmith was wrong about the law. But Comey told them that neither Ashcroft nor he, as acting attorney general, would certify that the program was legal so that it could be renewed.[29]

Then, around 8 p.m. on March 10, the night before the program was set to expire, Comey was being driven home from the Justice Department when he received an urgent call from Ashcroft's chief of staff, David Ayers. Ashcroft's wife had just called Ayers from the hospital and told him she had been called by the White House—apparently by Bush personally—and was informed that the president was sending Gonzales and White House chief of staff Andy Card to visit her ailing husband.

Suspecting that the White House was going to attempt to get Ashcroft to overrule the decision in his weakened condition, Comey said he had his driver turn on the car's siren and rush to the hospital. He also called his own chief of staff and urged him to get Goldsmith and Philbin to the hospital, too. And Comey called FBI director Robert Mueller, with whom he had consulted closely about the wiretapping program over the previous week, to tell him what was happening.

"I'll meet you at the hospital right now," Mueller told Comey.

When Comey reached the hospital, he and his guards ran up the stairs. They had beaten Card and Gonzales there. Comey entered the darkened room, where Ashcroft's wife was watching over her husband, now in his sixth day of intensive care. Comey said he was "shocked" at seeing Ashcroft's state and tried to get his boss to understand what was happening, despite the heavy pain medication. Unsure if he had succeeded, Comey went back out into the hallway and spoke with Mueller by phone. Mueller assured him he was on his way and then asked to speak to the head of the security force guarding Ashcroft.

"Director Mueller instructed the FBI agents present not to allow me to be removed from the room under any circumstances," Comey recalled.

Comey went back inside and was soon joined by Goldsmith and Philbin. They waited for a few minutes, and then the door opened and Card and Gonzales walked in, the latter carrying an envelope—apparently the order that he wanted Ashcroft to sign certifying the wiretapping program's legality.

Ignoring everyone else in the room, Gonzales asked Ashcroft, "How are you, General?"

"Not well," Ashcroft replied, according to Comey.

Moving quickly to business, Gonzales explained why they were there and what they wanted Ashcroft to approve. Then the patient, Comey recalled, stirred—and told them that he would not give the authorization they wanted.

"He lifted his head off the pillow and in very strong terms expressed his view of the matter, rich in both substance and fact, which stunned me, drawn from the hour-long meeting we'd had a week earlier, and in very strong terms expressed himself, and then laid his head back down on the pillow. He seemed spent, and said to them, 'But that doesn't matter, because I'm not the attorney general,'" Comey recalled.

Ashcroft pointed to Comey then and said, "There is the attorney general."

Without acknowledging Comey, Gonzales and Card turned to leave. "Be well," Card said as they walked out of the room. Moments after they left, Mueller arrived, and Comey angrily told him what had happened. "I thought I had just witnessed an effort to take advantage of a very sick man, who did not have the powers of the attorney general because they had been transferred to me," Comey later recalled.

Then an FBI agent came up to them and said that there was a call for Comey at a command center that had been set up next door to Ashcroft's room in the otherwise empty hallway. It was Card.

Comey took the call. The two had an angry exchange. Card ordered Comey to report immediately to the White House. Comey replied, "After what I just witnessed, I will not meet with you without a witness, and I intend that witness to be the solicitor general of the United States"—the No. 3 official at the Justice Department.

At that moment, the solicitor general of the United States, Ted Olson, was at a dinner party in Washington. When he heard what Comey had to say, he immediately left the dinner and headed for the Justice Department. Gathering in a conference room, Comey, Olson, Goldsmith, Philbin, and senior staff from both Comey's and Ashcroft's offices went over what was happening. Everyone, Comey said, seemed to feel the same way. "I felt like we were a team, we all understood what was going on and we were trying to do what was best for the country and the Department of Justice," he recalled. "But it was a very hard night."

At 11 p.m., Comey and Olson left the Justice Department and drove up Pennsylvania Avenue to the White House, where they entered the West Wing. Card would not allow Olson to enter his office, so Comey relented and went in alone. Calmer now, they argued for a few minutes, and then Gonzales walked in, bringing Olson with him, and the four continued to argue. By now, Card knew that it was possible that the Justice Department was threatening a cataclysmic response — mass resignations of the entire leadership team along with their top aides. He urged Comey to reconsider. But Comey again refused to back down, and the meeting ended.

The next day, Thursday, March 11, was the deadline for the program to be reauthorized. That was also the day that terrorists bombed commuter trains in Madrid, killing several hundred people. Bush decided to sign the order renewing the program, even though his own Justice Department was telling him it was illegal. Despite the drama of the Madrid bombing, Comey wrote a letter of resignation, intending to resign the next day.

"I believed that I couldn't stay if the administration was going to engage in conduct that the Department of Justice had said had no legal basis," Comey later explained to Congress. "I just simply couldn't stay."

Comey told Congress that from his conversations with other Justice Department officials, he believed many of them were prepared to resign with him — including FBI director Mueller, Comey's chief of staff, Chuck Rosenberg, Ashcroft's chief of staff, David Ayers, and Ashcroft himself.

"Mr. Ashcroft's chief of staff asked me something that meant a great deal to him, and that is that I not resign until Mr. Ashcroft was well enough to resign with me," Comey recounted. "He was very concerned that Mr. Ashcroft was not well enough to understand fully what was going on. And he begged me to wait until — this was Thursday that I was making this decision — to wait until Monday to give him the weekend to get oriented enough so that I wouldn't leave him behind, was his concern."

Comey agreed to wait until after the weekend so they could all leave together. But on the morning of Friday, March 12, Comey and Mueller went to the Oval Office for the daily Justice Department counterterrorism briefing. As they were leaving, Bush called Comey back to speak one-on-one for fifteen minutes in his study, the details of which Comey would not divulge to Congress. Then Bush asked Mueller to come in for another private conversation. And Mueller emerged and told Comey that at the end of his conversation, "we had the president's direction to do what we believed, what the Justice Department believed was necessary to put this matter on a footing where we could certify to its legality."

Comey, Goldsmith, and their colleagues spent the next several weeks making a series of undisclosed changes to the warrantless surveillance program—during which time the original program continued to operate, even though the president had been told it was illegal.

The changes that satisfied Ashcroft, Comey, Goldsmith, Mueller, and the rest of the rebels that the program now looked lawful enough that they no longer felt the need to resign have not been made public. But in mid-2007, after Comey's testimony about the dramatic events of March 2004, outside specialists in national security speculated that the program's scope may have been narrowed by imposing greater controls on whose communications the government could monitor without a warrant. One theory was that the revised program may have focused, for the first time, only on suspected Al Qaeda phone calls rather than on potentially "terrorist" calls generally, and that the legal justification for the program may have been rewritten so that it relied not just on the president's inherent powers as commander in chief, but also on Congress's authorization to use military force against Al Qaeda after 9/11.[30]

But in any case, because there was still no judge to independently review the military's decisions about which lines to monitor, the compromise was unenforceable. And most legal specialists agree that no changes, short of going back to warrants, could have brought the surveillance program into compliance with the FISA law—a pressing question that would, after the program's existence was later revealed, come before a federal judge.

4.

On April 28, 2004, Deputy Solicitor General Paul Clement came before the Supreme Court in the case of *Hamdi v. Rumsfeld* and urged the justices not to get the courts involved in any of the cases of the prisoners the Bush-Cheney administration was holding without trial as "enemy combatants." As the oral arguments unfolded, several of the justices wanted to know whether the Bush-Cheney administration considered itself bound to obey the Convention Against Torture when interrogating the detainees. Clement assured them that the administration would never allow interrogators to mistreat prisoners. "The United States is signatory to conventions that prohibit torture and that sort of thing, and the United States is going to honor its treaty obligations," Clement said, adding, "I wouldn't want there to be any misunderstanding about this. It's also the judgment of those involved in this process that the last thing you want to do is torture somebody or try to do something along those lines."[31]

That very evening, any Supreme Court justice who happened to tune in to *60 Minutes II* saw the first leaked images of U.S. troops graphically mistreating and sexually humiliating Iraqi prisoners at Abu Ghraib. Photographs depicted American guards leering and grinning as they forced naked detainees to simulate sex acts, beat them, piled them into a pyramid, put one on a leash, attached wires to a man in a pointed hood, menaced prisoners with vicious dogs, and subjected them to other abusive treatment. In one photograph, a prisoner lay dead, his corpse packed in ice.

Congress, the American public, and the world erupted. In the resulting tumult, several parts of the Bush-Cheney administration's legal strategy would be shaken loose from behind the veil of secrecy that had cloaked the executive branch.

On May 12, 2004, navy general counsel Mora was watching congressional hearings about the exploding Abu Ghraib torture scandal in Iraq on C-SPAN, when a witness made reference to the existence of a "Working Group Report on Detainee Interrogations in the Global War on Terrorism." Amazed, Mora made some calls and learned that it was true: The report had been secretly completed, and its legal conclusions had become the operational basis for military interrogations. This fact had been concealed from him, the JAGs, and other dissidents who had rejected Yoo's legal reasoning back in the winter of 2003. The revelation disgusted Mora, who later said that it intensified a "cooling" between him and Haynes, the Pentagon general counsel. (Mora would resign the following year.)

Mora learned another thing. Major General Geoffrey Miller, the commander of the Guantánamo prison, had been briefed about the contents of the working group report, including Yoo's legal analysis about torture laws, in the spring of 2003.[32] On August 29, 2003, five months after receiving the briefing and eight months before the notorious photographs of abuse at Abu Ghraib surfaced, Miller flew to Iraq for a ten-day consulting trip. His mission was to help interrogators at Abu Ghraib learn from the techniques developed at Guantánamo so they could get more intelligence about the growing Iraqi insurgency. Among other things, Miller recommended letting interrogators instruct guards about how to treat detainees in between questioning sessions. Major General Antonio Taguba, who investigated the Abu Ghraib scandal for the Pentagon, determined that Miller's recommendations had significantly contributed to the complete breakdown of discipline at the prison: "Interrogators actively requested that MP guards set physical and mental conditions for favorable interrogation of witnesses."[33] Critics charged that Miller's instructions amounted to asking guards to soften up detainees by treating them roughly so they would be less able to resist their interrogators. The photographed abuses began one month after Miller's consulting trip.

Miller would later reject the idea that his advice could have resulted in the extreme abuses that had been photographed at Abu Ghraib. In the same way, the Bush-Cheney administration condemned the torture and insisted that it had never authorized it.[34] This official line came under a cloud when someone leaked the administration's legal team's interrogation memos to several publications. The media organizations put the documents on their websites for the world to read, from the sections saying that Congress "may no more regulate the President's ability to detain and interrogate enemy combatants than it may regulate his ability to direct troop movements on the battlefield," to its extremely narrow definition of "torture." Further outrage ensued. Law professors and human rights groups around the country denounced the legal reasoning and conclusions of the documents as fatally flawed. As the clamor grew, Goldsmith decided to formally withdraw the memos, apparently repudiating the government's own legal findings—an extraordinary step in the midst of a war.

On June 22, 2004, Goldsmith, Comey, and Philbin held a briefing for reporters at the Justice Department to explain the decision.[35] Taking the lead, Comey said that the statements about potential defenses for torture charges and a commander in chief's power to bypass torture laws were nothing more than "broad academic theories," and he asserted that the theories had never been relied upon for an actual policy. But in any case, he also said, the August 2002 opinion was "under review and will be

replaced with analysis limited to the legality of actual Al Qaeda interrogation practices and the torture statute and other applicable laws."[36]

Goldsmith's decision to yank the interrogation memos caused a final
burst of apoplexy among the hard-liners on the Bush-Cheney legal team. As
Yoo later wrote in his memoir: "I thought this a terrible precedent. It showed
that Justice Department judgments on the law had become just one more political target open to partisan attack and political negotiations. The implication was that if one put enough pressure on the Justice Department it, like
any other part of the government, would bend. It also suggested to me that
the leadership in the Justice Department that had replaced the team there
on 9/11 was too worried about the public perceptions of its work."[37]

The rejection of the CIA interrogation memo after Abu Ghraib would
be Goldsmith's final move in his extraordinary but largely hidden struggle to bring the executive branch back within a traditional understanding
of the rule of law. The fierce bureaucratic war with Addington had required unrelenting long hours at the office at a time when he had young
children at home. It was also clear that Goldsmith's decision to stand up
to the White House had come at a price: There was no chance that he
would ever be made a federal appeals court judge, the reward the Bush-
Cheney White House had paid to his more of a "team player" predecessor
at the Office of Legal Counsel, Jay Bybee. But that spring, the Harvard
Law School faculty, seeking a conservative to diversify its roster of liberal-
leaning international law scholars, had voted to offer Goldsmith a tenured
position as a professor. Goldsmith decided to get out. On June 17,
2004 — five days before the interrogation memo press conference — the
Justice Department put out a press release announcing that Goldsmith
had decided to resign at the end of July to return to academia.

Ironically, because his stand against the White House's more extreme
vision was then largely unknown to the public, Goldsmith would find
himself facing something of a hostile workplace all over again when he arrived in Cambridge. Just over a month into the fall semester, the *Washington Post* reported the existence of a secret Office of Legal Counsel memo
about Iraqi detainees. Goldsmith had signed the memo on March 19,
2004 — just one week after the showdown in Ashcroft's hospital room
over the surveillance program, though that incident was not yet known to
the public. The memo said it was lawful for the CIA to temporarily take
Iraqi prisoners out of Iraq for interrogation, although it also said that any
such prisoners would retain a full right to humane treatment, no matter

where they were held.[38] Some international law specialists argued that any such deportation would violate the Geneva Conventions, and several liberal law scholars used the news to publicly question their new colleague's fitness to teach at Harvard. "I believe that the faculty was seriously at fault for not inquiring more deeply, prior to making this appointment, into any role Jack Goldsmith may have played in providing legal advice facilitating and justifying torture," Harvard public interest law professor Elizabeth Bartholet told the *Boston Globe*.[39]

It would take years before the full story of Jack Goldsmith would be revealed, showing just how mistaken such sentiments were.

5.

On June 28, 2004, just four days after Goldsmith and Comey called the press conference to announce that they were scrapping Yoo's interrogation memos in light of the Abu Ghraib controversy, the Supreme Court handed down its first major rulings about presidential power in the war on terrorism.

First, by a 6–3 vote, the justices decided that U.S. courts had jurisdiction to hear lawsuits filed on behalf of the accused enemy combatants being held at Guantánamo. This decision was hailed in the popular media as a rebuke to the Bush-Cheney administration, which had urged the justices not to intervene with the commander in chief's decisions in the midst of a war.

But, as the White House hastened to point out, the decision said nothing about what rights the detainees might get to invoke once they got into court. The administration adopted the position that they had no rights at all—that technically they could file lawsuits, but that any lawsuit would have to be dismissed for lack of anything to talk about. That stance set up years of further litigation, preventing the June 2004 ruling from resulting in tangible results for most of the prisoners. Later, as the lawsuits dragged on, the White House would persuade Congress to pass a law stripping courts of jurisdiction over Guantánamo lawsuits, effectively rolling back the adverse decision.

The other major decisions handed down on June 28, 2004, concerned the U.S. citizens who were being held without trial as enemy combatants. Because Yaser Hamdi and Jose Padilla were American citizens and imprisoned on U.S. soil, there was never any doubt that courts had jurisdiction over them. But the administration argued that it could imprison both men, without a trial or even access to a lawyer, for the duration of the open-ended war on terrorism. (After the Supreme Court agreed to hear their cases, the administration, however, abruptly declared that their interrogations had reached a point at which it was now safe to grant both prisoners their first limited access to an attorney—all while insisting that the government was not legally required to do so before it was ready.)

Here, the court delivered a mixed message. It made no decision in the case of Padilla, who had been arrested at the airport in Chicago. Instead, it ruled 5–4 that his case should have been brought in a different court district, using the technicality to kick the case back down without ruling on its merits.

As for Hamdi, who had been detained on the battlefield in Afghanistan, the court delivered a fractured and confusing set of opinions. (One surprise: Justice Antonin Scalia, who otherwise almost always supports executive power claims, wrote a dissent declaring Hamdi to be either charged with a crime or freed, since Congress had not suspended habeas corpus.) But the bottom line was that a majority of the justices said that the president did have the wartime authority to hold Hamdi without charges as an enemy combatant, even though he was a U.S. citizen. There was no need to decide whether the commander in chief's power to do so was "inherent," because Congress, via the war resolution of September 14, 2001, had voted to authorize the president to use all "necessary and appropriate" military force against Al Qaeda. Invoking "long-standing law-of-war principles," the court ruled that "detention to prevent a combatant's return to the battlefield is a fundamental incident of waging war."[40]

This presidential power was not, however, absolute: Hamdi's father had sworn that his son was a missionary, not a terrorist, and if that turned out to be true, then the president would have to let Hamdi go. The court ruled that while Hamdi was not entitled to a full trial, he should get some kind of hearing at which he could challenge the factual basis of his detention before a "neutral decision-maker." In this part of the main opinion, Justice Sandra Day O'Connor famously wrote, "It is during our most challenging and uncertain moments that our Nation's commitment to due process is most severely tested; and it is in those times that we must preserve our commitment at home to the principles for which we fight abroad. . . . We have long since made clear that a state of war is not a blank check for the President when it comes to the rights of the Nation's citizens."

The media largely focused on the ways in which the rulings were a setback for the Bush-Cheney administration. The court had intervened in wartime after the administration had asked it to stay out. The justices had extended court jurisdiction to Guantánamo after the administration had urged it to stay away. And they had required "enemy combatants" to get hearings after the administration had declared that its military judgments should not be second-guessed.

Nonetheless, the Bush-Cheney administration was generally pleased with the ruling in the Hamdi case. O'Connor had not specified that the hearings had to be before a civilian court, so the Pentagon swiftly designed its own quickie hearings before a panel of military officers. The prisoners would not be given a lawyer or the right to see the evidence for themselves if it was classified. These panels, the administration decided, were enough to satisfy the ruling. And the administration's legal team noted with quiet satisfaction that, so long as some kind of minimal hearing was involved, the Supreme Court had just signed off on giving presidents the wartime power to hold a U.S. citizen without charges or a trial—forever. "The Justice Department is pleased that the U.S. Supreme Court today upheld the authority of the president as commander in chief of the armed forces to detain enemy combatants, including U.S. citizens," said Mark Corallo, a department spokesman. "This power, which was contested by lawyers representing individuals captured in the war on terror, is one of the most essential authorities the U.S. Constitution grants the president to defend America from our enemies."[41]

## 6.

On November 2, 2004, Bush and Cheney won a second term in office. Six days later, a federal district judge in New York City handed down a ruling that seemed to sharply repudiate the legal theories the administration had spent its first four years carefully constructing.

The case involved a thirty-four-year-old Yemeni man named Salim Ahmed Hamdan, who was captured in Afghanistan in November 2001 and taken to Guantánamo. Hamdan admitted that he had worked on Osama bin Laden's farm in Kandahar before 9/11, serving as the Al Qaeda leader's personal driver for $200 a month. But the Guantánamo prisoner, who had only a fourth-grade education, insisted that he was only a laborer and not a terrorist. The Bush-Cheney administration accused Hamdan of being a full member of Al Qaeda and decided to make him one of the first detainees who would be tried before a military commission for conspiracy to commit acts of terrorism.

When Flanigan and Addington had hastily written up the military commission order in early November 2001, they had expected the tribunals to quickly start churning through cases and handing out sentences. To that end, the administration had crafted rules that would make it easy for prosecutors to win cases: Defendants had no right to see the evidence against them and no right to appeal any convictions in independent courts.

But the vision of swift justice had not materialized. Bush's new rules meant a new bureaucratic system was required. Endless delays ensued as the Pentagon tried to build a system of trial procedures from scratch, and as prosecutions took a backseat to interrogations. Two years passed before anyone was charged before the commission.

Then, when the process finally started moving forward in August 2004, a new roadblock appeared: The military defense lawyers appointed to represent the detainees took their assigned roles more seriously than anyone had expected. Hamdan's appointed defense lawyer, Lieutenant Commander Charles Swift, enlisted the help of a Georgetown University law professor, Neal Katyal, and together they filed a federal lawsuit seeking to have the military tribunal shut down. They argued that President Bush lacked the power to set up military commissions without explicit authorization from Congress, and that Bush lacked the power to declare that the Geneva Conventions did not apply to prisoners captured in the conflict in the Afghanistan war.

On November 8, 2004, a federal district judge in Washington, James Robertson, agreed with Swift and Katyal. Rejecting the administration's contention that the Geneva Conventions did not apply to Hamdan, he ruled that the military commission was illegal. "The government has asserted a position starkly different from the positions and behavior of the United States in previous conflicts, one that can only weaken the United States' own ability to demand application of the Geneva Conventions to Americans captured during armed conflicts abroad," wrote Robertson, a 1994 Clinton appointee.

News of Robertson's decision quickly reached Guantánamo, thirteen hundred miles away. That same day, in a retrofitted courtroom inside an old airfield control tower on a hill in the middle of the base, the commission was in the midst of a hearing on pretrial motions in Hamdan's case when it got the word. A marine in full battle dress brought a note to the presiding officer, Colonel Peter Brownback, as he sat at a dark-paneled wooden dais before the insignias of each military service. Brownback abruptly gaveled the hearing closed, declaring an "indefinite recess" for the three-colonel tribunal panel.[42]

Over the next eight months, the courtroom would sit empty while the Bush-Cheney administration appealed the ruling to the U.S. Court of Appeals for the District of Columbia. One of the three appeals court judges on the panel that would consider the case was a recent Bush appointee named John G. Roberts Jr.

### 7.

After Jack Goldsmith resigned from the Justice Department in the summer of 2004, Ashcroft installed his own counselor, a former FBI chief of staff named Daniel Levin, as the acting head of the Office of Legal Counsel. Levin's main task was to personally draft a replacement for Yoo's interrogation memo. A fierce new battle ensued over how far the replacement would go in repudiating the old memo's legal conclusions—and, by extension, how far it would go in implying that what the CIA had been doing for the past year and a half had been illegal.

Completed on December 30, 2004, the replacement interrogation memo was written to be released to the public, and it was immediately posted on the Justice Department's website. The advisory opinion adopted a slightly less restrictive definition of what level of pain would amount to torture, and it did not offer potential legal defenses to help officials who might be prosecuted for violating anti-torture laws. The new memo said nothing about whether the commander in chief could override interrogation laws—neither endorsing that view nor repudiating it—and, crucially, it contained a footnote declaring that everything the CIA and military had been doing under the old memo was still legal.[43] Largely overlooked, this footnote represented a bureaucratic triumph by Cheney and Addington. As Yoo pointed out in his memoir: "Though it criticized our earlier work, the 2004 opinion included a footnote to say that all interrogation methods that earlier opinions had found legal *were still legal*. In other words, the differences in the opinions were for appearances' sake. In the real world of interrogation policy nothing had changed. The new opinion just reread the statute to deliberately blur the interpretation of torture as a short-term political maneuver in response to public criticism."[44]

The rebels had lost, and soon few remained in positions of government power. Some parts of the great purge of internal dissidents left voluntarily; others were pushed after pointedly being denied promotions.

On June 24, 2004, a week after Jack Goldsmith's resignation was announced, solicitor general Ted Olson said that he, too, would step down that summer. Olson had been a towering figure in the conservative legal community since the Reagan administration. He would forever be associated with the Unitary Executive Theory as the plaintiff in the 1988 independent-counsel case, and he had spent the last several years defending the White House's agenda—including its war on terrorism policies—before the Supreme Court. But in March 2004, on the night of the Ashcroft hospital room showdown over the surveillance program, Olson had stood with Comey, accompanying him to the White House for the late-night fight with Card and Gonzales. (Comey did not list Olson, however, as one of the top officials who was prepared to resign over the incident.) Although Olson's role in the surveillance fight would not be revealed for another three years, there were hints that Olson had grown somewhat disillusioned with the Bush-Cheney legal team hard-liners. The *Washington Post* reported that Olson's departure did not surprise department insiders, citing an unnamed Justice official as saying that Olson was known to be "unhappy that he was not informed about controversial memos authored by the Office of Legal Counsel on the use of harsh interrogation methods on detainees overseas."[45]

John Ashcroft, who had quietly battled with the White House for control of the legal team from the start and who agreed with Goldsmith and Comey in March 2004 that the surveillance program was illegal, would also not be a part of the Bush-Cheney second term. Days after Bush won reelection in November 2004, Ashcroft announced his resignation. He would be replaced as attorney general by the very same man whom he had repudiated from his hospital bed for wanting to violate the rule of law: Alberto Gonzales. Once criticized by liberals, civil libertarians, and limited-government conservatives who saw him as virtually personifying the authoritarian impulses of the Bush-Cheney administration, Ashcroft would see his image somewhat rehabilitated among his former critics once the fuller story of his record became public in Comey's May 2007 testimony. The out-of-power Ashcroft kept his silence in the days following

Comey's disclosures but let his former deputy's account stand. And because Ashcroft could never be credibly accused of being weak on counterterrorism, the disclosure reverberated. As David Keene, the longtime national chairman of the American Conservative Union and a conservative critic of the administration's legal theories, said, "The importance of what has now come out about Ashcroft is that it undermines the continuing attempt to label as 'soft on terror' anyone who disagrees with the administration and says there ought to be constitutional guarantees. Ashcroft makes that impossible, and that is important."[46]

Patrick Philbin, who had written John Yoo–esque legal memos about military commissions and Guantánamo for the Office of Legal Counsel in 2001 but joined Goldsmith in hitting the brakes on the most extreme claims in 2003–2004, had been in line to become the principal deputy solicitor general after Paul Clement moved up to replace Olson as the new solicitor general. Gonzales, now the attorney general, favored giving Philbin the job even after he joined the rebellion over the lawfulness of the warrantless surveillance program. But Addington and Cheney opposed his promotion. Comey later told Congress that "the vice president's office blocked that appointment," sending word to Gonzales at his new office in the Justice Department that "the vice president would oppose" Philbin's promotion if Gonzales tried to pursue it.[47] Gonzales didn't. Philbin left government service to join a Washington law firm in 2005.

Daniel Levin had hoped he would be nominated permanent head of the Office of Legal Counsel in 2005 after he completed the new interrogation memo. But in his previous job as Ashcroft's counselor, he, too, had stood with those who were prepared to resign over the surveillance program in March 2004, according to Comey. And Levin had authored the replacement interrogation memo that, even though it included the critical footnote saying that the CIA had never done anything illegal, failed to fully embrace the Yoo-Addington theory of commander-in-chief powers. Levin, too, didn't get the job.* Levin would spend a brief period as legal

---

*The Office of Legal Counsel would go for years without a confirmed replacement for Goldsmith. In June 2005, nearly a year after Goldsmith left, President Bush nominated the attorney Goldsmith had hired to be his principal deputy, Steven Bradbury, for the position. Bradbury was a former clerk to Supreme Court justice Clarence Thomas, but he had no special expertise in national security legal issues. By the summer of 2007, the Senate had not confirmed Bradbury, who remained the office's acting head only and therefore had far less clout or independent standing than Goldsmith had wielded.

adviser to the National Security Council, then quit in 2005 to join a Washington law firm. It would later emerge that Gonzales's chief of staff, Kyle Sampson, briefly considered making Levin a replacement U.S. attorney for the northern district of California in early 2006, but ultimately Levin wouldn't get that job, either.

In April 2005, Jim Comey, who had embraced Goldsmith's rejection of the interrogation and warrantless surveillance policies and made Goldsmith's fight his own, would announce that he, too, was leaving government.[48] Four months later, on the eve of his departure to become the general counsel of Lockheed Martin, the outgoing deputy attorney general would deliver a farewell address in the Great Hall of the Justice Department. During the speech to his colleagues, Comey seemed to make a cryptic reference to the fights over the warrantless surveillance and torture issues that he had fought alongside Goldsmith and the other non–team players. Comey said that he had dealt with a few issues that, "although of consequence almost beyond my imagination, were invisible because the subject matter demanded it."

In such disputes, Comey would add, he had worked alongside several people whose loyalty "to the law . . . would shock people who are cynical about Washington." These people, he said, "came to my office, or my home, or called my cell phone late at night, to quietly tell me when I was about to make a mistake; they were the people committed to getting it right—and to doing the right thing—whatever the price. These people know who they are. Some of them did pay a price for their commitment to [do] right, but they wouldn't have it any other way."[49]

He was not referring to those still on the government payroll.[50]

## 8.

On October 9, 2004, the Bush-Cheney administration had deported Hamdi back to Saudi Arabia rather than giving him the hearing that the Supreme Court said he was entitled to receive if the president wanted to keep holding him as an enemy combatant. Hamdi's release meant that a prisoner who the White House had once sworn was too dangerous to be allowed access to a lawyer was now going free—just like hundreds of prisoners from Guantánamo who were held without trial for years and then quietly released. Critics said that the administration's legal strategy had been cynical: They appeared to have inflated the danger posed by

Hamdi in order to get a favorable precedent and then let him go once that precedent was in hand.

What happened next in the Padilla case added to such suspicions.

On September 9, 2005, the Fourth Circuit Court of Appeals in Richmond, Virginia, ruled that the commander in chief could hold an American arrested on U.S. soil as an enemy combatant, just like Americans captured on a foreign battlefield. The author of the ruling was Judge J. Michael Luttig, who had been one of the heads of the Office of Legal Counsel in the Bush-Quayle administration and who was often mentioned as a potential Bush Supreme Court nominee. "We can discern no difference in principle between Hamdi and Padilla," Luttig wrote, adding that the president's "powers include the power to detain identified and committed enemies such as Padilla, who associated with al Qaeda and the Taliban regime, who took up arms against this Nation in its war against these enemies, and who entered the United States for the avowed purpose of further prosecuting that war by attacking American citizens and targets on our own soil."[51]

Padilla's lawyers again appealed to the Supreme Court. But shortly before the justices were to decide whether they should take up the case, the Bush-Cheney administration suddenly announced that it was through holding Padilla as an enemy combatant and was ready to prosecute him in civilian court. When the administration released its criminal indictment against Padilla, it said nothing about a dirty bomb or a plot to blow up buildings using a natural gas line. Nor did it allege that Padilla had returned to the United States for the purpose of carrying out domestic terrorist attacks, as the government had sworn to the Fourth Circuit. Instead, the administration said that it had good evidence that Padilla had conspired to provide material support to terrorists operating overseas, such as in the breakaway Russian province of Chechnya.

The disconnect between what the appeals court had been told about Padilla and his far less alarming indictment incensed Luttig. In an extraordinary opinion issued December 21, 2005, Luttig — one of the most conservative and executive power–friendly judges on the federal bench — accused the Bush-Cheney administration of manipulating the judicial process to make sure that the Supreme Court would have no opportunity to evaluate the precedent Luttig himself had just written. The Padilla indictment, he said, raised serious questions about the credibility of the government's statements on which the judge had relied when crafting that precedent, and left "the impression that Padilla may have been held for these years, even if justifiably, by mistake."[52]

Hoping to prevent the case from being rendered moot before the Supreme Court could review and possibly reverse the now awkward precedent, Luttig and his colleagues refused to allow the government to transfer Padilla from military to civilian custody. It was a questionably bold gesture—Padilla himself wanted out of the military brig, and the government now was willing to let him go—and the Supreme Court quickly overruled them, allowing Padilla to be transferred to a civilian prison. The Court then dismissed Padilla's appeal as moot because he was no longer being held as an enemy combatant. Just as Luttig had feared, the maneuver ensured that his precedent—written on the assumption that the administration was telling the truth when it said it had good evidence that Padilla was plotting attacks on U.S. soil—was left intact.*

Luttig's ultimate refusal to go along with the presidential power maximalists doomed his prospects of being picked by the Bush-Cheney legal team for the Supreme Court. Shortly after his act of rebellion, Luttig resigned from his life-tenured appeals court seat and became the general counsel of Boeing.

## 9.

On December 20, 2005, as Judge Luttig was putting his finishing touches on the quixotic order refusing to transfer Padilla from military custody to the criminal justice system, Cheney gave a rare and extraordinary

---

*In a different case in June 2007, a three-judge panel on the Fourth Circuit would rule 2–1 that Bush lacked the power to hold civilians inside the United States as enemy combatants. The panel did not quarrel with the outcome of the Padilla case but held that Ali al-Marri, a citizen of Qatar being held as an enemy combatant on U.S. soil, was different from Padilla and had to be charged with a crime, held as a material witness to a grand jury investigation, or released. Marri was a computer science graduate student in Illinois who had been arrested in December 2001 by civilian authorities who accused him of credit-card fraud. On the eve of his trial, in June 2003, Bush had declared Marri to be an enemy combatant and had him transferred to a military brig. The administration said Marri had been sent as a sleeper agent by Al Qaeda to explore ways of disrupting the nation's financial system. Following the June 2007 ruling, the Bush administration asked the full appeals court to reverse the panel's decision. The two judges in the majority were Clinton appointees, while the dissent was a Bush appointee.

press conference. Although Cheney rarely spoke to reporters, he invited a group of journalists traveling with his entourage during a Middle East trip to have a conversation. Just four days earlier, the *New York Times* had published its story revealing the existence of the National Security Agency's warrantless surveillance program. The revelation had caused an immediate uproar, derailing a vote in Congress to reauthorize provisions of the USA Patriot Act that were set to expire. Several prominent Republicans had joined with the usual critics of the administration to question the legality of the program, which on its face violated the Foreign Intelligence Surveillance Act of 1978. Now that the program was in the open, Cheney was eager to explain why the critics were all wrong. Laying down his belief in a "strong, robust executive authority," Cheney explained to the reporters that authorizing the military to ignore the warrant law was "totally appropriate and consistent with the constitutional authority of the president."[53]

Cheney also elaborated at length about how the laws that Congress had enacted after Watergate and Vietnam had unconstitutionally "served to erode the authority, I think, the president needs to be effective, especially in a national security area." One of the post-Watergate laws was the warrant law, and Cheney made clear that he believed it was a good thing that the president had shown that the White House could flout it. And Cheney indicated that he hoped to establish further precedents for the expansion of presidential authority. Listing other statutory constraints on presidential power, such as the War Powers Resolution of 1973 and the anti-impoundment law of 1974, Cheney said they, too, "will be tested at some point." Cheney also brought up his nearly forgotten report from the 1987 Iran-Contra investigation, pointing out that in the minority views section lay a "robust view of the president's prerogatives" when it came to national security. (The following month, in January 2006, the Department of Justice would release a forty-two-page memo explaining that the president's "inherent" powers as commander in chief gave him the right to ignore the warrant law.[54] The forty-two-page memo echoed the arguments of Cheney's Iran-Contra report: The commander in chief is the "sole organ" of the country when it comes to foreign affairs and national security, it said, so Congress cannot pass laws that restrict how the president carries out his responsibilities.[55] It also made a separate argument—one Cheney had not made—that Congress had implicitly authorized Bush to bypass laws such as the warrant requirement when it approved the use of military force against Al Qaeda.)

On January 20, 2006, Bush's top political adviser, deputy White House chief of staff Karl Rove, told a meeting of the Republican National Committee that the warrantless-wiretapping controversy could be used to boost Republicans' standings in the polls heading into the 2006 midterm elections. By emphasizing that Bush was willing to use any means necessary to stop terrorism, Rove said, Republicans could reframe the controversy as the simpler question of whether the program's critics were weak on terrorism. "The United States faces a ruthless enemy, and we need a commander in chief and a Congress who understand the nature of the threat and the gravity of the moment America finds itself in," Rove said. "President Bush and the Republican Party do; unfortunately, the same cannot be said for many Democrats." And, referring specifically to the warrantless surveillance program, Rove said, "Let me be as clear as I can be: President Bush believes if Al Qaeda is calling somebody in America, it is in our national security interest to know who they're calling and why. Some important Democrats clearly disagree."[56]

Soon after Rove's speech, Bush launched a blitz of election-style campaigning around the country to build support for the wiretapping program—and his claimed power to bypass laws at his own discretion in the interest of national security. Speaking in Kansas on January 23, 2006, Bush declared before a cheering crowd of military families that he did not need to follow the warrant law because Congress authorized him to use military force against terrorists. "I'm not a lawyer, but I can tell you what it means," Bush said. "It means Congress gave me the authority to use necessary force to protect the American people but it didn't prescribe the tactics. . . . If [terrorism suspects] are making phone calls into the United States, we need to know why, to protect you."[57]

In his State of the Union address of January 31, 2006, Bush further insisted that the warrantless wiretapping program was legal because "previous presidents have used the same constitutional authority I have." He did not mention that all the warrantless wiretaps ordered by previous presidents were put in place *before* court orders were required for investigations involving national security. Since Congress passed the law requiring warrants in 1978, no president but Bush had defied it.[58]

David Cole, a Georgetown University law professor who volunteered to consult with a lawsuit aimed at shutting down the program, called Bush's statement "either intentionally misleading or downright false."[59] And the University of Chicago's Richard Epstein predicted that the Supreme Court would reject Bush's assertions that his wartime powers authorized him to override the law long after the initial emergency receded—if the Court ever got a chance to address the question. "I find every bit of this legal argument disingenuous," Epstein said.

Other conservative luminaries who publicly broke with the White House over its legal claims that month included syndicated columnist George F. Will, who denounced the administration's arguments as both "risible" and a "monarchical doctrine" that was "refuted by the plain text of the Constitution."[60] David Keene, chairman of the American Conservative Union, said the legal powers claimed by the White House could be used to justify anything: "Their argument is extremely dangerous. . . . The American system was set up on the assumption that you can't rely on the good will of people with power."[61] Grover Norquist of Americans for Tax Reform said, "There is no excuse for violating the rule of law."[62] Larry Pratt, executive director of Gun Owners of America, worried that the program created a risk that government surveillance would be used against the political opponents of whoever was in power. "Some liberals think of gun owners as terrorists," he said.[63] In the same way, Paul M. Weyrich of the conservative Free Congress Foundation said that even strong Bush supporters should consider the long-term implications of giving the White House the ability to ignore laws, explaining, "My criteria for judging this stuff is what would a President Hillary do with these same powers."[64] And Bruce Fein, a former Justice Department official under President Reagan, said that those siding with the administration had "a view that would cause the Founding Fathers to weep. The real conservatives are the ones who treasure the original understanding of the Constitution, and clearly this is inconsistent with the separation of powers."[65]

Reading about the revelation in his office a few blocks north of the White House, Brent Scowcroft was particularly troubled. Scowcroft shared many of the same formative experiences as Cheney and was a believer in robust presidential power, and he, too, viewed strong executive authority as a principle of good governance. As the national security adviser to President Ford, Scowcroft, like Cheney, had chafed when Congress imposed new restrictions on the White House after Vietnam and Watergate. In 1990, when Scowcroft reprised his role as national security adviser for the Bush-Quayle administration, he had joined Cheney in urging the first President Bush to launch the Gulf War without congressional permission. When Congress initially proposed the warrant law, Scowcroft urged Ford to oppose it. But because Ford endorsed it and Carter signed it, even Scowcroft said presidents were bound to obey it. "One should push one's position, but not to an excess—not to say that the Constitution, which carefully balances powers, gave to the commander in chief an authority that supersedes all the other powers," he said. "I just think that's fundamentally in error."[66]

The conservative repudiation of the Bush-Cheney legal position was not absolute, however. Several former executive branch lawyers joined the administration in defending the legality of the surveillance program. David Rivkin, a former associate White House counsel in the Bush-Quayle administration, dismissed the doubters as misguided libertarians who failed to understand that the nature of terrorism required treating the home front as a battlefield. "Most of the critics don't really agree that this is war, or if they do, they haven't thought through the implications," Rivkin said. "The rules in war are harsh rules, because the stakes are so high."[67]

Despite its dwindling allies, the Bush-Cheney administration insisted that the warrantless surveillance program would continue. The administration stonewalled when Senate Judiciary Committee chairman Arlen Specter, Republican of Pennsylvania, tried to probe the program's legality, saying it would provide details of the program only in classified briefings to the Senate Intelligence Committee. But the Republican Intelligence Committee chairman, Pat Roberts of Kansas, was not interested in an oversight investigation, and on March 7, 2006, the rest of the Republicans on the Intelligence Committee decided in a 10–8 party-line vote not to look into the program.[68]

The administration also fought a new battle inside the executive branch to quash dissidents. The Justice Department's Office of Professional Responsibility would try to launch an ethics investigation into the program. The internal watchdog office was headed by H. Marshall Jarrett, a former career prosecutor with two decades of experience going after corrupt public officials from both parties, and who had been appointed during the Clinton administration. Jarrett's investigation aimed at probing whether department lawyers such as John Yoo had knowingly signed off on an unreasonable interpretation of the law in order to give legal cover to an illegal program. His investigation ran into a brick wall when the National Security Agency refused to grant the ethics office lawyers the necessary security clearance to learn about the details of the program, even though it had promptly given such clearance to other department prosecutors and FBI agents who were assigned to figure out who leaked the program's existence to the *New York Times*.[69] In later congressional testimony, Alberto Gonzales revealed that Bush had personally made the decision not to grant the security clearances to the ethics investigators.[70]

Frustrated by the inaction of Congress and internal executive branch checks, several civil liberties groups filed a lawsuit trying to get a judge to review the legality of the program. The plaintiffs were a group of scholars, journalists, lawyers, and organizations that frequently communicated with people in the Middle East via telephone lines or e-mail. They argued that the program's existence violated their rights to free speech and to privacy, because people no longer wanted to communicate with them out of fear that their calls and e-mails could be monitored. The administration urged judges to dismiss the case, arguing that state secrets could be disclosed if the lawsuits went forward, and that since no one knew whose calls had been monitored, no particular person or group had standing to sue. One judge after another had agreed to dismiss other attempts to bring such cases. But federal district court judge Anna Diggs Taylor, a 1979 Carter appointee to the Eastern District of Michigan, let the lawsuit go forward, saying that there was enough information about the program, based only on what the Bush-Cheney administration had conceded in public about it, for her to issue a decision.

On August 17, 2006, Taylor ruled that the program illegally trampled on both free speech and privacy rights. "It was never the intent of the Framers to give the president such unfettered control, particularly where his actions blatantly disregard the parameters clearly enumerated in the Bill of Rights," Taylor wrote, ordering the program to be shut down immediately and for the government to start restricting itself to wiretapping only with a judge's approval again.[71]

But the White House refused to comply with the ruling, insisting that the program was both legal and a "vital tool" in the war on terrorism. The Bush-Cheney administration quickly filed an appeal, with law professors on both sides of the issue predicting that Taylor's decision was vulnerable to being reversed on legal technicalities, such as the plaintiffs' standing to sue. Pressure would mount sharply ten weeks later, when Democrats won a majority in both chambers of Congress in the 2006 midterm elections. After the new Congress was sworn in on January 2, 2007, Democrats vowed to reopen investigations into the program.

But before they had time to get going, Gonzales sent a surprise letter to the Senate Judiciary Committee on January 17, 2007, informing them that the issue was moot because the National Security Agency would now revert to operating under the supervision of the Foreign Intelligence Surveillance Court. After extensive negotiations, Gonzales said, the administration had convinced one of the judges on the national security court, which issues secret warrants under the Foreign Intelligence Surveillance Act, to issue an "innovative" and "complex" order that would allow the National Security Agency to continue what it had been doing, but now with the approval of the national security court—or at least with the approval of this particular judge. The details of this order were unclear, but administration attorneys used it to intensify an attack on Taylor's ruling. They asked an appeals court to dismiss the case as moot—and to erase the existence of Taylor's opinion from judicial history as a matter of "public interest."[72] But the extra dodge proved to be unnecessary. On July 6, 2007, the appeals court voted 2–1 simply to reverse Taylor and toss out the case. The two GOP-appointed judges in the majority explained that the State Secrets Privilege prevented the courts from learning whether the plaintiffs were personally wiretapped, and thus whether they had standing to sue.

Even as it maneuvered to avoid an official repudiation of its legal theories, the administration continued to insist that it always had been, and always would be, legal for the president to bypass the warrant law—it just wasn't necessary at the moment, thanks to the mysterious court order. "We commenced down this road five years ago because of a belief that we could not do what we felt was necessary to protect this country under FISA," Gonzales told the Senate on January 18, 2007. "That is why the president relied upon his inherent authority under the Constitution. My own judgment is, is that the president has shown maturity and wisdom here in this particular decision. He recognizes that there is a reservoir of inherent power that belongs to every president. You use it only when you have to. In this case, we don't have to [anymore]."[73]

Gonzales's explanation attracted criticism. Jack Balkin, a Yale Law School professor of constitutional law, observed that there is a "remarkable similarity between the Administration's behavior in the Padilla case and its behavior here. . . . Once again, the goal is to prevent a court from stating clearly that the President acted illegally and that his theories of executive power are self-serving hokum." The administration could have gone to Congress at the beginning to adjust the warrant law for the new needs of data collection and surveillance. Instead, it had used the law's perceived deficiencies—which, in light of the new agreement, evidently turned out not to be deficiencies after all—"as an excuse to disregard the law, so that it could make claims of unbridled Presidential authority to ignore FISA," Balkin said.[74]

Despite such criticism from the sidelines, however, the administration's strategy worked. Its assertion that the program had been legal all along would never be repudiated at a level higher than that of a district court judge, and Taylor's order never went into effect.

# 10.

At the start of the Bush-Cheney administration's second term in office, its legal team had systematically locked down a series of advisory opinions and policies that expanded presidential power, freeing the presidency from the burden of obeying statutes and treaties. It had declared and demonstrated that the president has the power to bypass a warrant law, unilaterally create military commission trials, pull out of treaties without consulting Congress, hold foreigners and U.S. citizens alike without charges or trials, and interrogate prisoners beyond the limits of anti-torture rules. It had beaten back internal revolts over the legality of its interrogation program and its still-secret warrantless wiretapping program, then purged itself of dissidents. When the surveillance program was revealed in the coming years, as noted above, the administration would hold the line against an attack on the underlying theory of an executive power to bypass laws, preserving it for future presidents to invoke.

But the story was not complete. The military commission case was still grinding on, and its path would illustrate the importance of the administration's effort to seed the federal judiciary with former executive branch lawyers who agreed with sweeping presidential powers. Fallout from the military commission case would also demonstrate the raw politics of presidential power in Congress.

And even before the military commission case reached its denouement, another issue would become the subject of a major, yearlong battle with Congress over the scope of presidential power. That fight, over a new and tighter ban on torture, proposed by Senator John McCain and hotly opposed by Cheney, would dominate the fifth year of the Bush-Cheney presidency.

# 9

## The Torture Ban

On January 6, 2005, White House Counsel Alberto Gonzales came before the Senate Judiciary Committee to be confirmed as the attorney general of the United States. The hearing on Gonzales's fitness to lead the Department of Justice focused on his participation in crafting the Bush-Cheney administration's position on torture. Sitting stiffly and reading from a prepared statement amid the whirring and clicking of high-speed camera shutters, Gonzales declared that he was committed to "ensuring that the United States government complies with all of its legal obligations as it fights the war on terror, whether those obligations arise from domestic or international law. These obligations include, of course, honoring the Geneva Conventions whenever they apply."[1]

The context for his remarks was the Abu Ghraib abuse scandal, which had come to light the previous spring. After initial expressions of outrage, Congress had been content to let the Pentagon investigate the matter internally. Those Department of Defense investigations put all the blame on a breakdown of discipline among low-ranking soldiers. Eclipsed by the larger drama of the presidential election, the torture issue had receded during the second half of 2004, but now it was returning to the fore. After President Bush narrowly defeated Democratic senator John F. Kerry on November 2, 2004, Attorney General John Ashcroft, as noted earlier, announced that he would not stay on for a second term. Secretary of State Colin Powell, another first-term cabinet member who had clashed with the Cheney faction

209

over such issues as respecting the Geneva Conventions, also said he was leaving. Bush had moved to replace them with White House loyalists who had kept their feet off the brakes during the first-term debates about presidential power. Bush's national security adviser, Condoleezza Rice, would take over State, and Gonzales would take over Justice.

With Republicans in control of the Senate, both nominations were virtually assured of confirmation. But Gonzales's connection to the interrogation controversy provided a belated opportunity for Democrats to bear down on the administration's handling of the Abu Ghraib scandal. Several secret memorandums had leaked to the press showing that Gonzales had been closely involved in crafting the post-9/11 interrogation policy. The most notorious of the secret advisory opinions was the August 1, 2002, memo in which John Yoo had concluded that the infliction of any pain short of that equal to "death, organ failure, or permanent damage resulting in a loss of significant bodily function" was not "torture" for legal purposes, that a variety of legal defenses could be mustered to exonerate a U.S. official who employed harsh interrogation techniques, and that the president, as commander in chief, had the power to authorize interrogators to ignore an anti-torture law. Yoo's memo had been personally commissioned by Gonzales on behalf of the CIA. It was addressed to Gonzales, and it evidently met with his approval, since he had not sent it back to the Office of Legal Counsel to be rewritten.

Seeking to preempt tough questions about its interrogation policy at Gonzales's confirmation hearing to be attorney general, the administration had publicly issued its less sweeping replacement interrogation memo a few days earlier, on December 30, 2004. And in the opening statement at his confirmation hearing one week later, Gonzales distanced himself and the administration from allegations of detainee abuse, characterizing the torture at Abu Ghraib as the rogue actions of a few bad apples, actions that had no connection to official policy.

"Like all of you, I have been deeply troubled and offended by reports of abuse," Gonzales said, still reading from his prepared remarks. "The photos from Abu Ghraib sickened and outraged me and left a stain on our nation's reputation. And the president has made clear that he condemns the conduct and that these activities are inconsistent with his policies. He has also made clear that America stands against and will not tolerate torture under any circumstances. I share his resolve that torture and abuse will not be tolerated by this administration and commit to you today that, if confirmed, I will ensure the Department of Justice aggressively pursues those responsible for such abhorrent actions."

Skeptics observed that Gonzales's words were carefully chosen. He loudly repudiated "torture" but left unanswered whether the administration was still defining "torture" narrowly enough to exclude the infliction of many kinds of cruel and painful techniques. He affirmed a commitment to obeying "the rule of law," leaving unanswered the question of whether he was referring to specific statutes against abuse or a commander in chief's inherent constitutional power to bypass such statutes. He pledged his respect for treaty obligations against the abuse of wartime prisoners but added the crucial qualifier "whenever they apply."

The next day, the Senate Judiciary Committee heard testimony from a panel of expert witnesses who weighed in on Gonzales's suitability to be the nation's top law enforcement officer. Among the most vocal of the critics who testified was Yale Law School dean Harold Koh.

Koh shared many attributes with Yoo. Koh, too, was of South Korean heritage; his parents had emigrated from Korea, although Koh himself was born in Boston. Like Yoo, Koh had worked in the Office of Legal Counsel for a Republican president, having been an attorney-adviser there under the Reagan administration. But Koh had also served as assistant secretary of state for democracy, human rights, and labor in the Clinton administration and was a critic of the Bush-Cheney policies at Guantánamo and elsewhere. Just over a decade earlier at Yale Law School, Koh had been Yoo's law professor and mentor. Yoo took three classes from Koh and worked both as Koh's research assistant and his teaching assistant.[2] The two even cowrote a paper. Now, in his presentation before Congress, Koh did not mention Yoo's name, but he made clear that he thought his former student had lost his way.

"Having worked in both Democratic and Republican administrations, and for more than two years as an attorney in the Office of Legal Counsel itself, I am familiar with how legal opinions like this are sought and drafted," Koh said. "I further sympathize with the tremendous pressures of time and crisis that government lawyers face while drafting such opinions. Nevertheless, in my professional opinion, the August 1, 2002, OLC memorandum is perhaps the most clearly erroneous legal opinion I have ever read."[3]

Koh proceeded to eviscerate his former student's work.[4] Among its other faults, Koh said, the memo "grossly overreads the inherent power of the President" as commander in chief. And, in what the dean characterized as "a stunning failure of lawyerly craft," Yoo's memo did not even mention *Youngstown,* the landmark 1952 Supreme Court decision in the Truman administration's steel seizure case. That precedent had spelled out clear limits on Truman's power to act contrary to the expressed will of Congress, even in a situation that could have an impact on his ability to carry out the Korean War.

Yoo continued to stand by the quality of his work. In his 2006 memoir, *War by Other Means,* he attacked critics who used Gonzales's hearings to "claim that the president cannot act against the wishes of Congress, even in wartime." What Koh failed to understand, Yoo wrote, is that a domestic labor dispute is different from "detention and interrogation policy," and that only the latter "are at the heart of the president's commander-in-chief power to wage war." If the Office of Legal Counsel "were to accept that *Youngstown* controlled the executive branch in war, the President's powers would be crippled," Yoo further explained.[5] Koh was unmoved. *Youngstown,* he noted, was about the president's ability to successfully wage a foreign war, not an ordinary domestic labor dispute. And, Koh said, checks and balances on presidential power do not evaporate just because the president is operating overseas.[6]

The shortcomings of the interrogation memo highlighted a striking characteristic of the administration's legal team. The Bush-Cheney legal team was largely made up of very bright, highly educated people with sterling academic credentials, yet few legal specialists of comparable expertise outside the government believed their legal theories. Nevertheless, the legal team's confidential advisory opinions—memos that were never intended to see the light of day—provided legal cover for the administration to safely proceed with policies that skirted laws and treaties. The memos eliminated the risk that some future Justice Department might try to prosecute an American interrogator: All the defendant need say is that he relied in good faith upon the legal advice provided by the Office of Legal Counsel. And if the OLC's interpretation of the law differed dramatically from the view of the overwhelming majority of independent legal scholars—well, that was just a dispute among academics.

Koh testified that the memo Yoo had written, Bybee had signed, and Gonzales had accepted, raised profound questions about the legal ethics of everyone involved. "If a client asks a lawyer how to break the law and escape liability, the lawyer's ethical duty is to say no. A lawyer has no obligation to aid, support, or justify the commission of an illegal act."[7]

In his memoir, Yoo rejected attacks on his ethics. He said that his only duty was to tell the commander in chief what the legal options were, not to set interrogation policy. "The complaint of the critics was, in essence, that government lawyers should impose specific policies upon the President, following their personal policy views on what the law ought to be," Yoo wrote. ". . . The law does not give us all the answers. The law requires our elected leaders to make policy judgments."[8]

## 2.

Eleven days after Koh's testimony, on January 17, 2005, Gonzales turned in his written answers to follow-up questions from members of the Senate Judiciary Committee. Lurking within them was an explosive new disclosure.

Pressed about the Convention Against Torture, a treaty that President Reagan had signed and that the Senate ratified in 1994, Gonzales revealed for the first time that the administration legal team had secretly concluded that the treaty had force only on domestic soil, where the U.S. Constitution applies.[9] Thus, for noncitizens held overseas, no rules applied.

Legal scholars were nearly universal in condemning the administration's interpretation of the treaty.[10] Judge Abe Sofaer, who negotiated the Convention Against Torture for President Reagan, sent a letter to Congress saying that the Reagan administration never intended the treaty's prohibitions against brutal treatment—including a ban on cruel, inhuman, and degrading treatment that falls short of "torture"—to apply only on U.S. soil. But the Bush-Cheney administration held fast to its position. The old interrogation memos may have been set aside with grand—if quietly ambivalent—flourish the previous month, but here was a new justification to provide legal cover for harsh interrogation policies.

The Bush-Cheney legal team's reinterpretation of the Convention Against Torture was the only real piece of information that came out of Gonzales's confirmation hearings. Democrats complained that the White House counsel had evaded their questions and refused to provide information to which Congress was entitled, but their minority numbers rendered them powerless to do anything about it. On February 3, 2005, the Senate confirmed Gonzales to be attorney general by a vote of 60–36.

But the claim that the torture treaty didn't apply to prisoners overseas was enough to set off one of the most dramatic fights over presidential power of the Bush-Cheney presidency — a fight that would be led by one of the most powerful Republicans in Congress, Senator John McCain of Arizona. A Vietnam War hero, McCain had survived torture himself as a seven-year prisoner of war at the notorious "Hanoi Hilton" prison. McCain was also a member of the Senate Armed Services Committee, where he had been shown classified details of the detainee operations, including searing pictures from Abu Ghraib that never leaked to the public. He was aware of the allegations of abusive treatment of detainees being held at Guantánamo and Bagram Air Base — as well as several open homicide investigations for prisoners who died while in U.S. custody. The Arizona senator had the clout, the image, and the moral authority to push back against the administration, and he made it his mission that year to do so.

### 3.

Whether torture and other coercive interrogation techniques actually work is a separate question from whether the president has the power to authorize the harsh treatment of wartime prisoners in defiance of laws and treaties. But the stakes are so dramatic that it is worth briefly pausing to examine why the military's professional interrogation experts, who after 9/11 were vastly outnumbered by untrained ad hoc interrogators, believed that the coercive interrogation policy unleashed by the Bush-Cheney legal team's theories was incompetent and a terrible mistake. These experts were opposed to harsh interrogations not primarily because they felt such tactics were immoral and illegal. (Very few professional military interrogators are bleeding-heart liberals.) Instead, the skeptics were focused on pragmatic results: extracting useful information from captured jihadists. They knew that there is no scientific evidence that coercive techniques produce information that is better than, or even as good as, the information obtained by other approaches, as the government's own Intelligence Science Board, a panel of experts established in August 2002 to advise the intelligence community, later concluded.[11]

In movies and shows such as Fox television's *24*, Hollywood has fostered a simplistic image of torture: Tough good guys beat up bad guys, and then the bad guys give up valuable information. When torture was debated in the United States after 9/11, this image was largely what sprang to mind among the public. But physical torture of this type is not what the Bush-Cheney administration signed off on. While some interrogations clearly got out of control, the official policy aimed at a far more subtle form of torture, one that left no physical scars on the suspected terrorists.

The techniques the Bush-Cheney administration approved after 9/11 included a range of disorienting and debilitating ordeals, including stripping prisoners naked; subjecting them to prolonged isolation and sleep disruption and deprivation; bombarding cells for long periods with very loud music and grating sounds; leaving bright lights on in a cell twenty-four hours a day; keeping cells stifling hot or freezing cold; shackling prisoners in painful "stress" positions for many hours; exploiting prisoners' phobias by such means as menacing them with fierce dogs; and—in the case of the CIA—water-boarding. Accounts by detainees and former interrogators indicate that interrogators also sometimes pushed detainees' religious buttons, desecrating the Koran in front of them and tormenting them sexually. Typically, several of these techniques were piled atop one another in carefully planned-out sessions that sometimes lasted weeks or even months. The rationale behind this approach was that if detainees were filled with exhaustion, fear, hopelessness, and confusion, then their sources of inner strength—their sense of personal identity, their ability to process what was happening to them, their religious fervor—would erode, and they would stop holding out on providing the critical information they were presumed to be harboring.

This coercive system of interrogation was put into widespread use following the 9/11 terrorist attacks. Eyewitness accounts put it all over—at Guantánamo, in Iraq, in Afghanistan, in CIA prisons, and, according to Jose Padilla's lawyers, in a military brig on U.S. soil. There were clearly hundreds and hundreds of U.S. officials employing these techniques in many contexts simultaneously around the globe. Yet before 9/11, the United States had no large-scale training program for teaching officials to interrogate prisoners in this way. What the nation instead had was a special program that trains troops at potential risk of being captured far behind enemy lines—primarily pilots, who might get shot down, and Special Forces—in how to "Survive, Evade, Resist, and Escape." (The CIA's covert paramilitary agents, many of whom are former Special Forces troops, are also experienced with SERE School for the same reasons.) SERE instructors put trainees through the types of torments described above in order to prepare them to resist brutal interrogations if they are captured by a foreign enemy who does not obey the Geneva Conventions.

After 9/11, there was a sudden widespread need for interrogating detainees, and the president had declared that the Geneva Conventions did not apply to the war on terrorism. In that context, troops and agents who had been through SERE School began inflicting on prisoners the techniques they had experienced in a controlled training setting. And in some cases the military pulled in SERE School instructors—who were not real interrogators with advanced degrees in psychology and real-world experience in questioning prisoners from other cultures, but rather noncommissioned officers taught to portray interrogators in simulated scenarios involving American trainees—and put them to work as real interrogators. In a June 2004 press conference after the Abu Ghraib scandal, for example, General James T. Hill, then the head of the U.S. Southern Command, which oversaw Guantánamo, remarked that prior to January 2002, his operation "never had to deal with this kind of strategic interrogation business." As Guantánamo struggled to begin systematically interrogating hundreds of prisoners, Hill said, officials tapped the "SERE School and developed a list of techniques." Hill added that he had been assured by the Pentagon that such techniques were "legally consistent with our laws."[12]

Professional interrogation experts were aghast at this policy. Because of their expertise, they fully understood something that the Special Forces troops, the SERE instructors, and the top generals and policy makers did not understand: where SERE techniques came from, and what they were really for.

SERE School was a by-product of the Korean War. During the war, Communist forces began producing elaborate propaganda films of American pilots who had been shot down and captured "confessing" to such heinous crimes as deliberately targeting civilians with chemical and biological weapons. The U.S. government knew that the confessions were false and that they had been coerced, but the prisoners of war did not seem to have been physically abused before making the "confessions." After the war, when the pilots were returned, they all told the same story: Chinese interrogators, working with the North Koreans, had put them through a series of sustained torments—the same list described above—until their minds had bent and they had made the false confessions.

This revelation about Communist "brainwashing" techniques had a

In this undated photo, White House chief of staff Dick Cheney speaks with President Gerald Ford in the Oval Office. Ford — and Cheney with him — came to power in the wake of Watergate and the Vietnam War as Congress moved to rein in the "imperial presidency." (GERALD R. FORD PRESIDENTIAL LIBRARY)

Secretary of Defense Cheney and General Colin Powell watch President George H. W. Bush speak at Arlington National Cemetery on November 16, 1990, during the run-up to the Gulf War. Cheney urged Bush to launch the war without getting congressional approval, but Bush rejected Cheney's advice. (DEPARTMENT OF DEFENSE, DEFENSE VISUAL INFORMATION CENTER)

During the terrorist attacks of September 11, 2001, Vice President Cheney and senior staff retreat to the White House bunker. Cheney authorized the military to shoot down any remaining hijacked planes, claiming that he had prior authorization from President George W. Bush to give such an order. The 9/11 Commission, however, found no documentary evidence for the alleged phone call with Bush. (WHITE HOUSE PHOTO BY DAVID BOHRER)

President Bush shakes Vice President Cheney's hand as they are sworn in for a second term on January 20, 2005. During preparations for the second inauguration, Cheney said he believed that the proper power of the presidency was finally being restored. (WHITE HOUSE PHOTO BY PAUL MORSE)

David Addington, a close aide to Cheney since the days of the Iran-Contra investigation, was the dominant leader of the Bush administration's legal team.
(WHITE HOUSE PHOTO BY DAVID BOHRER)

John Yoo, a deputy in the Justice Department's Office of Legal Counsel, wrote secret advisory opinions concluding that neither statutes nor treaties can bind the hands of the commander in chief.
(UNIVERSITY OF CALIFORNIA, BERKELEY, SCHOOL OF LAW, PHOTO BY JIM BLOCK)

Jack Goldsmith, who became the head of the Office of Legal Counsel in the fall of 2003, tried to roll back some of the most aggressive assertions of presidential power, including secret memos claiming that the commander in chief can set aside antitorture laws.
(HARVARD LAW SCHOOL)

The "enemy combatant" policy, under which the president claimed the power to imprison people indefinitely and without a trial or legal rights, began as a way to detain and interrogate foreigners held at Guantánamo without obeying the Geneva Conventions. (DEPARTMENT OF DEFENSE, DEFENSE VISUAL INFORMATION CENTER)

Within months, the enemy combatant policy spread to U.S. citizens arrested and imprisoned on U.S. soil, as in the case of Jose Padilla. (STILL FRAME FROM DEPARTMENT OF DEFENSE VIDEO, ENTERED INTO COURT RECORD, UNITED STATES V. JOSE PADILLA)

President Bush congratulates his former counsel and longtime friend Attorney General Alberto Gonzales after he was sworn in as the nation's top law enforcement official on February 14, 2005. During Gonzales's confirmation, he let slip the previously secret conclusion by the administration's legal team that the commander in chief need not obey the Convention Against Torture overseas. (WHITE HOUSE PHOTO)

President Bush announces on May 8, 2006, the nomination of General Michael Hayden *(right)* to be the new CIA director as the director of National Intelligence, John Negroponte, looks on According to Bush, Hayden — who headed the military's National Security Agency on 9/11 — proposed the program in which the president authorized the NSA to wiretap on U.S. soil without warrants, bypassing a 1978 surveillance law. (WHITE HOUSE PHOTO BY PAUL MORSE)

Using such stresses as sleep disruption and physical exhaustion—techniques adapted from torture-resistance training—American interrogators pressure this hooded and shackled prisoner to provide information about the insurgency. Coercive interrogation techniques were routinely employed after the Bush legal team declared that presidential power trumps the Geneva Conventions and other rules against treating detainees harshly. These previously unpublished photographs were taken in Iraq in the summer of 2003 and provided by a source with firsthand knowledge of the event. (AUTHOR'S FILES)

On December 15, 2005, President Bush invites Republican senators John McCain and John Warner *(left)* to the White House in order to declare that he is wholeheartedly accepting a new no-loopholes torture ban—even though he had earlier threatened to veto it. Fifteen days later, Bush would issue a signing statement claiming the right to bypass the law. (WHITE HOUSE PHOTO BY PAUL MORSE)

President Bush shakes hands with Arlen Specter, the chairman of the Senate Judiciary Committee, after signing the USA Patriot Improvement and Reauthorization bill on March 9, 2006. Hours later, Bush would issue a signing statement declaring that he could ignore oversight provisions in the bill, prompting Specter to ask, "What's the point of having a statute if the president can cherry-pick what he likes and what he doesn't like?" (WHITE HOUSE PHOTO BY KIMBERLEE HEWITT)

President Bush congratulates the future chief justice of the Supreme Court, John Roberts, after announcing Roberts's nomination on July 19, 2005. As a young lawyer in the Reagan administration, Roberts came of age marinating in disputes over executive power from the White House's vantage point. (WHITE HOUSE PHOTO BY ERIC DRAPER)

President Bush listens to future Supreme Court justice Samuel Alito acknowledge his nomination on October 31, 2005. Another former Reagan administration lawyer, Alito gave a speech to the Federalist Society in 2000 affirming his allegiance to the Unitary Executive Theory. (WHITE HOUSE PHOTO BY PAUL MORSE)

series of consequences. In popular culture, it filtered into such movies as 1962's *The Manchurian Candidate*. In the intelligence community, the CIA spent millions studying the techniques to see whether it could make use of them; it concluded in a 1963 interrogation manual that the coercive approach was not very helpful outside the context of producing false propaganda because "under sufficient pressure subjects usually yield but their ability to recall and communicate information accurately is as impaired as the will to resist."[13] (The interrogation manual suggests that it might have one extremely limited application—getting a suspected KGB double agent to admit his identity—but it is silent on the critical question of how a questioner can tell whether the confession is true or false.) And in the military, the revelation prompted the creation, in 1955, of SERE School—a program whose sole purpose was to prepare American troops to resist such treatment so that they never again produced false-propaganda confessions. The program's origins survive in its motto: "Return With Honor."

Almost half a century passed between the establishment of SERE School and 9/11, which prompted the sudden application of SERE techniques as part of a widespread American interrogation program. Over time, a subtle but critical distinction had been lost by all but the true professionals who studied and conducted strategic interrogation for a living. Neither SERE trainers, who run scenarios by following the instructions in basic military manuals, nor their Special Forces trainees understood that the coercive techniques used in the program were designed to make prisoners lose touch with reality so that they will falsely confess to what their captors want to hear, not for extracting accurate and reliable information. "People who defend this say 'we can make them talk,'" said Colonel Steve Kleinman, the former head of the air force's strategic interrogation program. "Yes, but what are they saying? The key is that most of the training is to try to resist the attempts to make you comply and do things such as create propaganda, to make these statements in either written or videotaped form. But to get people to comply, to do what you want them to do, even though it's not the truth—that is a whole different dynamic than getting people to provide accurate, useful intelligence."[14]

Dr. Michael Gelles, the navy's top forensic psychologist, who raised alarms about Guantánamo in December 2002, explained why coercive interrogations are bad policy. Abuse, Gelles said, inevitably introduces false information into the intelligence system because people will say anything to get relief from suffering and fear. Making matters worse, interrogators never know when to stop increasing the pressure because they don't know what their prisoners know and don't know; if a prisoner knows seven things but the interrogator believes he knows ten, then the interrogator will keep pushing until the prisoner has said ten things. And unless the prisoner is killed or locked up for life, eventually he will be released to tell the world what happened to him, undermining America's moral authority. Finally, Gelles said, inflicting pain and humiliation on a prisoner destroys the opportunity to build rapport with him in order to persuade—or trick, browbeat, insult, confront, challenge, or cajole—him into saying what he knows, the technique that professional, trained interrogation experts overwhelmingly prefer.

Gelles said his skepticism about coercive interrogation tactics approved by Pentagon policy makers was quietly supported by many government specialists, including fellow psychologists, intelligence analysts, linguists, and interrogators who have experience extracting information from captured Islamist militants and other enemies. "We do not believe—not just myself, but others who have to remain unnamed—that coercive methods with this adversary are effective," said Gelles. "If the goal is to get 'information,' then using coercive techniques may be effective. But if the goal is to get reliable and accurate information, looking at this adversary, rapport-building is the best approach." Gelles added, "Why would you terrify them with a dog? So they'll tell you anything to get the dog out of the room?"[15]

False confessions only exacerbate things, given how many prisoners are unlikely to be able to offer a true confession. For example, a Red Cross report in 2004 estimated that between 70 percent and 90 percent of military detainees in Iraq had been arrested by mistake in the confusion of the insurgency. That same year, the head of interrogations at Guantánamo said that the majority of the detainees there had no useful information. Hundreds of prisoners there were later released—including three British men who under duress had admitted to being in a video with Osama bin Laden but who were later cleared when the British government determined that they had been in England at the time the video was shot in Afghanistan. One of the three, Shafiq Rasul, later explained why he had falsely confessed: "Because of the previous five or six weeks of being held in isolation and being taken to interrogation for hours on end, short shackled and being treated in that way. I was going out of my mind and didn't know what was going on. I was desperate for it to end and therefore eventually I just gave in and admitted to being in the video."[16]

Perhaps not surprisingly, there is strong evidence that the violent interrogation tactics muddied American intelligence files with bad information. One of the worst examples was a Libyan trainer for Al Qaeda named
Ibn al-Shaykh al-Libbi. His CIA interrogators believed that he might have
knowledge of Al Qaeda involvement with the Iraqi government under
then-dictator Saddam Hussein. Libbi protested that he knew of no Iraq
connection. According to ABC News, Libbi was then subjected to increasingly harsh abuse for several weeks. He finally broke after being water-
boarded and then forced to stand naked in a cold cell all night and doused
regularly with cold water. Seeking to please his interrogators, Libbi told
them what they wanted to hear, admitting that Iraq had offered to train
Al Qaeda operatives in chemical and biological weapons. Libbi's statements became a key basis of the Bush-Cheney administration's claim, in
Secretary of State Colin Powell's prewar United Nations Security Council
presentation, that Iraq was working with Al Qaeda: "Al Qaida continues
to have a deep interest in acquiring weapons of mass destruction," Powell
said. ". . . I can trace the story of a senior terrorist operative telling how
Iraq provided training in these weapons to Al Qaida. Fortunately, this
operative is now detained, and he has told his story."

Libbi later recanted his statements, and the CIA determined that Libbi
"had no knowledge of such training or weapons and fabricated the statements because he was terrified of further harsh treatment,"[17] according
to ABC News.

Another particularly troubling example is the case of Al Qaeda member Abu Zubaydah, the Saudi who was captured in a suspected safe house
in Pakistan in March 2002. Zubaydah was described in public by Bush
the following month as "one of the top operatives plotting and planning
death and destruction on the United States." But, as the investigative
journalist Ron Suskind reported in his book *The One Percent Doctrine*,
CIA analysts came to the conclusion that Zubaydah was little more than
a travel agent for the organization who was kept out of the inner circle
and given no access to secret operational details. And there was a good
reason Zubaydah had not risen higher in the organization, Suskind reported: He was schizophrenic. Zubaydah's diary, seized at the time of his
arrest, was written in the voice of three different people, each with a dis-
tinct personality.

Nonetheless, Zubaydah was water-boarded, beaten, threatened, subjected to mock executions, and bombarded with continuous deafening

noise and harsh lighting. Under such duress, the already mentally ill prisoner said yes over and over again when asked if Al Qaeda was interested in bombing shopping malls, banks, supermarkets, nuclear plants, apartment buildings, and water systems, Suskind reported. After each vague affirmation, the "information" was quickly cabled back to Washington, where it ended up in the president's daily briefing and in FBI warnings that invariably leaked to the media. Many of the breathless and panicked warnings of Al Qaeda plots that marked the Bush-Cheney administration's first term, with its periodic orange alerts that came to nothing, came from Zubaydah's interrogation.[18]

Gelles, Kleinman, and other interrogation experts tried to raise alarms internally about the dangers and ineffectiveness of the SERE-style coercive techniques, but they were ignored and threatened. Civilian decision makers inside the Bush-Cheney administration viewed such criticisms as an attack on its claims of presidential power. And they dismissed the complaints as nothing more than another example of the misguided worries of a "law enforcement" mind-set too focused on gathering evidence that could be used in a civilian courtroom to understand that different rules apply in wartime.

## 4.

On July 24, 2005, John McCain introduced an amendment to the annual bill in which Congress authorizes the Pentagon's work. His amendment was cosponsored by Senate Armed Services Committee chairman John Warner, Republican of Virginia, and Senator Lindsey Graham, Republican of South Carolina and a reservist military lawyer. The amendment made clear that military interrogators could not exceed the limits set out in the Army Field Manual for the treatment of detainees—limits written specifically to comply with the Geneva Conventions—no matter what their superiors, leading up to the commander in chief, might purport to authorize. The amendment also made clear that all U.S. officials—including CIA agents—were prohibited from inflicting not just torture but all forms of "cruel, inhuman, and degrading treatment" on anyone in their custody, no matter where in the world the prisoner was held.

The text of McCain's proposal came to be known as the McCain Amendment or the McCain Torture Ban, and it would be the subject of a fierce wrestling match between the senator and the White House for months to come. Alarmed, Cheney went to Congress to lobby against the measure, meeting privately with Warner and Graham, among others. At Cheney's request, Senate majority leader Bill Frist of Tennessee pulled the Pentagon authorization bill from the floor to prevent the Senate from passing it with McCain's language attached.

The fight stalled for the next two months. Hurricane Katrina's devastation along the Gulf Coast occupied the nation's attention, and Frist kept from the Senate floor any legislation that could become a vehicle for the torture ban amendment. But by October, Frist's hand was forced by the need to pass a military budget. When Frist introduced a $440 billion Defense Department spending bill to the floor, McCain promptly introduced his torture ban as an amendment to that bill as well, reiterating his view that the administration's legal theories were "strange" and could be invoked by enemies in future wars to justify abusing American prisoners of war. "We are Americans, and we hold ourselves to humane standards of treatment of people no matter how evil or terrible they may be," McCain said, adding that the terrorists "don't deserve our sympathy. But this isn't about who they are. This is about who we are. These are the values that distinguish us from our enemies."[19]

By then, more than two dozen retired generals had signed a letter urging Congress to pass the McCain Amendment, including Colin Powell and John Shalikashvili, both former chairmen of the Joint Chiefs of Staff. But the Bush-Cheney administration was adamant that such a law not be passed. On October 5, 2005, White House press secretary Scott McClellan announced that Bush had decided he would use the first veto of his presidency against any bill passed by Congress that contained the torture ban, because "it would limit the president's ability as commander in chief to effectively carry out the war on terrorism."[20] Hours after McClellan's threat, the Senate, in a rare bipartisan rebuke to the White House, voted to approve McCain's amendment 90–9. The majority included forty-six of the chamber's fifty-five Republicans.

The House version of the bill did not contain the McCain Amendment because House GOP leaders, who imposed tighter control over their chamber on behalf of the White House than Frist, had refused to let members vote on it. Thus, a House-Senate conference committee, meeting to iron out differences between the two versions of the military spending bill, would decide whether the new (or newly clarified) torture law would live or die.

Once again, Cheney moved in, personally coming to the Capitol to lobby lawmakers not to pass the legislation. On October 20, he and the CIA director, Porter Goss, met with McCain for forty-five minutes and asked him to support a change that would impose the restrictions on military interrogators but exempt CIA interrogators from any limits when questioning foreign terrorists abroad.[21]

Cheney's proposal to exempt CIA interrogators was startling. Such a statute would for the first time clearly authorize the CIA to engage in abusive interrogations. In effect, it would *legalize* the abuse of detainees in CIA prisons, a matter that had previously been a gray area at best. McCain told Cheney his proposal was completely unacceptable. "I don't see how you could possibly agree to legitimizing an agent of the government engaging in torture," McCain said a few days later. "No amendment at all would be better than that."[22]

The next Tuesday, November 1, 2005, Cheney showed up at the weekly Republican senatorial luncheon in the Mansfield Room in the Capitol and spoke against the McCain Amendment, arguing that harsh interrogations by the CIA against captured Al Qaeda operatives had generated important information and that the president needed to preserve his flexibility in fighting terrorism. McCain rose to rebut Cheney at the closed-door meeting, arguing that the perception that the United States was using torture was damaging its standing with allies around the world.[23]

The next day, the *Washington Post* published an exposé detailing the CIA's use of secret interrogation prisons overseas, including in several new democracies in Eastern Europe where such prisons were illegal under local laws.[24] Continental lawmakers and human rights groups erupted. Even as President Bush repeated his mantra to reporters on a trip to South America that the United States did not "torture," Colin Powell's former chief of staff, Lawrence Wilkerson, went on CNN and declared, "There's no question in my mind where the philosophical guidance and the flexibility in order to do so [torture prisoners] originated — in the vice president of the United States' office."[25]

Desperate to bring the issue down, the White House sent national security adviser Stephen Hadley in Cheney's place to negotiate with McCain. McCain didn't budge. Then, in mid-December, the final piece of the puzzle seemed to fall into place: Republican leaders in the House of Representatives finally allowed a vote on the torture ban. It passed overwhelmingly — 308 to 122, with 107 Republicans voting against the

White House. The lopsided and bipartisan vote demonstrated that there was more than two-thirds support for the torture ban in both chambers—enough to override the threatened presidential veto.

The next day, on December 15, 2005, in a move that appeared to acknowledge Cheney's defeat, the White House announced that it would accept the torture ban after all. When Bush handed McCain his hard-fought victory, he did so with a flourish. Bush invited McCain and Warner to join him in the Oval Office, then invited camera crews and the White House press pool to come inside and film them shaking hands. Seated in a blue-and-white-striped chair before the office's marble fireplace, Bush sought to put the best face on his apparent defeat by embracing McCain's arguments as his own. "Senator McCain has been a leader to make sure that the United States of America upholds the values of America as we fight and win this war on terror. And we've been happy to work with him to achieve a common objective, and that is to make it clear to the world that this government does not torture and that we adhere to the International Convention of Torture[sic], whether it be here at home or abroad," Bush said, later adding, "I so appreciate your hard work, Senator. You're a good man who honors the values of America."

As the cameras continued to roll for the evening newscasts, McCain thanked Bush. "I want to take this opportunity to thank you for the effort that you made to resolve this very difficult issue," McCain said. "I'm very pleased that we reached this agreement, and now we can move forward and make sure that the whole world knows that, as the president has stated many times, that we do not practice cruel, inhuman treatment or torture."[26]

The message to Congress, to the world, and to the American public was clear. Bush would sign the bill. The law banning torture and other forms of cruel, inhuman, and degrading treatment for prisoners in U.S. custody would be absolute, with no exception for the CIA or overseas prisons. The long fight that erupted after 9/11 over whether America would employ torture and other forms of brutal tactics against prisoners was over. The next day's newspapers ran the story on their front pages. The *New York Times*, for example, portrayed the result as a "stinging defeat" for Bush and a "particularly significant setback for Vice President Dick Cheney, who since July has led the administration's fight to defeat the amendment or at least exempt the Central Intelligence Agency from its provisions."[27]

That was how the world looked on December 16, 2005. But Cheney and the administration's legal team weren't finished.

### 5.

Cathie Martin, the communications director for Vice President Cheney, once explained under oath that the Bush-Cheney White House often tried to dump bad news late on a Friday—in order to bury it. "Fewer people pay attention to it late on Friday," Martin testified at the perjury trial of Cheney's former chief of staff, I. Lewis "Scooter" Libby. "Fewer people pay attention when it's reported on Saturday."[28]

December 30, 2005, was a Friday—and a particularly quiet Friday in Washington. It was the day before New Year's Eve weekend, Congress was out of session, and President Bush was at his ranch in Crawford, Texas. Most of the national press corps was on vacation, and the few reporters who were on duty were doing their best to get out of the office early. Several news organizations made note of the fact that Bush signed several bills that day. One contained a five-week extension for the USA Patriot Act, which Bush was having trouble getting reauthorized without additional oversight protections that the White House opposed. Another bill signed by Bush was the military budget containing the McCain torture ban.[29]

The White House put out two statements that day about the new laws included in the huge military-spending package. The first statement was meant for public consumption. It was written in plain English, and it lauded the bill for the many good things it would accomplish. Among them, Bush noted the detainee amendment, remarking that his administration was "committed to treating all detainees held by the United States in a manner consistent with our Constitution, laws, and treaty obligations, which reflect the values we hold dear. U.S. law and policy already prohibit torture. Our policy has also been not to use cruel, inhuman or degrading treatment, at home or abroad. This legislation now makes that a matter of statute for practices abroad. . . . These provisions reaffirm the values we share as a Nation and our commitment to the rule of law."[30]

But around 8 p.m., the White House issued another statement about the bill. Given almost exactly the same title, this second document was not meant for public consumption, although it would be entered in the Federal Register. Written in dense legalistic language, and making frequent references to bill sections identified only by number, this "signing statement" contained instructions for CIA and military interrogators about how they were to interpret the new torture ban law: "The executive branch shall construe [the torture ban] in a manner consistent with the constitutional authority of the President to supervise the unitary executive branch and as Commander in Chief and consistent with the constitutional limitations on the judicial power, which will assist in achieving the shared objective of the Congress and the President . . . of protecting the American people from further terrorist attacks."[31]

On Monday, January 2, 2006, Georgetown law professor Martin Lederman, who had worked for the Justice Department's Office of Legal Counsel from 1994 to 2002, noted the signing statement in an entry on the law blog Balkinization. "So much for the president's assent to the McCain Amendment," Lederman wrote, adding, "You didn't think Cheney and Addington were going to go down quietly, did you?"[32]

The next day, a *Boston Globe* reporter called the White House to find out what the signing statement meant. Did the administration believe that Bush, as commander in chief, had the constitutional power to bypass the torture ban? Months later, when controversy surrounding Bush's use of signing statements reached a crescendo, administration lawyers would adopt a strategy of being far less candid about the plain-English meaning of their legal claims. But on that chilly day in early January, there was no public interest in the signing statements, and administration officials discussed the matter forthrightly. The White House press office put the reporter on the phone with an administration attorney and allowed him to explain the statement, on the condition that he be identified as a "senior administration official" rather than by name—a standard practice in the Bush-Cheney White House.

The senior administration official was frank. "There is some truth to what you are saying," he said. It wasn't that the torture ban had no meaning, he stressed: "We are not going to ignore this law. We consider it a valid statute. We consider ourselves bound by the prohibition on cruel, unusual, and degrading treatment." But, the official said, a situation could arise in which Bush might decide that the torture ban got in the way of his responsibilities to protect national security—for example, a "ticking time bomb" scenario in which a captured terror suspect is believed to have information that, if elicited, could thwart a planned attack. In that situation, the president would not consider himself bound to obey the torture ban—or, rather, he would "construe" the ban as giving him an unwritten waiver for special national security circumstances. Indeed, he said, if the president determined that using brutal techniques on a captured terrorist suspect could stop attacks, then it would be unconstitutional for Congress to pass a law stopping the commander in chief from authorizing interrogators to use such tactics.[33]

In other words, with this statement, Bush had officially instructed interrogators that despite the new law, he still had the power, as commander in chief, to waive the torture ban when he saw fit. He was telling the CIA and the military that if they received authorization to inflict suffering on a detainee, they should not worry about McCain's torture ban because the ban itself was an unconstitutional intrusion on his authority as president. John Yoo's August 1, 2002, interrogation memo may have been replaced, but its central claim endured: "In order to respect the president's inherent constitutional authority to manage a military campaign against Al Qaeda and its allies, [anti-torture laws] must be construed as not applying to interrogations undertaken pursuant to his commander-in-chief authority." The entire year's fight in Congress had been irrelevant, the White House had declared, because Congress lacked the constitutional authority to pass a law that tied the commander in chief's hands.

6.

While Congress was out of session, McCain had embarked on a trip to Antarctica to study global warming. The next day, his staff finally reached him by satellite phone to tell him what had happened. McCain conferred with Warner, whose office put out a joint statement on both senators' behalf repudiating the White House. "We believe the president understands Congress's intent in passing, by very large majorities, legislation governing the treatment of detainees," the two senators wrote. "The Congress declined when asked by administration officials to include a presidential waiver of the restrictions included in our legislation. Our committee intends through strict oversight to monitor the administration's implementation of the new law."[34]

Separately, the third primary sponsor of the detainee treatment law, Lindsey Graham, stated that he agreed with everything McCain and Warner had said and would go further. Bush's stance, he said, was endangering U.S. troops by setting a precedent that a leader could make an exception to the Geneva Conventions simply by declaring torture necessary to protect national security. "I do not believe that any political figure in the country has the ability to set aside any . . . law of armed conflict that we have adopted or treaties that we have ratified," Graham declared. "If we go down that road, it will cause great problems for our troops in future conflicts because [nothing] is to prevent other nations' leaders from doing the same."[35]

The White House did not respond to the senators' comments, and few other media outlets picked up on the story.

# 10

## Power of the Pen:
## Signing Statements

### 1.

Just before 3 p.m. on Thursday, March 9, 2006, President Bush stepped to a podium in the White House's East Room to thunderous applause. Standing before golden curtains and surrounded by lawmakers, Bush unleashed lavish praise on the USA Patriot Improvement and Reauthorization Act, calling it "a piece of legislation that's vital to win the war on terror and to protect the American people." Moments later, as cameras whirred, he stepped to a desk decorated with a sign proclaiming "Protecting the Homeland" and signed the legislation into law, extending and making permanent most of the original Patriot Act.[1]

It had taken a long political slog to get to this moment. Adopted overwhelmingly by Congress six weeks after 9/11, the Patriot Act had evolved into a symbol of civil liberties lost to those who feared that the government was going too far in trammeling individual rights in the name of stopping terrorism. The Bush-Cheney administration's pervasive secrecy over how the FBI was using its enhanced police powers to secretly search homes and to seize banking and Internet records without warrants had fueled a drive in Congress to add more oversight restrictions to the package, parts of which were set to expire without new legislation. The White House and its allies among the Republican leaders of the House of Representatives opposed the extra oversight measures, but several Republican senators joined with Democrats to filibuster the Patriot Act reauthorization bill. Finally, the administration agreed to accept some extra restrictions in exchange for getting the bill passed. The changes included several new legal mandates requiring the Justice Department to make regular and comprehensive reports to congressional oversight committees about how it was using its expanded powers. The compromise bill did not entirely please either civil libertarians or the White House, but the democratic process appeared to have worked. When the president put his signature on the bill, officially known as H.R. 3199, at the elaborate signing ceremony in the East Room, the saga seemed to be over.

But it wasn't over. Later that day, after the members of Congress and reporters had left, Bush issued a signing statement declaring that he did not consider himself bound to obey the new oversight requirements. Despite the law's mandatory provisions that the executive branch regularly give Congress a complete accounting of how the FBI was using the Patriot Act, Bush declared that he could withhold any such information if he decided that its disclosure would be undesirable. "The executive branch shall construe the provisions of H.R. 3199 that call for furnishing information to entities outside the executive branch . . . in a manner consistent with the President's constitutional authority to supervise the unitary executive branch and to withhold information the disclosure of which could impair foreign relations, national security, the deliberative processes of the Executive, or the performance of the Executive's constitutional duties," Bush said.[2] The administration's carefully worded statement left it to legal specialists to point out in plain English that Bush was claiming that only the parts of the bill that expanded his power were constitutional, essentially nullifying the parts of the bill that checked those new powers.

The Patriot Act signing statement, coming less than three months after the McCain Torture Ban signing statement, prompted a renewed outcry. Senator Patrick J. Leahy of Vermont, the ranking Democrat on the Senate Judiciary Committee, said that Bush's legal claims represented "nothing short of a radical effort to manipulate the constitutional separation of powers and evade accountability and responsibility for following the law. The president's signing statements are not the law, and Congress should not allow them to be the last word. The president's constitutional duty is to faithfully execute the laws as written by the Congress, not cherry-pick the laws he decides he wants to follow."[3] And Representatives Jane Harman of California and John Conyers of Michigan—the ranking Democrats on the Intelligence and Judiciary committees, respectively—sent a letter to Attorney General Alberto Gonzales asking that Bush follow the law. "We ask that the administration immediately rescind this statement and abide by the law," they wrote. "Many members who supported the final law did so based upon the guarantee of additional reporting and oversight. The administration cannot, after the fact, unilaterally repeal provisions of the law implementing such oversight. . . . The time to raise objections to laws Congress is [considering is] while they are pending. Once the president signs a bill, he and all of us are bound by it."[4]

The administration ignored the complaints.

## 2.

Bush was not the first occupant of the White House to issue signing statements instructing subordinates in the executive branch about how they were to interpret new laws. But he made by far the most aggressive use of the device. By the seventh year of the Bush-Cheney presidency, Bush had attached signing statements to about 150 bills enacted since he took office, challenging the constitutionality of well over 1,100 separate sections in the legislation. By contrast, all previous presidents in American history *combined* had used signing statements to challenge the constitutionality of about 600 sections of bills, according to historical data compiled by Christopher Kelley, a Miami University of Ohio political science professor who was one of the first to study signing statements. "What we haven't seen until this administration is the sheer number of objections that are being raised on every bill passed through the White House," Kelley said. "That is what is staggering. The numbers are well out of the norm from any previous administration."

Bush's record was different from his predecessors' in another way. He was also virtually abandoning his veto power. Well into the seventh year of his presidency, Bush had vetoed just two bills—a funding measure Congress passed in July 2006 for embryonic stem cell research and an Iraq war spending bill Congress passed in May 2007. No other modern president had made so little use of his veto power. Even as his immediate predecessors had increased their use of signing statements, they had also continued to veto a bill when they had serious problems with one or more of its provisions. Bill Clinton, for example, vetoed thirty-seven bills, George H. W. Bush forty-four, and Ronald Reagan seventy-eight. Not since the nineteenth century had any chief executive made as little use of his veto authority as did Bush during the first six years of his presidency.

For years, political observers had puzzled about why Bush, who was so aggressive about exerting his executive prerogatives in every other respect, was not vetoing bills. As the full scope of Bush's use of signing statements became clear, so did the answer to the mystery: Bush's legal team was using signing statements as something better than a veto—something close to a line-item veto. In 1998, the Supreme Court had ruled that line-item vetoes, even when Congress approves of them, are unconstitutional because the Founders wanted presidents to either veto an entire legislative package or accept it all. But the Bush-Cheney administration had figured out that if a president signed a bill and then instructed the government to consider selected provisions null, he could accomplish much the same thing. Moreover, it was an absolute power because, unlike when there is a regular veto, Congress had no opportunity to override his legal judgments.

Although signing statements are filed in the Federal Register, almost nobody in Washington outside the executive branch paid any attention to them until 2006.[5] Then, Bush's challenges to the torture ban and the Patriot Act oversight provisions prompted a closer look at the other instructions he had issued since taking office. Once deciphered, the signing statements were a road map to the full implications of his administration's agenda of concentrating ever more governmental power into the White House.

3.

Far back into the nineteenth century, presidents occasionally signed a large legislative package while declaring that some section of the bill was unconstitutional, so the statute created by that section of the bill need not be enforced as written. But the use of signing statements was rare until the mid-1980s, when a group of young conservative attorneys working in the Reagan administration realized that issuing the documents more frequently might be a way to expand presidential power.

The inspiration for taking a closer look at signing statements appears to have been a high-profile fight involving new procedures for government contractors. In 1984, Congress passed a bill called the Competition in Contracting Act. President Reagan signed the bill but issued a signing statement telling the executive branch that a section of it was unconstitutional, and he directed agencies not to obey the statute created by that section. A losing bidder who would have won a contract if the section had been obeyed sued the government, and a federal judge ruled in March 1985 that the Reagan administration had to obey all of the act's provisions. But Attorney General Ed Meese, insisting that the executive branch had independent power to interpret the Constitution, declared that the government would refuse to comply with the ruling. An appeals court upheld the ruling, chastising the Reagan administration for trying to seize a kind of line-item veto power for itself, and the House Judiciary Committee voted to cut off funding for Meese's office unless the executive branch obeyed the courts. In June 1985, Meese backed down.[6]

That same month, Steven Calabresi joined the Meese Justice Department after finishing up his clerkship year with appeals court judge Robert Bork, whom Reagan later unsuccessfully nominated for the Supreme Court. Calabresi (who, as mentioned earlier, had cofounded the Federalist Society in 1981 while a law student), linked up with another young conservative. His name was John Harrison, and he, like Calabresi, had recently graduated from Yale Law School and then clerked for Bork. As they brainstormed ways to advance Reagan's conservative agenda, Calabresi and Harrison hit upon a new use for signing statements. Despite the Competition in Contracting defeat earlier that summer, on August 23, 1985, the two young attorneys wrote a memo to Meese proposing that Reagan should start issuing signing statements much more frequently as part of an overall strategy of increasing the executive branch's influence over the law.[7]

Specifically, Calabresi and Harrison were interested in how "activist judges" used and abused legislative history—the transcript of debate by members of Congress as a bill was being crafted—when called upon later to interpret the meaning of a disputed statute. Signing statements, the two young lawyers argued, could be used to create a comparable record of the president's interpretation of potentially ambiguous laws so that his view could be taken into account as well. Meese liked their proposal, and in December 1985, the attorney general wrote to the West Publishing Company and asked them to include presidential signing statements in the *U.S. Code Congressional and Administration News,* the standard collection of bills' legislative history. The company agreed to begin doing so, a major step in increasing the perceived legitimacy of the device.[8]

In September 1985, a Meese aide, T. Kenneth Cribb, asked the acting head of the Office of Legal Counsel, Ralph Tarr, to draft a memo explaining how the government had issued signing statements up until that point,

and to suggest ways to improve the process, given Meese's interest in issuing them more systematically.[9] A month later, Tarr did that and more. In
a prescient seven-page manifesto, Tarr wrote that signing statements were
"presently underutilized and could become far more important as a tool
of Presidential management of the agencies, a device for preserving issues
of importance in the ongoing struggle for power with Congress, and an
aid to statutory interpretation for the courts." Indeed, Tarr pointed out, the
device was potentially powerful in ways that went far beyond simply adding
a president's views to a statute's legislative history in the hope that someday
a court might pay attention to it. "It might also give [the White House] an
additional tool—the threat of a potential signing statement—with which
to negotiate concessions from Congress." And, he said, the statements can
be used as a powerful device for telling executive branch agencies how to
interpret a new law: "The President can direct agencies to ignore unconstitutional provisions or to read provisions in a way that eliminates constitutional or policy problems. This direction permits the President to
seize the initiative in creating what will eventually be the agency's interpretation," Tarr wrote.[10]

Cribb also asked the Litigation Strategy Working Group, a brain trust
of about fifteen political appointees drawn from throughout the Justice
Department, to study the "theoretical and practical issues" raised by the
possibility of expanding the use of signing statements.[11] This request led
to a February 6, 1986, memo by Samuel A. Alito, a member of the Litigation Strategy Working Group, in which the future Supreme Court justice
laid out a proposal for a pilot project aimed at issuing signing statements
more frequently as a way to "increase the power of the executive to shape
the law."

Alito focused on the use of signing statements as legislative history, a
far more modest use of the mechanism than the Bush-Cheney administration's practice. But he still recognized that what they were playing
with was potentially revolutionary, predicting major problems if their
plan was sprung artlessly. Alito foresaw that congressional relations could
be frayed "due to the novelty of the procedure and the potential increase
of presidential power." And, he emphasized, "congress is likely to resent
the fact that the president will get in the last word on questions of
interpretation."

Therefore, Alito suggested, the plan should be unveiled in slow motion,
beginning with bills that concerned only the Department of Justice, and

gradually ramping the practice up over time to cover laws that affected the rest of the federal government. "As an introductory step, our interpretive statements should be of moderate size and scope," he wrote. "Only relatively important questions should be addressed. We should concentrate on points of true ambiguity, rather than issuing interpretations that may seem to conflict with those of Congress. The first step will be to convince the courts that Presidential signing statements are valuable interpretive tools."[12]

After several years, Calabresi and Harrison's original idea—getting judges to start citing the devices as a legitimate part of a statute's legislative history—did not pan out, but the effort had unintended consequences. As Tarr had foretold, Reagan and his successors discovered a different power that flowed from the practice of issuing signing statements more frequently, using them to instruct subordinates in the executive branch agencies about how they were to interpret laws—frequently by declaring, as in the Competition in Contracting Act dispute, that certain sections of bills were unconstitutional and need not be enforced or obeyed as written. "I initially thought of signing statements as presidential legislative history," said Calabresi, who is now a law professor at Northwestern University in Chicago. "I've subsequently come to think of them as being important vehicles by which presidents can control subordinates in the executive branch. They subsequently came to be important to the Unitary Executive."[13]

By the end of Reagan's second term, he had used statements to challenge, interpret, or rewrite ninety-five sections of bills—the most by any president in American history up to that point.[14] And when the Bush-Quayle administration's legal team inherited the newly important tool, they decided to expand upon it in order to meet what they perceived to be a mounting problem in the bills Congress was sending them.

In a January 1990 speech to the Federalist Society, Richard Thornburgh, George H. W. Bush's first attorney general, complained that the veto power the Founders gave the president was no longer good enough as a means for defending his prerogatives from congressional meddling, because lawmakers were increasingly lumping new restrictions on presidential power into large and important bills. "Today's legislative process has rendered the presidential veto a less effective check on congressional encroachments than was envisioned two centuries ago," Thornburgh said. "It is often very difficult for the President to veto legislation that contains sometimes blatantly unconstitutional provisions. For example, Congress has become fond of inserting substantive provisions in appropriations bills. This is what they call making the provision veto-proof."[15]

Thornburgh did not, in that speech at Washington's Mayflower Hotel, raise the possibility of using signing statements as a substitute line-item veto to solve the problem. But the record of the Bush-Quayle administration demonstrates that they hit upon using signing statements as precisely the solution to the problem Thornburgh described. During their four years in office, the use of signing statements ballooned again: The first President Bush used signing statements to challenge 232 sections of bills.

Bill Clinton's Democratic administration liked signing statements, too. In a November 1993 memo, Walter Dellinger, head of the Office of Legal Counsel for Clinton, wrote: "If the President may properly decline to enforce a law, at least when it unconstitutionally encroaches on his powers, then it arguably follows that he may properly announce to Congress and to the public that he will not enforce a provision of an enactment he is signing. If so, then a signing statement that challenges what the President determines to be an unconstitutional encroachment on his power, or that announces the President's unwillingness to enforce . . . such a provision, can be a valid and reasonable exercise of Presidential authority."[16]

Confronted by a Republican-controlled Congress for most of his presidency, Clinton used signing statements to challenge 140 sections of bills over eight years—not as many as the Bush-Quayle administration, but still the second most in history to that point. In 1997, for example, Congress passed a military budget bill that contained a section forbidding the transfer of American military equipment to United Nations peacekeeping forces unless Congress received fifteen days' advance notice. When Clinton signed the bill, he issued a signing statement saying that because he was the commander in chief and had independent authority to conduct the nation's foreign affairs, he need not obey the fifteen-day-notice law.[17]

But Clinton's legal team was inconsistent and hesitated to go all the way. For example, in February 1996, Congress passed a military budget bill that included a section requiring the Pentagon to discharge all HIV-positive soldiers, even if they were otherwise healthy. When Clinton signed the bill, he issued a signing statement declaring that he had "concluded that this discriminatory provision is unconstitutional."[18] He urged Congress to repeal the law and said he would not let the Justice Department defend the law in court if an HIV-positive soldier sued the government.

But Clinton's legal team—Dellinger and White House counsel Jack Quinn—explained to reporters that while the president felt HIV provision was unconstitutional, he could not refuse to enforce the HIV provision, because no court ruling had confirmed his view. Instead, they said, the executive branch was bound to enforce the law until a court intervened. "When the president's obligation to execute laws enacted by Congress is in tension with his responsibility to act in accordance to the Constitution, questions arise that really go to the very heart of the system, and the president can decline to comply with the law, in our view, only where there is a judgment that the Supreme Court has resolved the issue," Dellinger said.[19]

After the Bush-Cheney administration took office, the use of signing statements would undergo exponential growth. Behind the scenes, the chief architect of the administration's expanded use of signing statements was David Addington. Early on, Cheney made sure that all legislation would be routed through the Office of the Vice President for review before it reached the president's desk. Addington then scoured the bills for any new laws that he believed would infringe on the president's constitutional powers as he saw them, drafting signing statements for Bush to sign.

"Signing statements unite two of Addington's passions," said Brad Berenson, who also helped prepare signing statements as an associate White House counsel from 2001 to 2003. "One is executive power. And the other is the inner alleyways of bureaucratic combat. It's a way to advance executive power through those inner alleyways. . . . So he's a vigorous advocate of signing statements and including important objections in signing statements. Most lawyers in the White House regard the bill review process as a tedious but necessary bureaucratic aspect of the job. Addington regarded it with relish. He would dive into a two-hundred-page bill like it was a four-course meal."[20]

Knowing that Cheney's counsel was likely to review the bills, other White House and Justice Department lawyers began vetting legislation with Addington's views in mind, according to a second former lawyer in the Bush White House, who asked not to be named. The younger attorneys learned to be extremely careful to flag any provision that placed limits on presidential power. "You didn't want to miss something," he said.

The staff of previous vice presidents had neither the authority to review legislation nor interest in such a task, and other administrations had left the bill-vetting process to the White House counsel's office and the Justice Department's Office of Legal Counsel. "What's happening now is unprecedented on almost every level," said Ron Klain, who was chief of staff to Vice President Al Gore from 1995 to 1999. "Gore was a very active policy maker in the Clinton administration, but that didn't include picking through bills of Congress to find things to disagree with."[21]

## 4.

Among the laws Bush challenged included requirements that the government provide information to Congress, minimum qualifications for important positions in the executive branch, rules and regulations for the military, restrictions affecting the nation's foreign policy, and affirmative action rules for hiring. In his signing statements, Bush instructed his subordinates that the laws were unconstitutional constraints on his own inherent power as commander in chief and as the head of the "unitary" executive branch and thus need not be obeyed as written.

Many of the laws Bush said he could bypass—including the McCain Torture Ban—involved the military and intelligence agencies. On at least four occasions during the Bush-Cheney tenure, Congress passed laws forbidding U.S. troops from engaging in combat in Colombia, where the U.S. military was advising the government in its struggle against narcotics-funded Marxist rebels. It also capped the number of troops and civilian government contractors the United States could deploy to Colombia. After signing each bill into law, Bush used a signing statement to inform the military that he need not obey any of the Colombia restrictions because he was commander in chief. The combat ban and troop cap, he declared, would be interpreted merely "as advisory in nature."

Bush also said he could bypass laws requiring him to tell Congress before diverting money from an authorized program in order to start a secret operation, such as funding for new "black sites," where suspected terrorists were secretly imprisoned around the world. Congress also twice passed laws forbidding the military from using intelligence that was not "lawfully collected," including any information on Americans that was gathered in violation of the Fourth Amendment's protections against unreasonable searches. Congress first passed this provision in August 2004, when the National Security Agency's warrantless surveillance program was still a secret, and it passed it again after the program's existence was disclosed in December 2005. On both occasions, Bush used signing statements to tell the military that only the commander in chief could decide whether the use of such intelligence was acceptable.

In December 2006, Congress passed a postal service bill that restated an existing ban on opening first-class mail without a warrant, unless the letter or package is suspected of containing a letter bomb. Bush's signing statement said that the executive branch could nevertheless open mail without a warrant when "specifically authorized by law for foreign intelligence collection."[22] This qualifier rendered the warrant requirement effectively meaningless, since in the warrantless-wiretapping controversy, the administration had asserted it was authorized by the "law" of the president's inherent constitutional powers to intercept phone calls without a judge's approval.

In October 2004, five months after the Abu Ghraib torture scandal in Iraq came to light, Congress passed a bill containing a series of new rules and regulations for military prisons. Bush signed the bill, turning each of the sections into laws, and then he said he could ignore them all. One provision made clear that military lawyers can give their commanders independent advice on such issues as what would constitute torture. Bush ordered the military lawyers not to contradict his administration's politically appointed lawyers. Another post–Abu Ghraib law required the Pentagon to retrain military prison guards on the requirements for humane treatment of detainees under the Geneva Conventions, to perform background checks on civilian contractors in Iraq, and to limit such contractors' involvement in "security, intelligence, law enforcement, and criminal justice functions." Bush told the armed forces that as the commander in chief, he was not bound to obey the requirements—and by extension, since they were all part of the same "unitary" executive branch, neither were they.

Yet another post–Abu Ghraib law created the position of inspector general for Iraq. Bush sharply reduced the impact of this law by writing in his signing statement that the inspector general "shall refrain" from investigating any intelligence or national security matter, or any crime the Pentagon says it prefers to investigate for itself. He had placed similar limits on an inspector-general position created by Congress in November 2003 for the initial stage of the U.S. occupation of Iraq. The earlier law empowered the inspector general to notify Congress if a U.S. official refused to cooperate, but Bush told the inspector general that he could not give any information to Congress without permission from the administration.

Many of the other laws Bush asserted he could bypass imposed requirements on him to provide information to congressional oversight committees. In December 2004, for example, Congress passed an intelligence bill requiring the Justice Department to tell it how often, and in what situations, the FBI was using special national-security wiretaps on U.S. soil. The bill also contained language requiring the Justice Department to give oversight committees copies of administration memos outlining any new interpretations of domestic-spying laws. It further contained eleven other sections requiring reports about such issues as civil liberties, security clearances, border security, and counternarcotics efforts. After signing the bill, Bush issued a signing statement telling the executive branch that he could withhold all the information sought by Congress.

It went on. Also in December 2004, Bush signed a law saying that, when requested, scientific information "prepared by government researchers and scientists shall be transmitted [to Congress] uncensored and without delay." Bush then told researchers in a signing statement that he could order them to withhold any information from Congress if he decided its disclosure could impair foreign relations, national security, or the workings of the executive branch.

Likewise, when Congress created the Department of Homeland Security in 2002, it said oversight committees must be given information about vulnerabilities at chemical plants and with regard to the screening of checked bags at airports. The Homeland Security Act also said Congress must be shown unaltered reports about problems with visa services prepared by a new immigration ombudsman. But Bush instructed the executive branch that the president had a constitutional right to withhold the information and alter the reports.

In December 2006, Congress passed a law prohibiting the United States from transferring nuclear technology to India if that country violated international nonproliferation guidelines. Bush said only he got to determine what the country's foreign policy would be, so he would view the required ban merely as "advisory."

Bush also challenged laws that set minimum qualifications for who could be placed in important executive branch positions — positions often created by Congress. In October 2006, Congress passed a law in response to the revelation during Hurricane Katrina that Bush's choice to head the Federal Emergency Management Agency, Michael Brown, had been a politically connected hire whose prior experience was in managing a horse-racing association, not emergency management. The law said the president must nominate a candidate who has "a demonstrated ability in and knowledge of emergency management" and "not less than five years of executive leadership." Bush said that only he, as head of the executive branch, got to decide who to appoint to offices, so he could ignore the requirement.[23]

On several other occasions, Bush informed the executive branch that he was not bound to obey laws creating "whistle-blower" job protections for federal employees—laws in which Congress had assured the workers that they could not be fired or otherwise punished for telling a member of Congress about possible government wrongdoing. For example, when Congress passed a massive energy package in August 2005, it strengthened whistle-blower protections for employees at the Department of Energy and the Nuclear Regulatory Commission. Congress added the provision in the bill because lawmakers believed Bush appointees were intimidating nuclear specialists so that they would not testify about safety issues related to a planned nuclear-waste repository at Yucca Mountain in Nevada. The administration supported the facility, but both senators from Nevada—Republican John Ensign and Democrat Harry Reid—opposed it. After Bush signed the energy bill, he issued a signing statement declaring to the executive branch that he could ignore the whistle-blower protections.

Although the Supreme Court had rejected the Unitary Executive Theory as false, Bush invoked it eighty-two times during his first term alone, targeting many laws that gave government officials duties that might conflict with presidential control.[24] In November 2002, Congress sought to generate independent statistics about student performance. The lawmakers passed a statute setting up an educational research institute to conduct studies and publish reports "without the approval" of the secretary of education. When Bush signed the bill containing the research law, he instructed the executive branch to interpret it to mean the precise opposite of what Congress had written. Citing his authority to supervise a unitary executive branch, Bush decreed in his signing statement that the institute's director would be "subject to the supervision and direction of the Secretary of Education."

Similarly, the Supreme Court had repeatedly upheld affirmative action programs, as long as they did not include quotas. (In 2003, the Court voted 5–4 to uphold a race-conscious university admissions program over the strong objections of Bush, who argued that any such program should be struck down as unconstitutional.) Yet despite the Court's rulings, Bush took exception at least nine times to provisions that sought to ensure that minorities were represented among recipients of government jobs, contracts, and grants. In December 2004, for example, Congress passed a law requiring the new national intelligence director to recruit and train women and minorities to be spies, analysts, and translators in order to ensure diversity in the intelligence community. Bush signed the bill containing the new law but directed the executive branch to construe it "in a manner consistent with" the Constitution's guarantee of "equal protection" to all, thus pressing forward with his view that affirmative action programs amount to unconstitutional reverse discrimination—this even though the Supreme Court had recently rejected that precise argument.

5.

The gap between the legal claims in the Bush-Cheney signing statements and mainstream understandings of the Constitution threw new light on a potentially enormous problem lurking in the Constitution: If a president has the power to instruct the government not to *enforce* laws that he alone has declared to be unconstitutional, then he can free himself from the need to *obey* laws that he alone says restrict his actions unconstitutionally—even when the Supreme Court, were it given an opportunity to review his theory, would be unlikely to agree with it.

Legal disputes involving the balance of power between the president and Congress are very difficult to get before a court. As Supreme Court justice Robert Jackson noted in 1952, the office of the presidency is "relatively immune from judicial review."[25] Unlike in some other countries, in the American system of law, a court cannot offer an "advisory opinion" that resolves some abstract dispute. Instead, a specific victim of a law or policy, over whom courts have jurisdiction, must file a lawsuit for a question to get before the Supreme Court. But nobody has legal standing to sue over most of the important laws that Bush challenged. There is no individual victim, for legal purposes, if, hypothetically, a president sends more troops to Colombia than a statute allows. There might be a "victim" if a detainee is tortured in violation of the torture ban, but if that detainee is not a U.S. citizen and is not on U.S. soil, it would be very difficult for a civilian court to obtain jurisdiction to hear the case. In addition, the White House could invoke the State Secrets Privilege to get any such lawsuit dismissed without a ruling on the underlying legal dispute.

There were other difficulties for those inclined to attempt to push back against the Bush-Cheney signing statements. A misstatement of the law alone is not a crime, for example. Someone can falsely declare that they have a right to take a television home from the store without paying for it, but unless he actually follows through on that threat and steals the TV, there is nothing to prosecute. Moreover, it was very difficult to know which of the laws challenged Bush was actually violating—if any. The most important laws that Bush challenged nearly always involved classified foreign affairs and national security matters, where the executive branch's actions are secret from the public and often from a majority in Congress. Thus, his actions were often limited only by what his handpicked lawyers told him he could not do in their confidential advice. "There can't be judicial review if nobody knows about it," said Georgia State's Neil Kinkopf. "And if they avoid judicial review, they avoid having their constitutional theories rebuked."[26]

Allies of the Bush-Cheney administration argued that concerns about its signing statements were overblown, noting that just because the president had reserved a right to bypass a law didn't mean that he went on to disobey it. Indeed, in some cases, the administration clearly ended up following laws that Bush said he could bypass. For example, citing his power to "withhold information" in September 2002, Bush declared that he could ignore a law requiring the State Department to list the number of deaths of U.S. citizens in foreign countries. Nevertheless, the department still put a list on its website.

Skeptics replied that the administration had damaged credibility when it came to its assurances about what it was doing behind closed doors. At a government-sponsored rally to support the Patriot Act in 2004, for example, Bush told the public that "any time you hear the United States government talking about wiretap, it requires—a wiretap requires a court order. Nothing has changed, by the way. When we're talking about chasing down terrorists, we're talking about getting a court order before we do so."[27] But it later emerged that since 9/11, the government had been secretly intercepting phone calls and e-mails on U.S. soil without court orders.

Moreover, the Government Accountability Office (the agency formerly known as the General Accounting Office, which had changed its name in 2004 to better reflect its mission) later sampled a small number of the laws Bush had challenged. Although it did not look at any of the more controversial laws involving classified national security matters, the GAO found that agencies went on to disobey six out of sixteen provisions. For example, one such law required the border patrol to move its checkpoints for illegal immigrants near Tucson every seven days. In a signing statement, Bush asserted that only the president can decide how to deploy law enforcement officers, and he instructed the border patrol to view the law as merely "advisory." The border patrol had gone on to disobey the law, explaining to the GAO that it was only "advisory." In response to the report, a White House spokesman said, "The signing statements certainly do and should have an impact. They are real."[28]

Bruce Fein, a deputy attorney general in the Reagan administration, said the American system of government relies upon the leaders of each branch "to exercise some self-restraint." But Bush had declared himself the sole judge of his own powers and then ruled for himself every time. "This is an attempt by the president to have the final word on his own constitutional powers, which eliminates the checks and balances that keep the country a democracy," Fein said. "There is no way for an independent judiciary to check his assertions of power, and Congress isn't doing it, either. So this is moving us toward an unlimited executive power."[29]

Fein was not the only member of the Reagan legal team who criticized the way in which the Bush-Cheney legal team used signing statements. Even Calabresi, the coauthor of the original 1985 memo urging Meese to expand the use of signing statements, said that the Bush-Cheney team was no longer using the device in the way he originally had had in mind. A president, Calabresi concluded, should be able to decline to execute a law only when he has a "good faith" belief that it's unconstitutional — when it's "clear" to everyone that the law is invalid. "It can't be a really contested matter of constitutionality," he explained. "That's the tricky thing. It is clear that the president is not supposed to have a power to just suspend laws, or to just take a law that was on the books and freeze it."[30]

Moreover, Calabresi said, if a president is confronted with a bill that he believes is unconstitutional, his first duty in most cases is to veto the bill unless the country would be severely hurt by the failure to enact other provisions of the bill immediately. Calabresi said it is a "bad idea" for a president to regularly sign bills into law and then to issue signing statements declaring that portions of the bill are unconstitutional. "I think what the administration has done in issuing no vetoes and scores of signing statements is not the right way to approach this," Calabresi said.

And Douglas Kmiec, who headed the Office of Legal Counsel in Reagan's second term and was another key player in overseeing the growth of signing statements, said he disapproved of what he called the "provocative" and sometimes "disingenuous" manner in which the Bush-Cheney administration used signing statements. Kmiec, who is now a Pepperdine University law professor, said the Reagan team's goal was to leave a record of the president's understanding of new laws only in cases where an important statute was ambiguous. He rejected the idea of using signing statements to contradict the clear intent of Congress, as Bush and Cheney did. Presidents should either quietly tolerate provisions of bills they don't like or they should veto the bill, he said, adding that he thought the Bush-Cheney administration's use of signing statements had gone too far, needlessly antagonizing Congress. "The president is not well served by the lawyers who have been advising him," Kmiec said.[31]

6.

On June 4, 2006, the board of governors for the American Bar Association, meeting in flood-ravaged New Orleans, voted unanimously to investigate whether Bush had exceeded his constitutional authority when he asserted in his signing statements that he had the constitutional authority to ignore laws. The ABA president, Michael Greco, a Boston lawyer who had served on former Republican Massachusetts governor William F. Weld's Judicial Nominating Council, appointed a blue-ribbon and bipartisan task force of legal luminaries—including former officials from all three branches of government, prominent scholars, and a retired FBI director—to carry out the inquiry.*

---

*The ABA task force's members included several conservative Republican figures, including Mickey Edwards, a former member of Congress from Oklahoma; Bruce Fein; and William S. Sessions, a retired federal judge who was the director of the FBI under both Reagan and President George H. W. Bush. Other members included Patricia Wald, the retired chief judge of the U.S. Court of Appeals for the District of Columbia; Harold Koh, dean of Yale Law School; Kathleen Sullivan, former dean of Stanford Law School; Charles Ogletree, a Harvard law professor; Stephen Saltzburg, a George Washington University Law School professor who was a Justice Department official under Reagan and the first President Bush, as well as a prosecutor in the Iran-Contra scandal; Mark Agrast, a former legislative counsel for Representative William D. Delahunt, Democrat of Massachusetts; and Thomas Susman, who worked in the Justice Department under both Presidents Johnson and Nixon, and who was later counsel to the Senate Judiciary Committee. The task force was chaired by Neal Sonnett, a former federal prosecutor turned Miami defense attorney whose clients included Republican lobbyist Jack Abramoff.

The ABA Task Force on Presidential Signing Statements and the Separation of Powers Doctrine worked for nearly two months researching, debating among themselves, and crafting a thirty-two-page report and recommendations. They unveiled their findings before a packed press conference at the National Press Club on July 23, 2006.[32] Their conclusion: It is a violation of the Constitution for a president to sign a bill and then issue a signing statement declaring that some of its provisions are unconstitutional and need not be enforced (or obeyed) as written. The panel concluded that the Founders gave presidents only two options: veto a bill, or sign it and enforce all of it. "The president's constitutional duty is to enforce laws he has signed into being, unless and until they are held unconstitutional by the Supreme Court," the report said. "The Constitution is not what the president says it is."[33]

In its report, the ABA task force acknowledged that its work had been prompted by "the number and nature of the current president's signing statements," but it emphasized that its criticism was "not intended to be, and should not be viewed as, an attack on President George W. Bush." They noted that previous presidents had also used signing statements and they emphasized that their main concern was the future balance of power between Congress and the executive branch. Specifically, they warned that signing statements were evolving into a kind of back-door line-item veto, which the Founders never intended presidents to have — especially when Congress had no ability to override it. "A line-item veto is not a constitutionally permissible alternative, even when the president believes that some provisions of a bill are unconstitutional," they said. "A president could easily contrive a constitutional excuse to decline enforcement of any law he deplored, and transform his qualified veto into a monarch-like absolute veto."*

More than 150 newspaper editorial boards, columnists, and political cartoonists around the country joined in the call for an end to signing statements. But the ABA task force's findings met with a more controversial

---

*On August 7, 2006, the ABA House of Delegates adopted the task force's findings as the official position of the American Bar Association as a whole. The group declared that it "opposes, as contrary to the rule of law and our constitutional system of separation of powers, the misuse of presidential signing statements by claiming the authority or stating the intention to disregard or decline to enforce all or part of a law the president has signed, or to interpret such a law in a manner inconsistent with the clear intent of Congress."

reception among some legal scholars. Some critics argued that the task force was being unrealistic. As former attorney general Thornburgh had argued back in 1990, Congress sometimes includes flawed provisions in large and important bills, which are impractical to veto over small constitutional problems. For example, the Supreme Court made clear in 1983 that Congress cannot force the executive branch to get the prior approval of an oversight committee before taking an action. Nor can Congress give one of its chambers or committees the ability to veto an executive branch decision. The court explained that the only actions by Congress that have legal force are those in which majorities in both chambers have approved something and then given it to the president to sign or veto. But Congress had continued to include unconstitutional one-chamber or one-committee "legislative veto" provisions in numerous bills. Presidents had signed such bills but said they would interpret the legislative veto provision to be a mere request to notify the committee about the actions the executive branch was taking. Under this wink-and-nod system, life in Washington had gone on. If presidents instead had to veto bills every time they contained such a small flaw, critics said, the machinery of government would grind to a halt.

The ABA task force, however, said that the Constitution's limits on presidential power trump such pragmatic considerations. Congress could quickly fix a flawed bill and repass it within a few hours, they said. And they suggested that Congress would quickly clean up its act and pass tidier bills once presidents enforced the rules more rigidly.

Other scholarly critics rejected the notion that presidents can only either veto a bill or sign it and enforce all of it literally. They noted that most scholars agree that presidents *can* and *should* decline to enforce unconstitutional statutes that are already on the books from a previous administration. If that is the case, the critics said, then why can't a president also sign a large bill with small constitutional flaws and not enforce them instead of vetoing it? And in such a situation, the critics added, a signing statement is a good thing, because at least it lets people outside the executive branch know about the decision. Take away signing statements, and presidents will still sign bills and not enforce all of their sections, but it will be less transparent.

To this, ABA president Michael Greco and the members of the task force replied: Signing a bill is different from deciding whether to enforce a law that is already on the books. A president swears an oath to protect and defend the Constitution. When given an opportunity to keep off the books a statute that would violate the Constitution, the president must veto the bill.

Finally, some critics of the ABA argued that the task force, by bending over backwards to appear bipartisan and to avoid singling out President Bush for criticism, had missed the real target. These critics agreed that the Bush-Cheney signing statements were outrageous but said the problem was not the device itself, but instead the legal theories being expressed in the signing statements. The Bush-Cheney team was making imperious claims about what kinds of laws violated the president's powers. But future presidents with a more mainstream understanding of the Constitution ought to be able to keep signing flawed bills and issuing signing statements identifying any unconstitutional parts, they said.[34] The liberal Harvard Law School professor Laurence Tribe, for instance, said he agreed that Bush had "abused" the practice of issuing signing statements, but he also said that taking away from future presidents the power to sign a bill and then not enforce parts of it would do more harm than good. "We need to keep in mind that institutional remedies designed to fit pathological power-holders might themselves prove to be misfits in their overall impact on what should be an enduring system of checks and balances," Tribe wrote.[35]

But Mickey Edwards, the former Republican congressman from Oklahoma who also served on the ABA task force, said all the critics—both conservatives who accused the task force of being too anti-Bush, and liberals who accused it of being insufficiently anti-Bush—were missing the bigger picture. Thanks to the actions of recent presidential legal teams from both parties, the executive branch was prying open an ever-larger constitutional loophole in order to increase its power at the expense of Congress's. Under the Bush-Cheney administration, he said, the practice reached a tipping point that finally brought it into the spotlight. Now that everyone realized what was happening, he said, it was time to put the presidency back into the veto-it-or-sign-it box the Founders intended.

"It's not about Bush; it's about what should be the responsibility of a president," Edwards said. "We are saying that the president of the United States has an obligation to follow the Constitution and exercise only the authority the Constitution gives him. That's a central tenet of American conservatism—to constrain the centralization of power."[36]

7.

The controversy over the Bush-Cheney signing statements also prompted a sustained reaction in Congress.

At first, many of the lawmakers who stepped forward in 2006 to accuse the White House of usurping their institution's constitutional power to write the law were Democrats. "We're a government of laws, not men," said Senate minority leader Harry Reid, Democrat of Nevada, adding, "It is not for George W. Bush to disregard the Constitution and decide that he is above the law."[37] Patrick Leahy of Vermont declared, "The scope of the administration's assertions of power is stunning, and it is chilling."[38] Edward Kennedy of Massachusetts said that the Bush-Cheney administration, abetted by "a compliant Republican Congress," was undermining the checks and balances that "guard against abuses of power by any single branch of government."[39] Representatives Sheila Jackson-Lee of Texas and Barney Frank and Edward Markey, both of Massachusetts, proposed legislation to roll back the use of signing statements.[40]

But some Republicans, perhaps recognizing that the White House would not always be in GOP hands, joined in the criticism. Senate Judiciary Committee chairman Arlen Specter held a hearing on signing statements on June 27, 2006. Specter asked the administration to send Attorney General Alberto Gonzales or Steven Bradbury, the acting head of the Office of Legal Counsel. Instead, the administration sent Michelle Boardman, a lower-ranking deputy. Boardman sidestepped questions about the legal merits of specific signing statements. Instead, she argued that Bush had actually shown Congress *respect* by using signing statements instead of vetoes when he had concerns about parts of the bills they had passed. "Respect for the legislative branch is not shown through [making a] veto," she announced. "Respect for the legislative branch, when we have a well-crafted bill, the majority of which is constitutional, is shown when the president chooses to construe a particular statement in keeping with the Constitution, as opposed to defeating an entire bill that would serve the nation."[41]

Boardman also insisted the president has the power and responsibility to bypass any statute that conflicts with the Constitution, even in cases "where the Supreme Court has yet to rule on an issue, but the president has determined that a statutory law violates the Constitution." She also stressed that previous presidents had used signing statements to raise constitutional concerns about legislation they were signing as well.

But Senator Russ Feingold, Democrat of Wisconsin, pointed out that the administration had used that power "far more often" than any predecessor. Moreover, Feingold said, Bush had done so "to advance a view of executive power that, as far as I can tell, has no bounds." He added that the White House had "assigned itself the sole responsibility for deciding which laws it will comply with, and in the process has taken upon itself the powers of all three branches of government."

A month later, on July 26, 2006, Specter filed legislation that would give Congress the legal standing to sue a president over the claims he made in a signing statement so that a court could resolve whether or not a White House really had the power to set aside or rewrite a particular law. Specter's bill would also instruct courts to ignore presidential signing statements when interpreting the meaning of a statute.

Meanwhile, Bush continued to issue several high-profile and controversial signing statements in late 2006. And neither Specter's bill nor any of the related three House Democratic proposals received a vote before the Republican-controlled Congress adjourned at the end of 2006. But in early 2007, after Democrats regained power in both chambers of Congress, such measures were immediately revived. And as soon as Democrat John Conyers Jr. took over the gavel of the House Judiciary Committee in January 2007, he beefed up the committee staff by hiring a special "oversight and investigative unit" of about six attorneys to lead the panel's probes of the administration. Conyers said its first tasks would include attempting to determine whether the executive branch had gone on to violate the laws Bush had claimed a right to ignore. "This is a constitutional issue that no self-respecting federal legislature should tolerate," Conyers said.[42]

# 11

## "To Say What the Law Is": The Supreme Court

### 1.

On July 1, 2005, Supreme Court justice Sandra Day O'Connor—the author of the 2004 *Hamdi* opinion, which declared that "a state of war is not a blank check for the president"—sent President Bush a brief note. After nearly a quarter century of service on the bench, the justice was seventy-five years old, and her husband's health was failing. "This is to inform you of my decision to retire from my position as an associate justice of the Supreme Court of the United States, effective upon the nomination and confirmation of my successor," O'Connor wrote. "It has been a great privilege indeed to have served as a member of the court for 24 terms. I will leave it with enormous respect for the integrity of the court and its role under our constitutional structure."

O'Connor's retirement unleashed tumult in Washington. It had been more than a decade since the last Supreme Court vacancy, and well-funded interest groups among both liberals and conservatives had long been bracing for the next nomination fight. In addition to being the first woman ever to serve on the Court, O'Connor was also by far its most powerful member. The Court often decided important cases by a 5–4 vote—with four generally predictable liberal votes, four generally predictable conservative votes, and O'Connor as a swing vote who held the power to decide which faction to make a majority. Her replacement could help shift the Court's ideological balance for decades, affecting the outcome of a huge range of issues, including abortion, affirmative action,

250

civil rights, the death penalty, environmental regulations, gay marriage, police searches, and states' rights.

Eighteen days later, the press corps was told to assemble in a ceremonial space on the first floor of the White House dominated by marble walls, lush wine-red carpeting, and golden curtains. At 9:02 p.m., Bush appeared at the far end of the room and strode to a podium. By his side stood a fifty-year-old appeals court judge named John G. Roberts Jr.

"One of the most consequential decisions a president makes is his appointment of a justice to the Supreme Court," Bush said. "When a president chooses a justice, he's placing in human hands the authority and majesty of the law. The decisions of the Supreme Court affect the life of every American. And so a nominee to that Court must be a person of superb credentials and the highest integrity; a person who will faithfully apply the Constitution and keep our founding promise of equal justice under law. I have found such a person in Judge John Roberts."[1]

Polished and charismatic, Roberts had grown up the son of a steel-mill executive in Indiana before earning top grades at Harvard College and then Harvard Law School. He clerked on the Supreme Court for then–associate justice William Rehnquist before joining the Reagan administration in 1981 alongside a cohort of other young conservative attorneys. Roberts worked for both the Justice Department and the White House Counsel's office under Reagan and was deputy solicitor general in the Bush-Quayle administration. The first President Bush had nominated Roberts for an appeals court judgeship but then lost the White House to Bill Clinton before the Senate took up Roberts's nomination. Unconfirmed, Roberts spent the 1990s as a highly successful and well-paid appellate attorney, arguing dozens of times before the Supreme Court on behalf of private clients. When the second President Bush took office, he nominated Roberts for an appeals court seat again, and the Senate confirmed him in June 2003. Now, two years later, Roberts was in line for the promotion of a lifetime.

Only four days before Bush nominated Roberts to the Supreme Court, Roberts had voted to give the White House a sweeping victory in *Hamdan v. Rumsfeld*, a case challenging the president's wartime powers. In November 2004, a federal judge had struck down Bush's military commission trials at Guantánamo, saying that the president could not create such trials without involving Congress and that he had violated the Geneva Conventions. But on July 15, 2005, Roberts and two colleagues overturned the lower-court decision, ruling that Bush did not need to consult Congress before setting up his commissions. And in a separate part of the *Hamdan* case, which was decided by a 2–1 vote, Roberts cast the decisive vote to hold that the commander in chief has independent power to declare that the Geneva Conventions do not protect wartime detainees suspected of terrorism—calling this "the sort of political-military decision constitutionally committed to him."[2]

When Bush announced that he was picking Roberts for the Supreme Court, some observers noted the close proximity of Bush's decision and the military commissions ruling. But eyebrows really shot up the following month. On August 2, 2005, Roberts turned in a Senate Judiciary Committee questionnaire in preparation for his coming confirmation hearings. One of the questions the Senate asked was when he had met with administration officials to be interviewed as a potential candidate for the Court. Roberts told the Senate that he had met with Attorney General Alberto Gonzales on April 1, 2005—six days before he heard oral arguments in the case.[3] On May 3, as Roberts and his two colleagues were conferring about how to decide the case and what the opinion should say, Roberts had gone to Vice President Cheney's mansion at the U.S. Naval Observatory for a secret meeting with Cheney, Cheney's chief of staff I. Lewis "Scooter" Libby, White House chief of staff Andrew Card, Bush's political adviser Karl Rove, White House counsel Harriet Miers, and Gonzales. (The interview began when Cheney—who had been helping winnow down the list of possible Supreme Court nominees for months before O'Connor's announcement—told Gonzales, "Well, you're the lawyer. Let's begin."[4]) On May 23, Miers met with Roberts again. And Roberts's final interview had been with Bush himself—a meeting at which Bush, as he emphasized in introducing Roberts, had been "deeply impressed" by the judge. The meeting with Bush was on July 15, the very day Roberts and his colleague handed down the opinion backing broad executive powers for the president.

## 2.

Disputes over the scope of the president's constitutional powers, as previously noted, rarely get litigated, a reality that usually allows handpicked presidential legal teams to make their own pronouncements. On rare occasions, however, a plaintiff arises who has standing to sue a president, and such cases can result in an embarrassing and frustrating setback for aggressive White House legal teams. During these instances, a slight swing on the Supreme Court can make the difference. All other legal experts must make arguments about the text and history of the Constitution in order to convince others that their interpretation of the law is correct. But at the top of the American legal system, five justices on the Supreme Court don't need to convince anybody. Instead, five human beings in black robes, each bringing his or her own experiences and agendas to the courthouse, have the raw power simply "to say what the law is," as Chief Justice John Marshall wrote in *Marbury v. Madison*, the landmark 1803 case that established the principle that the court gets the final word on the meaning of the Constitution.

The power held by any bloc of five Supreme Court justices has at times proven controversial to liberals and conservatives alike. Prior to 1937, a bloc of conservatives on the Court kept striking down minimum-wage, work-week, and child-labor laws on the grounds that the Constitution contains an unwritten right to contract for one's labor as one might choose. Then a change of heart by one justice and a decision to retire by another meant that suddenly such New Deal laws were constitutional. In 1970, the Supreme Court held 6–3 that the government could not stop paying welfare benefits without first giving the recipient a full hearing.[5] Six years later, after four justices retired and were replaced by Nixon and Ford nominees, the Court held 6–2 that the government *could* cut off benefits without a pretermination hearing.[6] Prior to December 2000, the overwhelming consensus in the legal community was that states had a right to handle their own elections. Then, in the *Bush v. Gore* case, the five most states' rights–oriented justices voted to overrule the Florida Supreme Court's order for a full statewide recount in the disputed presidential election, a ruling that effectively made George W. Bush president.[7]

When Supreme Court vacancies arose during the Bush–Cheney era, Bush had many conservative lawyers to choose from, any of whom would have satisfied the Republican Party's base. When he announced his selections, the media and legal activist groups—conservative and liberal alike—focused overwhelmingly on the nominees' records on social and economic issues such as abortion rights, affirmative action, and environmental regulation. The coverage and questioning tended to overlook perhaps the single most important trait that all three nominees had in common from the perspective of the Bush-Cheney legal team. All three were conservatives of a very particular type. All three nominees had spent years working inside the executive branch, marinating in fights over presidential power from the point of view of the White House. Having developed their legal thinking alongside others dedicated to expanding the president's authority, all three nominees were a safe bet in the long-term project to achieve five votes on the Supreme Court—a new majority bloc ready to say that their theories of presidential power were true.

And in the midst of the Supreme Court nomination battles of 2005 and 2006, *Hamdan v. Rumsfeld,* one of the most important cases on presidential power to emerge from the Bush-Cheney era, reached the high court. Its fate would sharply illustrate the stakes in the administration's long-term efforts to build a voting bloc sympathetic to maximum executive power.

3.

In the weeks that followed President Bush's announcement that John Roberts would be the first Supreme Court nominee in more than a decade, the National Archives released tens of thousands of pages of Reagan administration files that had Roberts's name on them—memos about matters large and small, from abortion litigation strategy to whether Reagan ought to invite singer Michael Jackson to the White House in order to commend the "king of pop" for his charity work. As the media and Senate aides sifted through the cascade of documents for clues to Roberts's legal philosophy, they found traces of his thinking about an abundance of issues. Front-page headlines trumpeted the discovery that Roberts once contributed to a Reagan administration legal brief saying that *Roe v. Wade,* the abortion rights decision, had been wrongly decided because "the Constitution does not protect a right to an abortion." Roberts had privately denounced a version of the Equal Rights Amendment for women. He had worked assiduously to adopt a narrow reading of the Voting Rights Act. As a private attorney, he had represented mining interests seeking to evade environmental regulations and business groups seeking to avoid affirmative action requirements. As an appeals court judge, he had tried to restrict the ability of the federal government to protect an endangered species that lived in only one state.

Roberts was, in short, a conservative across a host of issues, and activist groups soon filled the airwaves with dire warnings of the "threat" his nomination posed to progressive causes. Almost lost amid the hubbub was something the papers revealed about an issue that was neither conservative nor liberal. Roberts, from the beginning of his legal career and straight through to the *Hamdan* decision, had demonstrated his unwavering commitment to the project to expand presidential power.

His views were shaped during his clerkship year under Rehnquist during the Supreme Court's 1980–1981 term. When, as part of the negotiations with the Ayatollah Khomeini to end the embassy-worker hostage crisis, President Carter had agreed to shut down lawsuits by American corporations that had lost property in Iran after the revolution, serious questions about executive power were raised. The American businesses wanted the courts to award them Iranian property in the United States as compensation for their lost property in Iran. Such lawsuits were authorized by a statute passed by Congress, but Carter had asserted he could shut them down on his own. The Supreme Court had unanimously backed Carter, declaring that broad deference was owed to a president's foreign policy decisions, and noting that Congress seemed to have acquiesced, because lawmakers did not pass new legislation to defend their statute.[8]

The opinion was written for the Court by Rehnquist. Although the behind-the-scenes input of law clerks is a closely held secret, *Legal Times* later reported that there was evidence Roberts had played a leading role in drafting Rehnquist's opinion.[9] And Roberts later would take steps to protect the decision's reputation. In August 1983, when he was working for the White House counsel's office, Roberts was asked to review the draft of an article by another administration attorney that placed the Iran case in a "rogue's gallery" of suspect decisions based on a false constitutional premise. Roberts wrote that while he would not "feign objectivity on the point," he strongly objected to allowing the official to criticize the case and requested it be removed from the article.[10]

Indeed, while the entire Reagan team was dedicated to preserving presidential prerogatives—a project that sometimes took the form of undermining the power of the rival branches of government—memos housed at the National Archives and the Reagan Presidential Library show that Roberts often took more extreme positions than his colleagues. In April 1982, less than a year after he joined the administration, Roberts reviewed a nine-page memo by Ted Olson, then the head of the Justice Department's Office of Legal Counsel. At the time, conservatives in Congress were considering legislation that would attempt to take away the Supreme Court's power to decide cases involving issues such as abortion rights or school desegregation busing. The Reagan administration was trying to decide whether it would support or oppose the jurisdiction-stripping legislation. In his memo, Olson argued that there were "sound political reasons to oppose these bills," including that it would make Reagan look "courageous and principled" to "oppose efforts, however well-intentioned, to weaken the Court's constitutional function." But Roberts disagreed with Olson. In his review copy of the draft, Roberts bracketed this paragraph and scrawled in the margins, "Real courage would be to read the Constitution as it should be read and not to kowtow" to liberal law professors.[11]

In June 1983, the Supreme Court handed down a decision that sharply undercut the power of Congress to check the presidency. For years, as noted earlier, Congress had passed laws delegating extra powers to the executive branch but also reserving the right to veto specific decisions the executive branch made with those powers if lawmakers did not like them. Often, these laws allowed just one chamber, or just one committee, to vote to override an executive branch decision. In *INS v. Chadha,* the Court struck down hundreds of these "legislative vetoes" scattered throughout federal law. Congress quickly convened hearings to determine how the government should respond to the ruling.

Inside the White House, Roberts was among a group of attorneys assigned to review the testimony administration officials were preparing to submit at those hearings. Some in the executive branch wanted to go further. They saw the fallout from the *Chadha* decision as an opening to seize power over the independent agencies, such as the Federal Reserve, the Food and Drug Administration, and the Federal Trade Commission. Congress had designed these agencies to be free from political interference by withholding from the president the power to direct their actions or to fire their officers. Such agencies were a thorn in the side of presidential power absolutists, who believed that the White House should be able to directly control all aspects of the federal bureaucracy—a belief that would soon be crystallized in the name Unitary Executive Theory.

On July 15, 1983, Roberts declared himself to be one of those who believed that the president was entitled to run the independent agencies. "With respect to independent agencies, the testimony suggests in a general way that the time may be ripe to reconsider the existence of such entities, and take action to bring them back within the executive branch," Roberts wrote. "Only this last point has generated controversy among those reviewing the testimony. I agree that the time is ripe to reconsider the Constitutional anomaly of independent agencies, and the testimony does no more than suggest such a fresh look in the broadest terms. More timid souls may, however, desire to see this deleted as provocative."[12]

Two weeks later, as the *Chadha* decision continued to roil the government, Roberts was again pushing further than his colleagues to seize even greater advantage for the power of the president. One of the laws affected by the ruling was the Foreign Assistance Act, which banned federal aid to certain nations but under certain conditions allowed a president to waive such a restriction. In its original form, the law had allowed Congress to veto a presidential waiver if both chambers voted to do so—a procedure the *Chadha* decision might still allow. But in 1981, Congress had replaced the two-chamber veto with a one-chamber veto, which *Chadha* said was clearly unconstitutional. State Department lawyers, reviewing this law, declared that the *Chadha* ruling had invalidated the 1981 changes, so the two-chamber veto was back. Roberts was livid. "This is absurd," he wrote on July 28, 1983. The better interpretation, he explained, was that no veto at all had survived the ruling, so presidents were now free to waive foreign assistance bans without any check-and-balance oversight from Congress.[13]

Roberts soon had another chance to demonstrate his views on presidential power. In October 1983, without asking Congress for authorization, Reagan ordered U.S. troops to invade the tiny country of Grenada in the Caribbean. Though many approved of the policy thinking behind the gesture, some critics called for Reagan to be impeached for breaking the law. As this debate unfolded in January 1984, Roberts was assigned to review a letter to the president and draft a reply. It was from a retired Supreme Court justice, Arthur Goldberg.

In his letter, Goldberg said he agreed that it was doubtful that the invasion of Grenada was constitutional, but he noted it had been a great success and helped the cause of democracy in that country. The former Supreme Court justice compared Reagan's actions to those of President Lincoln during the Civil War, arguing that Reagan should not be impeached even if the Grenada action was unconstitutional because he "acted in good faith and in the belief that this served our national interest." Roberts, drafting a reply to Goldberg for his boss's signature, thanked the former justice for defending Reagan but emphasized that the administration had no doubt that the invasion was legal. Citing a section of the Iran lawsuit decision he had helped write as Rehnquist's clerk, Roberts insisted that the president had "inherent authority in international affairs to defend American lives and interests and, as Commander-in-Chief, to use the military when necessary in discharging these responsibilities."[14]

Throughout the winter and spring of 1984, Roberts also demonstrated that he believed a president should enjoy strong powers to keep his administration's papers secret. One of the post-Watergate reforms passed by Congress was the Presidential Records Act in 1978. This law declared that, beginning with the administration that would follow Jimmy Carter's, all presidential papers would be considered government property and, with a few exceptions for classified national security–related materials, the documents must be made available to the public and researchers twelve years after a president leaves office. In a series of memos about this law, Roberts made clear that he loathed this law, believing it to be an unconstitutional infringement on the presidency's power to keep information secret.

Reviewing testimony about presidential archives, Roberts wrote on February 13, 1984, that the administration ought to challenge the act's twelve-year limit on disclosure. He returned to his worries about the future disclosure of presidential records on May 16, 1984, arguing that the administration should come out against a bill then pending in Congress that would make the National Archives a separate agency. Roberts said that the bill "*could* grant the Archivist some independence from Presidential control, with all the momentous constitutional consequences that would entail." Others in the administration disagreed with Roberts's interpretation, and the White House did not object to the bill. Realizing he could not overrule them, Roberts suggested attaching a signing statement to the bill making clear that the president would interpret the bill as allowing the president to fire an Archivist if he or she tried to disobey the White House about whether to release an historic presidential document.[15]

Roberts delivered his broadest attack on the Presidential Records Act on September 9, 1985. Warning of the need to do something about the flaws in the law, he noted that the problem was that it would not be possible for the executive branch to file a lawsuit challenging the act until twelve years after the Reagan administration—the first to be subject to its disclosure requirement—left office. But in 2001, it was possible that the sitting president, "whose views will be critical in an executive privilege dispute," would be someone with a political interest in making sensitive Reagan-era documents "open to the public."[16] Perhaps, Roberts suggested, it would be possible for the Reagan administration to challenge the constitutionality of the records law right then in 1985, arguing that the president's ability to receive candid advice was already being harmed.

"Twelve years is a brief time in public life," Roberts wrote in a draft memorandum that he suggested his boss, White House counsel Fred Fielding (who would reprise his role for the Bush-Cheney White House starting in 2007), might want to sign. "Many of the personalities candidly discussed in sensitive White House memoranda, and certainly many of the authors of the memoranda, will be active twelve years from now. My concern is not so much the embarrassment that might result in the year 2001 when comments made under different circumstances become public, but the danger that the prospect of disclosure after such a brief period might inhibit the free flow of candid advice and recommendations within the White House. That flow is protected by the constitutionally based doctrine of executive privilege, and a strong argument can be mounted that the statutory 12-year ceiling on restricting access is unconstitutional."[17]

Roberts lost his crusade; the Reagan administration did not challenge the Presidential Records Act. As it turned out, however, the Reagan team could not have had stronger future allies in keeping their papers secret than Vice President Cheney, who shared Roberts's view of the need for presidential advice to be secret and candid, and President George W. Bush, whose father's vice presidential papers were among those that were to be released in 2001. The Bush-Cheney team did not even bother to ask a court to strike down the law, as Roberts had envisioned; instead, as noted earlier, Bush issued an executive order that simply gutted the law without further ado. Yet, ironically, there were two members of the Reagan team who did not benefit from the Bush-Cheney attack on the Presidential Records Act, because Bush chose to nominate them to the Supreme Court, making it politically impossible to withhold their papers from the Senate Judiciary Committee.

The first of those who did find their papers at the National Archives open to the public for all to read, just as the young Roberts had worried would happen, was Roberts himself. And throughout the documentary trail, Roberts revealed himself to be a strong advocate of pushing the boundaries of presidential power. He pushed to resist congressional efforts to make recess appointees less powerful than officials who went through the Senate confirmation process. He pressed to expand the president's ability to govern in secret, pushing to roll back the Federal Advisory Committee Act (the very law Cheney would seek to circumvent in his energy task force case) and warning against even appearing to endorse the idea of "freedom of information," lest it be construed as suggesting that the Freedom of Information Act was a good thing. He opposed issuing any presidential documents in connection with the War Powers Resolution that were worded in such a way as to concede that Congress had a role in deciding when military hostilities could begin or end.[18]

To be sure, Roberts was an attorney working for a client—the president—and so was inclined to protect his client's interests. But Roberts's memos show that even by the standards of the Reagan administration, which had been full of attorneys dedicated to protecting presidential prerogatives, Roberts regularly took more extreme positions on presidential power than many of his colleagues.[19]

And in 2003, when he became a life-tenured judge on the appeals court and was beholden to no client, he continued to side with executive power. During his first year on the bench, for example, a three-judge panel on Roberts's appeals court disagreed with Vice President Cheney in his dispute over whether he had to disclose his secret energy task force records. Roberts voted to have the full court take a second look at the case, indicating that he thought the panel decided it wrongly. In a 2004 case involving whether Bush had the power to dismiss lawsuits against Iraq by a group of American soldiers who had been captured and tortured during the first Gulf War, Roberts alone among a panel of three judges embraced the administration's expansive reading of presidential power. Under the administration's interpretation of a statute, the president had the power to declare that courts could not hear such lawsuits. Only Roberts agreed, arguing that as long as "the President's interpretation of [the law] is at least a reasonable one," the courts should defer to it.[20]

## 4.

The importance of the Roberts nomination would soon intensify. On September 4, 2005, Supreme Court chief justice William Rehnquist died from thyroid cancer. Bush decided to change the nomination so that Roberts would fill Rehnquist's seat as chief justice rather than O'Connor's seat as an associate justice.

Many commentators suggested that the change lowered the stakes of the nomination because Rehnquist was perceived as a solid conservative vote, so even if Roberts turned out to be very conservative, his presence in Rehnquist's seat would not alter the outcome of any cases. These observers, however, were focused on social issues, such as abortion rights, giving little attention to how the change could affect rulings on presidential power. True, when compared with very liberal justices, Rehnquist was generally sympathetic to claims of broad presidential power, as one might expect from the former head of the Office of Legal Counsel for the Nixon administration. But Rehnquist came from an older generation of conservatives who remembered the fights Republicans in Congress had waged against Democratic presidents—Roosevelt and Truman—who were the first to expand executive power and set the "imperial presidency" in motion. Rehnquist, moreover, had clerked for Justice Robert Jackson in 1952, when Jackson penned his famous opinion laying out the limits of presidential power in the steel-seizure case. All of this made Rehnquist more suspicious of untrammeled presidential power than were the GOP activists who came of age during the Reagan years, such as Roberts. It had been Rehnquist, after all, who authored the 1987 decision rejecting the Unitary Executive Theory in the independent-counsel case. And in 2004, rejecting the views of the Bush-Cheney administration, Rehnquist had joined the O'Connor opinion holding that before the president can imprison a U.S. citizen as an "enemy combatant," the detainee must be given a fair hearing and legal representation.

Moreover, few in the media focused on the special administrative power wielded by the chief justice. Among his most important functions is the power to handpick which federal judges will sit on the secret Foreign Intelligence Surveillance Court, which must sign off on wiretaps and clandestine break-ins on U.S. soil conducted for counterintelligence and counterterrorism investigations. As chief justice, Roberts would be in a position to select judges for the national security court who were either likely to be skeptical or deferential to executive branch claims.

On September 29, 2005, the Senate voted 78–22 to confirm Roberts as the nation's seventeenth chief justice. Half of the chamber's forty-four Democrats ultimately voted for him, in acknowledgment of Roberts's stellar credentials, his smooth demeanor, and his polished testimony. Senator Leahy explained his decision to vote for Roberts like this: "Judge Roberts is a man of integrity. I can only take him at his word that he does not have an ideological agenda."[21]

Shortly after the Senate vote, Roberts went to the White House for a brief swearing-in ceremony at the center of executive power. Afterwards, he said, "I view the vote this morning as confirmation of what is for me a bedrock principle—that judging is different from politics." There would be decades to measure his voting record against that principle; Roberts was fifty years old on the day he took the oath, becoming the youngest man in more than two centuries to inherit the most powerful life-tenured position in U.S. government.[22]

A few months after he was installed as the new chief justice, Roberts got his first opportunity to pick a member of the Foreign Intelligence Surveillance Court. In December 2005, when it was revealed that Bush authorized the military to wiretap without warrants and circumvented the national security court, Judge James Robertson—the same federal district judge who struck down Bush's military commissions in the *Hamdan* case—resigned from his FISC seat in apparent protest of the program.[23] Roberts decided to fill the vacancy with Judge Robert Bates, the same federal district judge who sided with Cheney in dismissing the General Accounting Office's lawsuit seeking access to the energy task force records, a ruling that sharply undercut the congressional watchdog agency's ability to probe the executive branch.

5.

The lopsided confirmation of Roberts to be chief justice was a resounding political victory for the White House and a rare bright spot amid the fallout from the slow federal response to the Hurricane Katrina disaster along the Gulf Coast. Now, with Roberts installed in Rehnquist's seat, O'Connor still needed to be replaced. After more than ten years without a Supreme Court confirmation fight, the country was going to get two in a row. And there were signs that the second nomination battle was going to be tougher. Liberal activist groups such as the Alliance for Justice and People for the American Way had been preparing for years for the next Supreme Court vacancy, and they were outraged that Democrats had not put up a tougher fight against Roberts. Moreover, the second pick would have a greater impact on the outcome of a wider range of cases. While Roberts was unlikely to vote strikingly differently than his conservative predecessor Rehnquist had on social issues, O'Connor had been the Court's leading moderate and swing vote. If the justice who replaced her was more conservative on social issues, the outcome of cases involving such hotly disputed matters as affirmative action and the death penalty might flip.

Perhaps hoping to deflect some of the coming attacks, Bush signaled that he would pick a woman or a minority for the seat, telling reporters that he understood that "diversity is one of the strengths of the country." But very

few people on either side of the political aisle expected the choice he announced at just past 8 a.m. on October 3, 2005—the first day of the Supreme Court's term. Appearing beside Bush was his own White House
counsel and his longtime attorney dating back to his Texas days, Harriet
Miers.

At first glance, the choice seemed inexplicable. Miers had won respect as
a corporate attorney in Dallas, where she rose to the top of a major law firm
and was the head of the State Bar of Texas. But she had no constitutional law
experience and no reputation as a first-rate legal thinker, conservative or
otherwise. Educated at Southern Methodist University, a low-ranking law
school, Miers had never been a judge, nor published an academic law journal article. Almost nobody—liberals and conservatives alike—believed
that Miers was remotely qualified to hold one of nine life-tenured seats on
the Supreme Court. In the immediate wake of the Hurricane Katrina disaster and the questions it raised about Bush's choice of Michael Brown, who
had no emergency management experience, as director of the Federal Emergency Management Agency, Miers was immediately decried as yet another
unqualified crony.

The furor was particularly intense among conservative activists who
had helped shepherd Roberts's nomination to its successful conclusion.
The first blow was struck at 8:12 a.m., almost before Bush had finished
speaking. Reporters glanced down at their buzzing BlackBerrys to discover an e-mail from Manuel Miranda, who organized more than 150
grassroots groups of social conservatives to build support for confirming
Bush's judicial picks through the umbrella group Third Branch Conference. Miranda was brutal: "The reaction of many conservatives today will
be that the president has made possibly the most unqualified choice since
Abe Fortas who had been [President Lyndon B. Johnson's] lawyer. The
nomination of a nominee with no judicial record is a significant failure
for the advisers that the White House gathered around it."[24]

Conservative criticism would only grow more harsh. Former judge Robert Bork, the conservative jurist whose 1987 failed confirmation marked a
milestone in partisan rancor, told MSNBC that Miers's nomination was "a
disaster on every level" because she was "a woman who's undoubtedly as
wonderful a person as they say she is, but so far as anyone can tell she has
no experience with constitutional law whatever. Now it's a little late to
develop a constitutional philosophy or begin to work it out when you're

on the court already. So that—I'm afraid she's likely to be influenced by factors, such as personal sympathies and so forth, that she shouldn't be influenced by. I don't expect that she can be, as the president says, a great justice."[25] The day after the nomination, George F. Will turned in a column submitting that "the president's 'argument' for her amounts to: Trust me. There is no reason to, for several reasons. [Bush] has neither the inclination nor the ability to make sophisticated judgments about competing approaches to construing the Constitution. Few presidents acquire such abilities in the course of their pre-presidential careers, and this president particularly is not disposed to such reflections."[26]

Adding to the tensions, conflicting documents emerged indicating that Miers might harbor moderate views about abortion rights and affirmative action.[27] Evangelical groups protested that Miers could not be counted on to vote for their key goal: overturning *Roe v. Wade*. Bush sought to assure them otherwise, sending a thinly disguised message that they could trust her because she herself was an evangelical Christian.[28] But the campaign only further alienated many conservatives, who said it was inappropriate to make Miers's religion part of her credentials or to argue that she would vote for the "right" outcomes of cases. Soon, conservative-opinion leaders were openly calling for the Miers nomination to be defeated. Former White House speechwriter David Frum, who had drafted Bush's famous "axis of evil" speech, announced he would run campaign commercials calling for Miers to be rejected.

Then, amid the clamor, a dispute over executive power arose. The Senate asked to see Miers's White House memos in order to judge the quality of her legal work, and the White House said disclosing such documents would violate executive privilege. The dispute was roundly seen as a trumped-up face-saving reason for pulling the nomination, as such a request was obviously foreseeable before she was nominated, and because conservative commentator Charles Krauthammer had suggested engineering a scenario of "irreconcilable differences over documents" in an October 21 column entitled "The Only Exit Strategy."[29] Bush followed Krauthammer's advice when he withdrew Miers's nomination on October 27, 2005—just over three weeks after she was announced.

"It is clear that Senators would not be satisfied until they gained access to internal documents concerning advice provided during her tenure at the White House—disclosures that would undermine a President's ability to receive candid counsel," Bush said. "Harriet Miers's decision demonstrates her deep respect for this essential aspect of the Constitutional separation of powers—and confirms my deep respect and admiration for her."[30]

So, why did Bush nominate Miers? The conventional wisdom was that the fiasco was simply the result of Bush's feckless enjoyment of the power his office gave him to reward his friends. But in fact, Miers was a sound pick by the Bush-Cheney administration on an issue about which they cared deeply: executive power. Bush needed to pick a female justice for political reasons, but executive branch experience was almost nonexistent in the résumés of the female conservative appeals court judges and state supreme court judges favored by conservative legal activists.[31] Miers, however, could be counted on to embrace Bush's expansive view of presidential powers. First of all, she was deeply loyal to Bush and, through him, to the institution he represented. Among two thousand pages of official correspondence and personal notes released by the Texas State Library and Archives Commission after her nomination was a letter she had written then–Texas governor Bush for his fifty-first birthday in July 1997: "You are the best governor ever—deserving of great respect." Other papers had her pronouncing her patron "cool" and "the greatest!" and declaring Texas "blessed" for his leadership.[32] With such an adoring view, Miers could be easily envisioned as providing solid support for any presidential claim of power that might come before the Court.

Moreover, even though it was Cheney-associated lawyers such as David Addington and John Yoo who had done the heavy lifting of crafting legal arguments in favor of virtually unrestricted presidential power since the attacks of September 11, 2001, Miers, along with every other White House attorney, had been absorbing and internalizing those arguments for years.[33] Like Roberts before her, she was an executive branch lawyer who identified with the task of defending the prerogatives of the president.

To be sure, the evidence that Miers was likely to be another executive power absolutist was not completely without exception. Years earlier, she had argued against expanding government powers in the face of security threats. In July 1992, as the president of the Texas Bar Association, Miers warned against responding to a courtroom shooting spree by infringing "on precious, constitutionally guaranteed freedoms." Writing in *Texas Lawyer* magazine, Miers had argued, "The same liberties that ensure a free society make the innocent vulnerable to those who prevent rights and privileges and commit senseless and cruel acts. Those precious liberties include free speech, freedom to assemble, freedom of liberties, access to public places, the right to bear arms, and freedom from constant surveillance. We are not willing to sacrifice these rights because of the acts of maniacs." But Miers had written that column a decade before moving to Washington and going to work for a president she adored amid the new threats of the war on terrorism, where the maniac might be holding a suitcase nuke instead of a handgun. In a speech in April 2005 before a GOP lawyers' group, she sounded a different note, arguing that reauthorizing the USA Patriot Act was "critical," because it had been "used in so many ways to help protect this nation and its people and in the war on terror." She made this speech in the context of bipartisan calls to amend the law with checks on new surveillance powers. There were other signs that her views had changed. Bill Goodman, legal director of the Center for Constitutional Rights, which sued Bush on behalf of prisoners at Guantánamo, for example, tried to raise alarm about Miers's nomination in the wake of Roberts. "The fact that the president is now seeding the Supreme Court with people who have been handmaidens in his efforts to increase the power of the executive without any check or oversight whatsoever is very disturbing," he said. And Leonard Leo of the conservative Federalist Society, who was one of the few outside legal activists not to break with the White House over the Miers nomination, invoked her association with Bush's terrorism policies in a vain attempt to assuage fears among fellow conservatives that she was too moderate. "In her work respecting the War on Terror and the threats posed to our country by misuse of foreign and international law, Ms. Miers has applied the Constitution as the Framers wrote it," Leo wrote.[34]

One final incident from the last days of her doomed nomination may have revealed the extent to which Miers had come to identify with the administration's aggressive views of far-reaching executive powers. The Senate Judiciary Committee sent Miers a questionnaire to fill out listing her background and experiences with constitutional law, as is standard practice. When she returned the document, it was decried across party lines for being short on details and specifics. Specter and Leahy vowed to essentially make her redo the questionnaire, a humiliation she was spared by her withdrawal. But lost among the bipartisan insults over the depth of her answers was a telling detail of what Miers had said. Among her chief qualifications to sit on the Supreme Court, she wrote, was the fact that her time as counsel to Bush had given her significant constitutional experience in "presidential prerogatives, the separation of powers, executive authority, and the constitutionality of proposed regulations and statutes." And she later added, "My time serving in the White House, particularly as Counsel to the President, has given me a fuller appreciation of the role of the separation of powers in maintaining our constitutional system. In that role, I have frequently dealt with matters concerning the nature and role of the executive power."[35]

## 6.

On October 31, 2005, four days after Bush withdrew Miers's name, he called another 8 a.m. press conference. Standing in the White House's Cross Hall, he introduced a replacement nominee: Samuel Alito Jr., a judge on the Third Circuit Court of Appeals. Alito was well known in conservative legal circles—a member of the Federalist Society with more than a decade of written opinions as an appeals court judge and with a top-notch pedigree, including a Yale Law School degree. Conservative activist groups quickly closed ranks behind the White House and backed his nomination. Liberal activist groups, which had sat on the sidelines during the conservative meltdown in October, also geared back up into action, eager to portray Alito as a threat.

Bush made no direct mention of the Miers nomination debacle that Halloween morning, but his remarks introducing Alito emphasized the ways in which the replacement pick was strong in all the places where Miers had been inadequate. Bush emphasized Alito's intellect and experience, noting his Ivy League credentials and calling him "one of the most accomplished and respected judges in America," whose fifteen years on the bench gave him "more prior judicial experience than any Supreme Court nominee in more than seventy years."[36] All this was true. But in one key respect Alito was like Miers, just as Miers was like Roberts.

First, like Miers and Roberts before him, Alito had spent his formative years in the federal government as an executive branch attorney. Alito joined the Reagan administration solicitor general's office in August 1981, then switched to the Justice Department's Office of Legal Counsel four years later. Reagan named Alito to be a U.S. Attorney in March 1987, taking him out of the White House amid the Iran-Contra scandal, and in February 1990, Bush's father had made Alito a federal judge on the U.S. Court of Appeals for the Third Circuit. Because few cases involving the federal government go through the Third Circuit, which covers New Jersey and Pennsylvania, Alito had not made any decisions as directly on point to executive power as Roberts's votes in cases about the military tribunal and Cheney's energy papers. But in many other respects, his leanings as an executive power absolutist were even clearer in his record.

In June 1984, for example, while working in the solicitor general's office, Alito had argued that high-ranking executive branch officials should be immune from lawsuits by victims of any illegal actions they took while on the job. His comments came as the Supreme Court considered a case involving illegal wiretapping by the Nixon administration. In 1970, Nixon's attorney general, John Mitchell, gave the FBI permission to wiretap a group of Vietnam War protesters suspected of plotting to kidnap Henry Kissinger and to bomb utility tunnels near federal buildings. No judge had approved the decision to listen in on the group's phone calls. In 1972, a jury cleared the protesters of any wrongdoing. That same year, the Supreme Court ruled in a different case that it was unconstitutional for the government to place domestic wiretaps without a warrant, even in national security matters. Prompted by that ruling, a man who had talked with one of the antiwar activists on the wiretapped line sued Mitchell personally, seeking financial damages for violation of his rights.

Mitchell's lawyers argued that the suit should be dismissed. The courts had no power under the Constitution's separation of powers, they said, to intrude on the executive branch by allowing lawsuits against the president's top aides for actions they take in performing their official duties. The case wound through the courts for years. In 1982, in a different case, the Supreme Court ruled that, with rare exceptions, the president's top aides can be held liable in civil lawsuits, but Mitchell pressed on with his objections. In 1984, as his case came before the Supreme Court, the Reagan administration had to decide whether to support Mitchell's broader reading of executive branch immunity. Alito was assigned to review the case. In a seven-page memo dated June 12, 1984, Alito wrote that he agreed with Mitchell that executive branch officials should be immune from civil lawsuits, even when their actions are unconstitutional—although he also cautioned that the Reagan administration should be careful about using a Nixon-era case to push its views. He noted that Rehnquist would likely side with the Reagan administration over such a question but would have to recuse himself because he was a former Nixon official who had worked with Mitchell. "There are strong reasons to believe that our chances of success will be greater in future cases," Alito added. "In addition, our chances of persuading the Court to accept an absolute immunity argument would probably be improved in a case involving a less controversial official and a less controversial era."[37]

In November 1985, when Alito applied to move from the solicitor general's office to the Office of Legal Counsel in Meese's Justice Department, he wrote a fiery application letter intended to prove that he was "and always have been a conservative and an adherent to the same philosophical views that I believe are central to this administration." Press stories about Alito's 1985 application letter concentrated on the fact that he had written that he believed "the Constitution does not protect a right to an abortion" and that he had touted his membership in the Concerned Alumni of Princeton University, a group that had objected to admitting women to the formerly all-male school.[38] The coverage tended to overlook another fact: Throughout the two-page letter, Alito repeatedly suggested that courts should defer to the "elected branches of government" as a matter of constitutional principle, not just in the area of "protecting traditional values" but also in security matters—the central front in the project to expand presidential power. "I believe very strongly in . . . the need for a strong defense and effective law enforcement," he wrote. ". . . In the field of law, I disagree strenuously with the usurpation by the judiciary of decision-making authority that should be exercised by the branches of government responsible to the electorate."[39]

Alito's letter was convincing. The next month, he joined the Office of Legal Counsel and went to work answering constitutional questions that arose within the executive branch. One of his duties was to serve on the Litigation Strategy Working Group, a special committee of fifteen political appointees who served as a brain trust for the Reagan administration's efforts to reshape the law in line with its ideological agenda. A major front in that war was to strengthen the power of the executive branch and diminish the influence of the courts and Congress. Alito took an active role in helping the committee advance the presidential-power project and, as noted earlier, was a prime mover in pushing Reagan to issue more signing statements in order to, as he wrote, "increase the power of the executive to shape the law."[40]

Alito's work with the Litigation Strategy Working Group would give him regular opportunities to develop and internalize an expansive theory of presidential power. On September 4, 1986, for example, Alito and the rest of the group met in the Lands Division Conference Room at the Justice Department for the sole purpose of discussing ways to turn aside "challenges to executive power." According to a memo that laid out the day's agenda, the group looked at such issues as ways to roll back restrictions on a president's "military power and related emergency powers"; to undermine statutes that set up independent officials within the executive branch who could not be fired by the president; to defend and expand "executive privilege"; to expand the power of the president to enter into "executive agreements" with foreign powers instead of treaties in order to cut out the role of Senate ratification; and to expand the president's absolute power of "executive discretion in foreign affairs and national security matters." Also up for discussion that day was "judicial usurpation of power . . . against the executive branch." This included court interference in "military management" and, in an echo of the Nixon-vintage wiretapping case, rulings against civil lawsuit immunity for executive branch officials.[41]

That meeting of the Litigation Strategy Working Group was one of the last Alito would attend. A few months later, in March 1987, he became the U.S. Attorney for the District of New Jersey, where he focused on prosecuting criminals. Nevertheless, Alito kept a close eye on developments in the presidential-power project—including a major setback for advocates of the Unitary Executive Theory, the Supreme Court's 7–1 June 1988 ruling in the independent counsel case.

In 1989, Alito denounced the independent counsel decision during an introduction to a debate sponsored by the conservative Federalist Society. "The Supreme Court hit the doctrine of separation of powers about as hard as heavyweight champ Mike Tyson usually hits his opponents," Alito said. He characterized the decision as an endorsement of a "congressional pilfering" of presidential power, and he embraced Scalia's championing of the Unitary Executive Theory as a "brilliant but very lonely dissent."[42] At the same event, Alito also praised then–solicitor general Charles Fried, one of the speakers at the debate he was introducing, for having "argued and won a great separation of powers victory" in a 1986 case involving a law intended to end budget deficits. Until struck down, the law had given the comptroller general—a congressional official who could not be fired by the president—the power to impose automatic spending cuts on the federal budget to achieve deficit-reduction goals. The Court ruled that Congress could not give such an "executive" power to an official accountable to the legislative branch.

In November 2000, Alito spoke at another Federalist Society convention, this time in Washington's storied Mayflower Hotel. In his remarks, he said, "In the thirteen years since I left [the Reagan-era Office of Legal Counsel], I have not had much occasion in my day-to-day work to think about the constitutional powers of the Presidency," but he made it clear that his views had not changed. Calling the Unitary Executive Theory the "gospel according to OLC," Alito said that he was as firmly committed to advancing this basis for expanding presidential power as he had been when he worked for Meese. He acknowledged that the Unitary Executive Theory, by freeing the president of many checks and balances, "can be used to accomplish things that most probably would not favor." But, he said, he still favored such a presidency.[43]

## 7.

When the Senate Judiciary Committee held its confirmation hearings for John Roberts in September 2005, the issue of executive power had received scant attention amid the clamor over his views on abortion, civil rights, and other social issues. But two events on the eve of Alito's January 2006 confirmation hearings changed the atmosphere, sharply intensifying the Senate's interest in presidential authority. First, on December 16, 2005, the *New York Times* published its article revealing that the Bush-Cheney administration had authorized the military to monitor Americans' international phone calls and e-mails without obtaining a judge's approval, seemingly a direct violation of a Watergate-era law regulating domestic surveillance. Then, on December 30, Bush issued the signing statement that undermined the McCain Torture Ban. The two high-profile claims that a president has the power to defy federal laws set off a brief firestorm in Congress, ensuring that Alito would be questioned more closely about his views on executive power.

On the first day of the hearings, January 9, 2006, Senator Richard Durbin said in his opening statement that he would focus on Alito's endorsement of the Unitary Executive Theory. "That's a marginal theory at best, and yet it's one that you've said you believe," said the Illinois Democrat. "This is not an abstract debate. The Bush administration has repeatedly cited this theory to justify its most controversial policies in the war on terrorism. Under this theory, the Bush administration has claimed the right to seize American citizens in the United States and imprison them indefinitely without charge. They have claimed the right to engage in torture, even though American law makes torture a crime. Less than two weeks ago, the White House claimed the right to set aside the McCain torture amendment that passed the Senate ninety to nine. What was the rationale? The Unitary Executive Theory, which you have supported."

Durbin's colleague Senator Charles Schumer, Democrat of New York, also weighed in. "The president is not a king, free to take any action he chooses without limitation by law," he said. ". . . In the area of executive power, Judge Alito, you have embraced and endorsed the theory of the unitary executive. Your deferential and absolutist view of separation of powers raises questions. Under this view, in times of war the president would, for instance, seem to have inherent authority to wiretap American citizens without a warrant, to ignore congressional acts at will, or to take any other action he saw fit under his inherent powers. We need to know, when a president goes too far, will you be a check on his power or will you issue him a blank check to exercise whatever power alone he thinks appropriate?"

The next day, when questioning began, Senator Edward Kennedy was the first to quiz Alito about his endorsement of the Unitary Executive Theory. Alito, however, turned the question aside by saying that in his Federalist Society speech he had been talking only about the idea that a president should have total control over lesser executive branch officials, not whether a president has the inherent presidential power to act beyond the will of Congress. Similarly, when asked about Bush's signing statement on the McCain Torture Ban in light of Alito's 1986 memo advocating for expanded use of signing statements, Alito simply described what a signing statement was. His answers were enough to turn aside Kennedy's thrust, and it was a tactic he repeated throughout the hearings whenever the topic of his views of executive power came up. When asked about the Unitary Executive Theory, he simply and narrowly described what it was. Alito carefully never said that he disagreed with the concept of expansive inherent powers for the president. He said only that inherent powers had not been the subject of his 2000 speech.

As for many of the senators asking Alito questions, they seemingly failed to grasp that the basis for extraordinary power claims being advanced by the Bush-Cheney legal team lay in *combining* the Unitary Executive Theory with its vision of vast "inherent" powers. In other words, by merely describing the unitary executive chocolate without disclosing his view of the inherent power peanut butter, and what he believed the two could become if united, Alito got away with never telling the senators what they really wanted to know.

Throughout the hearings, the closest any senator got to pinning Alito down on executive power was an exchange on January 11 with Senator Patrick Leahy. Leahy bore in on the real questions. For example, citing the Unitary Executive Theory in the case of an independent agency, the Federal Election Commission, Leahy asked, "Could the president, if he didn't like somebody they were investigating, a contributor or something, could he order them to stop?" Alito responded that Congress could establish some independence for executive branch officials—but then provided an enormous potential loophole: Any restrictions on firing the officials would be constitutional only if they "don't interfere with the president's exercise of executive authority." Leahy pressed on:

LEAHY: Could [the president] order the FBI to conduct surveillance in a way not authorized by statute?

ALITO: . . . He has to follow the Constitution and the laws of the United States. He has to take care that the laws are faithfully executed. If a statute is unconstitutional, then the president—then the Constitution would trump the statute. But if the statute is not unconstitutional, then the statute is binding on the president and everyone else.

LEAHY: But does the president have unlimited power just to declare a statute—especially if it's a statute that he had signed into law—to then declare it unconstitutional, he's not going to follow it?

ALITO: If the matter is later challenged in court, of course the president isn't going to have the last word on that question, that's for sure. And the court would exercise absolutely independent judgment on that question. It's emphatically the duty of the courts to say what the law is when constitutional questions are raised in cases that come before the courts.

LEAHY: That's an answer I agree with. Thank you.

But Alito did not address whether a president could declare a statute unconstitutional and violate it in a case that was impossible to challenge in court, as would commonly be the situation in a matter involving the separation of powers. Alito similarly conceded little on unrelated areas of the law, such as whether he would vote in line with his 1985 statement "The Constitution does not protect a right to an abortion."

Democratic leaders, knowing that they did not have the votes to stop Alito, decided that the best strategy was to vote en masse against him to show a united front. But the two Massachusetts senators, Kennedy and John F. Kerry, defied party leaders and called for a filibuster. The effort was applauded by liberal activist groups — especially those focused on abortion rights — but in the end it succeeded only in splitting the Democratic Party. Dashing party leaders' hopes of at least looking united against Alito, 24 Democrats voted in favor of the filibuster and 19 voted against it, echoing the party's 22–22 split on the Roberts nomination a few months earlier.[44]

On January 31, 2006, the Senate confirmed Alito to be the nation's 110th Supreme Court justice by a vote of 58–42, a largely party-line count that was overshadowed by the failed filibuster. Alito was sworn in that same day, replacing O'Connor and joining the Court in the middle of its 2005–2006 term.

## 8.

Justice Alito arrived on the Supreme Court in time to participate in the most important case of the term — and one of the most important cases involving presidential power in years. On March 28, 2006, the case of *Hamdan v. Rumsfeld* — the Guantánamo military tribunals case that Roberts had ruled on at the appeals court level just prior to Bush's decision to nominate him as O'Connor's replacement — was argued before the Supreme Court. Before the arguments began, Roberts himself stood up and left the courtroom; because the Court was hearing an appeal of his own decision, he recused himself from participation. Alito stayed, listening intently in his black robe from the far end of the bench — the seat where the newest justice sits — as Hamdan's lawyer, Georgetown law professor Neal Katyal, urged the Court to overturn the Roberts panel's ruling.

Katyal argued, as he had before, that Bush had no authority to set up the tribunals without consulting Congress, that the detainees should be able to invoke the Geneva Conventions in court as a guide to their minimum rights, and that the charge of conspiracy to commit terrorism was invalid because conspiracy is not a war crime under international law. "This is a military commission that is literally unbounded by the laws, Constitution, and treaties of the United States," Katyal said.

Alito was skeptical. He pressed Katyal to explain why Hamdan should be able to challenge his military trial up front, instead of waiting to see whether he was convicted and then raising the issue on appeal. "In criminal litigation, review after a final decision is the general rule," Alito noted. Wasn't Katyal seeking to give this enemy combatant an extra right that normal civilian defendants don't get?

Replied Katyal: "Justice Alito, if this were like a criminal proceeding, we wouldn't be here. The whole point of this is to say we're challenging the lawfulness of the tribunal itself. This isn't a challenge to some *decision* that a court makes. This is a challenge *to the court itself,* and that's why it's different than the ordinary criminal context that you're positing."[45]

Three months later, the Supreme Court handed down its decision, delivering a definitive judgment on the presidential-power theories advanced by the Bush-Cheney legal team. Bush had sought to limit the rights given to the detainees, saying that as president in a time of war he could handle such cases as he saw fit. He had established the commissions by executive order in November 2001 without consulting Congress, and he had established rules that allowed prosecutors to use secret evidence and confessions obtained by coercive interrogations. He had declared that the Geneva Conventions did not protect detainees in the war on terrorism, not even the basic prohibition against "the passing of sentences and the carrying out of executions without previous judgment pronounced by a regularly constituted court affording all the judicial guarantees which are recognized as indispensable by civilized peoples."

Five justices on the Supreme Court said Bush had broken the law.[46]

## 9.

It was immediately clear that the impact of the 5–3 ruling could go far beyond the fate of Salim Hamdan and the handful of other Guantánamo detainees who were facing charges before the military commission. Broadly speaking, the Court had repudiated assertions by Bush's legal team that, as commander in chief, the president is not bound to obey laws and treaties that restrict his ability to fight terrorism. More specifically, the majority had ruled that the United States was bound by Common Article Three of the Geneva Conventions, which guarantees fair trials to all people captured in an armed conflict. But the same provision also outlaws "cruel treatment, torture [and] outrages upon personal dignity, in particular, humiliating and degrading treatment." If the United States was bound to obey that restriction as well, then some of the harsh interrogation techniques Bush had authorized might be war crimes.

"Focusing just on the commissions aspect of this misses the forest for the trees," argued Martin Lederman, a Georgetown law professor and former Justice Department official, hours after the Court handed down the decision. "This ruling means that what the CIA and the Pentagon have been doing is, as of now, a war crime, which means that it should stop immediately."

Critics of the administration's legal theories rejoiced at the decision, calling it a victory for the rule of law against an executive power overreach. "I think that the language in here is really quite clear and unequivocal," said Elisa Massimino of Human Rights First. "This is really a civics lesson. Here the court is playing the role the founding fathers intended it to play both checking executive power and also reminding the president of the role of Congress." Yale Law School dean Harold Koh added: "Today's opinion is a stunning rebuke to the extreme theory of executive power that has been put forward for the last five years. It is a reminder that checks and balances continue to be a necessary and vibrant principle, even in the war on terror."[47]

But John Yoo, now back at Berkeley, was furious. He accused the Supreme Court of judicial activism and "micromanagement," saying its "unprecedented" intrusion into the president's "traditional national security prerogatives" would make the country less safe in all future emergencies. "What makes this war different is not that the president acted while Congress watched but that the Supreme Court interfered while fighting was ongoing," Yoo wrote. "The court displays a lack of judicial restraint that would have shocked its predecessors. . . . Justices used to appreciate the inherent uncertainties and dire circumstances of war, and the limits of their own abilities. No longer."[48]

## 10.

But such celebrations and lamentations proved overly simplistic. Press stories about the *Hamdan v. Rumsfeld* decision naturally focused on the five-member majority decision and tended to overlook hugely significant factors nestled in the dissenting opinion—two developments that potentially held the seeds of eventual triumphs for the cause of boundless presidential power.

First, the decision paved the way for increasing the legitimacy of presidential signing statements on occasions when courts have an opportunity to interpret a disputed statute. During Alito's confirmation hearings, he had turned aside questions about his 1986 memo by saying he had simply been assigned to raise and explore "theoretical problems" about the mechanism as a Reagan administration attorney and was not personally invested in the topic. ("The role of signing statements in the interpretation of statutes is, I think, a territory that's been unexplored by the Supreme Court, and it certainly is not something that I have dealt with as a judge," Alito had testified.[49]) Now Alito joined a dissenting opinion in the *Hamdan* case that contained an explicit reference to a presidential signing statement.

One of the issues that had been before the Court was whether the whole case should be thrown out to begin with because Congress had passed a law in December 2005 curtailing the power of Guantánamo detainees to file lawsuits. Congress had not said whether it meant the lawsuit ban to apply retroactively to pending cases, such as *Hamdan,* or whether it should stop only future lawsuits from being filed.

When Bush had signed the law, he had attached a signing statement to this provision, saying that he interpreted it as terminating existing lawsuits by Guantánamo detainees. The five-justice majority on the Court ignored Bush's signing statement. They read over the congressional history of the law and determined that it applied only to future lawsuits—so the *Hamdan* case could go forward.

But three justices disagreed, saying the case should have been thrown out. And in making their case, the dissent's author, Antonin Scalia, gave Bush's signing statement equal weight with statements by the bill's authors in Congress, suggesting—as the Meese Justice Department team two decades earlier had hoped courts would start doing—that there was no legal difference between the views of Congress and the president about what a law meant.

Scalia, who has long been skeptical about looking at the congressional record for insight into what an ambiguous statute means, scolded the majority. He said his colleagues had selectively cited bits of the act's legislative history to support its view and downplayed contrary evidence. "Of course in its discussion of legislative history the court wholly ignores the president's signing statement, which explicitly set forth his understanding that the [new law] ousted jurisdiction over pending cases," Scalia wrote, joined in dissent by Samuel Alito and Clarence Thomas.

The second seed of potential victory for the expansive executive power that was overlooked after the Court handed down its ruling in *Hamdan* lay in the vote count.

Although Roberts had recused himself from participation at the Supreme Court level, the new chief justice as an appeals court judge had already sided with the Bush-Cheney administration's view of its own powers. With Alito and Roberts on the new-look Supreme Court, then, there were now four justices who had demonstrated that they were inclined to defer to a president's claims to have sweeping powers to act beyond the will of laws passed by Congress, treaty obligations, and other checks and balances on executive power.

And the odds that those four would someday become the majority were strong. The Court's three youngest members—Roberts, fifty-one, Alito, fifty-six, and Thomas, fifty-eight—were all among the four "presidentialists." When the seventy-year-old Scalia was factored in, the average age of the four was less than fifty-nine. By contrast, the two oldest members of the court—John Paul Stevens, eighty-six, and Ruth Bader Ginsburg, seventy-three—were both members of the narrow majority that declared that even a commander in chief "is bound to obey the rule of law." The average age of the five exceeded seventy-two.

Given the realities of the human life span and the ebbs and flows of American politics, President Bush or one of his successors would have ample opportunity to gain that fifth vote.[50] And in the American legal system, five votes for a proposition on the Supreme Court makes that proposition the truth. Rather than being the final word on the Bush-Cheney legal team's sweeping theories of presidential power, *Hamdan* may turn out to have been one of the last hurrahs for those who believe in preserving the traditional checks and balances on White House power.

# 12

## Discipline and Control:
## The Executive Branch

1.

Just before 9 a.m. on Friday, July 28, 2006, a month after the Supreme Court declared that President Bush's military commission trials were illegal, a dozen professional military attorneys arrived at the Department of Justice headquarters for a meeting with the Bush-Cheney legal team. As members of the Judge Advocate General corps, these visitors were highly specialized servicemen and women. JAGs are law school graduates, members of the bar, and have received extensive training in the laws of war. Members of the JAG corps run court-martial trials for American troops accused of crimes, and during wartime they advise military commanders about how to avoid becoming war criminals. At the core of the JAG training and ethos is a profound reverence for the Geneva Conventions.

The JAGs had vehemently resisted Bush's legal conclusions that it was lawful to bypass the Geneva Conventions, arguing that the policy was both illegal and unwise, because undermining the treaties would increase the risk that American soldiers taken prisoner in future wars might be abused. But the administration's politically appointed attorneys, most of whom had never served in the military and were bent on making aggressive assertions of executive power, had discounted the uniformed lawyers' views as closed minded, parochial, and simplistic.

The JAGs had seen the *Hamdan* ruling as vindication. And now, as the administration scrambled to draft a bill for Congress that would resurrect some form of military commission trials for terrorists, the Justice

Department was bending over backwards to consult with the JAGs about what the legislation should look like, in marked contrast to how things had played out before.

Or that, at least, was the official message the administration was trying to send, in response to pressure from several key Republican senators who said they wanted the JAGs' advice to guide the new bill. On August 2, 2006, a week after the Justice Department meeting with the JAGs, Attorney General Alberto Gonzales would assure the Senate that the administration had complied with the Senate's wishes, testifying that "our deliberations have included detailed discussion with members of the JAG corps," whose "multiple rounds of comments . . . will be reflected in the legislative package."[1]

The JAGs had one overriding concern when they walked into the July 28 meeting for their opportunity to have detailed discussion about the legislative package: that there be no secret evidence. For the trials to be fair and to comply with the Geneva Conventions, they believed, defendants had to see all the evidence that prosecutors introduced against them so that they would have an opportunity to rebut it—an essential right in the Anglo-Saxon system of law that predates the existence of the United States by centuries. Bush's original military commissions, now struck down by the Supreme Court, allowed the removal of defendants from the courtroom when prosecutors wanted to introduce classified evidence. The political appointees said this was necessary in order to protect intelligence methods and sources, but the military lawyers believed that such a move violated basic principles of justice. If the government didn't want to show a particular piece of evidence to a defendant, then it shouldn't get to show it to the court, either.

But as soon as the JAGs sat down around a long conference table in room 5710—on the fifth floor of main Justice, just down the hall from the Office of Legal Counsel warren and the room in which eight Nazi saboteurs had been tried before a military commission during World War II—the administration lawyers announced that there was no point in debating the secret-evidence question, because a determination would be made by more senior officials. With the JAGs' main issue ruled out-of-bounds, the subsequent discussions were limited to minor concerns—wording changes, typo corrections, and procedural matters. The meeting lasted a little more than five hours, ending at 2:30 p.m. without a break for lunch. It was followed by a few days of e-mail exchanges that stopped after the first week of August. Following the exchanges, the Bush-appointed attorneys completed the bill they would submit to Congress on their own.[2]

The preemptive move meant that the "detailed discussion" and "multiple rounds of comments" that Gonzales later cited to the Senate almost entirely avoided the core concern of the JAGs. Gonzales himself had discussed secret evidence with the most senior JAGs precisely once, in late July. The session ended in an impasse, and the JAGs never got an opportunity to raise the issue with Gonzales again.

In the end, Congress decided to invite the top JAG from each service to testify about what they believed should be in the Military Commissions Act. Given an opportunity to bypass the filter of the Bush-Cheney legal team, the JAGs told lawmakers that to be fair and legal, the trials must give defendants the right to see any evidence used against them. The administration continued to argue against such a plan, but Congress ultimately decided that the uniformed lawyers were right; the final bill outlawed the use of secret evidence.

Although the JAGs won that round, the limits that the political appointees on the Bush-Cheney legal team had placed on its discussion with the career military lawyers left lingering bitterness. "The [Justice Department] should have learned that a failure to involve the JAG community can lead to problems," said Major General Nolan Sklute, who retired as the air force's top lawyer in 1996. "If they are talking to the JAGs only about superficial matters . . . that indicates that this is about form instead of substance, and nobody has learned any lessons out of this."[3]

## 2.

The federal bureaucracy exploded in size and importance over the twentieth century as Congress set up many new executive branch agencies and gave them increasing power. As the head of the executive branch, the president can draw on this permanent machinery of the state as a massive resource for implementing his policies—a tremendous advantage, considering the very small staffs of Congress and the judiciary. Yet those very same career professionals sometimes throw up roadblocks to a president's agenda.

Career civil servants and professional military officers are an entrenched force within the executive branch: Most are hired before a president takes office and will outlast his tenure, and they might not share his political agenda—especially if that agenda includes undermining the very mission Congress gave their agencies. Moreover, bureaucracies tend to develop arcane rules and procedures that can bog down or block the outcomes a president hopes to achieve. And most important, career bureaucrats are often specialists whose technical expertise gives them the authority to make judgments independently of the political appointees who are their temporary supervisors.[4]

The Bush-Cheney administration took vigorous steps to impose greater discipline and control on the permanent government, seeking to stamp out pockets of independence inside the executive branch. The administration tried systematically to subjugate and circumvent career officials who raised objections to their policies, and it tried to game the system to make sure that any expert advice the professionals provided would support the president's preexisting policy preferences. This was the Unitary Executive Theory in action—enforcing the notion that every official inside the executive branch is nothing more than an appendage of the president and should take no action and offer no opinion opposed by the White House. And while the Bush-Cheney administration was not the first to look for ways to expand its control over the permanent government, some of its battles with the bureaucracy were marked by particular intensity and aggression.

The administration fought to impose greater White House control on bureaucrats who hand out federal grants, on civil rights attorneys at the Justice Department, on government scientists who research environmental and reproductive health issues, and on agencies that make regulations that affect corporations. Among the most revealing of such case studies were its repeated clashes with career military attorneys.

3.

The story of the fight to sideline the Judge Advocates General corps dates back to the early 1990s, when Dick Cheney was secretary of defense in the Bush-Quayle administration. With his aide David Addington, Cheney tried but failed to eliminate the JAG corps' independence from political control.

For generations, the military has had two separate legal staffs: one uniformed and one civilian. The most important has long been the uniformed set, which is much larger and is charged with handling both courts-martial and legal issues that affect operational and war-fighting matters. Under statutes enacted by Congress, each military department—the army, air force, and navy    has a JAG corps of between roughly 650 and 1,700 uniformed lawyers. These uniformed lawyers are overseen by a two-star officer—"The" Judge Advocate General. Congress carved out specific responsibilities for the JAGs in statute, declaring in law for example that the top army JAG is to be "the legal adviser of the Secretary of the Army." But each military department also has a general counsel, a civilian political appointee who works on legal policy matters and oversees an office of other civilian lawyers.

In 1986, Congress passed a major act reorganizing the Department of Defense. While working on the bill, Congress examined the dual systems of legal services inside the military. Some argued that the two should be consolidated, putting the JAG corps under the direct supervision of the general counsels. But lawmakers decided to leave the JAGs' independence alone. Congress did make two changes: It recognized the existence of the general counsels in statute for the first time and required that presidential nominees for the positions undergo Senate confirmation before taking office. Though this seemed to elevate the status of the general counsels, they were in fact given no new authority.

After Cheney became secretary of defense in 1989, he and his top aides decided that Congress had made a mistake. They tried to change the system in order to subordinate the JAGs to greater control by the president's political appointees.

Cheney's project was initially sparked by a simple personality conflict between the army's top JAG, Major General John Fugh, and the first-ever army general counsel to undergo Senate confirmation, William "Jim" Haynes II.

Fugh was born in Beijing in 1934. After Communists took over China, his family came under particular oppression because his father had worked with American dignitaries. The Fughs fled to the United States when Fugh was fifteen, adopting an unusual Westernized spelling for their last name. Fugh, who became a U.S. citizen in 1957, went to Georgetown University's School of Foreign Service as an undergraduate and then to George Washington University Law School. After graduating from law school in 1960, Fugh joined the army as a JAG officer; twenty-four years later, he became the first Chinese American ever to attain the rank of general officer. In 1990, he became a two-star general and the top

JAG for the army, overseeing a global network of several thousand army attorneys. During the Gulf War, Fugh published a report systematically documenting Iraqi war crimes. He also set up a human rights training program for developing countries.[5]

Haynes was twenty years Fugh's junior. Born in Texas in 1958, Haynes graduated from Dickinson College and Harvard Law School, clerked for a federal district judge for a year, and then served a little more than four years in the army with the rank of captain. Haynes spent his entire active-duty tenure working in the Pentagon as an assistant to the army general counsel, where, as a member of a Special Honors Program, he dressed and functioned more like a civilian than a JAG. There, Haynes first met Fugh, who was then his superior officer by four ranks. In early 1989, at the tail end of Haynes's army service, he was assigned to work on the team managing the handover from the Reagan administration to the Bush-Quayle administration — and with it the arrival of Dick Cheney as the new secretary of defense. During the transition, Haynes met and befriended David Addington. A mentor-protégé relationship developed between the two that would dramatically accelerate Haynes's career.

A few months later, Fugh got a surprising phone call from Haynes, who had become an associate at a corporate law firm after leaving the army. "He called me and said, 'Gee whiz, don't say anything, but I may become the army general counsel,'" Fugh recalled. "I was slightly taken aback. Here's a captain walking out the door and then coming back in as general counsel of the army. I treated it as braggadocio. But in any event, it came true. It was just a quirk, because he was put on the transition team, and that's how he met Dave Addington, who was close to Cheney."[6]

In their new roles, the fifty-two-year-old Fugh and his thirty-two-year-old former subordinate officer had a testy relationship. Fugh said Haynes repeatedly tried to assert his authority over issues that Fugh believed were war-fighting and operational in nature, and thus not a civilian lawyer's business. During the run-up to the Gulf War, for example, Fugh's JAG team had to decide how to handle the corpses of American soldiers if Saddam Hussein were to use chemical or biological weapons, making the corpses environmentally hazardous. Haynes wanted to take part in the deliberations, but Fugh told him that battlefield casualties were a uni-formed responsibility and not something that political appointees should get into. Haynes also wanted to play a role in making decisions about JAG training, individual JAG officer assignments, and contracting matters handled by uniformed lawyers. But Fugh, who saw Haynes as an empire builder and a meddler, rebuffed him, insisting that they both stay in their legally assigned lanes.[7]

Haynes has not spoken publicly about the early history of the JAG dispute. But in 1992, Haynes recorded his views in a twelve-page internal Pentagon memo explaining why he believed that the top JAGs in each service, such as Fugh, should be brought under the direct control of civilian general counsels, such as himself. Haynes said, "Our constitutional and statutory order . . . contemplates civilian administration and control of the military," arguing that it made sense to consolidate the JAG corps under the control of the army general counsel. And Haynes strongly objected to Fugh's contention that the top JAG is "capable of providing the secretary [of the army with] 'independent' and 'nonpolitical' advice, implying that civilian officers are not."[8]

As the conflicts with his former superior officer continued, Haynes went to Addington, then Cheney's special assistant, for help. On Addington's advice, Cheney embraced Haynes's cause. On June 13, 1991, after the Gulf War ended, Cheney signed a letter asking Congress to change the law in order to give general counsels direct supervisory control of the JAGs. Congress rejected Cheney's request, but the political appointees were undeterred. The next spring, they attempted to achieve their goal using internal administrative orders instead of legislation. On March 3, 1992, Cheney's deputy signed a memo declaring that each service's general counsel was henceforth to be its "single chief legal officer," responsible for ensuring "uniform" legal interpretations among both civilian and uniformed lawyers and empowered to issue "controlling legal opinions."

The administrative order directly defied the expressed will of Congress, and lawmakers soon found an outlet for their outrage. Later that same month, the first President Bush nominated Addington to be the Pentagon's general counsel, its top civilian lawyer. During Addington's confirmation review in June and July of 1992, Senate Armed Services Committee chairman Sam Nunn pressed the nominee on the JAG issue. In written questions to Addington, Nunn said disapprovingly that it looked like the Cheney team wanted to empower political lawyers to force JAGs to "reach a particular result on a question of law or a finding of fact," and that they wanted to create a politically appointed filter between the JAGs and top military decision makers.

Addington distanced himself from the controversial order. He told the

Senate that the order was perhaps being misinterpreted, and he assured lawmakers that JAGs should remain free to give dissenting advice about the law directly to military leaders. He promised lawmakers that if he was confirmed, he would recommend substantial revisions to the administrative memo to avoid any "broader interpretation" such as the one Nunn had suggested.

To make sure Addington followed through, the Senate three weeks later included a provision in a military authorization bill, directing the Pentagon to rescind or rewrite the order by Cheney's deputy. The order, they wrote, could disrupt the ability of uniformed lawyers to "serve as the conscience of the Department [of Defense], providing DOD officials with thorough, objective, and professional legal advice."[9] Under such pressure, Cheney's Pentagon replaced the March 3, 1992, order that August.

After Addington's hearing, Fugh said, Haynes accused him of betrayal. "Haynes was really upset with me and accused me of disloyalty," Fugh recalled. "I said, 'Listen Jim, my loyalty is owed to the Constitution of the United States and never to an individual and sure as hell never to a political party. You remember that.' You see, to them, loyalty is to whoever is your political boss. That's wrong."

The Senate ultimately confirmed Addington, but with Bill Clinton's victory that fall, his tenure was brief. Over the next eight years, the issue of JAG independence temporarily receded. But when Cheney and Addington headed to 1600 Pennsylvania Avenue in 2001, Haynes got Addington's old position—the Pentagon's general counsel. Soon, conflict between the political lawyers and the JAGs flared again—this time amid the much more dramatic stakes of the war on terrorism.

"This didn't start with the torture fight," said Georgetown's Martin Lederman. "They've believed in [eliminating JAG independence] as a matter of religious faith for a long time. They knew it was going to matter, even though they didn't yet know what it was going to matter for."[10]

## 4.

At the same moment that the JAGs had been trying to block the Bush-Cheney legal team's sanction for draconian military commissions and harsh interrogations at Guantánamo, the political team tried to erode the JAG corps' authority and independence—reviving the effort Cheney,

Addington, and Haynes had launched back during the Bush-Quayle administration.

First, in January 2003, the army's new general counsel, a political appointee named Steven Morello, proposed changing the way the top army JAG was selected. Under the established system, a panel of generals pick the top JAG. Morello suggested changing the process so that the career panel would merely propose three finalists, from whom political appointees would select their favorite. Morello's idea died amid uniformed objections that the change could result in JAGs becoming too compliant and politicized. But Haynes would later try to revive the idea department-wide, issuing an internal Pentagon memo on February 4, 2005, arguing that such a change would give each political appointee "a degree of discretion in the selection of legal advisors with whom he or she works so closely and in whom he or she must place immense trust." But Haynes's proposal, too, would not go forward.

Then, in May 2003, a month after the secret completion of the detainee interrogation policy report, Morello proposed turning a thousand of the army's fifteen hundred uniformed lawyers into civilian positions. Morello said his goal was to free up more active-duty positions to be soldiers, but the shift would also have the impact of transferring significant clout and power from the army JAG corps to the general counsel's office. The proposal never moved forward because the position of army secretary—who would have to approve the change—was vacant at the time, and not filled until after Morello left the Pentagon in 2004. Morello later explained that his idea had come from a little-known 1992 study that had been commissioned by Haynes when he was the army general counsel under Cheney. The proposal had never been implemented because the Bush-Quayle administration had come to an end just after the study was completed. "It was basically unfinished business," Morello said.[11]

It was not the only unfinished business from the Cheney Pentagon to make an encore appearance. On May 15, 2003, the secretary of the air force, James Roche, issued an order giving its general counsel, Mary Walker, the authority to supervise and review virtually every legal issue arising in the air force. The order subordinated the top air force JAG and his subordinates to Walker's control by turning him into her military deputy. (Earlier that year, Walker had led the Pentagon working group on the treatment of detainees at Guantánamo, during which time she and the then–no. 2 air force JAG, Jack Rives, had clashed over the legality of harsh interrogations.) Based on the Roche order, Walker floated a thirty-two-page draft of new operating instructions for the service in which she asserted the right to exercise legal oversight and review over every legal issue arising in the air force—including court-martial trials, which by statute were reserved to the JAGs alone.

Scott Silliman, a specialist in military law at Duke, said that the sequence of events revealed that the push to subordinate the JAGs to greater political control, which began in 1991 as an "ad hoc" personality-driven conflict, had evolved into a "systematic" project amid the higher stakes of disputes over the Geneva Conventions. "This administration, as a matter of policy, is trying to marginalize the uniformed lawyers and vest as much authority as possible in the civilian general counsels," concluded Silliman. "The administration believes that the political appointees will not contest what the president wants to do, whereas the uniformed lawyers . . . are going to push back."[12]

The air force and army proposals alarmed retired JAGs, who asked the Senate Armed Services Committee, which had helped them a decade before, to come to their assistance again. Nunn was now retired, but their cause was taken up by a new senator, Lindsey Graham, a South Carolina Republican who also happened to be a reservist air force colonel and a JAG officer himself.

Pushed by Graham, in October 2004 Congress passed a new law forbidding Defense Department employees from interfering with the ability of the JAGs to "give independent legal advice" directly to military leaders—both field commanders and the civilian service secretaries at the Pentagon. Congress also directed the air force to rescind its May 15, 2003, order subordinating the air force JAG to Walker. The lawmakers scolded the Pentagon for its attempts to sideline the JAGs in defiance of the will of Congress, noting in a report accompanying the new law, "This is the second time in 12 years that attempts to consolidate legal services in the Department of Defense have led to congressional action. . . . The Air Force situation, while the most aggravated, is not unique."[13]

The Bush-Cheney administration's legal team promptly worked to avoid complying with Congress's instructions. When Bush signed the new law protecting the JAGs' ability to "give independent legal advice" in October 2004, he issued a signing statement decreeing that the legal opinions reached by his political appointees would still "bind all civilian and military attorneys within the Department of Defense." Pentagon leaders ignored the direction to rescind the air force legal order until the Senate later passed a bill that would have cut off funds for air force legal services if the noncompliance continued. (The provision was dropped in the House-Senate conference committee after the Pentagon finally complied.)

Against that background, a group of retired JAGs beginning in 2004 urged Congress to enact a law elevating the top JAG in each service from a two-star to a three-star general or admiral. The retirees argued that giving the top uniformed lawyers a higher rank would fortify their clout in the Pentagon's bureaucratic battles, ensuring that they were invited to the most important meetings and that their objections received greater attention. The White House sent a policy statement to Congress arguing that a three-star JAG law would "undermine the flexibility of the President" to decide for himself whether JAGs deserved a third star, and that it would also "add unnecessary and rank-heavy bureaucracy." The JAGs, it added, didn't need a higher rank, because they "already participate fully" in Pentagon affairs. The House of Representatives backed the White House, killing the three-star idea.

## 5.

The fight to subordinate the JAGs was just one of many fronts the Bush-Cheney administration pushed to expand its power over the bureaucracy. Another important example involved Bush's aggressive use of executive orders to force government officials to change how they decided who should receive federal grants. The power play reshaped bureaucratic behavior, enabling taxpayer funds to flow to religious groups, which would not have qualified for them under long-established procedures protecting the separation of church and state.

On January 29, 2001, nine days after taking office, Bush issued the first two executive orders of his tenure. They established a new White House Office of Faith-Based and Community Initiatives, and instructed five cabinet departments to establish similar centers inside their own bureaucracies.[14] Their mandate, Bush said, was to knock down internal rules and regulations that were preventing churches and synagogues from winning government grants for welfare work, such as providing homeless shelters, addiction treatment, after-school programs, and soup kitchens.

Many faith-based groups, such as Habitat for Humanity and the Salvation

Army, already received millions of dollars in government grants. But to qualify, such groups had to obey strict rules for the separation of church and state. They could not proselytize in the same facility that they used for taxpayer-funded work, and they could not discriminate against people of other faiths when hiring for positions funded by taxpayers. But Bush said such rules amounted to discrimination against religious groups by forcing them to abandon their identities in order to compete for grants.

Before the faith-based offices could start reshaping the bureaucracy's behavior, the administration first needed to change the federal rules about who could receive taxpayer funds. The White House sent Congress a bill expanding religious groups' eligibility by allowing them to win federal grants even if they refused to hire people of other faiths, and even if they wanted to surround their delivery of services with religious symbols, such as hanging a cross over a table where it handed out meals paid for by taxpayers. Critics said such proposals would violate civil rights and take the government too close to using government money to subsidize religion. Supporters said that the constitutional need for a wall of separation between church and state was exaggerated, and touted the changes as the essence of the "compassionate conservatism" on which Bush had campaigned.

Whatever the merits of the issue, the controversy over the proposals was enough to sink the legislation. Its chances of passage were deemed to be so low that Congress did not even bring the bill up for a vote. But on December 12, 2002, Bush issued an executive order instructing the bureaucracy to make the changes without congressional approval. "Many acts of discrimination against faith-based groups are committed by executive branch agencies, and, as the leader of the executive branch, I'm going to make some changes, effective today," Bush said. "Every person in every government agency will know where the president stands. And every person will have the responsibility to ensure a level playing field for faith-based organizations in federal programs."[15]

Ten years earlier, Secretary of Defense Cheney had asked Congress to pass a law subordinating professional military lawyers to political control, and when Congress declined, he tried to make the bureaucratic changes on his own, using administrative orders. Now Bush was doing the same thing for grant-making officials. But there was a crucial difference: In 1992, Congress was controlled by the opposition party, and the Senate defended its right to make such decisions by forcing Cheney and Addington to rescind the order. In December 2002, the president's party held the House and had just retaken the Senate. Congress did nothing to defend its role, and the orders stood.

Bush's political appointees, filling out the new faith-based offices seeded throughout the federal bureaucracy, went to work enforcing their mandate by making sure that grant officials embraced Bush's orders. At the United States Agency for International Development, political appointees wrote rules allowing missionary groups to hold church services in the same spaces they used for handing out food or medicine, just prior to or just after dispensing the taxpayer-funded foreign aid, putting a Christian frame on American assistance to many foreign countries. The appointees also rejected requests that they establish a firm rule requiring faith-based groups to inform people that participation in religious services was not required to receive the food or medicine U.S. taxpayers were providing.[16]

Bush himself wanted it known that he was personally responsible for this reshaping of the bureaucracy's welfare programs. On March 3, 2004, he made a campaign stop at a government-sponsored conference on Faith-Based and Community Initiatives in Los Angeles. Many religious activists came to speak, and they applauded loudly when Bush told them that it took a president not afraid to take unilateral action to reshape the machinery of government as boldly as he had done. "I got a little frustrated in Washington because I couldn't get the bill passed out of the Congress," Bush said. "Congress wouldn't act, so I signed an executive order—that means I did it on my own."[17]

## 6.

In September 2002, top aides to Douglas Feith, the undersecretary of defense for policy and one of the leading advocates inside the Bush-Cheney administration for invading Iraq, came to the White House to deliver an intelligence briefing entitled "Assessing the Relationship Between Iraq and al-Qaida." The briefers told I. Lewis "Scooter" Libby, Cheney's chief of staff and top national security adviser, and Stephen Hadley, the No. 2 official on the National Security Council, that there was good intelligence that the religious terrorist network was working hand in hand with the secular Iraqi regime. In a PowerPoint presentation, the briefers said that "intelligence indicates cooperation in all categories; mature, symbiotic relationship," that there were "multiple areas of cooperation" between the two, that both shared an interest in pursuing weapons of mass destruction, and that there were "some indications of possible Iraqi coordination with al-Qaida specifically related to 9/11."[18]

The briefing, delivered as the administration was pressing Congress to pass a resolution supporting war with Iraq, was highly unusual. Under normal circumstances, top government officials making national security decisions are supposed to rely on information that has been thoroughly vetted by the career analysts at the Central Intelligence Agency, the bureaucracy set up by Congress to provide accurate and politically neutral information. Among the things the career professionals do is examine whether there is more than one source supporting an allegation, whether the source has been wrong about something before, and whether the source really has access to the information he is asserting. After 9/11, the CIA's professional intelligence analysts had found no meaningful link between Al Qaeda and Iraq. Although there were a few reports in the cacophony of raw intelligence that supported the possibility of such a relationship, the analysts had found strong reasons to be highly skeptical about such claims.

That conclusion, however, was rejected by Cheney and other advocates of invading Iraq, who — like everyone else — criticized the CIA for its failure to detect the 9/11 plot and to prevent the Al Qaeda attacks from taking place. In January 2002, Deputy Defense Secretary Paul Wolfowitz, another supporter of using the military to topple Saddam Hussein, had directed Feith's policy shop to develop an alternative analysis of raw intelligence that would critique and counter the CIA's muted findings about Iraq.

Feith's office became one of the key sites of a systematic push to bypass professional intelligence analysts and create an information "product" that supported the administration's suspicions about Iraq. In Feith's shop and elsewhere in the executive branch, neoconservative political appointees stitched together raw intelligence reports, often of dubious credibility, without any vetting or analysis by professional intelligence specialists. The officials cherry-picked the files for reports that supported the notion that Iraq had an active weapons-of-mass-destruction program and that it was working hand in hand with Al Qaeda, "stovepiping" such reports to top decision makers (and leaking them to the press) while discounting any skepticism mounted by the professionals.

On July 23, 2002, top officials in British prime minister Tony Blair's cabinet met to discuss America's policy on Iraq. According to secret minutes of that meeting that were later leaked to the media, the head of British intelligence said that in a recent visit to Washington to confer with top Bush-Cheney officials, he had learned that "military action was now seen as inevitable. Bush wanted to remove Saddam, through military action, justified by the conjunction of terrorism and [weapons of mass destruction]. But the intelligence and facts were being fixed around the policy."[19] The Pentagon's inspector general later said that Feith's operation "expanded its role and mission from formulating defense policy to analyzing and disseminating alternative intelligence," providing senior decision makers with "conclusions that were inconsistent with the consensus of the intelligence community."

The CIA did not just disagree with Feith's conclusions—they disagreed with the "facts" on which he based those conclusions. In August 2002, Feith's aides had delivered a version of their Iraq–Al Qaeda briefing to CIA director George Tenet and a cadre of professional analysts. The CIA analysts sharply disagreed with the majority of the policy shop's presentation, believing that more than half of the information in the briefing was false. Without the CIA's knowledge, however, Feith nonetheless sent his presentation on to the White House, where his aides said nothing about the CIA's objections. In addition, for the White House version, Feith's team added an extra slide to their PowerPoint presentation, declaring that there were "fundamental problems" with the way the CIA was assessing information concerning the relationship between Iraq and Al Qaeda.

Feith's briefing also declared that there had been a "known contact" between the lead 9/11 hijacker, Mohamed Atta, and an Iraqi intelligence officer in Prague on April 9, 2001—an allegation based on a single report to the Czech intelligence agency, which the CIA investigated and rejected as highly dubious. Such a claim, potentially implicating Saddam Hussein in 9/11, was a tremendous asset in the drive to attack Iraq, and Cheney himself would repeatedly reference it in public during the drumbeat to war. But the career professionals at the CIA were right. The 9/11 Commission later concluded that there was "no evidence" that the secular Iraqi regime and the jihadist Al Qaeda ever developed a "collaborative operational relationship." The commission also reported that the available evidence—as vetted by the CIA—did not support the original Czech report of any meeting between Atta and an Iraqi agent in Prague on April 9. Atta had been photographed by an ATM camera in Virginia Beach on April 4, and he was in Coral Springs, Florida, on April 11. On April 6, 9, 10, and 11, Atta's cell phone had made calls from other sites in Florida. There is no record of Atta, who traveled on his real passport on other occasions when he entered and left the United States, leaving the country during that time span. And, it was shown, the Iraqi intelligence officer in question was not even in Prague on the morning of the supposed meeting.[20]

What the Bush-Cheney people did, said Kenneth Pollack, a former CIA intelligence analyst and National Security Council expert on the Middle East who wrote a book supporting a military invasion of Iraq, was reach a conclusion that getting rid of Saddam Hussein was the right thing to do, and then they proceeded to "dismantle the existing filtering process that for fifty years had been preventing the policymakers from getting bad information."[21]

Whatever the merits of the decision to invade Iraq, the administration's handling of prewar intelligence illustrated another strategy in its push to alter the balance of power between the president and a key element of the bureaucracy. In setting up a politically controlled alternative filtering system, the administration succeeded in diminishing the power of the CIA's information bureaucracy to check the White House's desired course of action.

7.

In December 2002, Danielle Leonard, a young civil-service attorney at the Justice Department's Civil Rights Division, was going through résumés submitted by law students who wanted to work at the voting rights section the next summer. A recent graduate of Harvard Law School, Leonard had joined the section two months earlier, following a year as a clerk for a federal judge. She had developed a passion for civil rights law during a stint as a summer associate at a law firm where she worked on a racial discrimination lawsuit filed by a group of black Secret Service agents, and Leonard thought it would be her "dream job" to enforce the nation's civil rights laws for a living. But there had turned out to be little work going on in the division after she joined it, and out of boredom she had volunteered to help screen applicants for the division's summer internship program. Then the "front office," where the political appointees who oversaw the division worked, sent out surprise orders: From now on, only the political appointees would decide who should be picked as summer interns.

"I was going through all these résumés and had done a lot of work and they sent someone to my office to take them away," Leonard later recalled. "The front office had taken over the summer hiring and would not even let us have access to the résumés anymore. I had to remove all my Post-it notes with my comments on them."[22]

The Bush-Cheney administration's move to extend its control over the summer intern program turned out to be just a footnote in sweeping new political controls coming to hiring decisions at the Civil Rights Division.[23]

Established in 1957 as part of the first civil rights bill since Reconstruction, the Civil Rights Division enforces the nation's antidiscrimination laws by developing lawsuits against state and local governments, submitting "friend-of-the-court" briefs in other discrimination cases, and reviewing changes to election laws and redistricting to make sure they won't dilute minority voting. The division is managed by a president's appointees—the assistant attorney general for civil rights and his deputies—who are replaced when a new president takes office. Beneath the political appointees, most of the work is carried out by a permanent staff of about 350 lawyers. They take complaints, investigate problems, propose lawsuits, litigate cases, and negotiate settlements. And, until the fall of 2002, career attorneys also played an important role in deciding whom to hire when vacancies opened up in their ranks.

In an acknowledgment of the need to be nonpartisan, there was a long-standing tradition that hiring for career jobs in the Civil Rights Division was handled by civil servants—not by political appointees. For decades, under all previous administrations, Democratic and Republican, committees made up of career lawyers had screened thousands of résumés, interviewed candidates, and made recommendations that were only rarely rejected by the politically appointed supervisors.

"There was obviously oversight from the front office, but I don't remember a time when an individual went through that process and was not accepted," said Charles Cooper, a former deputy assistant attorney general for civil rights in the Reagan administration. "I just don't think there was any quarrel with the quality of individuals who were being hired. And we certainly weren't placing any kind of political litmus test on . . . the individuals who were ultimately determined to be best qualified."

But during the fall 2002 hiring cycle, Attorney General John Ashcroft changed the rules for hiring into the Justice Department. Longtime career attorneys say there was never an official announcement. In the Civil Rights Division, where the potential for political interference is greater than in divisions that enforce less controversial laws, the hiring committee simply was not convened, and eventually its members learned that it had been disbanded and that political appointees were taking full control of career hiring. And, as Leonard discovered, the new hiring controls extended even down to summer interns.

Joe Rich, who joined the division in 1968 and who was chief of the voting rights section until he left in 2005, said that the change reduced career attorneys' input on hiring decisions to virtually nothing. Once the political appointees screened résumés and decided on a finalist for a job in the voting rights section, they would invite Rich to sit in on the applicant's final interview—but, Rich said, they wouldn't tell him who else had applied or ask his opinion about whether to hire the attorney.

The result of the unprecedented change was a quiet remaking of the Civil Rights Division, effectively turning hundreds of career jobs into politically appointed positions. Under the little-noticed tactic, the Bush-Cheney administration was able to start filling the agency's permanent ranks with a different breed of attorney. Hires with traditional civil rights backgrounds—either civil rights litigators or members of civil rights groups—plunged. Only nineteen of the forty-five lawyers hired between 2003 and 2006 in the voting rights, employment litigation, and appellate sections were experienced in civil rights law, résumés showed. And of those nineteen, nine gained their experience either by defending employers *against* discrimination lawsuits or by fighting *against* race-conscious policies designed to help minorities. In the two years before the change, 77 percent of those who were hired had traditional civil rights backgrounds.

Meanwhile, even though a federal civil-service law prohibits taking partisan ideology into account when hiring for career positions, conservative credentials rose sharply. Between 2003 and 2006, the three sections hired eleven lawyers who said they were members of the conservative Federalist Society. Seven hires in the three sections were listed as members of the Republican National Lawyers Association, including two who had volunteered for Bush-Cheney campaigns. Several new hires had worked for prominent conservatives, including former Whitewater prosecutor Kenneth Starr, former attorney general Edwin Meese, Mississippi senator

Trent Lott, and Judge Charles Pickering. And six listed themselves as belonging to Christian political organizations that promote socially conservative views.

The academic credentials of the lawyers hired into the division also underwent a shift at this time, the documents show. Attorneys hired by the career hiring committees had come largely from law schools with elite reputations, a reflection of the large number of applications for every available position. Now the political appointees were instead hiring many more graduates of law schools with conservative reputations. The changes in the voting rights section were particularly dramatic: The average *U.S. News & World Report* ranking for the law school attended by new hires to enforce voting rights laws plummeted from 15 to 65 after the change.

Many lawyers in the division described a clear shift in agenda accompanying the new hires. The division began redeploying its resources, developing fewer voting rights and employment cases involving systematic discrimination against African Americans, and more cases alleging reverse discrimination against whites and religious discrimination against Christians.

One example of the impact of the changing profile of the career professionals came in 2005, when a five-member team in the Civil Rights Division reviewed a new law in Georgia requiring voters to present a photo ID card or to buy one for $20. Four of the five members said the law would disproportionately suppress the votes of blacks because they were less likely to have a driver's license or passport. Division supervisors approved the law anyway. A judge later blocked it, comparing it to a Jim Crow–era poll tax. The lone member of the review committee who favored the law was hired in May 2005. He was a graduate of the University of Mississippi Law School and a member of both the Federalist Society and the Christian Legal Society.

Another example of the new hires' impact came in 2006, when the Civil Rights Division threatened to sue Southern Illinois University over its paid fellowships for women and minorities on the grounds that it discriminated against white men. The university scrapped the fellowships. The case was developed by a February 2004 hire who was a member of the Federalist Society and who had previously worked for the Center for Individual Rights, a nonprofit group that has filed many lawsuits opposing affirmative action in higher education.

Also in 2006, a Christian group sued a public library for preventing religious organizations from using its facilities to hold worship services. The division filed a "friend-of-the-court" brief saying that the library policy violated the Christian group's civil rights. The brief was written by a Notre Dame University Law School graduate who was hired in November 2004. He was a member of two groups that seek to integrate Catholic faith into law and society and had clerked for then–appeals court judge Samuel Alito Jr.

Furthering the transition, political appointees assigned many experienced civil rights lawyers to spend much of their time defending deportation orders rather than pursuing discrimination claims. Justice officials defended that practice, saying that attorneys throughout the department were sharing the burden of a deportation case backlog.

As morale plunged, lawyers hired under the old system began leaving the division in droves. (Leonard, the last of the hires into the voting rights section under the old rules, left for a corporate job in the summer of 2003, having stayed for just ten months.) In 2005, the administration even offered longtime civil rights attorneys a buyout. Department figures show that sixty-three division attorneys left in 2005 — nearly twice the average annual number of departures since the late 1990s. With every new vacancy, the administration gained a new chance to use the new rules to hire another lawyer more in line with its political agenda.

At a 2006 NAACP hearing on the state of the Civil Rights Division, David Becker, who was a voting-rights section attorney for seven years before accepting the buyout offer, warned that the personnel changes threatened to permanently damage the nation's most important civil rights watchdog. "Even during other administrations that were perceived as being hostile to civil rights enforcement, career staff did not leave in numbers approaching this level," Becker said. "In the place of these experienced litigators and investigators, this administration has, all too often, hired inexperienced ideologues, virtually none of which have any civil rights or voting rights experiences."

Some defenders of the administration's Civil Rights Division practices said there was nothing improper about the winner of a presidential election staffing government positions with like-minded officials. And, they said, the old career staff at the division was partisan in its own way — an entrenched bureaucracy of liberals who did not support the president's view of civil rights policy. Roger Clegg, who was a deputy assistant attorney general for civil rights during the Reagan administration, said that the change in career hiring was appropriate to bring some "balance" to what he described as an overly liberal agency. "I don't think there is anything sinister about any of this. . . . You are not morally required to support racial preferences just because you are working for the Civil Rights Division," Clegg said.

But Jim Turner, who worked for the division from 1965 to 1994 and was the top-ranked professional in the division for the last twenty-five years of his career, said that hiring people who are enthusiastic about civil rights to enforce civil rights laws is not the same thing as trying to achieve a political result through hiring particular people. Laws put on the books by Congress are supposed to be endorsed whether the current occupant of the White House likes them or not, he said. "To say that the Civil Rights Division had a special penchant for hiring liberal lawyers is twisting things."

In the spring of 2007, the newly Democratic-controlled Congress began boring in on alleged politicization in the Justice Department amid an investigation into the controversial firing and replacements of at least nine U.S. attorneys, an affair that this book will address in greater detail later. The investigation into the affair threatened to extend into the hiring changes in the Civil Rights Division, in part because the first replacement U.S. attorney, Bradley Schlozman, had previously spent three years as one of the political appointees most responsible for hiring decisions in the division, according to former career officials.[24] Moreover, complaints about the personnel changes in the Civil Rights Division dovetailed with a report that another key figure in the U.S. attorney firings, the department's White House liaison, Monica Goodling, was under internal investigation for allegedly taking partisan affiliation into account when hiring career assistant prosecutors, contrary to federal law.[25] (After being granted immunity from prosecution in exchange for her testimony, Goodling later admitted to Congress that she had "crossed the line" and used a political litmus test in career hiring decisions. Schlozman, who also testified before Congress but without immunity, admitted under questioning that he may have boasted about hiring Republicans at the Justice Department. But he insisted that he never broke civil-service rules by asking about job applicants' political views or partisan affiliation.)

Then, in what critics said was likely an attempt to head off a damaging new front in oversight, the Justice Department abruptly reversed course on its hiring policy. On April 26, 2007, the department distributed an internal memorandum reversing Ashcroft's 2002 decision to give total control over career hiring to political appointees. The change meant that in the Civil Rights Division, control of screening applications, conducting interviews, and recommending hires was back in the hands of committees of career civil servants, as it had been for decades.[26]

But skeptics were pessimistic about whether the reversal meant that the Civil Rights Division was really freed from partisan control. After all, the career ranks were now very different than they had been back in 2002. Droves of longtime veteran civil rights lawyers had left. In their place were many members of the Federalist Society, the Republican National Lawyers Association, and other such organizations.

The Bush-Cheney administration's effort to assert greater control over the Civil Rights Division was the latest chapter in a long-running power struggle between the agency and conservative presidents. Richard Nixon tried unsuccessfully to delay implementation of school desegregation plans that had been negotiated under Lyndon Johnson. Ronald Reagan reversed the division's position on the tax-exempt status of racially discriminatory private schools and set a policy of opposing school busing and racial quotas. Still, neither Nixon nor Reagan changed the division's procedures for hiring career staff, meaning that career attorneys who were dedicated to enforcing civil rights laws continued to fill the ranks.

William Yeomans, a twenty-four-year career veteran who also took the 2005 buyout, said he believed the current administration learned a lesson from Nixon's and Reagan's experiences: To make changes permanent, it is necessary to reshape the civil rights bureaucracy. "Reagan had tried to bring about big changes in civil rights enforcement and to pursue a much more conservative approach, but it didn't stick," Yeomans said. "That was the goal here—to leave behind a bureaucracy that approached civil rights the same way the political appointees did."

## 8.

On May 6, 2004, the Food and Drug Administration announced that it had decided not to permit pharmacies to sell an emergency contraception pill, Plan B, without a prescription. The agency explained to the manufacturer of the "morning-after" drug, essentially a high-dose birth control pill that prevents fertilization and the implantation of an embryo, that the government was concerned about the possibility that teenage girls might not understand how to use it correctly without a doctor. This decision was a surprise. Five months earlier, a federal advisory panel of scientific experts had voted 23–4 to recommend approving the application to sell the drug over the counter, concluding that Plan B could be safely and correctly used by all women, including teenagers, without a doctor's supervision. And the agency's staff had recommended following the advisory panel's view. Normally, agencies such as the FDA base their decisions on the information provided by their expert advisory panels — but, strangely, not this time.[27]

Several women's groups accused the agency's political appointees of overruling the experts in order to please social conservatives who believed that Plan B encouraged promiscuity and was a form of abortion. One group, the Center for Reproductive Health, filed a lawsuit seeking to have the FDA's decision overturned. In depositions, two senior career scientists who worked on the application backed up the critics' accusations. One scientist said she was told by the deputy FDA commissioner that the over-the-counter application for Plan B needed to be rejected "to appease the administration's constituents," and that it could later be quietly approved for adults only. Another scientist said he had learned in early 2004 that then–FDA commissioner Mark McClellan—the brother of then–White House spokesman Scott McClellan—had already decided against approval, even though the FDA staff had not completed their analysis of Plan B. (McClellan, who left the FDA shortly before the decision was announced, denied the accusation.)

Government scientists and outside scientific experts who serve on advisory boards can pose a major obstacle to a president's ability to carry out his political agenda. Where Congress has instructed an agency to make decisions on the basis of accurate and neutral information, the scientific bureaucracy can, simply by presenting its findings, sway the outcome of regulatory decisions in a direction sometimes opposed by the president and his political appointees.

To undermine this threat to its control, the Bush-Cheney administration systematically allowed their political agenda to trump advice from government scientists across a wide range of issues, including reproductive health, global warming, environmental pollution, the protection of endangered species, and stem cell research. According to the Union of

Concerned Scientists, an advocacy group that documents political inter-ference with scientists, Bush-Cheney appointees censored or suppressed scientific reports, limited media access to government scientists, and ma-nipulated scientific advice by subjecting advisory panel nominees to politi-cal litmus tests, stacking the panels with industry representatives and religious activists with dubious credentials, and by simply ignoring or dis-banding scientific advisory committees whose findings ran contrary to the White House's political agenda.[28]

The administration's well-documented record of manipulating scien-tific information for policy reasons is long enough to fill a book by itself, as demonstrated by Chris Mooney's *The Republican War on Science*. But to give just a few examples:

In the summer of 2002, a federal advisory committee at the Centers for Disease Control and Prevention was preparing to vote on whether to lower the amount of lead exposure that would be considered poisonous to children. Since the level had last been set, in 1991, new research had shown that even smaller amounts of lead were harmful to children's cognitive development than previously thought, and the panel was widely expected to recommend adjusting the level downward—a ruling that could cost paint and gasoline companies in possible lawsuits. Bush's secretary of health and human services, Tommy Thompson, abruptly intervened to change the makeup of the panel, which had previously been appointed only by career staff. In unprecedented fashion, Thomp-son rejected five experts and replaced them with five others who critics said were likely to vote against tightening the regulation—including one who had testified in court on behalf of a paint company that he be-lieved children could withstand lead exposure at levels many times higher than that of the consensus view of other scientists. It later emerged that several of the nominees had been handpicked by the lead industry, and at least two had financial ties to it. The regulations were not tightened.[29]

In January 2004, the Environmental Protection Agency published a proposed new rule on the release of mercury into the air by coal-fired power plants. Awareness had been growing that even small amounts of mercury exposure in the womb can cause children to experience learning deficits and developmental delays, and coal-fired plants were the largest man-made source of mercury pollution. But the new rule allowed the power industry to keep pumping many tons of mercury into the atmosphere for decades to come, endangering public health but saving the power and coal industries billions of dollars. Soon after the EPA rule came out, it emerged that political appointees had pasted language into the rule that had been written by industry lobbyists.[30] Five career scientists at the EPA later told the *Los Angeles Times* that Bush's political appointees at the EPA had bypassed professional staff and a scientific advisory panel in crafting the rule. The Bush-Cheney administration chose a process "that would support the conclusion they wanted to reach," said John A. Paul, a Republican environmental regulator who cochaired the EPA's advisory panel.[31]

The mercury controversy was just one of many at the Environmental Protection Agency. Russell Train, who was the top administrator at the EPA under both Presidents Nixon and Ford, said that the level of political interference at the agency under the Bush-Cheney administration represented a stark break from the way things had been under earlier Republican presidents. "In all my time at the EPA, I don't recall any regulatory decision that was driven by political considerations," Train wrote. "More to the present point, never once, to my best recollection, did either the Nixon or Ford White House ever try to tell me how to make a decision."[32]

And in February 2004, the administration dismissed a scientist from the President's Council on Bioethics. The scientist, Dr. Elizabeth Blackburn, was one of the most prominent cancer researchers in the world, but she had been critical of the administration's position restricting the use of federal funds for stem cell research. The White House denied any political reason for axing Blackburn.[33]

The Bush-Cheney administration's record on manipulating science prompted an outpouring of protest by previously apolitical scientists. On February 18, 2004, more than sixty leading scientists, including Nobel laureates, university chairs and presidents, and former federal agency directors, signed a joint statement protesting the Bush-Cheney administration's politicization of science as unprecedented. In the years that followed, more than eleven thousand other scientists added their names to the statement.

"When scientific knowledge has been found to be in conflict with policy goals, the administration has often manipulated the process through which science enters into its decisions," they wrote. "Other administrations have, on occasion, engaged in such practices, but not so systematically nor on so wide a front."[34]

9.

Bush would also go further than any president in history to impose White House control on the executive agencies that create government health and safety regulations for businesses.

Throughout the twentieth century, Congress created a series of specialized agencies and outsourced to them lawmaking power over extremely technical subjects. These regulation-writing agencies exist within the executive branch and are supervised by political appointees, but they also serve as an extension of Congress and so are watched very closely by congressional oversight committees. Advocates of strong presidential power have long chafed at the White House's lack of total control over such agencies, believing that their close relationship with congressional oversight committees means that they are answering to the wrong master. And beginning with President Nixon, White Houses controlled by both parties have increasingly taken steps designed to bring such agencies under tighter presidential control.

During Nixon's first term, he created an Office of Management and Budget in the White House. This office was a brain trust of political loyalists who helped the president to manage the sprawling federal bureaucracy so that he could bend its work to his agenda. By the end of Nixon's first term, however, his top advisers were dissatisfied with the results and decided to take much more aggressive steps. Their strategy, Nixon administration memos show, was to politicize the bureaucracy by purging it and then restocking it with "Nixon loyalists" who would "retake the departments." Agency heads were to send regular reports to Nixon's chief of staff, H. R. Haldeman, about their progress in "gaining control of the bureaucracy."[35] But the effort was derailed by Watergate.[36]

Ronald Reagan, who ran against big government, revived Nixon's effort. In February 1981, shortly after Reagan took office, he issued an executive order requiring all agencies to submit proposed new policies to the White House's Office of Management and Budget for review before they could be published in the Federal Register. In January 1985 Reagan went further, issuing a second executive order, requiring agencies to annually submit to the White House a cost-benefit analysis of their proposed new rules, allowing the White House to make objections and to delay and quash regulations it opposed for ideological reasons. This tactic, wrote former Reagan administration attorney Douglas Kmiec in his memoir, was a major component of the White House's push to implement the Unitary Executive Theory by making the executive agencies respond to the president instead of to congressional oversight committees. Technically, Kmiec wrote, White House objections to proposed regulations had no legal weight because Congress had given the agencies the power to make rules by law—yet such objections by the president often carried the day, anyway.[37]

The Bush-Quayle administration kept Reagan's 1985 system in place while escalating its impact. President George H. W. Bush put Vice President Quayle in charge of a new "Council on Competitiveness" to review proposed regulations when they arrived at the White House. Quayle's council bottled up rules that industry opposed and occasionally moved to block them with a vague pronouncement that they were excessively burdensome to business.[38]

When Bill Clinton became president, he took the regulation controls that he inherited from the Reagan-Bush years and, on paper at least, intensified them. In a 1993 executive order, Clinton required agencies to make additional justifications for their proposed new regulations, such as identifying in detail the problem the proposed new rule was intended to fix. But the potential impact of Clinton's move was not immediately apparent because he was not ideologically opposed to government regulation of businesses, unlike his predecessors. As Yale Law School's Jack Balkin noted, Clinton's goal was to try to take political credit for new rules that would improve protections for the environment and consumers. He wanted to know what the career bureaucracy was doing ahead of time so he could announce the positive news himself—especially after Republicans retook Congress in 1994 and he was less able to achieve his agenda through legislation.[39]

But the system set up by Clinton's order could be put to more intrusive use by a White House that was politically opposed to government regulations. When the Bush-Cheney administration took office in 2001, its political appointees at the Office of Management and Budget began using Clinton's system to reject rules proposed by the agencies because they were allegedly too costly for the benefits they would generate, or because they were otherwise inconsistent with the administration's policy. For the first six years of the administration, the Bush-Cheney White House thus used Clinton's system to kill or water down scores of new health, safety, and environmental protection rules proposed by agency professionals.[40] Then, after losing control of Congress, the White House in January 2007 moved to take its influence over the regulatory agencies to an unprecedented level.

On January 18, 2007, two weeks after a newly Democratic-controlled Congress was sworn in, President Bush signed an executive order directing every agency head to "designate one of the agency's presidential appointees to be its Regulatory Policy Officer."[41] The order made clear that the new officials were to be the president's political enforcers, apparatchiks embedded inside each bureaucracy and empowered "to ensure the agency's compliance" with his mandates as the professionals went about making decisions on new regulations. Bush's order insisted that "no rulemaking shall commence nor be included" in each agency's plans without the approval of the new Regulatory Policy Officer—thereby allowing the political appointees to nip new regulations in the bud, before outsiders could learn that agency professionals had identified a health, safety, or environmental problem they thought was worth fixing.

Bush's new executive order also imposed steeper requirements on agencies as they developed regulations: No new rules would be allowed unless the agency was able to identify a specific "market failure" that justified government intervention instead of letting businesses decide for themselves how to handle the problem. As Georgetown's Lisa Heinzerling noted, the new "market failure" requirement opened another front in the White House's attack on the power of Congress to decide what the permanent government should be doing. By setting up each regulatory agency in statute, Congress had essentially already decided that certain kinds of problems—such as the health and safety of the workplace and consumer goods—are worth addressing through regulation, even when the market could theoretically handle those problems on its own. Now under Bush's executive order, White House political appointees got to second-guess the decision by Congress to have relatively permissive standards for when a regulation is justified.[42]

Business groups hailed Bush's executive order, saying that it was the most aggressive attempt by any president yet to reduce burdensome new regulations. Critics charged that Bush was seeking to reward special interests by choking off new rules opposed by corporate interests.[43] But beyond the policy debate, there was no doubt about one thing: The order represented a significant expansion of presidential power. As Peter L. Strauss, a professor at Columbia Law School, told one reporter, the executive order "achieves a major increase in White House control over domestic government." He added, "Having lost control of Congress, the president is doing what he can to increase his control of the executive branch."[44]

# 13

## The Politics of Presidential Power

### 1.

At just past lunchtime on Wednesday, September 6, 2006, President Bush stepped to a podium in the East Room of the White House to loud applause. Behind the president stood row upon row of American flags, and assembled before him were such officials as Vice President Cheney, Attorney General Alberto Gonzales, and Central Intelligence Agency director Michael Hayden, along with Republican leaders in Congress and some family members of victims of the 9/11 attacks. As news channels transmitted his image around the world, Bush spoke steadily for thirty-seven minutes, delivering a series of momentous announcements.[1] The president acknowledged for the first time that the CIA had been running secret overseas prisons for high-value captives in the war on terrorism. The prisoners had been kept hidden from the Red Cross and subjected, in the president's words, to "an alternative set of procedures" by their interrogators. Bush said the program was "one of the most vital tools in our war against the terrorists," but for now it was being put on hiatus. All fourteen of the CIA's current prisoners—including the accused mastermind of 9/11, Khalid Sheikh Mohammed—had just been transferred to military custody at Guantánamo, and they would now be granted Red Cross visits. (Bush made no mention of other prisoners who were believed to have been in the CIA's custody; Human Rights Watch would later identify more than forty missing CIA prisoners whose fate was unknown; most were presumed to have been handed off to foreign governments.) Nevertheless, the president quickly insisted, nothing that the U.S. government had previously done to the prisoners was illegal under "our laws, our Constitution, and our treaty obligations," and he reserved the option to put more prisoners in the CIA's hands in the future.

"This program has been subject to multiple legal reviews by the Department of Justice and CIA lawyers," Bush said. "They've determined it complied with our laws."

Bush also said that the fourteen former prisoners of the CIA would be put on trial for their alleged crimes as soon as Congress enacted a bill he was sending over that very day, the Military Commissions Act of 2006. One of the things the administration's bill would do, if it became law, was roll back the Supreme Court's two-month-old *Hamdan v. Rumsfeld* decision. Although five justices had declared that Bush's original military commission trials were illegal and ordered them to be shut down, they had also suggested that some form of military commissions would be legal under certain conditions. One such condition, the Supreme Court had said, was the president's getting explicit permission from Congress before setting them up.

"Today, I'm sending Congress legislation to specifically authorize the creation of military commissions to try terrorists for war crimes," Bush said. ". . . We're now approaching the five-year anniversary of the 9/11 attacks—and the families of those murdered that day have waited patiently for justice. Some of the families are with us today—they should have to wait no longer."

After the audience broke into another round of applause, Bush revealed that the administration hoped the Military Commissions Act would go beyond trials. It turned out that the White House wanted to erase another part of the *Hamdan* ruling as well. One of the reasons the Supreme Court had decided that Bush's military commissions were illegal was that the draconian trial rules violated a section of the Geneva Conventions requiring wartime courts to give defendants all the procedural rights "which are recognized as indispensable by civilized peoples." This holding meant that the Geneva Conventions restricted the president's options in the war on terrorism after all, contrary to the opinion of the Bush-Cheney legal team, and it had sweeping implications.

The same section of the Geneva Conventions that requires fair trials, as noted earlier, also bans "cruel treatment and torture" and "outrages upon personal dignity, in particular, humiliating and degrading treatment."

Thus, from the moment the *Hamdan* ruling made clear that the Geneva Conventions applied after all, any U.S. official who inflicted harsh interrogation tactics on detainees, and any Bush-Cheney administration figure who signed off on that treatment, might be considered a war criminal. Bush now announced that he wanted Congress, in the Military Commissions Act, to take that possibility off the table. "Some believe our military and intelligence personnel involved in capturing and questioning terrorists could now be at risk of prosecution under the War Crimes Act — simply for doing their jobs in a thorough and professional way," he said. "This is unacceptable. So today, I'm asking Congress to pass legislation that will clarify the rules for our personnel fighting the war on terror."

Wrapping up, Bush called upon Congress to pass the bill within the next few weeks, before lawmakers went home to finish campaigning for the midterm election. He explained that "the need for this legislation is urgent" and that "time is of the essence."

Political analysts said that Bush's move was a masterstroke. In just two months Americans were scheduled to go to the polls for midterm elections. Polls showed that Republican candidates were in trouble. The increasingly unpopular war in Iraq, the flawed response to Hurricane Katrina, spreading corruption scandals, and runaway pork barrel spending were combining to put Democrats within striking distance of retaking at least one chamber of Congress. By launching a new fight over granting dramatic powers to the president for use in the war on terrorism, Republican strategists hoped to change the subject on the eve of the vote — reuniting their party and once again portraying Democrats as weak on national security.

Sensing the political danger, Democrats stayed on the sidelines during the next three weeks, largely letting Republicans debate among themselves about what should be in the Military Commissions Act. But in late September, when the House of Representatives passed the bill, 160 Democrats — including all of the party's House leadership — voted against it. Immediately, as the pundits had predicted, Republicans pounced, seeking to use the vote to define the differences between the two parties in the starkest terms: The GOP backed strong presidential powers necessary to keep terrorists from destroying America, while Democrats were willing to put the security of the nation at risk by hamstringing the commander in chief. "Republicans are committed to ensuring the president has every resource at his disposal to stop terrorist plots and protect the American people," said House majority leader John Boehner, Republican of Ohio, immediately after the vote. "It is outrageous that House Democrats, at the urging of their leaders, continue to oppose giving President Bush the tools he needs to protect our country."[2] And at a campaign stop the next day, Bush delivered a fiery partisan speech declaring that congressional Democrats' distrust of executive power made them weak and unworthy of voters' faith. As the commander in chief, Bush announced, his "most solemn duty . . . is to protect the American people." But the Democrats, he said, were unwilling to give "those responsible for defending you . . . all the tools necessary to do so."[3]

## 2.

Ambitious presidents do not always have to resort to seizing extra power through secret and complex legal maneuvers. Under the right conditions, Congress sometimes willingly cedes extraordinary new authority to the White House. That extra power can become a permanent addition to the president's arsenal, even after political support for it in Congress and among the public has fallen away.

This "politics of presidential power" draws strength from two potential factors. First, when the same political party controls both Congress and the White House, the president is the party leader of the leaders of the legislative branch. This can make Congress behave more like a subordinate and deferential arm of the executive branch than like the independent and coequal institution the Founders intended it to be. Second, when there are pervasive fears about grave and imminent threats to national security, both the public and Congress historically have tended to be more willing to grant the president extra powers in order to protect the country—powers that later the president may not be willing to put down again, especially if it is still unclear whether the crisis is over. Both of these factors came into alignment during the first six years of the Bush-Cheney administration.

When Bush took the oath of office on January 20, 2001, the Republican Party found itself in full control of the White House and Congress for the first time since 1954. With the exception of a brief moment in the Senate (after Senator Jim Jeffords of Vermont left the Republican Party in mid-2001, giving Democrats a razor-thin majority in the Senate until the 2002 election), one-party rule prevailed in Washington until 2007. This extended partisan hegemony undercut a central pillar of the Founders' plan for maintaining the constitutional balance between the branches of government: Pride and ego would ensure that officials in each branch would resist encroachments by the other on their own institutional turf. "Ambition must be made to counteract ambition," James Madison explained in the *Federalist Papers*.[4] But as Thomas Mann and Norman Ornstein argued in their 2006 book *The Broken Branch,* the leaders of the Republican Congress saw themselves "as field lieutenants in the president's army far more than they [did] as members of a separate and independent branch of government,"[5] allowing party to trump institution. "The arrival of unified Republican government in 2001 transformed the aggressive and active GOP-led Congress of the Clinton years into a deferential and supine body, one extremely reluctant to demand information, scrub presidential proposals, or oversee the executive," they observed.[6]

One-party control of government alone, however, does not fully explain what happened from 2001 to 2006. After all, the United States had also seen one-party rule during the first two years of the Clinton administration, but Congress then retained a sense of independence from the White House's agenda—rejecting Clinton's health-care proposals, for example. One important difference is that Democrats had continuously controlled one or both chambers of Congress for four decades by 1993, so congressional leaders identified strongly with their institutional role and had the self-confidence that comes from feeling permanently entrenched in power. In 2001, by contrast, Republicans had controlled Congress for just six years. Moreover, their hold was tenuous, with only tiny majorities in both chambers and a brief loss of Senate control in 2002. Led by such avowedly partisan figures as House majority leader Tom DeLay of Texas, the GOP Congress responded to its precarious standing with a strategy of marching in lockstep in order to pass uncompromisingly conservative bills without much Democratic support. Such a tactic demanded strong centralized control of Congress by party leadership, giving Bush, as the head of the Republican Party, more leverage over the congressional majority than Clinton had enjoyed as leader of the Democratic Party in 1993–1994.

But the most dramatic factor bolstering the wholesale obeisance to the president by the Republican Congress was 9/11 and the subsequent wars in Afghanistan and Iraq. Clinton took office after the Cold War had ended, significantly diminishing his political standing as the official most responsible for defending the nation from foreign attack. But the sudden murder of nearly three thousand civilians on U.S. soil on 9/11 unleashed a new climate of extraordinary fear and uncertainty across the United States, recharging the office Bush held with full wartime prominence. Like many periods of national security emergency, the war on terrorism proved to be conducive to the logic of strongman politics: The stronger the president, the safer America supposedly would be.

Recognizing the political benefits that naturally accrue to a wartime leader, the Bush-Cheney White House went to great efforts to emphasize the president's role as commander in chief. "I'm a war president," Bush declared in the midst of the 2004 election, and he referred to his role as the commander in chief constantly when he gave political speeches around the country.[7] Examples of this were everywhere. When the president traveled outside Washington and wore more casual clothes, he was often photographed wearing a jacket with his name and the title "Commander in Chief" embroidered on its front. When Bush landed aboard an aircraft carrier off San Diego on May 1, 2003, and proclaimed the end of major combat in Iraq beneath a "Mission Accomplished" banner, both his flight suit and the navy plane flying him were emblazoned with the words "George W. Bush Commander-in-Chief."[8] Emulating a theatrical move made popular by Ronald Reagan, Bush always exchanged salutes with his marine honor guard when boarding a helicopter on the White House lawn. Yet, as the historian Gary Wills has pointed out, "Dwight Eisenhower, a real general, knew that the salute is for the uniform, and as president he was not wearing one. An exchange of salutes was out of order."[9]

Wills, writing in 2007, also lamented the increasing use of the constitutionally incorrect phrase "our commander in chief" or "the commander in chief of the United States" as synonyms for "the president." The Constitution makes the president the commander in chief only of the members of the armed forces, not of the nation's civilian population. As Wills noted: "The representative is accountable to citizens. Soldiers are accountable to their officer. The dynamics are different, and to blend them is to undermine the basic principles of our Constitution." That distinction had begun breaking down during the Cold War, as presidents of both parties fostered a cult of authority based around the sense that everyone had a patriotic duty to support the wartime leader. The war on terrorism allowed the Bush-Cheney White House and its supporters to revive and expand this theater of the president as everyone's "commander in chief," equating the president with both the military and the nation's security, and diminishing criticism of the president's policies as essentially unpatriotic and borderline treasonous. At the 2004 Republican National Convention, for example, Georgia senator Zell Miller, the erstwhile Democrat turned full-throated Bush supporter, thundered, "While young Americans are dying in the sands of Iraq and the mountains of Afghanistan, our nation is being torn apart and made weaker because of the Democrats' manic obsession to bring down our commander in chief."[10]

The Republican majorities in both chambers were driven by a desire to see the leader of their party succeed, by their need to march in lockstep in order to achieve partisan ends without having to compromise with Democrats, and by the sometimes overwhelming dynamic of wartime deference to "our commander in chief." For the nearly six years that these factors stood in alignment—a perfect storm of political pressures—Congress made only muted protests as the White House systematically accumulated greater powers, and at key moments Congress rallied around the president to pass legislation enabling the executive branch to consolidate and lock down its gains.

3.

In the years that followed 9/11, Congress often proved eager to hand the Bush-Cheney administration new powers when the White House asked for them. Shortly after the attacks, overwhelming bipartisan majorities had approved war on Al Qaeda and passed the USA Patriot Act. On the eve of the 2002 midterm election, Congress had gone along when Bush asked them to delegate to him the power to decide whether to attack Iraq if diplomacy later failed. After that election, lawmakers had passed the White House's version of the Homeland Security Act, giving presidential appointees the power to make personnel decisions about employees at the new department without the usual federal worker protections. And as the Iraq war had begun to go poorly and scandals such as Abu Ghraib arose, the GOP-led Congress had kept a light touch on its oversight hearings rather than holding the executive branch's feet to the fire.

The year 2006—the final year of one-party rule in Washington—would bring the politics of presidential power to a climax. The year began with two debates over the proper level of executive power. In late December 2005, as noted earlier, the *New York Times* revealed that Bush had authorized the National Security Agency to monitor Americans' international phone calls and e-mails without court oversight, violating a 1978 law. At the same time, Congress was debating a bill that would make permanent the USA Patriot Act. Almost everyone in the legislature supported reauthorizing the Patriot Act, but most Democrats and some Republicans wanted to amend the bill to include greater oversight provisions forcing the executive branch to periodically tell Congress how it was using its enhanced powers, a move the White House opposed. Seeking to pressure Congress over both issues, the Bush-Cheney administration attacked its critics for being soft on terrorism because they were unwilling to give the president the powers he needed in order to protect the country. It insisted that the wiretapping program was legal and necessary for fighting Al Qaeda, and it also insisted that Congress was endangering America by failing to pass its version of the Patriot Act reauthorization bill.

A very shaky foundation supported the White House's two-pronged attack on critics of the wiretapping program and the Patriot Act. Beneath the simplistic rhetoric, the administration's position was self-contradicting. The warrantless surveillance program was legal only if Bush could set his own rules for fighting Al Qaeda on U.S. soil—in which case it was unnecessary to reauthorize the Patriot Act, because the commander in chief could just issue an executive order doing the same thing as the bill. Likewise, if Congress was truly endangering the war on terrorism by holding up the Patriot Act, then statutes must matter after all—in which case the wiretapping program was illegal. In an unsigned, forty-two-page "white paper" about the wiretapping program issued by the Justice Department on January 19, 2006, the Bush-Cheney legal team acknowledged this gap in its logic and tried to paper it over.[11] A key 462-word footnote explained that while Bush had the wartime power to set his own rules for investigating Al Qaeda, the Patriot Act was still important because the government needed the act's extra police powers for "contexts unrelated to terrorism."[12] In other words, the administration's own position, hidden in the fine print, was that the Patriot Act was superfluous and irrelevant to the war on terrorism—a somewhat absurd stance made necessary by their desire to say the wiretapping program was legal.[13] But such nuances were lost amid the sweeping rhetoric as Bush traveled around the country before handpicked crowds and pounded on Congress for its criticism of his wiretapping program and its failure to pass his preferred version of the Patriot Act. "The Patriot Act may be set to expire, but the threats to the United States haven't expired," Bush declared at a rally in Kansas.[14]

Bush's campaign worked. The initial bipartisan outrage in Congress at the warrantless wiretapping program was blunted as Republicans closed ranks behind the White House. On a party-line vote, the Senate Intelligence Committee decided not to investigate the program. Senate Judiciary Committee chairman Arlen Specter, initially the most outspoken GOP critic of the program, ended up drafting legislation that would exempt the program from the warrant law. Although his bill went nowhere, the issue faded away for the rest of the congressional session.

Meanwhile, Congress was rushing to hand even more powers to the president, sometimes through stealth legislation that was discovered only much later. At just past 10 p.m. on November 9, 2005, a thirty-six-year-old member of the Senate Judiciary Committee's Republican staff, Brett Tolman, received an e-mail from the Justice Department's congressional liaison, William Moschella, asking him to insert into the USA Patriot Act reauthorization bill a provision that would eliminate a 120-day limit for "interim" U.S. attorneys to serve without Senate confirmation. Tolman replied fifty-seven minutes later: "I will get the comprehensive fix done."[15] He kept the promise, slipping the section into a draft of the bill while it was in conference committee. The change, which went unnoticed by members of Congress when they passed the final bill in March 2006, handed a sweeping new power to the executive branch. The provision allowed the attorney general to install anyone he liked as a permanent replacement U.S. attorney without any vetting by the Senate, a wholesale consolidation of power over federal law enforcement in the hands of the presidency. Bush soon nominated Tolman to be the new U.S. attorney for Utah, and he was already confirmed by the time the Patriot Act change came to light in early 2007. It prompted bipartisan outrage, and both chambers voted overwhelmingly to repeal it.

The power to bypass Congress in picking replacement U.S. attorneys was just one of several instances in which the GOP-led Congress enacted "stealth" provisions, slipped without debate into large bills, to hand the president greater executive authority. One of the most potentially momentous examples ceded extraordinary new powers to the president to impose martial law inside the United States over the objections of state governors.

In a little-noticed amendment attached to a massive military spending bill passed on September 30, 2006, Congress rewrote a two-century-old prohibition against the president's using federal troops (or state National Guard troops acting under federal command) to act as police on U.S. soil. This ban dated back to the Insurrection Act of 1807, when Congress said that there was only one circumstance in which a president could use troops to enforce the law against civilians: in the case of an armed revolt against the authority of the government. After the post–Civil War occupation of the South ended, Congress strengthened this taboo on martial law with the Posse Comitatus Act of 1878, which imposed criminal penalties — two years in prison — on anyone who tried to use the federal military as police without specific authorization from Congress.

These two laws were intended to keep as much day-to-day law-enforcement power out of the hands of the federal government as possible. The principle these laws defended was that the mission of the military is to subdue the nation's enemies, while the mission of the police is, in the words of the Los Angeles Police Department's famous motto, "to protect and to serve." Military troops could still be used for non–law enforcement operations, such as rescue efforts. And on rare occasions presidents used federal troops to quell riots — such as in 1957, when President Eisenhower federalized the Arkansas National Guard to enforce a school desegregation order in the face of a white mob, and in 1992, when President George H. W. Bush used federal troops, with the support of California's governor, to stop the "Rodney King" riots in Los Angeles. But beyond such narrowly limited circumstances, the Insurrection Act ensured for two centuries that even in major emergencies, local police or state National Guard units commanded by governors would handle any law-enforcement aspects of the situation — not federal troops commanded by the president.

But four days of chaos and lawlessness in New Orleans following the Hurricane Katrina floods of 2005 had generated widespread criticism that the response to the crisis by all levels of government was unsatisfactory. Amid the finger-pointing, the issue of presidential power emerged on Friday, September 2, four days after the storm. Bush asked the Democratic governor of Louisiana, Kathleen Blanco, to sign a legal document requesting a federal takeover of the New Orleans evacuation — a move that might have improved the effort by unifying a chain of command that was split among the mayor, the governor, and the president. But Blanco rejected the request to put city police and state National Guard units under the control of the Federal Emergency Management Agency. An unnamed state official told the *Washington Post* that she feared that the change would amount to martial law and would also allow the federal government to blame the locals for every problem that had happened until that point.[16]

Blanco's refusal to allow a federal takeover of the local elements of the rescue caused just a blip in the press, but it continued to resonate in the White House. On September 25, 2005, after receiving a military briefing in Texas about the response to Hurricane Rita, which hit the Gulf Coast right after Katrina, Bush first floated the idea in public of allowing the president to impose martial law in situations other than insurrections, even if a state governor didn't want to cede control. And, Bush made clear, he wasn't just talking about civilians at FEMA running things—he was talking about full military control, martial law leading to the commander in chief himself.

"The other question, of course, I asked, was, is there a circumstance in which the Department of Defense becomes the lead agency?" Bush mused to reporters. "Clearly, in the case of a terrorist attack, that would be the case, but is there a natural disaster which—of a certain size that would then enable the Defense Department to become the lead agency in coordinating and leading the response effort? That's going to be a very important consideration for Congress to think about."[17]

Bush's suggestion provoked a brief flurry of commentary. Some critics said that easing the standards for imposing martial law would be a threat to civil liberties. Meanwhile, former Bush-Cheney attorney John Yoo penned an op-ed arguing that "Congress doesn't need to pass new laws because Bush already had the power to send federal troops to New Orleans," in defiance of the Insurrection Act and the Posse Comitatus Act, based on the president's inherent constitutional powers as commander in chief.[18] That was essentially the last the public heard about the question for a year.

Then, in September 2006, the GOP-led Congress slipped into the coming year's military budget bill a wholesale change to the two-hundred-year-old rules surrounding martial law. With virtually no debate, Congress granted wide new powers for the president to use federal troops as police, over the objections of state governors and at the president's sole discretion. The conditions that can trigger such powers for the presidency now include not only major riots, but *any* emergency situation in which, "as a result of a natural disaster, epidemic, or other serious public health emergency, terrorist attack or incident, or other condition in any State or possession of the United States, the President determines that domestic violence has occurred to such an extent that the constituted authorities of the State or possession are incapable of maintaining public order."[19]

Bush made no mention of this truly historic expansion of the president's power to impose martial law when he signed the military budget bill into law on October 17, 2006. Nor had the White House or Congress drawn attention to the change in the weeks leading up to the bill signing. Instead, most of the public debate in Washington that month had centered on another bill that Bush also signed on October 17, one in which the Republican Congress delivered even more sweeping powers to the president than the martial law changes.

This second bill was the Military Commissions Act—and its enactment into law represented the apotheosis of the Bush-Cheney politics of presidential power.

4.

Members of the public who watched news coverage of the debate in Congress over the Military Commissions Act received a very misleading portrait of the bill's impact. Most of the attention placed on the legislation concerned a dispute between factions of Republicans about trials for foreign terrorism suspects at Guantánamo. But other provisions in the bill that had nothing to do with military commissions and went virtually undiscussed were far more sweeping. The Republican-led Congress used the Military Commissions Act to virtually eliminate the possibility that the Supreme Court could ever again act as a check on a president's power in the war on terrorism. The bill also granted a congressional blessing, in statute, for many of the hugely expanded executive powers that the Bush-Cheney administration had previously seized on its own, ensuring that they would be even more difficult to roll back.

As Congress rushed to hand these powers to the White House in September 2006, neither lawmakers nor most observers spent much time discussing them. Instead, the spotlight stayed on a high-profile dispute between the White House and several leading Republican senators—including John McCain of Arizona, John Warner of Virginia, and Lindsey Graham of South Carolina, the same trio who had pushed for the torture ban in 2005—over the kinds of evidence that prosecutors should be able to introduce. The White House insisted that prosecutors needed to be able to use classified evidence, which would be kept secret from defendants for national security reasons. The administration also wanted prosecutors to be able to use evidence that had been obtained through coercive interrogations. McCain and his allies, endorsing the view of the military Judge Advocate General lawyers, questioned whether a trial that relied upon such evidence would be fair. In the end, the skeptics won on secret evidence, which was banned, but lost on evidence obtained from coercive interrogations, which was allowed as long as a military judge decided that the evidence was reliable. The compromise brought to an end a debate that had raged for several weeks, and Congress quickly passed the bill.

Other provisions of the Military Commissions Act received far less attention but were arguably much more important. For example, one of the things Congress did in the Military Commissions Act was help undermine the Geneva Conventions as a check on the power of the commander in chief. The act allowed the executive branch to go back to what it had been doing before the Supreme Court's *Hamdan* decision declared that the Geneva Conventions applied to the war on terrorism. Instead of following the treaty's all-encompassing prohibitions against detainee abuse, the United States instead would pledge not to inflict only a specific list of extreme acts on detainees, such as murder, rape, biological experiments, and "serious" pain and suffering. Crucially, Congress delegated to the president alone the power to decide whether any particular coercive interrogation technique was prohibited by the list, and it stripped the courts of the power to hear lawsuits based on the Geneva Conventions, meaning the president's word was final.

This push was strongly opposed by the military community. They argued that by relaxing the taboo against abusing wartime prisoners, the chances would increase that enemies in future conflicts would feel free to mistreat American prisoners of war. More than fifty retired admirals and generals, including five former chairmen of the Joint Chiefs of Staff, sent Congress letters urging them not to alter the nation's understanding of the Geneva Conventions. Among the most prominent was Colin Powell. "The world is beginning to doubt the moral basis of our fight against terrorism," he wrote. "To redefine [the Geneva Conventions protections] would add to those doubts. Furthermore, it would put our own troops at risk."[20] But Congress made the changes anyway.

Lawmakers took other steps, too, to keep the courts from interfering in how the president decides to treat detainees. The Military Commissions

Act stripped federal courts of jurisdiction to hear all existing and future habeas corpus lawsuits filed by noncitizen enemy combatants, eliminating their ability to challenge the basis for their detention in court. This restriction extended even to noncitizens who might be arrested on U.S. soil—including permanent legal residents, the millions of green-card holders who, until the Military Commissions Act, had long enjoyed the same legal rights as citizens.

By eliminating habeas corpus, the Military Commissions Act essentially reversed *Rasul v. Bush*, the landmark 2004 Supreme Court decision holding that courts had jurisdiction to hear lawsuits by Guantánamo detainees. There were hundreds of prisoners in Cuba who were unlikely to be prosecuted by a military commission, because the government lacked specific evidence that they had committed any war crimes. But the new legislation meant that declaring such detainees "enemy combatants" was final, and they now faced the prospect of life imprisonment at the discretion of the executive alone. Based on the change, a federal appeals court in February 2007 threw out dozens of suits filed by individual detainees who wanted a judge to review the evidence on which they were being imprisoned without trial.[21] Four months later, the Supreme Court announced that it would review that decision — and the section of the Military Commissions Act upon which it was based — in its 2007–08 term, setting up a weighty test of presidential power before the new Roberts court.

But perhaps the most important provision of all in the Military Commissions Act concerned the president's power to seize American citizens as enemy combatants. In the *Hamdi* case, the Supreme Court voted 5–4 that the president had the power to imprison without trial a citizen seized on a foreign battlefield, allegedly fighting U.S. troops and U.S. allies alongside the Taliban and Al Qaeda. In the *Padilla* case, a federal appeals court extended that presidential power to a U.S. citizen arrested on U.S. soil while allegedly planning terrorist attacks. But the Supreme Court had never decided whether the *Padilla* ruling was correct. Now it wouldn't have to. Pouring reinforced cement around the *Hamdi* and *Padilla* precedents, Congress locked down the president's power to arrest U.S. citizens on U.S. soil and imprison them in a military brig without a trial if he or she thinks they pose a terror threat. In fact, Congress went even further than the Bush-Cheney administration had: Under the Military Commissions Act, the president can seize citizens as enemy combatants even if they have nothing to do with Al Qaeda. Instead, an enemy combatant can be anyone who "has engaged in hostilities or who has purposefully and materially supported hostilities against the United States."

Under this broad definition, the president can potentially imprison without trial any citizen who is accused of donating money to a Middle East charity that the government decides is linked to a terrorist group. The president can potentially imprison without trial citizens who are associated with militant fringe groups, such as the left-wing Black Panthers and the right-wing militia movement. The president could even imprison without trial citizens accused of helping domestic terrorists, such as the rural mountain dwellers of North Carolina who are suspected of helping Eric Rudolph, the abortion-clinic bomber, survive as a fugitive for five years. Yale's Bruce Ackerman wrote that the election-year bill amounted to a "massive congressional expansion of the class of enemy combatants." And the Military Commissions Act, he warned, could "haunt all of us on the morning after the next terrorist attack" by paving the way for a new round of heavy-handed mass detentions, such as the military imprisonment of Japanese-Americans during World War II.[22]

The Military Commissions Act, in short, was revolutionary. And when placed alongside all the other powers that the Bush-Cheney administration had seized for the presidency during the preceding six years, it became the crowning achievement of the project to expand executive power—embracing and entrenching many of the new presidential powers in statute.

The few observers who were paying close attention to the guts of the bill agreed that it was momentous. In an op-ed published two days after Bush signed the Military Commissions Act into law, Yoo celebrated. "Congress . . . told the courts, in effect, to get out of the war on terror," he wrote. "It is the first time since the New Deal that Congress had so completely divested the courts of power over a category of cases. It is also the first time since the Civil War that Congress saw fit to narrow the court's habeas powers in wartime because it disagreed with its decisions. The law goes farther. It restores to the president command over the management of the war on terror. It directly reverses *Hamdan* by making clear that the courts cannot take up the Geneva Conventions. Except for some clearly defined war crimes, whose prosecution would also be up to executive discretion, it leaves interpretation and enforcement of the treaties up to the president. It even forbids courts from relying on foreign or international legal decisions in any decisions involving military commissions."[23]

Yoo said that this wholesale elimination of the power of the judiciary to check the president was the Military Commissions Act's real substance, giving "current and future administrations, whether Democrat or Republican, the powers needed to win this war." Yoo's critics, such as Georgetown law professor and fellow Office of Legal Counsel veteran Martin Lederman, went one step further: Because of the Military Commissions Act, the Bush-Cheney legal team's dubious theories about a president's vast wartime powers were now completely safe from any further judicial repudiation. And in the future, other presidential legal teams, charged with writing secret Office of Legal Counsel memos telling the president what he can and cannot do, can similarly go down radical paths with the impunity that comes from having no fear of judicial review. Now more than ever before, the law would be simply whatever the president's handpicked lawyers said it was. "The reason John [Yoo] and his colleagues are so spooked by the prospect of judicial review is that they want the President to be able to act in accord with very radical and questionable legal interpretations, *without any risk that anyone will ever call them on it*," Lederman wrote.[24]

Some critics of the Bush-Cheney administration's policies vowed to challenge the Military Commissions Act in court. But the fact that Congress put the statute on the books left the executive branch in a very strong legal position. The Supreme Court has long held that the president's authority is at its maximum when he is acting with explicit congressional support. After all, under the Constitution Congress has the power to pass laws making all the rules and regulations for how the executive branch carries out its responsibility of protecting national security. Congress also has the power to change the government's understanding of treaties. And Congress can limit the jurisdiction of courts. It would not be easy to persuade the Roberts Court that Congress had gone too far in empowering the president.

5.

On November 7, 2006, just twenty-two days after President Bush signed the Military Commissions Act into law, American voters went to the polls to decide the fate of the Congress that had passed the bill. The results of the midterm election were overwhelming. Voters across the country resoundingly turned against the Republican Congress that had, for six years, acted as little more than an extension of the White House. After it became clear that Democrats would retake control of both chambers, the opposition party made bold pronouncements about how it was going to aggressively reverse its predecessors' pattern of subservience to the executive branch.

"Six years there's been no checks and balances," said the incoming Senate majority leader, Harry Reid of Nevada, immediately after meeting with Bush and Cheney on the Friday after the election. "They'll be there now."[25]

Some lawmakers signaled that they would try to undo some of the recent statutes, reversing some of the powers Congress had handed the executive branch. With a flourish, bills were introduced that would take such steps as restoring habeas corpus rights for enemy combatants; tightening the definition of "enemy combatant" to mean only those who personally engaged in direct hostilities against the United States; erasing the law allowing a president to impose martial law against the will of state governors; and bolstering the Freedom of Information Act and the Presidential Records Act against the administration's secrecy moves.

But despite the pageantry surrounding the introduction of such bills, most had almost no chance of becoming law. President Bush's veto pen, though virtually unused amid the explosion of signing statements during the six years of the Republican Congress, remained a potent weapon for the purpose of defending existing laws that he wanted to keep on the books. With it, Bush could require Congress to muster a two-thirds majority in both chambers to change an existing statute. If supporters of the White House had one-third plus one in either chamber, the statute would stay on the books. Since Democrats had only fifty-one senators in the Senate—with the now "independent" Joe Lieberman of Connecticut barely a Democrat and Tim Johnson of South Dakota hospitalized by a stroke and thus unable to vote—an override of any presidential veto appeared highly unlikely. The old Congress may have been gone, but much of its legacy of endorsing extraordinary expansions of presidential power seemed destined to remain locked in federal law.

Still, control of Congress also brought the opposition the power to hold oversight hearings and subpoena documents and officials. Some committees quickly launched an ambitious series of probes, pledging to make up for years of neglect by uncovering any mismanagement or scandal that had been allowed to fester inside the government. The new oversight energies centered on the mysterious firings of at least nine U.S. attorneys in 2006, including seven who had been dismissed on a single day just one month after the midterm election. One of the fired prosecutors, Carol Lam of Southern California, had been leading an aggressive probe into corruption by Republican officials, including now-jailed U.S. representative Randall "Duke" Cunningham. Another, David Iglesias of New Mexico, had refused to speed up the indictment of a prominent Democrat on the eve of the 2006 election, despite pressure from the state's senior U.S. senator, Republican Pete Domenici. And many of the fired attorneys—or those who were discovered to have been considered for firing but survived—turned out to be in "battleground" states, where White House political adviser Karl Rove was pressing for more vote-fraud investigations against Democratic organizers.

The congressional investigation of the firings dominated domestic headlines as the new Congress picked up steam. It led to the discovery of the provision that had been sneaked into the Patriot Act, allowing Gonzales to install permanent-replacement U.S. attorneys without Senate confirmation. The Justice Department had used the provision to install several replacements who did not have prosecutorial experience or the support of the home-state senators—normally a prerequisite to pass Senate vetting—and e-mails showed that Gonzales's chief of staff, Kyle Sampson, had urged aggressive use of the new provision as the plan came together. Both chambers voted overwhelmingly to repeal the provision in a rare bipartisan rebuke of the White House.

The affair also led to the resignations of several top Justice Department officials, including Sampson and the Justice Department's White House liaison, Monica Goodling, who, documents and testimony showed, had worked closely with the White House in evaluating which U.S. attorneys were "loyal Bushies," in Sampson's words, and so should be retained, and which should be fired. The probe also led to increasing pressure on Gonzales himself to resign. Gonzales initially said he had no involvement in the plan, but his account was contradicted by Sampson and various documents. By the late spring of 2007, many Republican lawmakers were joining in calls for Gonzales to be ousted, while Bush insisted that his old friend from Texas would stay. It was clear that the story of the controversy surrounding the U.S. attorney firings would not be over soon.

Amid mounting pressure from Congress, the Bush-Cheney administration began to pick its executive-power targets more carefully. The administration turned over several thousand pages of documents about the U.S. attorney firings from the Justice Department. But it balked at allowing

White House officials such as Rove, former White House counsel Harriet Miers, or their staff to testify about their role in the firings, citing the president's need for a zone of secrecy around his advisers.

In June 2007, Congress intensified the conflict. It issued subpoenas for two former White House officials involved in the U.S. attorney firings—Miers and Sara Taylor, a top Rove aide. Soon after, it issued subpoenas for documents related to the warrantless surveillance program, addressing them to the White House, Cheney's office, the Justice Department, and the National Security Council. The showdown appeared to be headed for a lengthy court battle over executive privilege that might simply run out the clock.

Relations with Congress deteriorated further the following month. On July 2, 2007, a federal appeals court denied a request by Cheney's former chief of staff, Scooter Libby, to be allowed to stay out of prison while he appealed his conviction for perjury and obstruction of justice in the CIA leak case. But hours later, Bush overturned the sentence on his own. Circumventing the usual Justice Department process for clemency applications, Bush declared that Libby's punishment was "excessive" and signed an order wiping away the entire thirty-month prison sentence, although he left a fine intact.

Administration defenders lauded Bush's move, deriding the prosecution of Libby as "political." They noted that Libby had not been charged with leaking Valerie Plame Wilson's identity, and some also said that Libby was being scapegoated by those who were angry at how the Bush-Cheney administration had taken the country into Iraq. But critics of the commutation argued that politics had had nothing to do with what had happened inside the courtroom, noting that Libby had been prosecuted by a Bush-appointed U.S. attorney and sentenced by a Bush-appointed district judge. Moreover, the punishment was in accordance with federal sentencing guidelines, which the Bush administration otherwise strongly backed. As special prosecutor Patrick Fitzgerald said in response to Bush's claim that Libby's sentence was "excessive": "In this case, an experienced federal judge considered extensive argument from the parties and then imposed a sentence consistent with the applicable laws. It is fundamental to the rule of law that all citizens stand before the bar of justice as equals. That principle guided the judge during both the trial and the sentencing."

Democratic leaders in Congress were blunter. No one questioned that the plain text of the Constitution gives presidents the authority to grant clemency. But critics accused Bush of abusing his prerogative to grant mercy—by using it not to correct an egregious miscarriage of justice, but to place the White House beyond accountability for lawbreaking. Reid called Bush's decision "disgraceful" and said that "history will judge him harshly." And House Speaker Nancy Pelosi called the move "a betrayal of trust," saying Bush had put his administration above the rule of law.

Other battles received less front-page notice. In May, the now-Democratic-controlled House Intelligence Committee issued a report saying that the CIA had violated a post-Watergate oversight law in 2006 when it failed to tell the panel about a "significant covert action activity." The committee did not say what the covert action was, but, in an echo of the 1988 aftermath of the Iran-Contra scandal, the disclosure led to calls to tighten reporting requirements on intelligence activities. Committee members filed a bill requiring the CIA's inspector general to audit every covert action at least once every three years and then to submit a report to Congress. Digging in its heels, the Bush-Cheney administration said it would veto any such bill because such a requirement "impermissibly intrudes on the president's constitutional authority to protect and control access to sensitive national security information."[26]

Still, the threat to *veto* such a bill, rather than to sign it and then issue a signing statement declaring the provision to be null and void, symbolized a seemingly changed attitude at the White House. Indeed, just a few days before issuing the veto threat on the CIA bill, Bush had exercised his veto power for only the second time in his presidency after Congress passed an Iraq war funding bill that included requirements to begin drawing down U.S. troop levels by the fall. In his veto message, Bush invoked language that was familiar from his signing statements, declaring that "this legislation is unconstitutional because it purports to direct the conduct of the operations of the war in a way that infringes upon the powers vested in the Presidency by the Constitution, including as Commander in Chief of the Armed Forces."[27] Such an executive-power claim was legally debatable, but by making it in a veto message instead of a signing statement, Bush was at least giving Congress an opportunity to override his judgment, as the Founders intended. (Congress failed to muster enough votes to override the veto.)

Indeed, the Bush-Cheney administration was starting to make a series of quiet retreats from some of its more aggressive claims of executive power. As noted earlier, in January 2007, Gonzales suddenly announced that the warrantless wiretapping program would be brought back under court oversight, as the 1978 warrant law required. In April 2007, also noted earlier, the Justice Department went back to the old way of hiring career lawyers in the Civil Rights Division and elsewhere, ending political appointee involvement in the selection process. The White House also said it would have no objection to Congress's repealing the Patriot Act provision that allowed "interim" U.S. attorneys to stay in office permanently without Senate confirmation, even though it had earlier said that the old system — under which a federal court could select a new U.S. attorney if the Senate failed to confirm one within 120 days — was an unconstitutional violation of executive power.

But many of these retreats were tactical, not permanent. The administration did not repudiate the aggressive claims of executive power it had made in the past; rather, it said only that there was no need to exercise them at that moment, and it reserved the right to revive them at any time in the future. In this way, the final two years of the Bush-Cheney presidency fit into a larger pattern since World War II in which the "imperial presidency" has waxed and waned. Whenever presidentialists have gained control of the White House, they have tended to make increasingly grandiose claims of presidential power. Then, when scandals and misgovernment have arisen, the presidentialists have temporarily retreated, only to slowly retake the ground they lost. The Korean War, the Vietnam War and the Watergate scandal, the Iran-Contra scandal, and now the Iraq war and the war on terrorism are all chapters in this history. Each one has also been a difficult time for America.

6.

While clashes over presidential power seem likely to dominate the final two years of the Bush-Cheney presidency, the administration's lame-duck status also raises the important question of what will come next. On January 20, 2009, a new president will be sworn in. Whether a Democrat or a Republican, he or she will inherit all the new and expanded executive powers created by the Bush-Cheney White House. As this next president fights political battles to implement his or her policy agenda, whether liberal or conservative, there will inevitably come a time when the Bush-Cheney precedents will offer a tempting solution to a difficult situation.

The next president's choices, and those of his or her legal team, will thus play an important role in the unfolding story of the executive branch's attempted takeover of the American government.

With that in mind, some political activists have begun to push for presidential power to be a major focus of the 2008 election—a drive to get presidential candidates to say what limits on the powers of their office they would obey before voters decide whom to entrust with the tremendous authority of the White House. This emerging drive cuts across ideological lines. In the spring of 2007, for example, a group of prominent Washington conservatives came together to form a new group, the American Freedom Agenda, which lobbied debate moderators to ask questions about executive power and which asked candidates to sign a ten-point pledge promising to take a restrained attitude toward executive power if elected. One of the founders, the direct-mail pioneer Richard Viguerie, said that conservative critics of the Bush-Cheney approach to executive power had had a difficult time getting their "constitutionalist" message across in recent years because Republicans controlled the government. But with everything up for grabs in 2008, he said, the time was ripe for the "traditional Barry Goldwater conservative," which he described as a conservative who believes in limited government and preserving checks and balances on those who wield power, to regain a voice.

"As it becomes more and more clear that Hillary Clinton could be the president of the United States, that is going to get a lot of conservatives' attention in a way this hasn't done before in recent years," Viguerie predicted.[28]

Yet even if the victor in the 2008 presidential election declines to make use of the aggrandized executive powers established by the Bush-Cheney administration, in the long run such forbearance might make little difference. The accretion of presidential power, history has shown, often acts like a one-way ratchet: It can be increased far more easily than it can be reduced. The annals of American history are now filled with new precedents in which a White House has claimed the power to bypass laws and then acted upon that claim, especially in matters of national security. The zone of secrecy surrounding the executive branch has been dramatically widened. The Supreme Court has been sharply tilted toward a sympathetic view of executive power, and the White House's political control of the permanent government has been dramatically expanded. The federal statute books are now riddled with asterisks, thanks to the explosive growth of signing statements, which have made it clear that a president can routinely sign legislation while declaring himself free to ignore sections that restrain his own powers—a dramatic change that has the potential to take away from Congress its constitutional right to override a president's decision to reject a new law.

The expansive presidential powers claimed and exercised by the Bush-Cheney White House are now an immutable part of American history—not controversies, but facts. The importance of such precedents is difficult to overstate. As Supreme Court justice Robert Jackson once warned, any new claim of executive power, once validated into precedent, "lies about like a loaded weapon ready for the hand of any authority that can bring forward a plausible claim of an urgent need. Every repetition imbeds that principle more deeply in our law and thinking and expands it to new purposes."[29]

Sooner or later, there will always be another urgent need.

# Acknowledgments

I begin by thanking my lovely wife and brilliant fellow journalist, Luiza Ch. Savage, who is the Washington correspondent for the Canadian newsweekly magazine *Maclean's*. Luiza provided intellectual and emotional support at every step toward the completion of this manuscript. It was she who first encouraged me to expand my work on presidential power into a book. From that moment to the production of initially clumsy chapter drafts and throughout the seemingly endless revisions process, Luiza was my first, repeated, and most important reader. Her countless edits measurably improved every page—and excised many more pages of material that did not make the grade. I am truly blessed to have Luiza as my partner in life.

At the *Boston Globe*, Peter Canellos is my bureau chief, editor, and friend, and his stalwart fellowship extended in many ways to this book. Peter was enormously supportive of the project, offering to let me keep using my office as a place to write even though I was on leave. A law school graduate as well as an ingenious editor, Peter volunteered his time to wade through early drafts of many chapters and provided critical advice. In this way he carried over our deeply collaborative efforts in the newspaper world, and I am grateful for his help and friendship.

This project would not have been possible without the support of the *Boston Globe* as an institution, including the backing of top editors Martin Baron, Helen Donovan, and Mary Jane Wilkinson. In addition to granting a leave of absence and offering logistical assistance, the *Globe* provided legal permission to draw on ideas and material I developed while on its payroll. I also want to express sincere appreciation for my many talented colleagues who have helped me grow as a journalist as I worked alongside them, both at the *Globe* and at the *Miami Herald*.

I was fortunate to be represented by the peerless Amanda Urban of ICM Talent. It is widely acknowledged that there is no better agent than

Binky in this industry, a reputation which I can now personally attest to and celebrate. Her guidance in finding an appropriate publisher for this project was invaluable, and I thank her for her professional expertise and her wise counsel.

This book was edited by Geoff Shandler at Little, Brown. I thank Geoff for taking a gamble on a first-time author, and for his keen insights and sound suggestions. Geoff's superb assistant, Junie Dahn, was a steady anchor throughout the project. Attorney Chris Nolan provided excellent advice. And nearly every paragraph in this book was sharpened and polished by the vigilant attentions of copyeditor Pamela Marshall.

During the writing and revisions of the manuscript, I had the advantage of the advice and suggestions of several experts steeped in some of the complex topics covered by this book. I thank them all, including Harold Koh of Yale Law School, Steven Aftergood of the Federation of American Scientists' Project on Government Secrecy, Peter Shane of Ohio State University's Moritz College of Law, Edward Rodriguez of the Judge Advocates Association, and Louis Fisher of the Library of Congress. In addition, this book benefited from the time I spent at the Gerald R. Ford Presidential Library in Ann Arbor, Michigan, and at the National Archives annex in College Park, Maryland. I am grateful to the research librarians at those facilities for their expert assistance, including Stacy Davis and Nancy Mirshah.

This book was also shaped by many interviews with former government officials who have firsthand knowledge of the events and topics it covers. Most allowed me to use their names, and they are cited in the text and endnotes. Several others helped me with my understanding of this material but asked not to be named. In every case, the interviews were productive, helpful, and fascinating, and I thank all who gave me their time and perspectives.

Finally, I would like to thank my parents, Robert and Sarah Savage, who fostered in me an interest in writing and politics from an early age. Both are teachers in professional life, and I continue to learn from them to this day.

# Notes

## 1. INSIDE THE BUNKER

1. For one of several available descriptions of the Presidential Emergency Operations Center, see Richard Clarke, *Against All Enemies* (New York: Free Press, 2004), 18.
2. "The Vice President Appears on *Meet the Press* with Tim Russert," September 16, 2001, http://www.whitehouse.gov/vicepresident/news-speeches/speeches/vp20010916.html.
3. "Cheney Recalls Taking Charge from Bunker," CNN, September 11, 2002, http://archives.cnn.com/2002/ALLPOLITICS/09/11/ar911.king.cheney/index.html.
4. *Final Report of the National Commission on Terrorist Attacks Upon the United States,* July 22, 2004, 40–42.
5. Ibid., 464 (footnote, 211).
6. Ibid., 41.
7. Ibid., 30, 43.
8. Ibid., 43.
9. According to the commission report, National Security Adviser Condoleezza Rice and Cheney's military aide, alone among those present in the bunker, told the commission investigators that they had a vague recollection of some kind of earlier call between Cheney and Bush, but no one else remembered such a call and there was no written record of it in call logs or notes. Ibid., 40–41.
10. Ibid., 41.
11. Ibid., 464–465 (footnotes, 216–221).
12. In the weeks and months following the attacks, Cheney and Bush gave numerous interviews about their performances on the morning of 9/11, and the 9/11 Commission obtained the full unreleased transcripts of each interview. A careful reading of the commission report's footnotes shows that no one mentioned any earlier phone call for more than three months. The dubious story first surfaced on December 17, 2001, when Bush sat down with reporters Bob Woodward and Dan Balz for an article the *Washington Post* published the following month. Ibid., 464 (footnote, 213).
13. See, e.g., Nicholas Lemann, "The Quiet Man: Dick Cheney's Rise to Unprecedented Power," *The New Yorker,* May 7, 2001.

14. John Kascht, "The Dick Cheney You Don't Know," *Talk,* May 2001, 88.
15. "Vice President's Remarks at the Gerald R. Ford Journalism Prize Luncheon, Followed by Q&A," June 19, 2006, http://www.whitehouse.gov/news/releases/2006/06/20060619-10.html.

## 2. THE FALL OF THE IMPERIAL PRESIDENCY AND THE RISE OF DICK CHENEY: 1789–1976

1. "Interview of the Vice President and Mrs. Cheney by KCWY News-13," May 27, 2006, http://www.whitehouse.gov/news/releases/2006/05/20060527-3.html.
2. John Kascht, "The Dick Cheney You Don't Know," *Talk,* May 2001, 88.
3. Ibid., 91.
4. Lee Davidson, "Lynne Cheney's Ancestors," *Deseret News,* January 22, 2006.
5. "Interview of the Vice President and Mrs. Cheney by KCWY News-13."
6. Nicholas Lemann, "The Quiet Man: Dick Cheney's Rise to Unprecedented Power," *The New Yorker,* May 7, 2001.
7. Kascht, "The Dick Cheney You Don't Know," 92.
8. Lemann, "The Quiet Man."
9. Davidson, "Lynne Cheney's Ancestors."
10. Lemann, "The Quiet Man."
11. Katharine Q. Seelye, "Cheney's Five Draft Deferments During the Vietnam Era Emerge as a Campaign Issue," *New York Times,* May 1, 2004.
12. Aage R. Clausen and Richard B. Cheney, "A Comparative Analysis of Senate House Voting on Economic and Welfare Policy: 1953–1964," *The American Political Science Review* 64, no. 1 (March 1970): 138–152.
13. Arthur Schlesinger, *The Imperial Presidency* (New York: Houghton Mifflin, 1973).
14. Michael B. Oren, *Power, Faith, and Fantasy* (New York: Norton, 2007), 29–32.
15. See, e.g., *Federalist 51* and *Federalist 75.*
16. This and the paragraphs that follow are largely derived from Schlesinger's *Imperial Presidency;* see also Louis Fisher, *Presidential War Power* (Lawrence: University of Kansas Press, 2004).
17. Schlesinger, *Imperial Presidency,* 50.
18. Abraham Lincoln, "Special Session Message," July 4, 1861, http://www.whitehousehistory.org/04/subs/activities_03/c02_04.html.
19. *Ex Parte Milligan,* 71 U.S. 2, 120–121 (1866).
20. Louis Fisher has argued that while Taft's view of presidential power differed rhetorically from Roosevelt's, on a practical level there was less difference between the two than historians conventionally say.
21. Alexander Hamilton, *Federalist 69.*
22. James Madison, "Helvidius No. 1," *Philadelphia Gazette,* August 31, 1793, reproduced in *The Mind of the Founder,* rev. ed., ed. Marvin Meyers (Indianapolis: Bobbs-Merrill Co., 1981), 206–207.

23. Some supporters of strong presidential war powers have argued that when the U.S. Senate ratifies treaties that give multinational groups the power to authorize the use of military force, such as with the United Nations charter and the North Atlantic Treaty Organization, Congress is delegating—to the foreign governments that sit on the United Nations Security Council or NATO—its constitutional power to decide when to take the United States from peace to war. But as Louis Fisher has pointed out, this argument is nonsense for multiple reasons. Among them, the Constitution gives the House of Representatives the power to block a war by refusing to authorize it, and the House does not get to vote on whether to ratify a treaty. The argument that such treaties eliminate the need for the president to obtain "advance congressional authorization would mean that the President and the Senate, through the treaty process, can obliterate the constitutional power of the House of Representatives to decide whether to take the nation to war. That position, no matter how asserted, is untenable." Fisher, *Presidential War Power*, 185.

24. *Youngstown Sheet & Tube Co. v. Sawyer*, 343 U.S. 579 (1952).

25. Schlesinger, *Imperial Presidency*, 153.

26. See, e.g., the Church Committee reports, http://www.aarclibrary.org/publib/church/reports/contents.htm

27. The Nixon-Frost interview was republished in several places, including in the *New York Times*, May 20, 1977.

28. See, e.g., Richard Nathan, *The Plot That Failed: Nixon and the Administrative Presidency* (New York: Wiley & Sons, 1975).

29. On December 13, 1969, for example, Nixon's chief of staff, H. R. Haldeman, recorded in his diary a conversation between Nixon and Rumsfeld in which the president said he wanted the Office of Economic Opportunity reorganized so that "everything clears through one place and there is some degree of control." Nixon also urged Rumsfeld to consider layoffs and "moved hard on cutting the OEO programs he doesn't like, i.e., Legal Services, Head Start, etc." H. R. Haldeman, *The Haldeman Diaries* (New York: Putnam, 2004), 114–115.

30. Author interview with Paul O'Neill, January 9, 2007.

31. *U.S. Code* 42 (1970), § 2809.

32. See, e.g., Clark Holmes, "The Poverty Lawyers' Work Is So Good, It Has to Be Stopped," *Washington Monthly*, June 1970, 50; see also David Wilson to John Dean, memorandum re: "Office of Legal Services of OEO," March 4, 1971, National Archives, Nixon Presidential Materials, John Dean Materials, Subject Files, box 53, folder: Office of Legal Services.

33. Holmes, "The Poverty Lawyers' Work."

34. Author interview with Terry Lenzner, October 3, 2006.

35. In October 1970, however, Rumsfeld did personally order Lenzner to shut down grants to programs in New Orleans, Dallas, and Los Angeles for allegedly violating Legal Services guidelines by, for example, providing legal assistance to a Black Panthers group. Taylor Branch, "The Ordeal of Legal Services: How Poor People Won in Court but Lost in OEO," *Washington Monthly*, January 1971.

36. Lenzner interview.

37. Kascht, "The Dick Cheney You Don't Know," 93.

38. Lenzner interview. (One dispute from the late spring of 1970 serves to illustrate the mounting political interference in the Legal Services program—and Cheney's growing role in carrying out Nixon's agenda of imposing greater control over the antipoverty bureaucracy. It began when a Legal Services lawyer in Charlotte, North Carolina, filed a police misconduct suit against the city on behalf of poor black people. The local board for the Charlotte program fired the lawyer, violating the program's rules against political interference. Lenzner promptly cut off federal funding for the Charlotte program to punish its board. A powerful Republican congressman from Charlotte, Rep. Charles Jonas, was infuriated by the loss of the grant for his district and met privately with Cheney to demand that it be reinstated. When Lenzner found out that Jonas was meeting with Cheney, the Legal Services director was angry that he had been cut out of the process. But Cheney told Lenzner to back off. A week after the Jonas meeting, on June 2, 1970, Cheney wrote: "Terry, you and I need to sit down and chat about Charlotte Legal Services at your convenience. Congressman Jonas called [Rumsfeld] again and we need to get squared away on what our position is so we can tell him the same story." Over Lenzner's strong objections, Charlotte got its grant back—without any new conditions on its board. After Lenzner figured out what had happened, he sent Rumsfeld a memo protesting the way Cheney had handled the Charlotte dispute. In the July 3, 1970, memo, Lenzner said the result "can only be a conclusion in the minds of those present that a decision, for political reasons, can be reversed simply by going to the 8th floor [where Cheney's and Rumsfeld's offices were] and requesting it." In the future, Lenzner added, he hoped that Rumsfeld would order Cheney to go through Lenzner's office first before acting on his own. These memo excerpts are quoted in Paul Clancy, "Charlotte Legal Services Flap Got OEO Aide Fired," *Charlotte Observer,* January 17, 1971, photocopy of article located in National Archives, Nixon Presidential Materials, John Dean Materials, Subject Files, box 53, folder: Office of Legal Services.)

39. Branch, "The Ordeal of Legal Services."

40. Later, Nixon tried a more frontal assault: refusing to spend money Congress had appropriated to fund the agency. In response, Congress in 1974 turned the program into the Legal Services Corporation, a federally funded private nonprofit that would be better shielded from political interference. Twenty-two years later, a newly Republican-controlled Congress and Democratic president Bill Clinton imposed new restrictions on the Legal Services Corporation. The 1996 changes, which echoed what the Nixon administration had wanted to do without congressional involvement, banned LSC-funded programs from filing "class actions, challenges to welfare reform . . . litigation on behalf of prisoners, representation in drug-related public housing evictions" and for certain noncitizens—even if they used private donations for such activities. http://www.lsc.gov/about/lsc.php.

41. Barry Werth, *31 Days* (New York: Doubleday, 2006), 20.

42. Bob Woodward, "Cheney Upholds Power of the President," *Washington Post,* January 20, 2005.

43. The anger in Congress was so great that Ford would take the unheard-of step of personally appearing before Congress to testify about his decision to grant the pardon, swearing that there had been no "deal" to give him the presidency in exchange for the promise of a pardon for Nixon. Ford for years would say that he wanted to spare the country the pain of a long trial for the former president. Then, on his deathbed, he would change his story, saying that his decision—which probably cost him the 1976 presidential election—had been based mostly on his personal feelings of friendship with Nixon. "I looked upon him as my personal friend. And I always treasured our relationship. And I had no hesitancy about granting the pardon, because I felt that we had this relationship and that I didn't want to see my real friend have the stigma," Ford confessed on condition that his words not be made public until after his death. See Bob Woodward, "Ford, Nixon Sustained Friendship for Decades," *Washington Post,* December 27, 2006.

44. Roy L. Ash to the president, memorandum re: "Freedom of Information Act Amendments (H.R. 12571)," August 12, 1974, Ford Presidential Library, Presidential Handwriting File, box 28, folder: Legislation (1).

45. See, e.g., unsigned and undated Office of Legal Counsel memorandum re: "Constitutional and Policy Questions Raised by the Senate Bill Amending the Freedom of Information Act," Ford Presidential Library, Philip Buchen Files, box 17, folder: Freedom of Information Legislation (3); and "Fact Sheet on Freedom of Information Act Amendments" and November 13 cover letter identifying them as being by Scalia, Ford Presidential Library, O'Donnell and Jenckes Files, box 5, folder: Freedom of Information 10–12/74.

46. Ken Cole to the president, memorandum re: "H.R. 12471, Amendments to Freedom of Information Act," October 9, 1974, Ford Presidential Library, Presidential Handwriting File, box 8, folder: Federal Government—Freedom of Information.

47. Veto message to the House of Representatives, October 17, 1974, Ford Presidential Library, Philip Buchen Files, box 17, folder: Freedom of Information Legislation (3).

48. A White House liaison to Congress clipped and saved a newspaper article that deemed the result a sign of the new president's "humiliating" lack of clout in Congress. The tilt toward Congress was dipping so far that Rumsfeld soon felt compelled to emphasize at a staff meeting "the need for all staffs to be certain that they held firmly to the administration positions when talking to Congress—not seek to 'get along' at the president's expense." Lyle Denniston, "Diminished Clout on Capitol Hill," *Washington Star-News,* November 23, 1974, Ford Presidential Library, O'Donnell and Jenckes Files, box 5, folder: Freedom of Information 10–12/74. (This newspaper closed in 1981, and there are no electronic archives for it. It appears that the headline on the clipping is actually a subheadline and that the full headline is missing, but its final word is "growing.") Mike Dunn to Bill Seidman,

memorandum re: "Senior Staff Meeting, December 13th, at 8:00 a.m.," December 13, 1974, Ford Presidential Library, L. William Seidman Files, box 90, folder: Senior Staff Meeting 12/13/74.

49. Memorandum of conversation, January 4, 1975, Ford Presidential Library, National Security Adviser Memoranda of Conversations, box 8, folder: January 4, 1975—Ford, Kissinger, Rockefeller, Marsh, Rumsfeld, Buchen.

50. Handwritten memorandum, "CIA—The Colby Report," December 27, 1974, Ford Presidential Library, Richard Cheney Files, box 5, folder: Intelligence—Colby Report.

51. Kascht, "The Dick Cheney You Don't Know," 93.

52. Rod Gramer, "Frank Church: Cerebral, Superior, Brilliant to Some; Cold, Misguided, Inconsistent to Others," *Idaho Statesman,* July 20, 1980, quoted in "Frank Church: Idaho's Man," Idaho Oral History Project, Boise State University, http://idahooratory.boisestate.edu/Churchbio2.htm.

53. Senate Select Committee to Study Governmental Operations with Respect to Intelligence Activities, *Intelligence Activities and the Rights of Americans,* April 26, 1976.

54. In 1976, as he was completing this report, Church ran for president. He won several Democratic primaries but eventually ceded the nomination to Jimmy Carter and contented himself with being the Senate Foreign Relations Committee chairman. His career came to an end in the 1980 election, when he topped a hit list of liberal senators whose reelection campaigns were targeted by out-of-state conservative funding. Accused of being soft on defense amid the conservative tide led by Ronald Reagan, Church lost his seat by less than a percentage point to Republican Steve Symms. Church worked for a few more years as a lawyer in Washington. His cancer returned, and he died in 1984 at the age of fifty-nine. Years later, after the 9/11 attacks, some conservatives would blame the Church Committee for making CIA officers too risk averse as they hunted for terrorists. "Frank Church: Idaho's Man."

55. Author interview with Jack Marsh, November 29, 2006.

56. Ron Nessen, *It Sure Looks Different from the Inside* (Playboy Publications, 1979), 58.

57. Memorandum of conversation, February 21, 1975, Ford Presidential Library, National Security Adviser Memoranda of Conversations, box 9, folder: February 21, 1975—Ford, Kissinger, Rumsfeld, Marsh.

58. Antonin Scalia, speech to the International Conference on the Administration of Justice and National Security in Democracies, Ottawa, Canada, June 12, 2007.

59. Untitled handwritten note, circa March 12, 1975, Ford Presidential Library, Richard Cheney Files, box 6, folder: Intelligence—Congressional Investigations.

60. Marsh interview.

61. Memorandum of conversation, May 14, 1975, Ford Presidential Library, National Security Adviser Memoranda of Conversations, box 11, folder: May 14, 1975—Ford, Kissinger, Bipartisan Congressional Leadership.

62. Peter Goldman, "Ford's Rescue Operation," *Newsweek,* May 26, 1975.

63. "The *Mayagüez*—What Went Right, What Went Wrong," *U.S. News & World Report*, June 2, 1975, 29. For the timing of the radio broadcast and the release of the crew, see Henry Kissinger, *Years of Renewal* (New York: Simon & Schuster, 1999), 567–570.

64. Goldman, "Ford's Rescue Operation."

65. President Richard M. Nixon to President Nguyen Van Thieu of the Republic of Vietnam, January 3, 1973, Ford Presidential Library, Richard Cheney Files, box 13, folder: Vietnam—Correspondence from Richard Nixon to Nguyen Van Thieu 10/72–12/72.

66. President Richard M. Nixon to President Nguyen Van Thieu of the Republic of Vietnam, October 16, 1972, Ford Presidential Library, Richard Cheney Files, box 13, folder: Vietnam—Correspondence from Richard Nixon to Nguyen Van Thieu 10/72–12/72.

67. Antonin Scalia, Assistant Attorney General, Office of Legal Counsel, statement on executive Agreements (S. 1251 and S. 632), before the Senate Subcommittee on Separation of Powers, Committee on Judiciary, May 15, 1975, Ford Presidential Library, Edward Schmults Files, box 17, folder: Legislative Encroachment Testimony.

68. Philip Buchen to Jeanne Davis, memorandum re: "Senate Foreign Relations Committee Request for Presidential Correspondence on Saudi Arabia," May 16, 1975, Ford Presidential Library, Philip Buchen Files, box 26, folder: National Security Chronological File (2).

69. National Security Council Memorandum for the Record re: "Executive Agreements," May 17, 1975, Ford Presidential Library, Philip Buchen Files, box 12, folder: Executive Agreements (2).

70. Handwritten notes, May 29, 1975, Ford Presidential Library, Richard Cheney Files, box 6, folder: Intelligence—*New York Times* Articles by Seymour Hersh 5/75–6/75 (1).

71. Donald Rumsfeld to Richard Cheney, memorandum re: "WH 50988," May 30, 1975, Ford Presidential Library, Richard Cheney Files, box 6, folder: Intelligence—*New York Times* Articles by Seymour Hersh 5/75–6/75 (2).

72. Richard Cheney to Donald Rumsfeld, memorandum re: "Status Report—*New York Times* Story of Sunday, May 25, 1975," May 29, 1975, Ford Presidential Library, Richard Cheney Files, box 6, folder: Intelligence—*New York Times* Articles by Seymour Hersh 5/75–6/75 (1).

73. The available files do not reveal whether such private conversations with newspaper publishers took place. Richard Cheney to Donald Rumsfeld, draft memorandum, May 30, 1975, Ford Presidential Library, Richard Cheney Files, box 6, folder: Intelligence—*New York Times* Articles by Seymour Hersh 5/75 6/75 (1).

74. Philip Buchen to the president, memorandum re: "Release of the Colby Report," July 7, 1975, Ford Presidential Library, Presidential Handwriting File, box 30, folder: National Security Intelligence (1).

75. Jack Marsh to the president, memorandum re: "Claim of Executive Privilege," November 13, 1975, Ford Presidential Library, Presidential Handwriting File, box 31, folder: National Security Intelligence (8).

76. The following February, on Antonin Scalia's advice, Ford asserted executive privilege to prevent FBI agents and Western Union officials from testifying about a program in which the telegram agency had been turning over cables to the government without warrants. Memorandum of conversation, November 21, 1975, Ford Presidential Library, National Security Adviser Memoranda of Conversations, box 16, folder: November 21, 1975—Ford, Kissinger; Antonin Scalia to Philip Buchen, memorandum re: "Claim of Executive Privilege with Respect to Materials Subpoenaed by the Committee on Government Operations, House of Representatives," February 17, 1976, Ford Presidential Library, Presidential Handwriting File, box 31, folder: National Security Intelligence (13).

77. Gerald Ford, *A Time to Heal* (New York: Harper & Row, 1979), 324. In 2004, however, after Cheney became vice president, Ford would say that his old aide had changed since the days of their close working relationship. "He was an excellent chief of staff. First class," Ford told Bob Woodward. "But I think Cheney has become much more pugnacious" as vice president. Ford said he agreed with Colin Powell's claim that Cheney seemed to have developed a "fever" about the threat of terrorism and Iraq. Bob Woodward, "Ford Disagreed with Bush About Invading Iraq," *Washington Post,* December 28, 2006.

78. Quoted in James Bamford, "Bush Is Not Above the Law," *New York Times,* February 1, 2007.

79. Philip Buchen to the president, memorandum re: "Intelligence Legislation Proposed by the Justice Department," February 13, 1976, Ford Presidential Library, Philip Buchen Files, box 26, folder: National Security Chronological File (6).

80. Philip Buchen to the president, memorandum re: "Intelligence Legislation Proposed by the Justice Department," February 13, 1976, and appendix A (note from the attorney general), Ford Presidential Library, Philip Buchen Files, box 26, folder: National Security Chronological File (6).

81. Philip Buchen to Richard Ober, memorandum re: "Draft Preamble for NSCIDs," March 17, 1976, Ford Presidential Library, Philip Buchen Files, box 26, folder: National Security Chronological File (6).

82. Philip Buchen to the president, memorandum re: "Legislation on Electronic Surveillance for Foreign Intelligence Purposes," March 15, 1976, Ford Presidential Library, Philip Buchen Files, box 26, folder: National Security Chronological File (6).

83. Cheney also took a greater leadership role in handling intelligence matters inside the administration, and to advance a tougher stance on the Cold War that he had been developing even before becoming chief of staff. In June 1975, for example, when Vice President Nelson Rockefeller's commission on CIA activities inside the United States came out with its report detailing many abuses by the agency, most ignored the report as a whitewash when compared with the more aggressive investigation the Church Committee was undertaking. But Cheney thought Rockefeller had gone too far, scrawling on the cover of his copy a question indicating that he thought the vice president had blundered in describing the CIA's conduct as illegal. "Does criticism of CIA hurt V.P. with conservatives?" Cheney wrote to himself. Later, after taking

the lead in Ford's 1976 election campaign, Cheney helped convince Ford to drop Rockefeller as his vice presidential nominee and replace him with the more conservative Senator Bob Dole of Kansas. Cheney used his position to steer the Ford administration toward his own hard-line views about the Soviet Union. Undercutting Kissinger's policy of détente, Cheney pressed for a sharper confrontation with Moscow. For example, Cheney urged Ford to meet with the dissident Alexander Solzhenitsyn in order to demonstrate that despite détente, the United States' relationship with the Soviet Union was not "all sweetness and light." See, e.g., Richard Cheney to Donald Rumsfeld, memorandum re: "Solzhenitsyn," Ford Presidential Library, Richard Cheney Files, box 10, folder: Solzhenitsyn, Alexander; Jack Marsh to Richard Cheney, memorandum, September 23, 1976, Ford Presidential Library, John Marsh Files, box 76, folder: Cheney, Richard 8/76–9/76.

84. He added, "Although he kept a low public profile, Cheney had accumulated as much control as some of the better-known chiefs of staff. Some reporters privately started calling him the Grand Teuton — a complex pun referring to his mountainous home state of Wyoming and the Germanic style of his predecessor, H. R. Haldeman." Nessen, *It Sure Looks Different,* 248–249.

85. Michael Medved, *The Shadow Presidents: The Secret History of the Chief Executives and Their Top Aides* (New York: Times Books, 1979), 339.

## 3. "A CABAL OF ZEALOTS": 1977–2000

1. T. R. Reid, "White House Staff Chief, in Love with Governing, Now Runs for Congress," *Washington Post,* August 28, 1978.
2. *Congressional Record,* accessed via http://public.CQ.com.
3. Michael Medved, *The Shadow Presidents: The Secret History of the Chief Executives and Their Top Aides* (New York: Times Books, 1979), 347.
4. Antonin Scalia, speech to the International Conference on the Administration of Justice and National Security in Democracies, Ottawa, Canada, June 12, 2007.
5. Edward Walsh, "Legislative Veto Trend Denounced by President," *Washington Post,* June 22, 1978.
6. *INS v. Chadha,* 462 U.S. 919 (1983).
7. Kenneth Bredemeier, "Goldwater, Other Lawmakers File Suit over Repeal of Taiwan Defense Pact," *Washington Post,* December 23, 1978.
8. "11/18 Cheney," handwritten notes of James A. Baker, The James A. Baker III Papers, Seeley G. Mudd Library, Princeton University, http://media .washingtonpost.com/wp srv/politics/interactives/cheney/docs/baker_ notes.pdf.
9. Charles Fried, *Order and Law* (New York: Simon & Schuster, 1991), 16.
10. See, e.g., Jeffrey Rosen, "Power of One," *The New Republic,* July 24, 2006.
11. Author interview with Steven Calabresi, January 3, 2007.
12. Author interview with Edwin Meese, January 2007.
13. Fried, *Order and Law,* 49–51.

14. See, e.g., John C. Keeney to the attorney general, memorandum re: "Status Report on Independent Counsel Matter: Preliminary Investigation of Allegations in House Judiciary Committee Report," March 10, 1986, National Archives, Records Group 60, Edwin Meese Subject Files (1985–1988), box 20, folder: Independent-Counsel (1986).

15. "Separation of Powers: Legislative-Executive Relations," National Archives, Department of Justice Files, Records Group 60, Edwin Meese Component Correspondence Files, folder: OLP (April–May 1986).

16. Stephen J. Markman to Edwin Meese III, memorandum re: "Separation of Powers," April 30, 1986, National Archives, Department of Justice Files, Edwin Meese Component Correspondence Files, folder: OLP (April–May 1986).

17. *Federalist 70.*

18. *Humphrey's Executor v. United States,* 295 U.S. 602 (1935).

19. Adding to their confidence, on July 7, 1986, the Court struck down a law that gave the comptroller general, an official who could be fired only by Congress, the right to impose across-the-board spending cuts in order to lower the deficit. The Court ruled that Congress had no right to give such an "executive" power to an official accountable to the legislative branch. The ruling seemed to open the door for a challenge to laws giving executive power to officials who were not accountable to the president. *Bowsher v. Synar,* 478 U.S. 714 (1986).

20. Jan Crawford Greenburg, *Supreme Conflict* (New York: Penguin Press, 2007), 200.

21. Richard Cheney to the president, memorandum re: "Ken Cole's Views on the Domestic Council," January 20, 1975, Ford Presidential Library, Richard Cheney Files, box 3, folder: Domestic Council — Vice President's Role 1/75– 12/75; memorandum of conversation, February 21, 1975, Ford Presidential Library, National Security Adviser Memoranda of Conversations, box 9, folder: February 21, 1975 — Ford, Kissinger, Rumsfeld, Marsh.

22. *Morrison v. Olson,* 487 U.S. 654 (1988).

23. Fried, *Order and Law,* 160–161.

24. Ibid., 170.

25. Author interview with former representative Mickey Edwards, November 13, 2006.

26. Ibid.

27. Julia Malone, "Congress Calls for Security for Marines amid Skepticism," *The Christian Science Monitor,* October 25, 1983.

28. See, e.g., Richard F. Grimmett, "The War Powers Resolution: After Thirty Years," Congressional Research Service, RL32267, March 11, 2004, http:// www.fas.org/man/crs/RL32267.html.

29. Robert Parry, "Congressional Trip to Grenada Boosts Reagan," Associated Press, November 8, 1983.

30. James Mann, *Rise of the Vulcans: The History of Bush's War Cabinet* (New York: Viking, 2004), 138–145.

31. "Dick Cheney Recalls the Ford Presidency," *National Journal* 17, no. 2 (January 12, 1985).

32. *The MacNeil/Lehrer NewsHour,* PBS, April 11, 1986.

33. Theodore Draper, *A Very Thin Line* (New York: Hill and Wang, 1991), 17–24.

34. Ibid., 24.

35. Jane Mayer, "The Hidden Power," *The New Yorker,* July 3, 2006.

36. *Hearing of the U.S. House of Representatives Select Committee to Investigate Covert Arms Transactions with Iran and the U.S. Senate Select Committee on Secret Military Assistance to Iran and the Nicaraguan Opposition,* July 20, 1987.

37. *Report of the Congressional Committees Investigating the Iran-Contra Affair,* 100th Cong., 1st sess., November 1987, H. Rept. 100–433, S. Rept. 100–216, 16–21.

38. Ibid., 457.

39. Gary Thatcher, "Minority Report Takes Strong Issue," *The Christian Science Monitor,* November 19, 1987.

40. Richard Cheney, "Covert Operations: Who's in Charge?" *Wall Street Journal,* May 8, 1988. Cheney and his allies succeeded in blocking the bill in 1988, although Congress passed a watered-down version of the forty-eight-hour bill two years later. By then, Cheney was back in the executive branch, serving as secretary of defense to the new president, George H. W. Bush.

41. "Vice President's Remarks to the Traveling Press," December 20, 2005, http://www.whitehouse.gov/news/releases/2005/12/20051220-9.html.

42. For a fuller treatment of the first Bush administration's efforts to govern unilaterally, see Charles Tiefer, *The Semi-Sovereign Presidency: The Bush Administration's Strategy for Governing Without Congress* (Boulder: Westview, 1994).

43. William P. Barr, "Common Legislative Encroachments on Executive Branch Authority," July 27, 1989, 13 U.S. Op. Off. Legal Counsel 248, 1989 WL 595833 (OLC).

44. Neil Kinkopf, "Furious George," *Legal Affairs,* September/October 2005.

45. "Remarks at Dedication Ceremony of the Social Sciences Complex at Princeton University in Princeton, New Jersey," 27 Weekly Comp. Pres. Doc. 589, May 10, 1991.

46. Richard Cheney, "Congressional Overreaching in Foreign Policy," draft prepared for March 14–15, 1989, American Enterprise Institute conference Foreign Policy and the Constitution, on file with the author.

47. "The Gulf War — Oral History — Dick Cheney," *Frontline,* http://www.pbs.org/wgbh/pages/frontline/gulf/oral/cheney/1.html.

48. Ibid.

49. Author interview with Lawrence Wilkerson, November 30, 2006.

50. Senate Committee on Armed Services, *Nominations of David S. Addington, to Be General Counsel of the Department of Defense, and Robert S. Silberman, to Be Assistant Secretary of the Army for Manpower and Reserve Affairs; to Consider Certain Pending Civilian Nominations; to Consider Certain Pending Army and Air Force Nominations; and to Discuss, and Possibly Consider, Certain Pending Navy and Marine Corps Nominations,* July 1, 1992.

51. Rosen, "Power of One."

52. Robert Pear, "Ending Its Secrecy, White House Lists Health Care Panel," *New York Times,* March 27, 1993.

53. Phyllis Schlafly, "Clinton's Power Grab Through Executive Orders," *Eagle Forum*, January 20, 1999, http://www.eagleforum.org/column/1999/jan99/99-01-20.html.

54. See, e.g., Walter Dellinger to Alan J. Kreczko, memorandum re: "Placing of United States Armed Forces Under United Nations Operational or Tactical Control," May 8, 1996.

55. *Chamber of Commerce of the United States v. Reich*, 74 F.3d 1322 (D.C. Cir. 1996).

56. "War Powers Resolution, RIP," *National Review*, August 23, 1993.

57. Randolph Moss to the attorney general, memorandum re: "Authorization for Continuing Hostilities in Kosovo," December 19, 2000, http://biotech.law.lsu.edu/blaw/olc/final.htm.

58. Guy Gugliotta, "Whipping Up a Role Reversal," *Washington Post*, May 4, 1999.

59. Ibid.

60. Eric Schmitt and Steven Lee Myers, "Clinton Lawyers Give a Go-Ahead to Missile Shield," *New York Times*, June 15, 2000.

61. Video available at http://www.cato.org/realaudio/con-07-12-00p4.ram. The George Washington University law professor Orin Kerr wrote about this presentation on the legal blog *Volokh Conspiracy* on September 18, 2006.

62. Mayer, "The Hidden Power."

63. Rita Beamish, "Cheney Says He Won't Run for President in '06," Associated Press, January 3, 1995.

64. Michelle Mittelstadt, "Bush Builds Campaign Brain Trust," Associated Press, February 25, 1999.

65. Rick Klein, "Cheney Will Lead Search for Bush's Running Mate," *Dallas Morning News*, April 26, 2000.

66. Governor George W. Bush, statement re: "Selection of Former Defense Secretary Richard B. Cheney to Be the Republican Vice Presidential Candidate," July 25, 2000.

## 4. THE AGENDA

1. Author interviews with Bradford Berenson, November 14, November 28, and December 1, 2006.

2. The official count in Florida gave Bush a victory over Gore by 537 votes out of more than six million cast. The tiny margin put a spotlight on the lack of precision in the state's voting system, which relied on punch-card ballots in some counties and fill-in-the-bubble optical-scan ballots in others. Hanging chads and sloppily filled-in ballots meant that machine counters had discarded many thousands of votes across Florida. In normal elections, with larger margins, the slight fuzziness made no difference, so there was no need to inspect such ballots by hand. But in 2000, a recount could easily shift the balance to Gore, who had won the popular vote nationally but needed Florida's electoral votes to become president. Lawyers from both parties de-

scended upon every county in Florida. Democrats pushed for a recount and had early success in a few counties whose second looks shrank Bush's margin of victory. Then Republicans dug in, asking courts to halt the recounts and accept a decision by Secretary of State Katherine Harris, who was also the cochair of Bush's Florida campaign, to certify the results as they stood, with Bush still slightly ahead. The Florida Supreme Court ordered a full statewide recount. But on December 12, 2000, the Supreme Court stepped in. By a 5–4 vote, the slight conservative majority bloc reversed the state court decision and halted the recount, ensuring that Bush and Cheney would take over the White House.

3. Alan Berlow, "The Texas Clemency Memos," *The Atlantic Monthly*, July/August 2003.
4. Berenson interviews.
5. Andrew Rudalevige, *The New Imperial Presidency* (Ann Arbor: University of Michigan Press, 2006), 208.
6. Berenson interviews.
7. *This Week*, ABC, January 27, 2002.
8. Author interview with a knowledgeable source.
9. Author interview with John Yoo, March 8, 2007.
10. Nicholas Horrock, "Bush Nominates Prof for a Top DOJ Post," *United Press International*, July 10, 2001.
11. Carri Geer Thevenot, "UNLV Law Professor Ready for DC Job," *Las Vegas Review-Journal*, November 19, 2001.
12. "Attorney General Ashcroft Welcomes White House Nominee for Assistant Attorney General for the Office of Legal Counsel," July 10, 2001, http://www.usdoj.gov/opa/pr/2001/July/315ag.htm.
13. Jay S. Bybee, Assistant Attorney General, Office of Legal Counsel, statement before the Subcommittee on Commercial and Administrative Law and the Subcommittee on Courts, the Internet, and Intellectual Property, House Judiciary Committee, concerning settlement of the *NextWave* case, December 6, 2001.
14. Peter Slevin, "Scholar Stands by Post-9/11 Writings on Torture, Domestic Eavesdropping," *Washington Post*, December 26, 2005.
15. "Two Korean-Americans Nominated for White House Office Positions," *Korea Times*, April 21, 2001.
16. Yoo interview.
17. John C. Yoo, "The Continuation of Politics by Other Means: The Original Understanding of War Powers," 84 *Cal. L. Rev.* 167, 196–241 (1996).
18. This more traditional understanding of war power, rejected by Yoo, is further supported by the Founders' explicit purpose in giving Congress the power to raise armies. The Founders did not anticipate that the United States would someday maintain a large standing military force in peacetime, so they believed that presidents' need to go to Congress to obtain a war-fighting force would help ensure that presidents did not disobey the Founders' decision that only Congress could decide whether the country should go to war.

19. James Madison, "Political Observations," April 20, 1795, in *The Papers of James Madison,* vol. 15 (March 24, 1793–April 20, 1795), ed. Thomas A. Mason and others (Charlottsville: University Press of Virginia, 1985), 518–521.
20. Slevin, "Scholar."
21. Cass Sunstein, "The 9/11 Constitution," *The New Republic,* January 16, 2006.
22. Yoo interview.
23. R. Jeffrey Smith and Dan Eggen, "Gonzales Helped Set the Course for Detainees," *Washington Post,* January 5, 2005.
24. Author interview with a knowledgeable source.
25. Author interview with Lawrence Wilkerson, November 30, 2006.
26. Daniel Klaidman and others, "Palace Revolt," *Newsweek,* February 6, 2006.

## 5. "BEHIND CLOSED DOORS": SECRECY I

1. "Remarks by the President at Energy Policy Meeting," January 29, 2001, http://www.whitehouse.gov/news/releases/20010129-1.html.
2. Jeffrey Birnbaum, "Fat and Happy in DC," *Fortune,* May 28, 2001.
3. Haley Barbour to Vice President Richard Cheney, memorandum re: "Bush-Cheney Energy Policy and $CO_2$," March 1, 2001, obtained by Judicial Watch through Freedom of Information Act lawsuit against the Department of Commerce, on file with Judicial Watch and with the author.
4. Joseph Kelliher to Dana Contratto, e-mail re: "National Energy Policy," March 18, 2001, on file with Judicial Watch and with the author. Bush would later make Kelliher, who was then a top adviser to the secretary of energy, the chairman of the Federal Energy Regulatory Commission.
5. After the task force finished its report, Lundquist would stay on as the White House's director of energy policy, working with Congress as it turned Cheney's task force report into an impenetrable, phone book–sized bill. Lundquist would leave government service on March 26, 2002, and open a lobbying business the next day. The Lundquist Group set up shop in a "posh office building perched kitty-corner from the Capitol" at 101 Constitution Avenue and began taking in hundreds of thousands of dollars annually from clients such as British Petroleum and Duke Energy Corporation. Susan Milligan and Maud Beeman, "Cheney Aide Now Lobbyist on Energy," *Boston Globe,* April 25, 2004.
6. John Dingell and Henry Waxman to Andrew Lundquist, April 19, 2001, http://www.house.gov/commerce_democrats/press/107ltr42.shtml.
7. David Addington to Billy Tauzin and others, May 4, 2001, http://www.house.gov/commerce_democrats/press/lundquist.pdf.
8. Walker switched his party registration from Republican to Independent in 1996. Author interview with David Walker, March 8, 2007.
9. David Addington to Anthony Gamboa, May 16, 2001, http://www.house.gov/commerce_democrats/press/vp.ltr.pdf.
10. "Chronology of GAO's Efforts to Obtain NEPDG Documents from the

Office of the Vice President, April 19, 2001–August 25, 2003," http://www.gao.gov/press/chronologynepdg.8.21.03_1.pdf.

11. "Energy Task Force: Process Used to Develop the National Energy Policy," U.S. General Accounting Office, August 2003, 22, http://www.gao.gov/new.items/d03894.pdf.

12. Louis Brandeis, *Other People's Money, and How the Bankers Use It,* rev. ed. (1933; repr., Bedford / St. Martin's, 1999).

13. Bob Woodward, "Cheney Upholds Power of the President," *Washington Post,* January 20, 2005.

14. Charlie Savage, "In Terror War's Name, Public Loses Information," *Boston Globe,* April 24, 2005.

15. Author interviews with Bradford Berenson, November 14, November 28, and December 1, 2006.

16. Author interview with Christopher Farrell, December 15, 2006.

17. Larry Klayman and Thomas Fitton to Richard B. Cheney, re: "National Energy Policy Development Group, a De Facto Federal Advisory Committee," June 25, 2001, on file with the author.

18. David S. Addington to Larry Klayman, July 5, 2001, on file with the author.

19. Quoted in Byron York, "GAO vs. Cheney: Coming Soon," *National Review,* February 20, 2002, http://www.nationalreview.com/york/york022002.shtml; see also "Chronology of GAO's Efforts."

20. "Chronology of GAO's Efforts."

21. *Grosjean v. Am. Press Co.,* 297 U.S. 233 (1936).

22. *U.S. v. Sinclair,* 321 F. Supp. 1074 (E.D. Mich. 1971).

23. "Damon J. Keith Biography," Wayne State University, Walter P. Reuther Library, http://www.reuther.wayne.edu/keith_bio.html.

24. *Detroit Free Press v. Ashcroft,* 303 F.3d 681 (6th Cir. 2002); internal quotation marks omitted.

25. *North Jersey Media Group v. Ashcroft,* 308 F.3d 198 (3rd Cir. 2002). The dissenting vote was cast by Judge Anthony Scirica, another Reagan appointee.

26. Savage, "In Terror War's Name."

27. Alberto Gonzales to John Carlin, August 1, 2001, http://www.fas.org/sgp/news/2001/09/presrecs.html.

28. Neil Lewis, "Bush Claims Executive Privilege in Response to House Inquiry," *New York Times,* December 14, 2001.

29. Glen Johnson, "Bush Denies Congress Papers for FBI Probe," *Boston Globe,* December 14, 2001.

30. Edwin Chen, "Bush Refuses to Turn Over Justice Records to Congress," *Los Angeles Times,* December 14, 2001.

31. Pete Yost, "Bush Invokes Executive Privilege to Keep Justice Department Investigative Documents Secret," Associated Press, December 14, 2001.

32. George Lardner Jr., "White House Request to Restrict Clinton Pardon Data Upheld," *Washington Post,* April 2, 2003.

33. *This Week,* ABC, January 27, 2002.

34. York, "GAO vs. Cheney."

35. Walker interview.

36. Dana Milbank, "GAO Ends Fight with Cheney over Files; Weakening of Hill's Oversight Decried," *Washington Post,* February 8, 2003.

37. Andrew Card to the heads of executive departments and agencies, memorandum re: "Action to Safeguard Information Regarding Weapons of Mass Destruction and Other Sensitive Documents Related to Homeland Security," March 19, 2002, http://www.usdoj.gov/oip/foiapost/2002foiapost10.htm.

38. The following section is all adapted from Savage, "In Terror War's Name."

39. Tomas Kellner and others, "Informer," *Forbes,* July 26, 2004.

40. "Nuclear Security Changes at NRC Provide Cover for Industry and Regulatory Failures," Public Citizen press release, August 4, 2004, http://www.citizen.org/cmep/energy_enviro_nuclear/nuclear_power_plants/security/articles.cfm?ID=12137.

41. Savage, "In Terror War's Name."

42. Ibid.

43. Ibid.

44. Andrew Revkin, "Bush Aide Softened Greenhouse Gas Links to Global Warming," *New York Times,* June 8, 2005.

45. Kirsten Downey, "U.S. Drops Report on Mass Layoffs," *Washington Post,* January 2, 2003.

46. Dana Milbank, "Seek and Ye Shall Not Find," *Washington Post,* March 11, 2003.

47. David Johnson and Eric Lichtblau, "A Critical Study, Minus Criticism," *New York Times,* October 30, 2003.

48. Two hundred eighty-eight of the pictures were of the remains of soldiers killed in Iraq; the other seventy-three were of the astronauts killed in the Columbia space shuttle disaster. http://www.thememoryhole.org/war/coffin_photos/dover/.

49. "Pentagon: Families Want Photo Ban," Associated Press, April 23, 2004.

50. Diana Jean Schemo, "Nation's Charter Schools Lagging Behind, U.S. Test Scores Reveal," *New York Times,* August 17, 2004.

51. Diana Jean Schemo, "U.S. Cutting Back on Details in Data About Charter Schools," *New York Times,* August 29, 2004.

52. Andrew Revkin, "Climate Expert Says NASA Tried to Silence Him," *New York Times,* January 29, 2006.

53. Andrew Keegan, "Feds Yank Gay Health Site," *Southern Voice,* March 10, 2006, http://www.sovo.com/2006/3-10/view/actionalert/aa.cfm.

54. "New Controls on Publishing Research Worry U.S. Government Geological Unit's Scientists," Associated Press, December 13, 2006.

55. Andrew Revkin, "Memos Tell Officials How to Discuss Climate," *New York Times,* March 8, 2007.

56. See, e.g., Jesselyn Radack, "Whistle-Blowing in Washington," *Reform Judaism,* spring 2006, http://reformjudaismmag.org/Articles/index.cfm?id=1104; Douglas McCollam, "The Trials of Jesselyn Radack," *The American Lawyer,* July 14, 2003, http://www.law.com/jsp/article.jsp?id=1056139907383.

57. Author interview with Jesselyn Radack, March 12, 2007.

58. Jesselyn Radack, "Broken Wings: The Indignities of Being on the No-Fly

List," *Buffalo Report,* April 15, 2004, http://buffaloreport.com/2004/040415
.radack.nofly.html.

59. Radack worked for a while as an adjunct law professor at American University, then found a job representing whistle-blowers. The complaint filed against her with the Maryland bar association was dismissed. Three and a half years after it was filed, the ethics complaint in the District of Columbia bar association was still pending. Ironically, even as the DC bar disciplinary committee kept her file open, the bar group also elected to have her sit on its ethics committee.

60. H.R. 5005, *Homeland Security Act of 2002,* signed November 25, 2002.

61. Charlie Savage, "Bush Was Told of Qaeda Steps," *Boston Globe,* April 11, 2004.

62. "Statement of Congressman John D. Dingell on the GAO Lawsuit Decision," December 9, 2002, http://www.house.gov/commerce_democrats/press/107st163.shtml.

63. Milbank, "GAO Ends Fight."

64. Peter Brand and Alexander Bolton, "Stevens Threat Halted GAO Cheney Case," *The Hill,* February 19, 2003.

65. Walker interview.

66. Ashcroft told the committees that he would talk about the Patriot Act only in private with the intelligence committees — which weren't charged with monitoring his department, weren't conducting such oversight, and did not ask for the information.

67. Steve Schultze, "Sensenbrenner Wants Answer on Law," *Milwaukee Journal Sentinel,* August 20, 2002.

68. Jim Hughes, "Lawmaker, Rights Group Differ on Patriot Act Data," *Denver Post,* October 18, 2002.

69. William Safire, "You Are a Suspect," *New York Times,* November 14, 2002.

70. Senator Jay Rockefeller to Vice President Cheney, July 17, 2003, http://a9.g
.akamai.net/7/9/8082/v002/democratic1.download.akamai.com/8082/pdfs/20051219_Rockfellerletter.pdf.

71. Tony Pugh, "Bush Administration Ordered Medicare Plan Cost Estimates Withheld," Knight Ridder, March 12, 2004.

72. Amy Goldsmith, "Official Says He Was Told to Withhold Data," *Washington Post,* March 14, 2004.

73. Reps. Henry Waxman and John Tierney to Defense Secretary Donald Rumsfeld, March 25, 2004, http:// www.cdi.org/news/missile-defense/HAW-JFT-Letter-to-Rumsfeld%2003-25-04.pdf.

74. Susan Milligan, "Classified Intelligence Bills Are Often Unread," *Boston Globe,* August 6, 2006.

75. Ibid.

76. Ibid.

## 6. THE UNLEASHING: LAWS AND TREATIES I

1. James Bamford, *A Pretext for War* (New York: Doubleday, 2004).

2. "President's Remarks at National Day of Prayer and Remembrance," September

14, 2001, http://www.whitehouse.gov/news/releases/2001/09/20010914-2
.html.

3. H.J. Res. 64, *Authorizing Use of United States Armed Forces Against Those Responsible for Recent Attacks Against the United States,* September 14, 2001.

4. "Statement by the President," September 14, 2001, http://www.whitehouse .gov/news/releases/2001/09/20010914-14.html.

5. "Remarks by the President to Police, Firemen, and Rescue Workers," September 14, 2001, http://www.whitehouse.gov/news/releases/2001/09/20010914-9.html.

6. Author interviews with Bradford Berenson, November 14, November 28, and December 1, 2006.

7. Tom Daschle, "Power We Didn't Grant," *Washington Post,* December 23, 2005.

8. Ibid.

9. The memo was quietly posted deep inside the Justice Department's website in late December 2004, after Bush and Cheney won reelection. The disclosure, which was not announced to the press, was part of preparations for then–White House counsel Alberto Gonzales's coming confirmation hearings to replace John Ashcroft as attorney general.

10. The memorandum did reserve one power for Congress: If lawmakers objected to a president's already-begun war, they could vote to cut off funds for the military effort — if they had the political will to take responsibility for ensuring that the United States would lose a war already in progress.

11. John Yoo to deputy counsel to the president, memorandum opinion re: "The President's Constitutional Authority to Conduct Military Operations Against Terrorists and Nations Supporting Them," September 25, 2001, http://www.usdoj.gov/olc/warpowers925.htm.

12. *Youngstown Sheet & Tube Co. v. Sawyer,* 343 U.S. 579 (1952). Truman's successors tried to work around the steel-seizure ruling with a series of awkward legal arguments. In some cases, presidents attempted to creatively declare that some statute contained implicit permission to ignore specific legal limits Congress had previously enacted in other bills. In other cases, presidents claimed that what they wanted to do was part of their "core" powers as commander in chief, beyond the reach of congressional regulation. The Bush-Cheney legal team would adopt both of these strategies for bolstering its claims of "inherent" power—but they would also go further in solving the problem, as they saw it, of congressional meddling on the president's exclusive turf.

13. Ironically, this use of the Unitary Executive Theory—the Bush-Cheney legal team's second punch—turned one of its core attractions to the Reagan legal team on its head. The Reaganites were not going after the independent agencies simply as a means to expand presidential power. Instead, they rooted their push in the principle of accountability. The idea was that someone who is elected by voters should oversee any government bureaucracy; as Charles Fried, Reagan's solicitor general, wrote in his memoir, presidential control

over the independent agencies would serve the principles of democracy by letting the "ordinary citizen know who it is that exercises power over him" (Charles Fried, *Order and Law* [New York: Simon & Schuster, 1991], 151–152). But the Bush-Cheney legal team turned the Unitary Executive Theory into a means for making the executive branch not more but *less* accountable, using it to target procedural safeguards Congress set up inside the executive branch to limit the arbitrary exercise of power.

14. Constitution of Massachusetts, art. 7, sec. 1, http://www.nhinet.org/ccs/docs/ma-1780.htm.

15. "Legal Authorities Supporting the Activities of the National Security Agency Described by the President," U.S. Department of Justice, January 19, 2006, http://www.usdoj.gov/opa/whitepaperonnsalegalauthorities.pdf.

16. John Yoo, *The Powers of War and Peace* (Chicago: University of Chicago Press, 2003), 122–124.

17. John Yoo to the author, e-mail, May 31, 2006.

18. Author interview with David Golove, May 31, 2006.

19. President to congressional leaders, re: "Reporting on Combat Action in Afghanistan Against Al Qaida Terrorists and Their Taliban Supporters," October 9, 2001.

20. "President Discusses War on Terrorism and Operation Iraqi Freedom, Cleveland, Ohio," March 20, 2006, http://www.whitehouse.gov/news/releases/2006/03/20060320-7.html.

21. See, e.g., Charlie Savage, "NSA Said to Be Monitoring All Overseas Contacts," *Boston Globe*, December 23, 2005; James Bamford, "NSA: The Agency That Could Be Big Brother," *New York Times*, December 25, 2005. The *Times* has also explained that the agency targeted a watch list of people who were suspected of links to terrorism on evidence that would be insufficient for a normal warrant. According to the *Times*, the watch list was limited to about five hundred people at a time, but because the list constantly changed, thousands of Americans were secretly monitored over the course of the program. James Risen and Eric Lichtblau, "Bush Lets U.S. Spy on Callers Without Courts," *New York Times*, December 16, 2005.

22. If engaged in "hot pursuit," the government may lawfully eavesdrop first and submit the paperwork to a judge for retroactive permission later, but there still must be evidence to justify the eavesdropping.

23. Even at 1975-vintage levels of computer-processing power and data storage, the National Security Agency, Church said, had the technological capacity to take away every American's privacy—by monitoring every telephone conversation and telegram. If a dictatorship were ever to arise in America, Church said, the government could use the NSA to ensure that security forces knew of any attempt to resist the state. "I don't want to see this country ever go across the bridge," Church warned. "I know the capacity that is there to make tyranny total in America, and we must see to it that this agency and all agencies that possess this technology operate within the law and under proper supervision, so that we never cross over that abyss. That is

the abyss from which there is no return." *Meet the Press*, NBC, October 29, 1975, quoted in James Bamford, *The Puzzle Palace* (Boston: Houghton Mifflin, 1982), 477.

24. "Press Briefing by Attorney General Alberto Gonzales and General Michael Hayden, Principal Deputy Director for National Intelligence," December 19, 2005, http://www.whitehouse.gov/news/releases/2005/12/20051219-1.html. Administration officials would also later say that they feared if they asked Congress to change the law in order to allow their program, the details of what they were planning to do would leak and alert terrorists, who could then avoid being caught in its snare.

25. This memo was cowritten with Roger Delahunty, another Office of Legal Counsel attorney.

26. The date and title of this memo were referenced in several later OLC opinions. See footnote 16 of Jay Bybee to William J. Haynes, memorandum re: "Potential Legal Constraints Applicable to Interrogations of Persons Captured by U.S. Armed Forces in Afghanistan," February 26, 2002, reproduced in Joshua L. Dratel and Karen J. Greenberg, eds., *The Torture Papers: The Road to Abu Ghraib* (New York: Cambridge University Press, 2005), 163. In its initial report, the *New York Times* also said that Yoo had written a memo arguing that the president could authorize electronic surveillance without warrants in light of the terrorist attacks. The paper quoted the memo as saying that "the government may be justified in taking measures which in less troubled conditions could be seen as infringements of individual liberties." It was unclear whether the reporters had seen the entire memo or had it in their possession; no further excerpts from the memo made it into print. Risen and Lichtblau, "Bush Lets U.S. Spy."

27. The absence of any statutory limit would still leave the Fourth Amendment's bar to unreasonable search and seizure. But in another memo, dated September 21, 2001, the legal team had also made short work of the Fourth Amendment. Given the potential devastation of further terrorist attacks, they said, it was "reasonable" for the president to deploy the military on U.S. soil—to shoot down hijacked civilian airliners, to set up military checkpoints inside U.S. cities, to launch attacks on suspected terrorist hideouts despite the risk of civilian casualties, and to use the high-tech surveillance techniques that went far beyond conventional wiretaps. "The government may be justified in taking measures which in less troubled conditions could be seen as infringements of civil liberties," the legal team wrote. ". . . We think that the Fourth Amendment should be no more relevant than it would be in cases of invasion or insurrection." The full text of this September 21, 2001, memo has not been made public, but excerpts of it were quoted by Tim Golden, "After Terror, a Secret Rewriting of Military Law," *New York Times*, October 24, 2004.

28. Author interview with John Yoo, March 8, 2007. Yoo emphasized in this conversation that he was unable to discuss the October 17 memo specifically because it remains classified but agreed to elucidate his general reasoning about the president's authority to use military force to combat terrorism inside the United States.

29. John Yoo interview transcript, "Spying on the Home Front," *Frontline*, http://www.pbs.org/wgbh/pages/frontline/homefront/interviews/yoo.html.
30. Author interview with a knowledgeable source.
31. Scott Shane and Eric Lichtblau, "Cheney Pushed U.S. to Widen Eavesdropping," *New York Times*, May 14, 2006.
32. "President Discusses War on Terrorism." On another occasion, Bush put it this way: "FISA is for long-term monitoring. What is needed in order to protect the American people is the ability to move quickly to detect. Now, having suggested this idea, I then, obviously, went to the question, is it legal to do so? I am—I swore to uphold the laws. Do I have the legal authority to do this? And the answer is, absolutely." "Press Conference of the President," December 19, 2005, http://www.whitehouse.gov/news/releases/2005/12/20051219-2.html.
33. Except, of course, in the rare case when two-thirds of each chamber of Congress vote to override a presidential veto.
34. Bruce Fein, opening statement, Senate Judiciary Committee, *Wartime Executive Power and the NSA's Surveillance Authority II*, February 28, 2006.
35. Author interview with Bradford Berenson, January 12, 2007.
36. The text of this memo has not been made public, but its contents were described to the author by several knowledgeable sources. Moreover, its author, date, and title were referenced in Jay Bybee to Alberto R. Gonzales, memorandum re: "Standards of Conduct for Interrogation Under 18 U.S.C. §§ 2340–2340A," August 1, 2002, reproduced in Dratel and Greenberg, *Torture Papers*, 172 (hereafter "August 1, 2002, interrogation memo").
37. Louis Fisher, *Presidential War Power* (Lawrence: University of Kansas Press, 2004), 206–207.
38. Author interview with Tom Romig, February 14, 2007.
39. Barton Gellman and Jo Becker, "A Different Understanding with the President," *Washington Post*, June 24, 2007.
40. Golden, "After Terror."
41. "Remarks by the President on National Missile Defense," December 13, 2001, http://www.whitehouse.gov/news/releases/2001/12/20011213-4.html.
42. George W. Bush, speech to the Republican National Convention, August 2000.
43. *Federalist 75*.
44. Bruce Ackerman, "Treaties Don't Belong to Presidents Alone," *New York Times*, August 29, 2001.
45. Proponents also noted that the president is able to fire members of his cabinet on his own, even though such officials need Senate approval to take office, although a cabinet member and a treaty are very different things. The power to fire a secretary of defense is not the same as the power to wipe away a major foreign policy commitment that has the status of the "supreme law of the land." See, e.g., John Dean, "The Termination Debate," *Findlaw*, August 31, 2001, http://writ.news.findlaw.com/scripts/printer_friendly. pl?page=/dean/20010831.htm.
46. *Goldwater v. Carter*, 444 U.S. 996 (1979).

47. In 1985, amid the secret and congressionally unauthorized conflict between the United States and the Soviet-supported government of Nicaragua, President Reagan picked up on Carter's precedent by unilaterally terminating the 1956 Friendship, Commerce, and Navigation Treaty with Nicaragua. Reagan also unilaterally ended the United States' acceptance of compulsory jurisdiction for disputes heard by the United Nations International Court of Justice, which had cited the treaty in a ruling against the United States in a case involving the mining of Nicaraguan harbors. Neither treaty move, however, was as high-profile as Carter's termination of the Taiwan treaty, and the executive power implications of Reagan's actions attracted little notice in Congress or the press.

48. David Sanger and Elisabeth Bumiller, "U.S. to Pull Out of ABM Treaty," *New York Times,* December 12, 2001.

49. The general description of Guantánamo is based on the author's notes from reporting trips to Guantánamo Bay Navy Base in July 2003, November 2003, and January 2005. For specific details of the unloading operation, see Carol Rosenberg, "Taliban Prisoners Arrive at Guantánamo to Sparse Conditions," *Miami Herald,* January 12, 2002.

50. Alex Perry, "Inside the Battle at Qala-I-Jangi," *Time,* December 1, 2001, http://www.cnn.com/CNN/Programs/presents/index.house.of.war.html.

51. Author interview with Pierre-Richard Prosper, January 17, 2007.

52. "DoD News Briefing—Secretary Rumsfeld and Gen. Myers," December 27, 2001, http://www.defenselink.mil/Transcripts/Transcript.aspx?TranscriptID=2696.

53. Courts had split over whether or not Guantánamo was within their jurisdiction in a pair of cases from the 1990s concerning migrants held at the base. A federal district court ruled that it did have jurisdiction to hear a lawsuit brought by a group of Haitians on the base, but the Clinton administration struck a deal with lawyers for the group—including a team of Yale law students led by Harold Koh—to vacate the decision in exchange for allowing the Haitians to come to the United States. But in another case, a federal appeals court later ruled that it did not have jurisdiction to hear a similar lawsuit brought by a group of Cubans being held on the base. The latter decision stayed on the books.

54. In his memoir, John Yoo reports that the "one thing we all agreed on was that any detention facility should be located outside the United States." John Yoo, *War by Other Means* (New York: Atlantic Monthly Press, 2006), 142.

55. The memo argued that Al Qaeda was not a nation-state and so not a party to the Geneva Conventions, and that Afghanistan was a "failed state" and the Taliban was not a legitimate government, so neither were covered by the treaty. It also argued that both Al Qaeda and the Taliban militias violated the laws of war by attacking civilians and failing to wear uniforms, so that even if the treaty did apply to the conflict, the president could determine that none of the Al Qaeda and Taliban fighters had earned the right to prisoner of war protections. The rebuttal to this argument is that the U.S. military is

bound to obey the Geneva Conventions regardless of whom it is fighting, and even if Al Qaeda and Taliban prisoners were not POWs, they were still entitled to the minimum standards of humane treatment covered under Common Article III of the conventions. The memo went on to argue, however, that because Common Article III covers wars that are "not of an international nature," this refers only to internal civil wars, as opposed to conflicts that cross borders but are not between nations. In June 2006, the Supreme Court rejected this interpretation, holding that the minimum standards of humane treatment in Common Article III were meant to cover all military conflicts.

56. John Yoo and Robert J. Delahunty to William J. Haynes II, memorandum re: "Application of Treaties and Laws to Detainees," January 9, 2002, reproduced in Dratel and Greenberg, *Torture Papers*, 38.

57. R. Jeffrey Smith and Dan Eggen, "Gonzales Helped Set the Course for Detainees," *Washington Post*, January 5, 2005.

58. Alberto R. Gonzales to the president, memorandum re: "Decision Re: Application of the Geneva Convention on Prisoners of War to the Conflict with Al Qaeda and the Taliban," January 25, 2002, reproduced in Dratel and Greenberg, *Torture Papers*, 118.

59. William H. Taft IV to counsel to the president, memorandum re: "Comments on Your Paper on the Geneva Convention," February 2, 2002, reproduced in Dratel and Greenberg, *Torture Papers*, 129.

60. Memorandum for the vice president and others re: "Humane Treatment of al Qaeda and Taliban Detainees," February 7, 2002, reproduced in Dratel and Greenberg, *Torture Papers*, 134. Buttressing his decision, Bush pointedly endorsed the assertion that he had "the authority under the Constitution to suspend Geneva as between the United States and Afghanistan." However, Bush said, there was no need for him to formally suspend the Geneva Conventions in this case, since he could simply declare that the treaty did not apply to the detainees in question—a classic distinction without a difference.

61. "Rumsfeld: Afghan Prisoners Will Not Be Treated as POWs," *Fox News*, January 28, 2002, http://www.foxnews.com/story/0,2933,44084,00.html.

62. "Secretary Rumsfeld Media Availability En Route to Guantánamo Bay, Cuba," January 27, 2002, http://www.defenselink.mil/transcripts/2002/t01282002_t0127enr.html.

63. Mark Denbeaux and Joshua Denbeaux, "Report on Guantánamo Detainees," Seton Hall University School of Law, February 7, 2006, http://law.shu.edu/aaafinal.pdf.

64. President's message to the Senate and the text of the Convention Against Torture and Other Cruel, Inhuman, or Degrading Treatment or Punishment, May 20, 1988.

65. The text of this memo has not been released, but its title, date, author, and addressee, and a quote from it—"The Commander-in-Chief Clause constitutes an independent grant of substantive authority to engage in the detention and transfer of prisoners engaged in armed conflicts"—were included in the August 1, 2002, interrogation memo. The administration later made

two other arguments in public: that the treaty did not apply to aliens overseas and that it applied only to prisoners being deported from U.S. soil. The United Nations Committee Against Torture, which governs the treaty's implementation, rejected the arguments as legally incorrect. See, e.g., http://www.usmission.ch/Press2006/CAT-May5.pdf.

66. "Extraordinary Rendition in U.S. Counterterrorism Policy: The Impact on Transatlantic Relations," Joint hearing before the Subcommittee on International Organizations, Human Rights, and Oversight, and the Subcommittee on Europe, of the Committee on Foreign Affairs, House of Representatives, April 17, 2007.

67. Technically, Arar's transfer was a summary deportation rather than an extraordinary rendition, as he was detained on U.S. soil rather than captured overseas. However, this is a distinction without a difference in the context of transferring terrorism suspects to foreign governments that are known to torture.

68. *Report of the Events Related to Maher Arar,* Commission of Inquiry into the Actions of Canadian Officials in Relation to Maher Arar, September 18, 2006, http://www.ararcommission.ca/eng/AR_English.pdf.

69. John Mintz, "Detainee Moved from Cuba to Va. Brig," *Washington Post,* April 6, 2002.

70. "Ashcroft Statement on 'Dirty Bomb' Suspect," CNN, June 10, 2002, http://archives.cnn.com/2002/US/06/10/ashcroft.announcement/.

71. The government cited two primary precedents. First, it cited a 1950 Supreme Court ruling that dismissed a lawsuit by some German soldiers in China who wanted to be released from an overseas military prison. The U.S. Army said it was holding them without trial because they had continued to fight after Berlin surrendered in 1945, making them illegal combatants. Taking the army's word for it without any independent inquiry into the facts, the Supreme Court refused to review the Germans' case. The administration brief cited this 1950 precedent ten times, presenting it as one of their strongest precedents. But unlike Hamdi and Padilla, the Nazis weren't U.S. citizens, and they were neither arrested nor imprisoned on U.S. soil. The administration's other major precedent involved a group of eight German-born Nazi saboteurs who were arrested on U.S. soil during World War II. One of the eight had become a naturalized U.S. citizen before the war. After they were tried and convicted by a military tribunal, the saboteurs asked the Court to overturn their sentences because they had a right to a trial in a regular civilian court. But in 1942, the Supreme Court upheld the military tribunal. The administration brief cited this precedent thirteen times. But also unlike Hamdi and Padilla, the Nazi saboteurs received a trial. Brief for Respondents-Appellants, *Hamdi v. Rumsfeld,* filed with United States Court of Appeals for the Fourth Circuit, June 19, 2002, http://news.findlaw.com/hdocs/docs/hamdi/hamdirums61902gbrf.pdf.

72. *Hamdi v. Rumsfeld,* 296 F.3d 278 (4th Cir. 2002).

73. *Padilla v. Rumsfeld,* 352 F.3d 695 (2nd Cir. 2003).

74. Smith and Eggen, "Gonzales Helped Set the Course for Detainees."

75. Michael Hirsh and others, "A Tortured Debate," *Newsweek,* June 21, 2004.

76. *Meet the Press,* NBC, September 16, 2001.

77. "Interview of the Vice President by Scott Hennen, WDAY at Radio Day at the White House," October 24, 2006, http://www.whitehouse.gov/news/releases/2006/10/20061024-7.html.

78. 18 U.S.C. § 2340.

79. Jay Bybee to Alberto R. Gonzales, memorandum re: "Standards of Conduct for Interrogation under 18 U.S.C. §§ 2340–2340A," August 1, 2002, reproduced in Dratel and Greenberg, *Torture Papers,* 172.

80. Mike Allen and Juliet Eilperin, "Bush Aides Say Iraq War Needs No Hill Vote," *Washington Post,* August 26, 2002.

81. This sudden surge had been crafted by the White House Iraq Group, or WHIG, which had secretly formed in August 2002 to coordinate a strategy for the coming confrontation with Iraq. Its members included Card; Bush's top political adviser, Karl Rove; Cheney's chief of staff, I. Lewis "Scooter" Libby; National Security Adviser Condoleezza Rice; and Rice's deputy, Stephen Hadley. The group also developed a "white paper" to educate Congress and the public about the "grave and gathering danger" of "Saddam Hussein's quest for nuclear weapons." Three unnamed officials who followed the paper's development later told the *Washington Post* that the WHIG participants "wanted gripping images and stories not available in the hedged and austere language of intelligence"—a stark display of the political benefits that come with the power to control information. Barton Gellman and Walter Pincus, "Depiction of Threat Outgrew Supporting Evidence," *Washington Post,* August 10, 2003.

82. Elisabeth Bumiller, "Bush Aides Set Strategy to Sell Policy on Iraq," *New York Times,* September 7, 2002.

83. *The NewsHour with Jim Lehrer,* PBS, September 9, 2002.

84. However, the White House initially refused to share its allegedly definitive intelligence with most in Congress. In a television interview, Cheney explained that briefing the 535 lawmakers about such "highly classified" intelligence would inevitably result in leaks that would compromise national security, so lawmakers who were not leaders or members of the Intelligence committees would have to vote on the basis of the more limited briefings the White House thought they could handle. The administration surrounded those briefings, delivered by Secretary of Defense Donald Rumsfeld, with a theatrical display of secrecy, holding them in a windowless room that was swept for bugs and making lawmakers swear oaths not to talk about the contents of the briefings. But lawmakers from both parties said the information they were given in the briefings was the same or even less than what was already in the newspapers. Senator John McCain, a strong supporter of the war authorization, walked out of one of the briefings, pronouncing it a "joke," and many lawmakers decided not to be briefed so that they could openly debate the Iraq policy on the basis of what was in the media (Jim VandeHei, "Iraq Briefings: Don't Ask, Don't Tell," *Washington Post,* September 15, 2002). Later that month, the administration slammed together a National

Intelligence Estimate for Iraq, completing in two weeks what usually takes months to prepare. The poor quality of this document, including its propensity for overstating claims that were not supported by the fine print, would later be the subject of an independent investigation by the conservative Judge Laurence Silberman and former Democratic senator and governor Chuck Robb.

85. See, e.g., William M. Welch, "Republicans Using Iraq Issue to Slam Election Opponents," *USA Today,* October 13, 2002.

86. President Bush to congressional leaders, re: "Reporting on the Commencement of Military Operations Against Iraq," March 21, 2003.

87. "Inside the Presidency with Bob Woodward," History Channel, originally broadcast January 20, 2005.

# 7. "A HOLLOW SHELL": SECRECY II

1. "Judge Emmet G. Sullivan," U.S. District Court for the District of Columbia website, http://www.dcd.uscourts.gov/sullivan-bio.html.

2. "Judge Resists Efforts to Block Energy Records," Associated Press, August 3, 2002.

3. Author interview with Christopher Farrell, December 15, 2006.

4. Executive order, *Further Amendment to Executive Order 12958, as Amended, Classified National Security Information,* March 25, 2003.

5. The order bolstered a previously more limited program that had begun in 1999 with the Clinton administration under which officials from the CIA, the Department of Energy, the Pentagon, and other agencies were looking through declassified records at the National Archives and quietly removing files.

6. "National Archives Information Security Oversight Office Releases Audit on Withdrawal of Records from Public Access," Information Security Oversight Office press release, April 26, 2006, http://www.archives.gov/press/press-releases/2006/nr06-96.html.

7. Information Security Oversight Office reports. By 2005, the last year for which numbers were available as of this writing, the peaks reached in 2004 had eased slightly — 258,633 secrets were classified, and thirty million pages of documents were declassified. At the same time, the government's willingness to declassify historic documents plummeted. Some seventy-five million individual pages of historically valuable documents had been made available for the first time in 2000. In 2004, by contrast, the figure was just twenty-eight million. http://www.archives.gov/isoo/reports/.

8. J. William Leonard, statement before the House Committee on Government Reform, Subcommittee on National Security, Emerging Threats, and International Relations, August 24, 2004.

9. Charlie Savage, "Bush Team Takes Hit on Secret Files," *Boston Globe,* May 4, 2004.

10. Steven Aftergood of the Federation of American Scientists' Project on Government Secrecy has argued that while the wording of Bush's executive order clearly gives the vice president the power to classify anything, it does not

definitively say whether the vice president, like the president, can declassify something that was stamped secret by an agency outside his office. Cheney himself, however, in an interview with *Fox News*, said that the order gave him complete declassification power equal to that of the president. See Steven Aftergood, "The Vice President's Declassification Authority," *Secrecy News*, February 16, 2006, http://www.fas.org/blog/secrecy/2006/02/the_vice_presidents_declassifi.html; and transcript of interview with the vice president by Brit Hume, *Fox News*, February 15, 2006, http://www.whitehouse.gov/news/releases/2006/02/20060215-3.html.

11. Mark Silva, "Bush Team Imposes Thick Veil of Secrecy," *Chicago Tribune*, April 30, 2006.

12. By the summer of 2007, the dispute had attracted the attention of the new Democratic-run Congress, and the legal claim that the vice president was not part of the executive branch became the subject of public ridicule. Amid the late-night laughter, Addington partially backed away from the claim, arguing that it was unnecessary to delve into constitutional issues because it was sufficient that the executive order "makes clear that the Vice President is treated like the President." Letter from Rep. Henry Waxman to Vice President Cheney, June 21, 2007, http://www.fas.org/irp/congress/2007_cr/waxman062107.pdf. Letter from David Addington to Senator John Kerry, June 26, 2007, http://kerry.senate.gov/newsroom/pdf/Addington_Letter.pdf.

13. Cheney also repeatedly touted Iraq's supposed nuclear programs, as when, on March 16, 2003, he told viewers of NBC's *Meet the Press*, "We know [Saddam Hussein]'s out trying once again to produce nuclear weapons." *Meet the Press*, NBC, March 16, 2003.

14. "Government's Response to Defendant's Third Motion to Compel Discovery," *United States v. I. Lewis Libby*, U.S. District Court for the District of Columbia, C.R. NO 05-394 (RBW), April 15, 2006.

15. The episode, Libby added, was very unusual. He testified that the July 8 meeting was the "only time he recalled in his government experience when he disclosed a document to a reporter that was effectively declassified" in such a manner. But he pressed on. Four days later, Libby provided similar information to Matt Cooper of *Time* and Tim Russert of NBC. Cheney, he said, had "specifically selected him to talk to the press about the NIE and Mr. Wilson" in place of the usual press contact for his office. Meanwhile, no one else in the White House, the CIA, or the State Department knew that the key judgments of the National Intelligence Estimate had been cleared for release, and they were continuing their own efforts to get them declassified. Ibid., 23.

16. Charlie Savage, "Ashcroft and Evans Resign from Cabinet," *Boston Globe*, November 10, 2004.

17. See, e.g., David Savage, "Justices Appear to Support Cheney Task Force Secrecy," *Los Angeles Times*, April 28, 2004; Lyle Denniston, "Justices Give Cheney Sympathetic Ear but Question Timing," *Boston Globe*, April 28, 2004.

18. The technical legal issue on which the case turned was whether Cheney had a right to appeal the discovery order without first officially invoking executive privilege and letting lower courts issue a final judgment on whether it

applied. The appeals court had said that his appeal was premature because he had not formally invoked executive privilege.

19. 542 U.S. 367 (2004).

20. Shannen Coffin, "Victory for the Executive," *National Review,* June 25, 2004, http://www.nationalreview.com/coffin/coffin200406250942.asp.

21. Warren Richey, "Security or Cover-Up?" *The Christian Science Monitor,* June 8, 2006.

22. Ibid.

23. Michael Freedman, "Daughters of the Cold War," *Legal Affairs,* January/February 2004.

24. Richey, "Security or Cover-Up?"

25. See, e.g., Louis Fisher, *In the Name of National Security: Unchecked Presidential Power and the Reynolds Case* (Lawrence: University of Kansas Press, 2006).

26. Gregg Toppo, "Education Dept. Paid Commentator to Promote Law," *USA Today,* January 7, 2005.

27. Robert Pear, "Buying of News by Bush's Aides Ruled Illegal," *New York Times,* October 1, 2005.

28. Christopher Lee, "Administration Rejects Ruling on PR Videos," *Washington Post,* March 15, 2005.

29. Michael Gerber, "GAO Calls Medicare Video News Releases Illegal Propaganda," *The Hill,* May 20, 2004.

30. Lee, "Administration Rejects Ruling."

31. Pear, "Buying of News."

32. Eli Lake, "Why an Espionage Investigation Is Terrible News for Journalists," *The New Republic,* October 10, 2005.

33. Walter Pincus, "Prosecution of Journalists Is Possible in NSA Leaks Case," *Washington Post,* May 22, 2006.

34. Three months later, the GOP-led Congress finally passed a 1,724-page bill based on Cheney's report. The Energy Policy Act of 2005 provided $14.5 billion in tax breaks, primarily benefiting the fossil fuel and nuclear power companies, and contained myriad obscure provisions helping industrialists. Conservationists called the bill bad policy because it did nothing to discourage consumption by raising fuel efficiency standards; small-government conservatives called the bill an enormous giveaway to an industry that was already making record profits on its own; and economists said the bill would do little in the short term to improve the then $63-a-barrel price of oil. Bookbinder quote is from Carol Leonnig and Jim VandeHei, "Cheney Wins Court Ruling on Energy Panel Records," *Washington Post,* May 11, 2005.

## 8. THE PERSEVERANCE AND THE PURGE: LAWS AND TREATIES II

1. See Lt. Col. Jerald Phifer to commander, Joint Task Force 170, memorandum re: "Request for Approval of Counter-Resistance Strategies," October 11,

2002, reproduced in Joshua L. Dratel and Karen J. Greenberg, eds., *The Torture Papers: The Road to Abu Ghraib* (New York: Cambridge University Press, 2005), 227.

2. LTC Diane Beaver to commander, Joint Task Force 170, memorandum re: "Legal Brief on Proposed Counter-Resistance Strategies," October 11, 2002, reproduced in Dratel and Greenberg, *Torture Papers,* 229.

3. William J. Haynes II to the secretary of defense, action memorandum re: "Counter-Resistance Techniques," November 27, 2002, reproduced in Dratel and Greenberg, *Torture Papers,* 237.

4. Author interview with Alberto Mora, February 7, 2007.

5. Ibid.

6. Mora also strongly disputed the arguments made by the Beaver legal brief, and he cautioned that even the "misperception that the U.S. government authorizes or condones detention or interrogation practices that do not comply with our domestic and international legal obligations . . . probably will cause significant harm to our national legal, political, military, and diplomatic interests." Alberto Mora to the inspector general, Department of the Navy, memorandum re: "Statement for the Record: Office of General Counsel Involvement in Detainee Legal Issues," July 7, 2004, http://www.newyorker.com/images/pdfs/moramemo.pdf.

7. Charlie Savage, "Abuse Led Navy to Consider Pulling Cuba Interrogators," *Boston Globe,* March 16, 2005; Charlie Savage, "Split Seen on Interrogation Techniques," *Boston Globe,* March 31, 2005; see also Jane Mayer, "The Memo," *The New Yorker,* February 27, 2006.

8. Mora to the inspector general, "Statement for the Record."

9. Rives's views were echoed by the top JAGs in every other service as well. Each warned that Yoo's interpretation of the law was wrong. Approving a policy of coercive interrogations, they said, would put U.S. troops at risk of prosecution or of being personally sued by any prisoners they abused. And, internal memos show, they cautioned that undermining the Geneva Conventions was a bad idea in general, because it could make other countries less willing to obey the treaty when handling captured American prisoners of war in future conflicts. MG Jack Rives to general counsel of the air force, memorandum, February 6, 2003; see also BG Kevin M. Sandkuhler to general counsel of the air force, memorandum, February 27, 2003; MG Thomas J. Romig to general counsel of the air force, memorandum, March 3, 2003, http://www.humanrightsfirst.org/us_law/etn/pdf/jag memos 072505.pdf.

10. Senator Carl Levin, opening statement, *Personnel Subcommittee Hearing on Military Commissions, Detainees, and Interrogation Procedures,* July 14, 2005, http://www.senate.gov/~levin/newsroom/release.cfm?id=240601.

11. *Hearing of the Senate Judiciary Committee on the Authority to Prosecute Terrorists Under the War Crime Provisions of Title 18,* August 2, 2006.

12. Donald Rumsfeld to Commander, U.S. Southern Command, memorandum re: "Counter-Resistance Techniques in the War on Terrorism," April 16, 2003, reproduced in *The Torture Papers,* 360.

13. Also, in January 2003, Brad Berenson, who had helped Flanigan and

Addington draft the military commissions order, left to become a partner at a Washington law firm. By the spring, the administration also lost Viet Dinh, the Justice Department official who wrote substantial portions of the USA Patriot Act, and Michael Chertoff, the department's criminal division chief who oversaw the post-9/11 sweeps that detained hundreds of Muslims on immigration charges. Dinh became a law professor and Chertoff became an appeals court judge, although he would later return as secretary of Homeland Security.

14. The Bybee nomination was slowed in part because of Democratic concerns about his involvement in "Iraq-gate," a now nearly forgotten scandal involving the Bush-Quayle administration's support for Iraqi dictator Saddam Hussein prior to the Gulf War. In 1989, Bybee—then an associate White House counsel—called a federal prosecutor and asked about an ongoing corruption case involving Iraq. Congressional Democrats later called for a special independent prosecutor to investigate whether Bybee had improperly attempted to influence the case on behalf of Iraq. But the matter faded away after the Bush-Quayle administration lost the 1992 election.

15. "U.S. Secretary of State Colin Powell Addresses the U.N. Security Council," February 5, 2003, http://www.whitehouse.gov/news/releases/2003/02/20030205-1 .html.

16. Steve Tetreault, "No-Shows Smooth Judicial Nominee's Path," *Las Vegas Review-Journal,* February 6, 2003.

17. Daniel Klaidman and others, "Palace Revolt," *Newsweek,* February 6, 2006. Yoo denied cutting Ashcroft out of the loop but also acknowledged that he and the attorney general had a testy relationship. "We were never buddies. I wasn't an Ashcroft guy from before the Justice Department, and the Justice Department and the White House had a history of tension" over appointments. Author interview with John Yoo, March 8, 2007. In his memoir, Yoo sharply criticized Ashcroft for being "ever a defender of his bureaucratic turf," for unwisely pushing to prosecute Zacarias Moussaoui in civilian court instead of before a military commission, for "going too far" in his political rhetoric, and for flinching instead of standing firm when the interrogation memos were leaked and criticized.

18. Jack Goldsmith and John Yoo, "Seattle and Sovereignty," *Wall Street Journal,* December 6, 1999.

19. John Yoo and Jack Goldsmith, "Missile Defense Defense," *American Lawyer* 23, no. 4 (2001).

20. William Glaberson, "Closer Look at New Plan for Trying Terrorists," *New York Times,* November 15, 2001.

21. Patrick Philbin was hardly modest about executive power: He was the author of the November 6, 2001, memo saying that the president had the power to convene military commissions, and the coauthor, with Yoo, of the December 28, 2001, memo saying that U.S. courts had no jurisdiction to review Guantánamo. Like Yoo, Philbin had also interviewed to replace Bybee as head of the Office of Legal Counsel but didn't get the job. Seeking a change, he asked Thompson to hire him as the top national security adviser for the

deputy attorney general's office—landing the position a few months before Thompson announced he was resigning.

22. The fourth Geneva Convention takes explicit note of combatants who hide among civilians and fight out of uniform, saying that spies and saboteurs who are captured by an occupying power forfeit the right to communicate with family members but that they otherwise must be treated with the full rights and privileges of a protected person under the conventions. Philbin and Goldsmith decided that it was too much of a stretch to ignore this provision in Iraq, where the United States was formally an occupying power. (In Afghanistan, the United States was not formally an occupying power, which made it easier to overlook this provision for that theater of war—though few independent legal scholars supported the administration's view that it was free to ignore the treaties for Afghanistan.)

23. Klaidman and others, "Palace Revolt."

24. The first to piece together this chain of events was Georgetown's Martin Lederman. See "Silver Linings, or Strange but True," Balkinization, September 21, 2005, http://balkin.blogspot.com/2005/09/silver-linings-or-strange-but-true.html.

25. Klaidman and others, "Palace Revolt."

26. Thompson signed off on sending Maher Arar, the dual Canadian-Syrian citizen falsely suspected of ties to terrorists, to Syria for interrogation, despite a treaty that obliged the United States not to send prisoners to foreign governments known to use torture. See, e.g., Dana Priest, "Top Justice Aide Approved Sending Suspect to Syria," *Washington Post,* November 19, 2003.

27. Unless otherwise noted, the remainder of this section is derived from Transcript, Hearing of the Senate Judiciary Committee, "Preserving Prosecutorial Independence: Is the Department of Justice Politicizing the Hiring and Firing of U.S. Attorneys?—Part IV," May 15, 2007. See also Klaidman and others, "Palace Revolt."

28. Michael Barnett, "Ashcroft in 'Guarded Condition' After Surgery at GW Hospital," *GW Hatchet Online,* March 9, 2004. http://media.www.gwhatchet.com/media/storage/paper332/news/2004/03/08/MetroNews/Web-Extra.Ashcroft.In.guarded.Condition.After.Surgery.At.Gw.Hospital-630291.shtml.

29. "Written Questions to Former Deputy Attorney General James B. Comey Submitted by Senator Patrick Leahy, May 22, 2007," delivered to the Senate Judiciary Committee June 6, 2007.

30. See, e.g., Orin Kerr, "What Led DOJ to Oppose the NSA Surveillance Program?" The Volokh Conspiracy, May 16, 2007, http://volokh.com/posts/1179350507.shtml.

31. Transcript of *Hamdi v. Rumsfeld* oral argument, April 28, 2004, http://www.supremecourtus.gov/oral_arguments/argument_transcripts/03-6696.pdf.

32. Mora to the inspector general, "Statement for the Record."

33. "Article 15-6 Investigation of the 800th Military Police Brigade," aka "The Taguba Report," March 9, 2004, http://news.findlaw.com/nytimes/docs/iraq/tagubarpt.html.

34. The available evidence suggests that the truth lies somewhere in between: Interrogators in Iraq were widely encouraged to use coercive techniques, including forced nudity, menacing dogs, sleep deprivation, and shackling into stress positions, to break the will of detainees. The abuses at Abu Ghraib included the routine use of such things. But the Abu Ghraib tortures also went further, as shown by the picture of naked men being piled into a pyramid. In their most extreme manifestations, the Abu Ghraib abuses reflected an official policy spiraling out of control and becoming something more extreme in the hands of a poorly trained, poorly supervised night-shift unit of reservists from rural West Virginia. Nevertheless, even when the official policy was being followed as planned—with no naked-prisoner pyramids but plenty of sleep deprivation, stress positions, isolation, and the rest—American interrogators were well into territory prohibited by laws and treaties, according to most scholars. And by lifting the taboo against coercive interrogations, the Bush-Cheney legal team put the country far down a slippery slope toward the ravine of Abu Ghraib. The goodwill of executive branch officials, critics concluded, was no substitute for the rule of law.

35. The author was one of the journalists who covered the background briefing under Justice Department–imposed ground rules that none of the participants could be identified by name or title in news coverage. However, *Newsweek* subsequently disclosed their identities in its article "Palace Revolt," breaking the embargo.

36. Bryan Bender and Charlie Savage, "Memos Detail Debate on Prisoners," *Boston Globe*, June 23, 2004.

37. John Yoo, *War by Other Means* (New York: Atlantic Monthly Press, 2006), 182.

38. Dana Priest, "Memo Lets CIA Take Detainees out of Iraq," *Washington Post*, October 24, 2004.

39. Marcella Bombardieri, "Harvard Hire's Detainee Memo Stirs Debate," *Boston Globe*, December 9, 2004.

40. *Hamdi v. Rumsfeld*, 542 U.S. 507 (2004).

41. Charlie Savage, "High Court Ruling Affords Detainees Their Day in Court," *Boston Globe*, June 29, 2004.

42. Description of commission chamber from author's visit to Guantánamo, January 2005. For description of Brownback receiving the note, see Carol Rosenberg, "Judge Halts Trial of Bin Laden's Chauffeur," *Miami Herald*, November 9, 2004.

43. Daniel Levin to James Comey, memorandum re: "Interrogation Standards under 18 USC 2340–2340A," December 30, 2004, http://www.usdoj.gov/olc/18usc23402340a2.htm.

44. Yoo, *War by Other Means*, 183.

45. Dan Eggan and Susan Schmidt, "Solicitor General Theodore Olson to Step Down," *Washington Post*, June 25, 2004.

46. Author interview with David Keene, May 24, 2007.

47. Answer to "Written Questions to Former Deputy Attorney General James B. Comey Submitted by Patrick Leahy," May 22, 2007.

48. A month later, Bush nominated Timothy Flanigan—the former deputy White House counsel and Addington ally who left in December 2002 to become an executive at Tyco—to replace Comey as deputy attorney general. But Flanigan's political comeback was derailed by the growing corruption investigation surrounding the Republican lobbyist Jack Abramoff. In one of his first acts at Tyco, Flanigan had hired Abramoff for $2 million to ensure that Congress preserved a tax loophole that allowed Tyco to avoid paying some U.S. taxes by registering as a Bermuda company. Abramoff had also persuaded Flanigan to have Tyco donate several million dollars to another lobbying firm, most of which was diverted to unrelated Abramoff-controlled entities. See, e.g., Thomas Mann and Norman Ornstein, *The Broken Branch* (Oxford University Press, 2006), 187–188. In October 2005, Flanigan withdrew his name from consideration for the position. Dan Eggen and R. Jeffrey Smith, "Flanigan Withdraws as Nominee for Deputy Attorney General," *Washington Post*, October 5, 2005.

49. James Comey, "Farewell Address," August 15, 2005, http://www.usdoj.gov/dag/speech/2005/dagfarewell.htm.

50. Comey would later tell Congress that he was thinking specifically of Patrick Philbin when he said this.

51. *Padilla v. Hanft*, 423 F.3d 386 (4th Cir. 2005).

52. Order, December 21, 2005, *Padilla v. Hanft*, no. 05-6396 (4th Cir.).

53. "Vice President's Remarks to the Traveling Press," December 20, 2005, http://www.whitehouse.gov/news/releases/2005/12/20051220-9.html.

54. "Legal Authorities Supporting the Activities of the National Security Agency Described by the President," U.S. Department of Justice, January 19, 2006, http://www.usdoj.gov/opa/whitepaperonnsalegalauthorities.pdf.

55. The administration also claimed that Congress had unknowingly given the president an additional grant of authority to bypass the warrant law when it voted to authorize the use of military force against the perpetrators of 9/11. Many commentators, comparing the January 2006 brief to the legal opinions drafted in the months after 9/11, believed that the Authorization for Use of Military Force argument, rather than being part of the original thinking behind the program, had been thrown in after the program was revealed. As the conservative commentator George F. Will wrote, the "assertion is implausible: None of the 518 legislators who voted for the AUMF has said that he or she then thought it contained the permissiveness the administration discerns in it. Did the administration, until the program became known two months ago? Or was the AUMF then seized upon as a justification? . . . Anyway, the argument that the AUMF contained a completely unexpressed congressional intent to empower the president to disregard the FISA regime is risible coming from this administration. It famously opposes those who discover unstated meanings in the Constitution's text and do not strictly construe the language of statutes." George F. Will, "No Checks, Many Imbalances," *Washington Post*, February 16, 2006.

56. Karl Rove, address to Republican National Committee, January 20, 2006, http://www.freerepublic.com/focus/f-news/1562337/posts.

57. "President Discusses Global War on Terror at Kansas State University," January 23, 2006, http://www.whitehouse.gov/news/releases/2006/01/20060123-4.html.

58. Administration officials also repeatedly pointed to a 2002 opinion by the Foreign Intelligence Surveillance Court of Review, which noted, in passing, that it took "for granted" that the president has "inherent authority to conduct warrantless searches to obtain intelligence information," adding, "Assuming that is so, FISA could not encroach on the president's constitutional powers." (The case involved a challenge to a provision of the Patriot Act that had nothing to do with warrantless wiretaps.) The officials tended not to note that this opinion was written by Appeals Court judge Laurence Silberman, the former Nixon and Ford administration official who had tried, in 1988, to recognize the Unitary Executive Theory as a constitutionally correct "doctrine," only to be summarily overturned by a 7–1 Supreme Court ruling. Silberman's aside in the 2002 opinion was not just dicta but also legally questionable: Even if a president has an *inherent* power to do something, it does not follow that such a power is automatically *exclusive* and thus may not be regulated by Congress. But because of the unique way the Foreign Intelligence Surveillance Court is set up, the Supreme Court had no opportunity to review his 2002 opinion, allowing Silberman to say anything with impunity.

59. Charlie Savage, "Specialists Doubt Legality of Wiretaps," *Boston Globe*, February 2, 2006.

60. Will, "No Checks, Many Imbalances."

61. Author interview with David Keene, January 27, 2006.

62. Author interview with Grover Norquist, January 27, 2006.

63. Author interview with Larry Pratt, January 27, 2006.

64. Author interview with Paul Weyrich, January 27, 2006.

65. Author interview with Bruce Fein, January 27, 2006.

66. Author interview with Brent Scowcroft, November 28, 2006.

67. Author interview with David Rivkin, January 27, 2006.

68. Rick Klein and Charlie Savage, "GOP Senators Refuse Eavesdropping Inquiry," *Boston Globe*, March 8, 2006.

69. On April 21, 2006, Jarrett wrote an angry memo to Deputy Attorney General Paul McNulty, Jim Comey's replacement. The memo, which was later obtained and released to the public by the Senate Judiciary Committee, said that Jarrett's investigators were being prevented from doing their jobs. "Since its creation some thirty-one years ago, OPR has conducted many highly sensitive investigations involving executive branch programs and has obtained access to information classified at the highest levels," Jarrett wrote. "In all those years, OPR has never been prevented from initiating or pursuing an investigation." Charlie Savage, "Bush Blocked Probe, AG Testifies," *Boston Globe*, July 19, 2006.

70. Ibid.

71. *American Civil Liberties Union v. National Security Agency*, 438 F. Supp 2d 754 (E.D. Mich. 2006).

72. "Government's Supplemental Submission Discussing the Implications of

the Intervening FISA Court Orders of January 10, 2007," *American Civil Liberties Union v. National Security Agency,* U.S. Court of Appeals for the Sixth Circuit, no. 06-2095, January 2007, http://www.scotusblog.com/movabletype/archives/DOJ%20on%20NSA%20mootness.pdf.

73. *Senate Judiciary Committee Hearing on Oversight of the Department of Justice,* January 18, 2007.

74. Jack Balkin, "The Bally Presidency," Balkinization, January 18, 2007, http://balkin.blogspot.com/2007/01/bally-presidency.html.

## 9. THE TORTURE BAN

1. *Hearing of the Senate Judiciary Committee on the Nomination of Alberto Gonzales to Be Attorney General,* January 6, 2005.

2. Author interview with John Yoo, March 8, 2007.

3. Harold Hongju Koh, statement before the Senate Judiciary Committee regarding the nomination of the Honorable Alberto R. Gonzales as attorney general of the United States, January 7, 2005, http://judiciary.senate.gov/testimony.cfm?id=1345&wit_id=3938.

4. Other faults, according to Koh: Yoo's memo never mentioned human rights. It adopted an "absurdly narrow" definition of torture that "flies in the face of the plain meaning of the term." It said that military and CIA interrogators could escape prosecution for torture because they were following the president's orders, ignoring the Nuremberg precedent that "just following orders" is no excuse. It employed a contorted and absurd interpretation of the international treaty that bans torture and other forms of cruel, inhuman, and degrading treatment, saying that the treaty bans *only* torture and actually *allows* lesser forms of abuse.

5. John Yoo, *War by Other Means* (New York: Atlantic Monthly Press, 2006), 184–186.

6. Author interview with Harold Koh, May 18, 2007.

7. Koh, statement before the Senate Judiciary Committee.

8. Yoo, *War by Other Means,* 180, 202.

9. When the Senate ratified the antitorture treaty in 1994, lawmakers simultaneously declared that the United States would interpret the treaty's phrase "torture and all other forms of cruel, inhuman, and degrading treatment" as referring to the same kinds of abuse already covered by the U.S. Constitution's Eighth Amendment prohibition against "cruel and unusual punishment." This made a great deal of sense. There was already a well-developed body of domestic law to explain what was meant by the Constitution's "cruel and unusual" terminology, and by relying on it, the Senate could avoid confusion. Gonzales's disclosure revealed that the Bush-Cheney legal team had seized on the Senate's reservation as a wide-open loophole, making the declaration mean something else entirely. If the treaty refers only to what the Constitution prohibits, they concluded, then it restricts the president's power to authorize harsh interrogations only where the Constitution *applies*—on U.S. soil.

10. The disclosure of this creative interpretation solved a pressing mystery. From the mid-2004 moment that Yoo's August 1, 2002, interrogation memo had leaked to the media, legal scholars had wondered why Yoo had spent so much time identifying the alleged distinction between the level of pain and suffering that would constitute torture for legal purposes and the level of harsh treatment that fell short of that term. This emphasis on drawing the line between torture and lesser forms of abuse was puzzling because the lesser forms of abuse were illegal, too. There was a specific statute banning torture, and there was also the Convention Against Torture, which in addition to banning torture also prohibited all forms of "cruel, inhuman, or degrading treatment or punishment which do not amount to torture." But if the United States was under no legal obligation to obey the Convention Against Torture overseas—that is, if only the statute and not the treaty mattered—then the president could authorize interrogators to inflict all kinds of pain and suffering on overseas prisoners by simply declaring that those tactics did not rise to "torture." Thus, there was a need to define "torture" narrowly and precisely.

11. "Educing Information—Interrogation: Science and Art, Foundations for the Future," Intelligence Science Board, December 2006, http://www.fas.org/irp/dni/educing.pdf.

12. "Media Availability with Commander, U.S. Southern Command General James T. Hill," June 3, 2004, http://www.defenselink.mil/Transcripts/Transcript.aspx?TranscriptID=3153.

13. "KUBARK Counterintelligence Interrogation," training manual of the Central Intelligence Agency, July 1963, 82–104, http://www.gwu.edu/~nsarchiv/NSAEBB/NSAEBB27/01-01.htm.

14. Author interview with Col. Steve Kleinman, January 16, 2007.

15. Charlie Savage, "Split Seen on Interrogation Techniques," *Boston Globe*, March 31, 2005.

16. Shafiq Rasul and others, "Composite Statement: Detention in Afghanistan and Guantánamo Bay," Center for Constitutional Rights, July 23, 2004, http://www.ccr-ny.org/v2/reports/docs/Gitmo-compositestatementFINAL23july04.pdf.

17. Brian Ross and Richard Esposito, "CIA's Harsh Interrogation Techniques Described," *ABC News*, November 18, 2005, http://abcnews.go.com/WNT/Investigation/story?id=1322866.

18. Ron Suskind, *The One Percent Doctrine* (New York: Simon & Schuster, 2006), 111. Underscoring the point, the CIA eventually dropped the abuse tactics with Zubaydah and tried the rapport-building approach. An agent who was well versed in the Koran talked at length with Zubaydah, using passages from the Muslim holy book to convince him that he had survived the shoot-out in Pakistan because Allah wanted him to tell his captors what he knew. Zubaydah provided two real pieces of information. He talked to the CIA about Al Qaeda's real operational commander, Khalid Sheikh Mohammed, letting slip that Khalid Sheikh Mohammed's code name was Mukhtar. Using that bit of information, agents managed to track the terrorist leader down and arrest him in a Pakistani safe house in March

2003. Thus, under the rapport-building style of questioning, endorsed by professionals such as Gelles and allowed by the Geneva Conventions, the CIA finally got useful information out of its somewhat addled captive. Ibid., 117.

19. "McCain Statement on Detainee Amendments," October 5, 2005, http://mccain.senate.gov/press_office/view_article.cfm?id=135.

20. "Press Briefing with Scott McClellan," October 5, 2005, http://www.whitehouse.gov/news/releases/2005/10/20051005-4.html.

21. Eric Schmitt, "Exception Sought in Detainee Abuse Ban," *New York Times,* October 25, 2005. Schmitt reported that the text of Cheney's proposal would have amended McCain's no-exceptions ban on cruelty with a provision stating that it would not apply to "clandestine counterterrorism operations conducted abroad, with respect to terrorists who are not citizens of the United States, that are carried out by an element of the United States government other than the Department of Defense and are consistent with the Constitution and the laws of the United States and the treaties to which the United States is a party, if the president determines that such operations are vital to the protection of the United States or its citizens from terrorist attack."

22. Charlie Savage, "McCain Fights Exception to Torture Ban," *Boston Globe,* October 26, 2005.

23. Dana Priest, "Cheney Fights for Detainee Policy," *Washington Post,* November 7, 2005.

24. Dana Priest, "CIA Holds Terror Suspects in Secret Prisons," *Washington Post,* November 2, 2005.

25. *Late Edition with Wolf Blitzer,* CNN, November 20, 2005.

26. "President Meets with McCain and Warner, Discusses Position on Interrogation," December 15, 2005, http://www.whitehouse.gov/news/releases/2005/12/20051215-3.html.

27. Eric Schmitt, "President Backs McCain Measure on Inmate Abuse," *New York Times,* December 16, 2005.

28. Dana Milbank, "In Ex-Aide's Testimony, a Spin Through VP's PR," *Washington Post,* January 26, 2007.

29. Martha Angle, "Bush Signs Last Two Spending Bills, Patriot Act Extensions," *CQ Today,* December 30, 2005.

30. "President's Statement on the Department of Defense, Emergency Supplemental Appropriations to Address Hurricanes in the Gulf of Mexico, and Pandemic Influenza Act, 2006," December 30, 2005, http: //www.whitehouse.gov/news/releases /2005 /12/20051230-9.html.

31. "President's Statement on Signing of H.R. 2863, the Department of Defense, Emergency Supplemental Appropriations to Address Hurricanes in the Gulf of Mexico, and Pandemic Influenza Act, 2006," December 30, 2005, http://www.whitehouse.gov/news/releases/2005/12/20051230-8.html.

32. Martin Lederman, "So Much for the President's Assent to the McCain Amendment," Balkinization, January 2, 2006, http://balkin.blogspot.com/2006/01/so-much-for-presidents-assent-to.html.

33. Author interview with a senior administration official, January 3, 2006; some excerpts from this interview appeared in Charlie Savage, "Bush Could Bypass New Torture Ban," *Boston Globe,* January 4, 2006.
34. Charlie Savage, "Three GOP Senators Blast Bush Bid to Bypass Torture Ban," *Boston Globe,* January 5, 2006.
35. Author interview with Senator Lindsey Graham, January 4, 2006; some excerpts from this interview appeared in Savage, "Three GOP Senators."

## 10. POWER OF THE PEN: SIGNING STATEMENTS

1. "President Signs USA Patriot Improvement and Reauthorization Act," March 9, 2006, http://www.whitehouse.gov/news/releases/2006/03/20060309-4.html.
2. "President's Statement on H.R. 3199, the USA Patriot Improvement and Reauthorization Act of 2005," March 9, 2006, http://www.whitehouse.gov/news/releases/2006/03/20060309-8.html.
3. Charlie Savage, "Bush Shuns Patriot Act Requirement," *Boston Globe,* March 24, 2006.
4. Charlie Savage, "Two Lawmakers Demand Bush Obey Laws," *Boston Globe,* March 26, 2006.
5. Two political science professors, Phillip J. Cooper of Portland State University and Christopher Kelley of Miami University of Ohio, had written about signing statements prior to 2006, although their work had not yet come to the broader public attention it merited. They were ahead of their time.
6. For a fuller account of this sequence, see Phillip J. Cooper, *By Order of the President* (Lawrence: University of Kansas Press, 2002), 225–227.
7. Steven Calabresi and John Harrison to the attorney general, memorandum re: "Presidential Signing Statements," August 23, 1985, Records Group 60, Department of Justice Files of Stephen Galebach, 1985–1987, 060-89-269, box 3, folder: SG/Chronological File.
8. Attorney General Edwin Meese III to President and CEO of West Publishing Co. Dwight D. Opperman, December 13, 1985; Opperman to Meese, December 26, 1985, Records Group 60, Department of Justice Files of Stephen Galebach, 1985–1987, 060-89-269, box 3, folder: SG/Chronological File.
9. T. Kenneth Cribb to Ralph Tarr, memorandum re: "Presidential Signing Statements," September 3, 1985, Records Group 60, Department of Justice Files of Stephen Galebach, 1985–1987, 060-89-269, box 3, folder: SG/Chronological File.
10. Ralph Tarr to T. Kenneth Cribb, memorandum re: "Presidential Signing Statements," October 28, 1985, Records Group 60, Department of Justice Files of Stephen Galebach, 1985–1987, 060-89-269, box 3, folder: SG/Chronological File.
11. T. Kenneth Cribb to Charles Fried, memorandum re: "Presidential Signing Statements," September 3, 1985, Records Group 60, Department of Justice Files of Stephen Galebach, 1985–1987, 060-89-269, box 3, folder: SG/Chronological File.

12. Although he counseled initial caution, Alito also foreshadowed, through phrases such as "an introductory step" and "the first step," the more aggressive use to which future presidents would put signing statements. And, without mentioning the term, he seemed to suggest the question of whether a president could use signing statements more aggressively to give himself a line-item veto: "What happens when there is a clear conflict between the congressional and presidential understanding? Whose intent controls? Is the law totally void? Is it inoperative only to the extent that there is a disagreement?"

13. Author interview with Steven Calabresi, January 3, 2007.

14. Research of Christopher Kelley.

15. Richard Thornburgh, remarks to the Federalist Society conference The Presidency and Congress: Constitutionally Separated and Shared Powers, January 19, 1990.

16. Walter Dellinger to Bernard N. Nussbaum, memorandum re: "The Legal Significance of Presidential Signing Statements," November 3, 1993, http://www.usdoj.gov/olc/signing.htm.

17. "Statement on Signing the Department of Defense Appropriations Act, 1998," October 8, 1997, http://www.presidency.ucsb.edu/ws/index.php?pid=53368.

18. "Statement on Signing the National Defense Authorization Act for Fiscal Year 1996," February 10, 1996, http://www.presidency.ucsb.edu/ws/index.php?pid=52387.

19. As it turned out, Congress revoked the HIV law before any court challenge could take place. *Special White House Briefing Re: Provision in the FY 1996 Defense Authorization Bill Relating to HIV-Positive Armed Services Members,* February 9, 1996.

20. Author interview with Bradford Berenson, May 4, 2006; excerpts appeared in Charlie Savage, "Cheney Aide Is Screening Legislation," *Boston Globe,* May 28, 2006. (Berenson subsequently granted permission to make his quotation on the record instead of on background.)

21. Savage, "Cheney Aide Is Screening Legislation."

22. "Statement on Signing the Postal Accountability and Enhancement Act," December 20, 2006, http://www.whitehouse.gov/news/releases/2006/12/20061220-6.html.

23. Charlie Savage, "Bush Cites Authority to Bypass FEMA Law," *Boston Globe,* October 6, 2006.

24. Phillip J. Cooper, "George W. Bush, Edgar Allan Poe, and the Use and Abuse of Presidential Signing Statements," *Presidential Studies Quarterly* 35, no. 3 (September 2005): 515.

25. *Youngstown Sheet & Tube Co. v. Sawyer,* 343 U.S. 579 (1952).

26. Charlie Savage, "Bush Challenges Hundreds of Laws," *Boston Globe,* April 30, 2006.

27. "President Bush: Information Sharing, Patriot Act Vital to Homeland Security," April 20, 2004, http://www.whitehouse.gov/news/releases/2004/04/20040420-2.html.

28. Charlie Savage, "U.S. Agencies Disobey Six Laws That President Challenged," *Boston Globe,* June 19, 2007.

29. Savage, "Bush Challenges Hundreds of Laws."
30. Calabresi interview.
31. Savage, "Cheney Aide Is Screening Legislation."
32. Charlie Savage, "Panel Chides Bush on Bypassing Laws," *Boston Globe,* July 24, 2006.
33. *Report of the American Bar Association Task Force on Presidential Signing Statements and the Separation of Powers Doctrine,* http://www.abanet.org/media/docs/signstatereport.pdf.
34. Charlie Savage, "Group Opposes Loss of Signing Statements," *Boston Globe,* August 5, 2006.
35. Laurence Tribe, "Larry Tribe on the ABA Signing Statements Report," Balkinization, August 6, 2006, http://balkin.blogspot.com/2006/08/larry-tribe-on-aba-signing-statements.html.
36. Savage, "Panel Chides Bush on Bypassing Laws."
37. Charlie Savage, "Three Democrats Slam Bush over Defying Statutes," *Boston Globe,* May 2, 2006.
38. Ibid.
39. Ibid.
40. Charlie Savage, "Two in Congress Rip Bush on Bypassing of Laws," *Boston Globe,* May 5, 2006.
41. Transcript, Senate Judiciary Committee, "Presidential Signing Statements," June 27, 2006.
42. Charlie Savage, "House Panel Probing Bush's Record on Signing Statements," *Boston Globe,* February 1, 2007.

## 11. "TO SAY WHAT THE LAW IS": THE SUPREME COURT

*A note on sources: Many of the archival documents cited in this chapter were culled from Reagan-era White House and Department of Justice files by officials at the National Archives and Records Administration during the Supreme Court confirmation battles of 2005–2006. Many thousands of documents that had the name John Roberts or Samuel Alito on them, most of which come from record groups that have not yet been opened to the public, were pulled and made available to reporters for photocopying. The author has drawn on his personal stacks of such photocopies in writing this chapter, but unfortunately many of them lack the full citations — file series, box number, and folder name — since making note of that at the time did not seem important. Each endnote includes as much information as possible.*

1. "President Announces Judge John Roberts as Supreme Court Nominee," July 19, 2005, http://www.whitehouse.gov/news/releases/2005/07/20050719-7.html.
2. *Hamdan v. Rumsfeld,* 415 F.3d 33 (D.C. Cir. 2005), some internal citations omitted. The opinion was written by Randolph and joined by Roberts.
3. John Roberts, Senate Judiciary Committee questionnaire, August 3, 2005.

4. Jan Crawford Greenburg, *Supreme Conflict* (New York: Penguin Press, 2007), 22, 189–90.
5. *Goldberg v. Kelly,* 397 U.S. 254 (1970).
6. *Mathews v. Eldridge,* 424 U.S. 319 (1976).
7. *Bush v. Gore,* 531 U.S. 98 (2000).
8. *Dames and Moore v. Regan,* 453 U.S. 654 (1981).
9. Tony Mauro, "The Year Roberts Had Rehnquist's Ear," *Legal Times,* August 1, 2005.
10. John G. Roberts to Fred F. Fielding, memorandum re: "Article on Legislative Acquiescence as a Tool of Statutory Interpretation: An Affront to the Constitution, Logic, and Common Sense," August 31, 1983.
11. Theodore Olson to the attorney general, memorandum re: "Policy Implications of Legislation Withdrawing Supreme Court Appellate Jurisdiction over Classes of Constitutional Cases," April 12, 1982.
12. John G. Roberts to Fred F. Fielding, memorandum re: "Proposed Testimony of Edward C. Schmults Concerning Legislative Veto," July 15, 1983, box 61.
13. John G. Roberts to Fred F. Fielding, memorandum re: "Draft State Department Q&As on Legislative Veto," July 28, 1983, box 61.
14. John G. Roberts to Fred F. Fielding, memorandum re: "Arthur Goldberg Correspondence on Grenada," January 13, 1984; Fred F. Fielding to Arthur Goldberg, draft letter, January 13, 1984, box 62.
15. John G. Roberts to Fred F. Fielding, memorandum re: "Draft Testimony of the General Services Administration on Presidential Libraries," February 13, 1984, box 53; John G. Roberts to Fred F. Fielding, memorandum re: "Proposed OMB Responses to Senator Hatfield Regarding S. 905 / National Archives and Records Service," May 16, 1984, box 33; John G. Roberts to Fred F. Fielding, memorandum re: "Enrolled Bill S. 905 — The National Archives and Records Administration Act of 1984 — and Signing Statement," October 17, 1984, box 33.
16. John G. Roberts to Fred F. Fielding, memorandum re: "Threat to Deliberative Privilege Posed by the Presidential Records Act," September 9, 1985.
17. Fred F. Fielding to [blank], draft memorandum re: "Threat to Deliberative Privilege Posed by the Presidential Records Act," September 9, 1985.
18. For a further look at other memos bearing on executive power, see *Report on the Nomination of John G. Roberts to the United States Supreme Court,* Alliance for Justice, 71–85, http://www.supremecourtwatch.org/robertsprehearing.pdf.
19. Roberts left the administration in mid-1986, before the Iran-Contra scandal, so we have no record of his views on whether the administration's actions were illegal or whether the laws the administration broke were unconstitutional. There are several memos from early 1986 in which Roberts cautioned against overtly involving the White House in efforts to encourage private groups to donate money to the Contras or to pressure Congress to lift restrictions on aid to the anti-Marxist rebels in Nicaragua. In this correspondence, written before the administration's efforts to secretly help the rebels became known outside a small clique in the National Security Council, Roberts does not question the validity of the laws in question.
20. *Acree v. Republic of Iraq,* 370 F.3d 41 (D.C. Cir. 2004).

21. Charlie Savage, "Leahy, in Surprise, Voices Support for Roberts," *Boston Globe*, September 22, 2005.

22. Charlie Savage, "Roberts Becomes Nation's Seventeenth Chief Justice," *Boston Globe*, September 30, 2005.

23. Carol D. Leonnig and Dafna Linzer, "Judges on Surveillance Court to Be Briefed on Spy Program," *Washington Post*, December 22, 2005.

24. Manuel Miranda, 8:12 a.m. e-mail re: "Statement of the Third Branch Conference," October 3, 2005.

25. Interview of Robert Bork by Tucker Carlson, MSNBC, October 14, 2005, http://www.msnbc.msn.com/id/9623345/.

26. George Will, "Can This Nomination Be Justified?" *Washington Post*, October 5, 2005.

27. Charlie Savage, "President's Pick Has Leaned Left and Right," *Boston Globe*, October 4, 2005.

28. Bush told reporters, "People are interested to know why I picked Harriet Miers. They want to know Harriet Miers's background. They want to know as much as they possibly can before they form opinions. And part of Harriet Miers's life is her religion." On that same day, James Dobson, head of the conservative Christian political activist group Focus on the Family, told his national radio audience that Bush's deputy chief of staff, Karl Rove, had assured him Miers was an "evangelical Christian" and a member of a "very conservative church which is almost universally pro-life." Charlie Savage, "Bush, Promoting Miers, Invokes Her Faith," *Boston Globe*, October 13, 2005.

29. Charles Krauthammer, "The Only Exit Strategy," *Washington Post*, October 21, 2005.

30. "President's Statement on Harriet Miers's Supreme Court Nomination Withdrawal," October 27, 2005, http://www.whitehouse.gov/news/releases/2005/10/20051027-2.html.

31. Federal appeals court judges Janice Rogers Brown, Edith Brown Clement, Edith Jones, Priscilla Owen, Diane Sykes, and Karen Williams had never worked in the executive branch, nor had Colorado Supreme Court justice Allison Eid, another conservative favorite. One exception to this rule was Michigan Supreme Court justice Maura Corrigan, but she had only been a federal prosecutor, a position that gave her no personal involvement with efforts to protect and magnify presidential power. The other exception was prominent appellate lawyer Maureen Mahoney, who had been deputy solicitor general in the Bush-Quayle administration, but she had been out of government for more than a decade. All of these women were strongly conservative in other matters, but none of them had much in the way of proven executive-power bona fides in comparison with the nominees Bush selected.

32. Ralph Blumenthal and Simon Romero, "Documents Show Supreme Court Nominee's Close Ties to Bush," *New York Times*, October 11, 2005.

33. Yoo himself seemed unsure about the scope of Miers's commitment to the legal positions he had crafted. The day after her nomination was announced,

he wrote in a *Washington Post* op-ed that her nomination was a missed opportunity because of her lack of a record of constitutional views. Yoo noted that Miers might shore up conservative support if the White House disclosed her private advice to the president about the extent of his executive power since she became White House counsel in January 2005. But Yoo also wrote that such a document release would be impossible. "She may be one of the key supporters in the Bush administration of staying the course on legal issues arising from the war on terrorism," Yoo wrote. "But it is hard to see how the administration could reveal Miers's position on these issues, given its tough, five-year struggle to preserve the confidentiality of executive-branch deliberations." John Yoo, "Opportunity Squandered," *Washington Post*, October 4, 2005.

34. Charlie Savage, "Miers Has Backed Wide Executive Role," *Boston Globe*, October 5, 2005.

35. Charlie Savage, "Panelists Demand More Data from Miers," *Boston Globe*, October 20, 2005; see also Miers's Senate Judiciary Committee questionnaire, October 18, 2004, http://www.washingtonpost.com/wp-dyn/content/article/2005/10/18/AR2005101800616_pf.html.

36. "President Nominates Judge Samuel A. Alito as Supreme Court Justice," October 31, 2005, http://www.whitehouse.gov/news/releases/2005/10/20051031.html.

37. Samuel A. Alito to the solicitor general, memorandum re: "*Forsyth v. Kleindienst*," June 12, 1984. Ultimately the case against Mitchell was dismissed—not on the grounds that the former attorney general had immunity from such a lawsuit but because he had ordered the wiretaps two years before a Supreme Court ruling made clear that warrants were required for domestic national-security wiretaps.

38. During his confirmation hearings, Alito claimed not to remember ever being a member of the Concerned Alumni of Princeton, despite having prominently listed it on his 1985 application. He also said that to the extent he was interested in the CAP cause, it would have been only in regard to their support for keeping a Reserve Officers' Training Corps on campus amid calls to expel them, not for their opposition to admitting female students. Alito himself had been an ROTC student as an undergraduate.

39. Samuel A. Alito Jr., "Personnel Qualification Statement," November 15, 1985, http://www.archives.gov/news/samuel-alito/accession-060-97-761/.

40. The memorandum raised concerns when it emerged almost at the same time as Bush's signing statement on the torture ban. Senator Patrick Leahy declared in advance of Alito's January 2006 confirmation hearings, "It is disturbing that President Bush seeks authority to dictate the interpretation of laws written and passed by Congress. Tellingly, this president's current choice for the Supreme Court was instrumental in developing this strategy 20 years ago while serving in the Meese Justice Department. I will be interested to hear Judge Alito's current thoughts on presidential signing statements as a device to expand presidential power and to minimize congressional intent." But Alito was defended by Meese, who said in a telephone interview that there's nothing wrong with

the idea that presidents should leave a record of their understanding of new laws. In addition, he said, Alito was simply carrying out administration policy. "All Alito was doing as a subordinate member of the Department of Justice was . . . contributing his legal scholarship to the departmental policy at the time," Meese said. Charlie Savage and Rick Klein, "Alito Foes Consider Presidential Powers the Defining Issue," *Boston Globe,* January 6, 2006.

41. Deputy Solicitor General Donald B. Ayer and Attorney-Adviser Lowell V. Sturgill Jr. to Samuel A. Alito and others, memorandum re: "Litigation Strategy Working Group," September 2, 1986. Includes Donald B. Ayer to the Litigation Strategy Working Group, memorandum re: "Possible Separation of Powers Issues," September 2, 1986, http://www.archives.gov/news/samuel-alito/accession-060-89-1/Acc060-89-1-box9-memoAyer-LSWG-Sep1986.pdf.

42. Samuel Alito, introduction to debate, After the Independent Counsel Decision: Is Separation of Powers Dead? *Am. Crim. L. Rev.* 26 (1989): 1667.

43. *Engage: The Journal of the Federalist Society's Practice Groups,* November 2001, 12.

44. Charlie Savage and Rick Klein, "Mass. Senators to Filibuster Alito," *Boston Globe,* January 27, 2006; Charlie Savage, "Alito Filibuster Effort Falls Short," *Boston Globe,* January 31, 2006.

45. *Hamdan v. Rumsfeld,* oral argument transcript, March 28, 2006.

46. *Hamdan v. Rumsfeld,* 546 U.S. ___ (2006).

47. Charlie Savage, "Justices Deal Bush Setback on Tribunals," *Boston Globe,* June 30, 2006.

48. John Yoo, "The High Court's Hamdan Power Grab," *Los Angeles Times,* July 7, 2006.

49. Senate Judiciary Committee, *Hearing on the Nomination of Samuel Alito to Be Associate Justice of the Supreme Court,* January 10, 2006.

50. The trend, moreover, was likely to shape the behavior of lower court judges as well. With the trait of deference to executive power playing an increasingly open role in presidents' decisions about which judges to nominate to the Supreme Court, any ambitious jurist would have extra incentive to build a record as a believer in letting the president do whatever he wanted to do.

## 12. DISCIPLINE AND CONTROL: THE EXECUTIVE BRANCH

1. *Hearing of the Senate Armed Services Committee on the Future of Military Commissions,* August 2, 2006.

2. Author interview with two knowledgeable sources.

3. Author interview with Nolan Sklute, August 25, 2006.

4. It is important to note that while the capacity of career professionals to resist a president's agenda is an important reality of modern government, it does not necessarily "make the bureaucracy a hero," as Yale's Jack Balkin has observed. An obstinate and unelected bureaucracy is just as capable of erecting roadblocks to ideas that would serve the public interest as they are

to bad ideas. But when a particularly aggressive presidential team is in office, one that seeks to push the limits of laws enacted by Congress about how the government should operate, career professionals can sometimes serve the interests of democracy by slowing things down and making sure issues are well considered, Balkin wrote. Jack Balkin, "Presidential Caesarism: The Executive Versus the Bureaucracy," Balkinization, December 8, 2006, http://balkin.blogspot.com/2006/12/presidential-caesarism-executive.html.

5. "Accomplished Chinese American: John Liu Fugh," *St. Louis Chinese American News*, June 2003, http://www.scanews.com/spot/2003/june/s667/english-news/caf-news.txt.
6. Author interview with John Fugh, July 28, 2006.
7. "Accomplished Chinese American."
8. William J. Haynes II to the judge advocate general, memorandum re: "Ensuring Effective Execution of the Law and Efficient Delivery of Legal Services," May 14, 2002, on file with the author.
9. Congress eliminated the provision in conference committee because by then the Pentagon had already rescinded the memorandum, as Addington promised. The quote is taken from the Senate report 103-352, authorizing appropriations for fiscal year 1993 for military activities of the Department of Defense, July 31, 1992.
10. Charlie Savage, "Military Lawyers See Limits on Trial Input," *Boston Globe*, August 27, 2006.
11. Author interview with Steven Morello, August 22, 2006.
12. Author interview with Scott Silliman, August 1, 2006.
13. Conference report to accompany H.R. 4200, the Ronald W. Reagan National Defense Authorization Act for Fiscal Year 2005, October 8, 2004.
14. Executive order, *Establishment of White House Office of Faith-Based and Community Initiatives*, January 29, 2001.
15. "President Bush Implements Key Elements of his Faith-Based Initiative," December 12, 2002, http://www.whitehouse.gov/news/releases/2002/12/20021212-3.html.
16. Farah Stockman and others, "Bush Brings Faith to Foreign Aid," *Boston Globe*, October 8, 2006.
17. "President's Remarks at Faith-Based and Community Initiatives Conference," March 3, 2004, http://www.whitehouse.gov/news/releases/2004/03/20040303-13.html.
18. *Report on Review of the Pre-Iraqi War Activities of the Office of the Under Secretary of Defense for Policy*, Department of Defense Inspector General Report no. 07 INTEL 04, February 9, 2007, http://levin.senate.gov/newsroom/supporting/2007/DODIG.slides.020907.pdf.
19. Matthew Rycroft to David Manning, memorandum re: "Iraq, Prime Minister's Meeting," July 23, 2002, http://www.michaelsmithwriter.com/memos.html.
20. *Final Report of the National Commission on Terrorist Attacks Upon the United States*, July 22, 2004, 228–229.

21. Quoted in Seymour Hersh, "The Stovepipe," *The New Yorker,* October 27, 2003.
22. Author interview with Danielle Leonard, July 10, 2006.
23. Most of the information in this section appeared, under a different form, in the following article: Charlie Savage, "Civil Rights Hiring Shifted in Bush Era," *Boston Globe,* July 23, 2006.
24. See, e.g., Charlie Savage, "Missouri Attorney a Focus in Firings," *Boston Globe,* May 6, 2007.
25. Dan Eggen and Amy Goldstein, "Ex-Aide to Gonzales Accused of Bias," *Washington Post,* May 3, 2007.
26. Dan Eggen and Amy Goldstein, "Political Appointees No Longer to Pick Justice Interns," *Washington Post,* April 28, 2007.
27. Gardiner Harris, "U.S. Rules Morning-After Pill Can't Be Sold over the Counter," *New York Times,* May 7, 2004.
28. Francesca T. Grifo, PhD, senior scientist with the Union of Concerned Scientists Scientific Integrity Program, statement before the House Committee on Oversight and Government Reform, *Hearing on Allegations of Political Interference with the Work of Government Climate Change Scientists,* January 30, 2007.
29. Jonathan Cohn, "Toxic," *The New Republic,* December 23, 2002.
30. Eric Pianin, "Proposed Mercury Rules Bear Industry Mark," *Washington Post,* January 31, 2004.
31. Tom Hamburger and Alan C. Miller, "Mercury Emissions Rule Geared to Benefit Industry, Staffers Say," *Los Angeles Times,* March 16, 2004.
32. Russell Train, "E.P.-eh?" *Grist,* September 22, 2003, http://www.grist.org/comments/soapbox/2003/09/22/epeh/index.html.
33. Paul Elias, "Scientist Lauded After Gov't Fires Her," Associated Press, March 20, 2004.
34. "Restoring Scientific Integrity in Policy Making," February 18, 2004, http://www.ucsusa.org/scientific_integrity/interference/scientists-signon-statement.html.
35. Andrew Rudalevige, "The Plot That Thickened: Inheriting the Administrative Presidency" (presented at the 2006 annual meeting of the American Political Science Association, Philadelphia, PA, August 31–September 3, 2006).
36. Richard Nathan, *The Plot That Failed: Nixon and the Administrative Presidency* (New York: Wiley & Sons, 1975).
37. Douglas Kmiec, *The Attorney General's Lawyer: Inside the Meese Justice Department* (Westport, CT: Praeger Publishers, 1992), 81.
38. Michael Weisskopf, "EPA Proposal on Recycling Is Trashed; White House Panel Opposes Agency Plan," *Washington Post,* December 20, 1990.
39. Jack Balkin, "Tightening Control over the Federal Bureaucracy," Balkinization, January 30, 2007, http://balkin.blogspot.com/2007/01/tightening-control-over-federal.html.
40. Lisa Heinzerling, "Balkin on Bush's Bureaucracy," Georgetown Law Faculty Blog, February 7, 2007.
41. Executive order, *Further Amendment to Executive Order 12866 on Regulatory*

*Planning and Review,* January 18, 2007, http://www.whitehouse.gov/news/releases/2007/01/20070118.html.

42. Lisa Heinzerling, "Deregulatory Review," Georgetown Law Faculty Blog, January 23, 2007, http://gulcfac.typepad.com/georgetown_university_law/2007/01/deregulatory_re.html.

43. "Bush Executive Order on Regulatory Authority Is Latest White House Power Grab," Public Citizen press release, January 18, 2007, http://www.citizen.org/hot_issues/issue.cfm?ID=1534; "Undermining Public Protections: Preliminary Analysis of the Amendments to Executive Order 12866," OMB Watch press release, January 18, 2007, http://www.ombwatch.org/article/articleview/3685/1/132?TopicID=3.

44. Quoted in Robert Pear, "Bush Directive Increases Sway on Regulation," *New York Times,* January 30, 2007.

## 13. THE POLITICS OF PRESIDENTIAL POWER

1. "President Discusses Creation of Military Commissions to Try Suspected Terrorists," September 6, 2006, http://www.whitehouse.gov/news/releases/2006/09/20060906-3.html.

2. Statement by House majority leader John Boehner, September 27, 2006.

3. "Remarks by the President at Bob Riley for Governor Luncheon," September 28, 2006, http://www.whitehouse.gov/news/releases/2006/09/text/20060928-8.html.

4. *Federalist 51.*

5. Thomas E. Mann and Norman J. Ornstein, *The Broken Branch* (Oxford University Press, 2006), 155.

6. Ibid., 215.

7. *Meet the Press,* NBC, February 8, 2004, http://www.msnbc.msn.com/id/4179618/.

8. "Commander in Chief Lands on USS *Lincoln,*" CNN, May 1, 2003, http://www.cnn.com/2003/ALLPOLITICS/05/01/bush.carrier.landing/.

9. Gary Wills, "At Ease, Mr. President," *New York Times,* January 27, 2007.

10. Text of speech by Democratic senator Zell Miller of Georgia as prepared for delivery at the Republican National Convention, September 2, 2004.

11. "Legal Authorities Supporting the Activities of the National Security Agency Described by the President," U.S. Department of Justice, January 19, 2006, http://www.usdoj.gov/opa/whitepaperonnsalegalauthorities.pdf.

12. Charlie Savage, "AG's Memo Raises Questions on Patriot Act," *Boston Globe,* January 25, 2006.

13. The Justice Department, pressed to explain itself, further argued that re authorizing the Patriot Act was necessary because it had torn down the wall separating criminal and counterintelligence investigators from sharing information. However, a federal appeals court had already ruled in 2002 that the "wall" was never legally required in the first place, so no legislation was required to keep it down.

14. "President Discusses Global War on Terror at Kansas State University," January 23, 2006, http://www.whitehouse.gov/news/releases/2006/01/20060123-4.html.
15. E-mail exchange between William Moschella and Brent Tolman, re: "Dan Collins Special," November 9, 2005, http://www.realcities.com/multimedia/nationalchannel/archive/mcw/pdf/usattorneys/032307/_3.pdf.
16. Manuel Roig-Franzia and Spencer Hsu, "Many Evacuated, but Thousands Still Waiting," *Washington Post,* September 4, 2005.
17. "President's Remarks During Hurricane Rita Briefing in Texas," September 25, 2005, http://www.whitehouse.gov/news/releases/2005/09/20050925.html.
18. John Yoo, "Trigger Power," *Los Angeles Times,* October 2, 2005.
19. Section 333 of H.R. 5122, *John Warner National Defense Authorization Act for Fiscal Year 2007.*
20. Colin Powell to Senator John McCain, September 14, 2006.
21. *Boumediene v. Bush,* no. 05-5062, U.S. Court of Appeals for the District of Columbia Circuit, February 20, 2007.
22. Bruce Ackerman, "The White House Warden," *Los Angeles Times,* September 28, 2006.
23. John Yoo, "Sending a Message," *Wall Street Journal,* October 19, 2006.
24. (His italics.) Martin Lederman, "John Yoo on Court-Stripping," Balkinization, October 19, 2006, http://balkin.blogspot.com/2006/10/john-yoo-on-court-stripping.html.
25. "Media Availability with Senator Harry Reid (D-NV), Senate Minority Leader, Following His Meeting at the White House with the President and Vice President," November 10, 2006.
26. Walter Pincus, "CIA Cited for Not Disclosing Covert Action," *Washington Post,* May 10, 2007.
27. Message to the House of Representatives, May 1, 2007, http://www.whitehouse.gov/news/releases/2007/05/20070502-1.html.
28. Author interview with Richard Viguerie, May 16, 2007.
29. *Korematsu v. United States,* 321 U.S. 760 (1944).

# Index

# About the Author

Pulitzer Prize–winning journalist Charlie Savage is a Washington correspondent for the *Boston Globe*. He covers national legal affairs with a focus on issues related to counterterrorism and executive power.

A native of Fort Wayne, Indiana, Savage graduated summa cum laude from Harvard College in 1998. He began his career as a local government and politics reporter for the *Miami Herald*. Savage later earned a master's degree from Yale Law School while on a Knight Foundation journalism fellowship. He joined the *Boston Globe*'s Washington bureau in the fall of 2003.

Savage's work on the Bush-Cheney administration's signing statements and other efforts to expand presidential power has been widely recognized. In addition to the 2007 Pulitzer Prize for National Reporting, he has received the American Bar Association's Silver Gavel Award and the Gerald R. Ford Prize for Distinguished Reporting on the Presidency.

Savage lives in Washington, DC, with his wife, the journalist Luiza Ch. Savage, and their son. He can be reached at charlie.savage@gmail.com.